KOPASSUS

KEN CONBOY

KOPASSUS

INSIDE INDONESIA'S SPECIAL FORCES

EQUINOX
PUBLISHING
JAKARTA SINGAPORE

EQUINOX PUBLISHING (ASIA) PTE. LTD.
PO BOX 6179 JKSGN
JAKARTA 12062
INDONESIA

WWW.EQUINOXPUBLISHING.COM

ISBN 979-95898-8-6

FIRST EQUINOX EDITION 2003

3 5 7 9 10 8 6 4

CONTENTS

PREFACE V

1. THE GREEN CAPS 3

2. INFANCY 13

3. POLITICAL INTRIGUE 28

4. SECESSION 37

5. MERDEKA 53

6. WEST NEW GUINEA 61

7. GLORIOUS VICTORY 81

8. LESSONS NOT LEARNED 91

9. STORMCLOUDS 109

10. BLACK SEPTEMBER 127

11. SPECIAL WARFARE 145

12. THE GOLDEN BOYS 166

13. FREE CHOICE 179

14. FLAMBOYAN 188

15. WAVES IN A BACKWATER 205

16. PHASE TWO 223

17. SEROJA 236

18. NANGGALA 255

19. WOYLA 277

20. KOPASSUS 305

GLOSSARY 317

INDEX 320

PREFACE

In April 2002, the Indonesian Army Special Forces—currently known as Kopassus—celebrated their half-century mark. The anniversary festivities at their Cijantung headquarters—including freefall parachute jumps, a self-defense exhibition by several hundred commandos, and a shooting demonstration—were upbeat and impressive.

Behind the scenes, however, Kopassus has long been on the defensive. Ever since the end of President Suharto's three-decade New Order government in 1998, the number of human rights violations attributed to special forces members has increased exponentially. Blaming the unit for Indonesia's legion of social ills has almost become reflexive. Some of this may be warranted, some is probably groundless, and most is based on an incomplete understanding of the unit, its leaders, and its abilities.

Here for the first time, the history of Kopassus is chronicled in a detailed, objective account. The story has been told before—in official Indonesian military publications—but this is an unauthorized rendition that attempts to show the unit in unbiased fashion, warts and all. It is important that this story be told for several reasons. First, the Indonesian Army Special Forces can be seen as a microcosm of that country's armed forces as a whole. Kopassus, after all, had a lead role in nearly all of Indonesia's major military campaigns since independence. Kopassus also came to disproportionately influence Indonesia's senior military leadership (even though the active strength at its height never exceeded seven thousand members) and by the early 1990s the majority of the most influential slots in the Indonesian army went to officers who held Kopassus as their alma mater.

Second, the story of Kopassus has an important international dimension. Members of the Indonesian Army Special Forces have at various times battled the militaries—or proxies—of the Commonwealth, the Netherlands, Portugal and United States. For each of these foreign powers, this account will add to a complete understanding of their contemporary military histories.

Lastly, the Indonesian Army Special Forces has influenced the development of unconventional warfare doctrine. At different times, Kopassus has been exposed to East, West, and non-aligned mentors. This has given Indonesia's military elite a unique perspective. And given the large number of brushfire conflicts across the archipelago, it has been able to test this blended doctrine in combat. What's more, Kopassus has passed on its understanding of unconventional warfare to other nations—by training commando cadres from Cambodia, for example—making the Kopassus story relevant for those militaries as well.

Looking ahead, Kopassus retains a profound effect on Indonesia as this vast insular nation lurches forward along the path toward democratization. It has had a particularly strong influence—both positive and negative—over bilateral military ties with the West. Kopassus is also on the vanguard of the country's counter-terrorism campaign. It is hoped that this history of the unit will allow its influence to be better understood. It must be noted that the following account stops at 1993. Though it could be argued that some of the most significant, and controversial, developments in Kopassus have taken place since that time, objectively documenting its operations since 1993 would be all but impossible given the number of existing vested interests and the lack of historical perspective. A post-1993 analysis will have to await a future volume.

This book is based upon both written sources and extensive oral interviews. In the United States, the written sources were gathered from the *Foreign Relations of the United States* series, as well as releases in the *Declassified Documents Reference System* and relevant media transcripts recorded by the *Foreign Broadcast Information Service*.

Among oral sources, Widjojo Soejono (General, ret.) and H. Djajadiningrat (Colonel, ret.) were especially generous and patient with their assistance. Darwin Nasution, too, went out of his way to offer much appreciated insights. Iswahjudi Karim lent invaluable help in tracking down source material. Luis A.M. Grao provided key documents on East Timor, and Richard Lasut volunteered much time in translating Dutch material.

Although all books are a collaborative effort, the author takes responsibility for everything in these pages. Any errors in fact or interpretation are my own.

Ken Conboy
Jakarta
November 2002

KOPASSUS

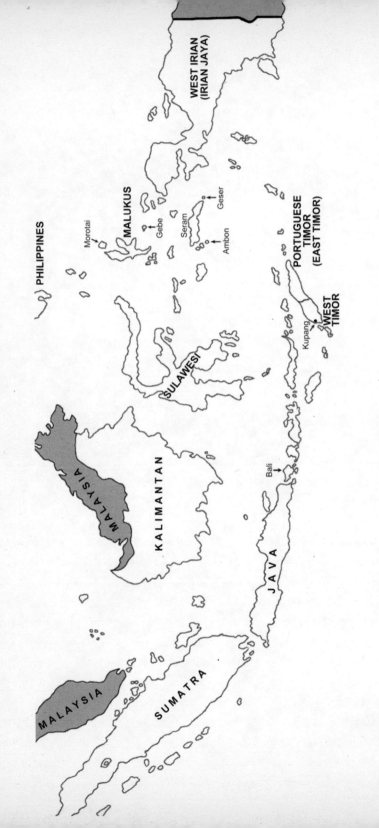

CHAPTER ONE

THE GREEN CAPS

Among the more than seventeen thousand islands that encompass the Indonesian archipelago, Ambon is rather unremarkable. Even in the context of the thousand-plus islands, islets, and atolls that form the Maluku chain, it commands little geographic significance.

In terms of world history, however, Ambon has been pivotal. The reason derives from nutmeg and cloves, two spices that spurred the great Age of Exploration in the fifteenth century. Literally worth their weight in gold, these condiments prompted the Portuguese, Spanish, Dutch, and British to spar over the so-called Spice Islands in an effort to corner their harvest.

Greed among these European competitors led to cruel excesses. In this, Holland had few equals. Looking to eclipse Portuguese influence, the Dutch in 1605 captured the Iberian fort on Ambon and renamed the surrounding town New Victoria—then set about desecrating Catholic churches and deporting locals with mixed blood. Eighteen years later, looking to expel a British foothold on the same island, they trumped up charges against eighteen English merchants as a pretext for torturing and beheading the group.

Using such ruthless practices, the Dutch were able to consolidate their hold over clove cultivation in the Malukus and convert Ambon into their regional trading hub. Reflecting this status, Ambon came to take on more colonial comforts, earning it the title "Queen of the East."

Its reign was not to last. Inevitably, clove cultivation spread to other parts of the world. With its Maluku monopoly irrevocably shattered, the Dutch had little reason to maintain Ambon. By the nineteenth century, it was a financial drain and expensive relic. By the beginning of the twentieth century, it was a stale backwater.[1]

But while Ambon itself was relegated to a colonial footnote, the people of Ambon were taking on significance far disproportionate to their numbers. With two-thirds of the natives on the island having converted to Christianity, they came to mimic the Dutch in both manner and dress. Their European overlords suddenly took note, offering Ambonese the best educational system in the archipelago. By the end of the nineteenth century, thousands were working for the colonial administration; three decades later, ten percent of Ambon's population had emigrated to serve the Dutch elsewhere in the archipelago. As loyal subjects, they had few peers.

Perhaps the area where the Ambonese contribution was felt greatest was in the Dutch colonial army. Founded in 1830, the *Koninklijk Nederlands-Indisch Leger* (KNIL) merged European cadres with local recruits primarily from eastern Indonesia to enforce control across Holland's Indonesian holdings. Of the local troops, fully half were Ambonese Christians.

In 1942, the symbiosis between Dutch and the people of Ambon was suddenly shattered by the Imperial Japanese. Seizing the island in a single day, Japan forever altered the local image of European omnipotence. The Japanese also turned on the island's Christians, who suffered tremendously under their hand.

Two years later, the situation worsened still. When the Japanese established significant military facilities across the Malukus, especially Ambon, the islands loomed large as an Allied target. U.S. bombers eventually zeroed in on the Japanese installations at New Victoria, leveling the town.

The end of World War II offered little reprieve. Looking to retake their Indonesian colony, the Dutch poured in troops from the Royal Dutch Army and resurrected the KNIL. Once again, the Ambonese came to dominate the KNIL ranks. But unlike the low-level disturbances of previous decades, Holland now faced a full-blown guerrilla insurgency spearheaded by revolutionaries intent on winning Indonesian independence.

Through mid-1949, both sides fought a bloody war with little quarter given. While outnumbered, the Dutch regular army and KNIL were generally successful in battlefields across the archipelago. Around the negotiating table, however, the Dutch were being trumped. That December, after strong diplomatic intervention from the U.S. (which threatened to withhold European reconstruction funds to Holland under the Marshall Plan), the nationalists emerged victorious. The Dutch agreed to transfer control to the Federated States of Indonesia; this included a semi-independent *Negara Indonesia Timur* (East Indonesian Nation), which the colonialists had earlier created for their most loyal subjects in the Malukus and Sulawesi. Also part of the agreement, the 80,000-man Royal Dutch military contingent would be immediately withdrawn and the 65,000-strong KNIL was to be demobilized and dissolved by the following summer; some of the latter would then theoretically be merged with the disparate pro-independence forces they had been fighting.

The divorce, it turned out, was hardly smooth. Resentment among hard-line Dutch military officers and politicians began to mount almost immediately, especially given that their defeat had come during negotiations and not on the battlefield. With the ink on the accords barely dry, they began to plot against the nascent independent Indonesia.

In January 1950, the plotters put their words into action. In the town of Bandung in West Java, hundreds of KNIL troops fanned out in the early morning hours. They hailed primarily from the *Regiment Speciale Troepen*—the Special Troop Regiment—an elite Dutch unit with a decidedly mixed past. The regiment traced its origins back to 1946, when it was raised as a Special Troop Depot in Batavia (the colonial name for Jakarta). That December, it deployed to southern Sulawesi to quell an early nationalist outbreak. With them went the depot commander, Captain Raymond "Turk" Westerling.

What followed was a dark chapter in Dutch military history. Westerling, a British-trained commando of Dutch and Turkish parentage, had thousands of Indonesian males between fifteen and fifty rounded up and executed.[2] By February 1947, the insurrection in southern Sulawesi was crushed and the special troops were withdrawn to Batavia. On account of their ruthless counter-insurgency success, the unit in November shifted to a new base at Batu Jajar—a village near Bandung—and was given permission to wear distinctive green berets. Two months later, they were expanded into a Special Troop Corps; one of its three commando companies was subsequently upgraded to airborne status.

Westerling did not share in their rewards. With word of the Sulawesi massacre reaching higher command, criticism mounted against the controversial captain. In November 1948, he was expelled from the unit. His troops, meanwhile, were merged in July 1949 with a separate (and untainted) company of paratroopers and renamed the Special Troop Regiment.[3]

While the regiment's paratroopers were not blamed for further excesses, they could not live down their earlier reputation. Among nationalist fighters, the special troops—dubbed Green Caps because of their headgear—were derided as dogs, a particularly harsh insult in Indonesia. Not surprisingly, there was some concern about reprisals when the Dutch agreed to leave.

It was at that point that Captain Westerling made a reappearance at Batu Jajar. Though run out of the corps more than a year earlier, he retained considerable loyalty among his Ambonese commandos and had the unofficial backing of several high-ranking compatriots. Seeking to defy diplomatic pressure to grant Indonesia its independence, Westerling and his patrons had already enticed almost eight thousand KNIL troops into giving titular support to a shadowy anti-nationalist rebel force. Ironically, this force took the name *Angkatan Perang Ratu Adil*—the War Force of the Just King. According to Indonesian legend, a Just King would some day lead them from colonial servitude.[4]

On 23 January 1950, Westerling moved past rhetoric and ordered eight hundred of his loyalists to seize Bandung. In making the attempt, they held several advantages. Many of the nationalist troops in Bandung—grouped under the *Siliwangi* "division" strung across West Java—were still on leave after the exhausting independence struggle. For those still in town, relations between them and the remaining Dutch troops, who were awaiting repatriation, were cool but proper; seeing little need to remain on a state of alert, both Indonesian and European troops normally strolled around Bandung without weapons.

Shattering this peace, Westerling and his men pushed easily across town. To their credit, the Indonesians recovered almost instantly from their initial shock and recalled troops on leave from neighboring villages. Very quickly, the numbers turned heavily against Westerling. Though he held the nationalists at bay for several hours—and killed seventy-two in the process—he was soon looking to arrange an escape. Drawing favors from high-ranking Dutch officers, the captain fled Java, leaving his rebels to the tender mercies of the nationalists.

Indonesia's reprieve was not to last. Almost immediately, Indonesia's first president, the dynamic but mercurial Sukarno, distanced himself from the country's proposed federal structure in favor of a unitary republic ruled from Jakarta. Just as quickly, resistance began to mushroom in those areas that fell under the Dutch-supported East Indonesian Nation. Denied their semi-independent status, a rebellion broke out in southern Sulawesi. And on 25 April, political leaders on Ambon seceded to form the *Republik Maluku Selatan* (South Moluccan Republic, or RMS).

Nobody was more surprised by the April declaration than the KNIL troops still spread across the archipelago. Apart from Westerling's short-lived uprising in Bandung, most of the colonial soldiers were demobilizing as scheduled. After April, however, many began to rethink if their defeat was a *fait accompli*. Itching to once again take up arms against the nationalists, hundreds shifted to the Dutch-held territory of West New Guinea (which, according to the December 1949 agreement, was not being turned over to Indonesia) to regroup. Others, especially from the Green Caps, made their way to Ambon to bolster the fledgling RMS.

For Sukarno and the Indonesian armed forces, these multiple tests in the east could not have come at a worse time. The nationalist military was still little more than a confusing patchwork of hundreds of thousands of revolutionary fighters and KNIL troops that had yet to be incorporated into a single, rationalized structure. Levels of training among the combatants varied widely, from militiamen taught by the Japanese, to those that had tutored under the Dutch, to guerrillas with no formal instruction. Its officer corps was impossibly young; their supreme commander, General R. Soedirman, had passed away from tuberculosis in January just short of his twenty-eighth birthday. Few had any comprehension of how to operate the military hardware—armor, ships, aircraft—turned over by the departing Dutch, much less how to effectively incorporate this equipment in a combined arms operation.

There was also the issue of national cohesion. With a few exceptions, the revolution had been fought as a series of local battles. This was not surprising given the country's island geography and myriad of ethnic groups. Loyalty among the revolutionary soldiers usually extended to the village or district, but rarely beyond. While there was general recognition of the top revolutionary leaders, a sense of binding national identity was far from fixed. This was especially the case outside of Java, where aversion to Javanese cultural chauvinism was commonplace.

Finally, there was the problem of logistics. The unrest in the east was physically far from nationalist troop concentrations on Java. Given Indonesia's shortage of aircraft and serviceable runways, maritime transportation was the only viable option to get to the front. Though Indonesia had just been handed a diverse inventory of amphibious landing craft from the departing Dutch, they had yet to properly train on these vessels.

But with the future of the unitary state hanging in the balance, Sukarno and his youthful officers had little choice but to move decisively against the rebels. Heading the campaign was the newly designated regional commander for East Indonesia, Alex Kawilarang. The son of Christians from Minahasa— the northernmost tip of Sulawesi—Kawilarang was in many respects similar to the rebels he was about to confront. Second only to the Ambonese, Minahasans were coddled by the Dutch and had proved a fertile recruiting ground for the KNIL. Kawilarang's father had been in the colonial army, as had Kawilarang himself. Defecting during the Japanese occupation, he had pledged loyalty to the revolutionary cause and—due to his relatively complete Dutch schooling and military experience—rose quickly up the rebel ranks.[5]

By the end of the revolutionary war, Kawilarang was counted among Indonesia's most competent field officers. In December 1949, he was rewarded with a promotion to colonel and assignment as the first military commander for North Sumatra. The post was a challenge: he faced spreading discontent among demobilized guerrillas, not to mention simmering secessionist sentiment in the far north. But before making headway, the high command in Jakarta recalled him from Sumatra in April 1950 to spearhead operations across the east.

By month's end, Kawilarang—barely past his thirtieth birthday—was leading Indonesia's first post-independence expeditionary force out of Java. Scrapping together a modest naval armada and borrowing several Javanese infantry battalions, he headed for the southern tip of Sulawesi. The threat there was relatively minor—a company of former KNIL were holding the port town of Makassar—and it was considered a good proving ground to test nationalist mettle. The gamble proved correct: with minimal opposition, a series of landings took place and Makassar was in government hands.

The Malukus were a wholly different matter. Because the RMS rebels were concentrated on Ambon, Kawilarang established a blockade by leapfrogging across the lesser-defended islands to its north and east in July. There he waited for the weather to subside—the calmest seas came in October—and for reinforcements to arrive. By the close of September, he had on hand over five infantry battalions, nearly the navy's entire complement of twenty-eight war vessels, and four aircraft. Ironically, the ships and planes had been turned over by the Dutch, and were now about to be used against some of Holland's most loyal native subjects.

Commander of government forces in the Maluku sector was Lieutenant Colonel Slamet Riyadi. A cherubic, twenty-three year old Catholic from Central Java, Riyadi divided his Ambon landing force in two. Personally taking half of the troops around the eastern side of the island, he approached shore on 28 September. After softening the beach with naval cannon fire, the first battalion transferred to native canoes and made a beachhead. More infantry and armor followed; they were all unopposed.[6]

The second half of the landing force did not have it so good. Targeting the north shore of the island, they came under immediate fire from RMS rebels. The government troops suffered seventeen casualties in the first hours, including a fatal injury to the ranking officer.[7]

On 3 October, Colonel Kawilarang himself landed on the island and linked up with Riyadi. Their target was New Victoria, the former Queen of the East that had been leveled during World War II. Now little more than a colorless collection of post-war waterfront structures, it was serving as the makeshift RMS capital. According to reworked government plans, Riyadi's task force would push southwest across the island toward New Victoria, while the hard-pressed task force at the northern beachhead would attempt a link-up. At the same time, the bulk of the naval armada would sail into Ambon harbor and land directly at the RMS stronghold.

On the map, Riyadi's troops had to cover little more than twenty kilometers to New Victoria. In reality, it promised to be a trying crawl. Vast stretches of the island were inhospitable mangrove swamps, which kept the government troops channeled—and vulnerable—along a handful of muddy roads. Most of the roadside villages were eerily barren, the inhabitants giving a wide berth to the predominantly Muslim troops from Java. More than a few had yet to be rebuilt following bombardment in World War II.

Riyadi's men had not gotten far when the first rebel shots rang out. From atop trees, behind huts, and out of roadside foliage, sniper fire began to pelt the government column. The RMS guerrillas remained invisible, melting into the jungle before the nationalists could concentrate their superior firepower.

Kawilarang quickly sized up the rebels. He knew that the Green Caps were prepared for a final stand, and he knew of their abilities both by reputation and his own experiences on Java during the revolutionary war. While prepared to laud their individual tenacity, he gave them little credit as a unit. "The Green Caps were not sportsmanlike," he sniffed.[8]

Riyadi was more impressed. Pressed against the mud as sniper bullets flew overhead, he saw his vastly superior force pinned down by a handful of diehard commandos. "I want some of those for myself," he told Kawilarang.[9]

Eventually, quantity won out over quality. On the morning of 3 November, after a grueling, month-long slog across the island, government troops converged on New Victoria. On the following afternoon, Lieutenant Colonel Riyadi was leading a column from atop a tank as his men approached the final RMS holdouts at the town's stone fort.

He did not live to see the rebels capitulate. During literally the final hour of the final day of the campaign, a lone Green Cap commando near the roadside zeroed his machinegun on the tank. A volley ricocheted off the armor skin, with one round tearing through the lieutenant colonel's abdomen. Rushed to a hospital ship and pumped full of morphine, Riyadi used his final conscious moments to demand he be returned to the front. Spirited to the end, his heart stopped beating later that night.[10]

1   Kal Muller, *Maluku* (Singapore: Periplus Editions, 1997), p. 45.

2   An official Indonesian military account, written in 1968, implausibly claims that Westerling's men executed 40,000 civilians in Sulawesi. Sedjarah Militer Kodam VI, *Siliwangi Dari Masa Kemasa* (Djakarta: Fakta Mahjuma, 1968), p. 375.

3   Alex Krijger and Martin Eland, *Het Korps Commandotroepen, 1942-1997* (The Hague: Historical Section of the Royal Netherlands Army, 1997), p. 60.

4   *Sejarah TNI*, Jilid II (Jakarta: Pusat Sejarah dan Tradisi TNI, 2000), p. 111.

5   Ramadhan K.H., *A.E. Kawilarang, Untuk Sang Merah Putih* (Jakarta: Pustaka Sinar Harapan, 1988), p. 13.

6   Interview with A. Sugiyanto, 25 May 2001. Sugiyanto served as Riyadi's adjutant during the Ambon operation.

7   Direktorat Perawatan Personil TNI-AL, *Sejarah Tentara Nasional Indonesia Angkatan Laut, 1950-1959* (Jakarta: Sub Direktorat Sejarah, 1987), p. 181.

8   Interview with Alex Kawilarang, 15 August 1997.

9   Kawilarang interview; Sugiyanto interview.

10 Direktorat, *Sejarah Tentara Nasional Indonesia Angkatan Laut*, p. 198; Ramadhan, *A.E. Kawilarang*, p. 236; Sugiyanto interview.

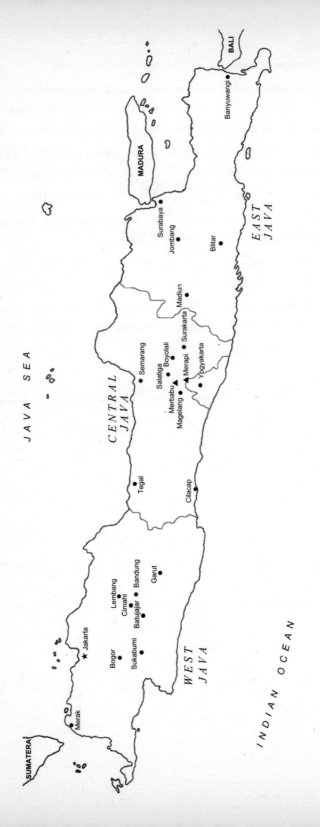

CHAPTER TWO
INFANCY

With the fall of New Victoria—renamed the town of Ambon, on the island of the same name—the RMS rebellion was effectively spent. Alex Kawilarang remained at his eastern Indonesia post for the next year, confronting sporadic rebel outbursts in the province of South Sulawesi before venturing to Jakarta in October 1951. This time the reason for his trip to the capital was personal, not professional. A national Olympics was being held that month, and the colonel was entering the fencing tournament. Predictably, he crushed the competition.

Intending to return to his post, Kawilarang was instead held back by the army leadership. Having proven himself in the east, he was now told to head for Bandung to take over the critical *Tentara & Territorium III*, the territorial military command encompassing West Java. In effect, this seat was synonymous with control of the army's Siliwangi division. Though labeled a division, Siliwangi was more accurately a loose umbrella command for five infantry brigades (each comprised of up to four battalions) strung across the western third of Java.

West Java, Kawilarang knew, was a province under siege. Confronting the Siliwangi division was a grassroots uprising known as Darul Islam. Translated as "House of Islam," DI was in many respects a social reaction by the people of West Java against the rest of the island. Culturally and linguistically, the province's ethnic Sundanese majority bristled at historically laboring in the shadows of the more powerful Javanese kingdoms further east. To differentiate themselves, the Sundanese shunned the heavily stratified societies—and resultant class conflicts—favored by the Javanese. While this made them less receptive to the precepts of communism (which had made deep inroads in rural Java), many had instead embraced Islamic extremism as a means of expressing nationalist sentiment.

Heading the DI movement was a Sundanese leader named Sekarmaji Marijan Kartosuwiryo. An early member of the Islamic League—a nationalist organization formed at the start of the twentieth century—Kartosuwiryo had risen to become its secretary general by 1931. Nine years later, opportunities for him and the league mushroomed during the Japanese occupation of World War II. After initially persecuting nationalists across Southeast Asia, the Japanese reversed themselves and encouraged the growth of religious organizations and independence movements—even to the point of training indigenous armies—as a means of currying local favor and frustrating attempts by the Allies to reassert colonial domination in Asia.

Wearing religious and political hats, Kartosuwiryo appealed to the Japanese on both counts. Stoking his activism, the Japanese allowed him to set up a training camp in West Java for a fledgling militant Islamic wing. By the time World War II ended, and renewed hostilities against the Dutch looked set to begin, his loyalists had a significant armed presence across the Sundanese heartland in West Java.

During the war of independence that followed, Kartosuwiryo's partisans fought dozens of pitched battles against the colonialists. In this, they formed a loose alliance with the nationalist guerrillas in the Siliwangi division. Neither faction lost sight of the fact that theirs was a marriage of convenience. Whereas the nationalists were fighting for an independent, secular state, the religious warriors made no secret that they envisioned an Islamic Indonesia.

Midway through the war, Kartosuwiryo got a lucky break. When the Dutch agreed to a ceasefire, the Siliwangi division conducted an extended march into Central Java to regroup. But after the ceasefire collapsed and the division moved back toward its home province in August 1949, they discovered Kartosuwiryo's men had expanded their area of operations across West Java during their absence. Later that month, Kartosuwiryo formally founded the DI and proclaimed himself head of an Indonesian Islamic State.

Exhausted by their extended march and again pummeled by the Dutch, the nationalists could offer only a limited response to the DI challenge. Once independence was granted in December, a response was delayed further by

the need to counter the Westerling uprising in January 1950, then by the need
to export troops to confront the RMS rebellion. As a result, when Sukarno
formally announced the formation of a republican government that August,
the DI felt sufficiently confident to disavow Jakarta's sovereign right to rule.[1]

By the time Kawilarang took command of West Java in November 1951,
the DI effectively displaced the government across much of rural West Java.
The extremists were not above inflicting bloodshed across the provincial
countryside. During the last three months of 1951, Islamic guerrillas were accused
of killing over four hundred and burning more than four thousand houses.[2]

Compared with previous threats—most notably the RMS rebellion—
the DI was a far more serious affront to the fledgling republic. Not only were
they operating close to the center of power on Java, but combating such a deeply-
rooted guerrilla insurgency required a nuanced, non-conventional campaign—
something the Indonesian military (despite its guerrilla origins) was ill equipped
to conduct. Consciously making strides to transform itself into a modern armed
forces, the army—especially the Siliwangi division—was neither organized
nor equipped to tackle a partisan DI opponent even though they were drawn
from the same Sundanese population.

Groping for unconventional remedies, Kawilarang began to contemplate
a specialized unit that could perform beyond the abilities of the typical Siliwangi
infantryman. Specifically, he wanted troops that could conduct long-range
patrols for extended periods. Though his Siliwangi troops were conducting
regular sweeps, they returned to base at short, predictable intervals that allowed
them to be easily sidestepped.[3]

This was not the first time such a specialized unit had been discussed.
Back in October 1950, the army chief of staff had mandated a panel to plan the
future size and shape of the military. That panel had advocated creation of
both a ranger regiment and an airborne commando regiment directly under
the army headquarters. Besieged by higher priorities, however, neither concept
had been adopted.[4]

Kawilarang himself had flirted with a similar but more modest concept
in early 1950 while in command of northern Sumatra. Raising an elite
commando formation on paper, he had gone as far as allocating troops and
giving it the name Ki-Pas-Ko (*Kompi Pasukan Komando*, or Commando Force
Company). But with no qualified instructors on hand, and Kawilarang getting
his transfer to eastern Indonesia, the company was stillborn.

Once in eastern Indonesia, Kawilarang again had fleeting exposure to the idea of a commando unit when confronting the Green Caps on Ambon. During that campaign, it had been Slamet Riyadi who voiced enthusiasm toward raising elite troops. But again caught up in more pressing matters, and with Riyadi shot dead, the plan failed to fire imaginations further up the chain of command.

This time, Kawilarang had reason to believe the effort might bear fruit. Whereas his Ki-Pas-Ko experiment had been frustrated by the lack of a qualified instructor, word had reached Bandung of a seasoned commando within their midst. His name was Mochamad Idjon Djanbi.

Mochamad Idjon Djanbi was born Rokus Bernardus Visser, the son of a successful Dutch tulip farmer. Fresh from college, the young Visser had been helping his father sell bulbs in London when World War II broke out. Unable to return to his Nazi-occupied homeland, he instead enlisted in the exiled Dutch army taking shape in England and was assigned as the personal driver for Queen Willamena.

Out of patriotism, or boredom, or both, Sergeant Visser left his cushy chauffeur post after a year and instead volunteered as a radioman for the 2 Dutch Troop. Part of the Inter-Allied Commando—which pooled segregated units of Polish, Norwegian, and French troops—it was an elite outfit being organized to support the retake of mainland Europe.

Along with most of his Dutch peers, Visser had his first taste of action during the overly ambitious Operation Market Garden in September 1944. Divided among the operation's multiple Allied task forces, Visser's portion of 2 Dutch Troop was attached to the U.S. 82 Airborne Division during its glider-borne landing in Holland. Unlike Market Garden's other prongs that were savaged by the Germans, Visser and his American paratroopers sidestepped the heaviest Nazi concentrations. Regrouping two months later, he was attached to another Allied drive, this time an amphibious landing along the southern Dutch coast at Walcheren.[5]

On account of good service, Visser was selected to undergo officer training before heading toward Asia near the war's end. Schooled at British airborne facilities in India, he was to be part of a special operations unit meant to combat the Imperial Japanese occupying the Dutch East Indies. As it turned out, the war ended and the Japanese withdrew in defeat before he could be deployed.

Japan's exit gave the Netherlands an opportunity to reassert control over its Indonesian colony. But with their home turf razed during the liberation of Europe, the Dutch could barely muster an expeditionary force for the Far East. Scrounged up whatever soldiers they could find, the Royal Dutch Army repackaged the special operations unit on India as a *School voor Opleiding van Parachutisten*—Airborne Training School—and sent it to Batavia in March 1946.

Commanded by Lieutenant Visser, the paratrooper school soon shifted to the abandoned U.S. Army hospital complex in Hollandia on Dutch West Guinea. Even by Indonesian standards, Hollandia was a primitive backwater. Surrounded by dense triple canopy and populated by stone-age Melanesian tribesmen that favored penis gourds over pants, the school was considered a true hardship post.

But for all its detractions, Visser became smitten with rural Indonesia. Returning to Europe on leave, he urged his wife—a British woman he married during the war—to move to the Far East with their four children. When she said no, he said yes to a divorce.

Returning to his airborne school, which in 1947 had shifted yet again from remote Hollandia to the relatively more civilized setting of Bandung, the newly promoted Captain Visser kept churning out paratroopers through the end of 1949. But with the colonial era set to end with Indonesia's independence, he reached an impasse in his life. Having grown more comfortable with the Asian lifestyle—its culture, its food, its women—he saw little point in going back to Europe. At the same time, remaining behind in an independent Indonesia posed problems. For one thing, there was no way to predict how the emancipated Indonesians would react to a former Dutch military officer living in their midst. Though Visser's airborne graduates were not tainted by atrocities—unlike the Green Caps—there was always the chance of retribution by a vengeful nationalist.

For another thing, some of Visser's colleagues viewed their former subjects with contempt. For them, his desire to turn his back on Holland and remain in Indonesia was nothing more than treason.

In the end, Visser took his chances and went native. Settling near Bandung, he looked to make his emigration more palatable by taking

Indonesian citizenship, marrying his Sundanese girlfriend, and converting to her Muslim faith. With his conversion came the new name of Mochamad Idjon Djanbi.

To that point in his life, Djanbi knew only two professions: soldiering and horticulture. Focusing on the latter, he began cultivating tulips on his wife's modest plot in a small village north of Bandung. It was not long, however, before word of his former military specialty spread among the Indonesians. The army's small military intelligence office in Jakarta went as far as compiling a short dossier on Djanbi, noting his qualifications as a commando and paratroop instructor.

In mid-1951, that dossier was handed to Lieutenant Aloysius Sugiyanto. A 23-year old Catholic from Yogyakarta, Sugiyanto had earlier been adjutant to another young Catholic officer, the late Slamet Riyadi. When Riyadi was killed in Ambon, Sugiyanto was temporarily out of a job. Eventually making his way back to Jakarta in late 1950, he happened to be readily available when the army was looking for volunteers to fill the pilot class of a Combat Intelligence course.

One of the first thirty young officers and non-commissioned officers to make the cut, Sugiyanto was tutored for the next four months in the basics of military intelligence. As an added bonus to boost morale, the entire group was dispatched to Bandung for a final round of airborne training. Again, this was the first time Indonesians were receiving such instruction in the post-independence era.[6]

By the spring of 1951, this initial class had concluded the course and most of the participants went back to their parent units. But rating the project a success, five of the graduates—including Sugiyanto—were retained as training cadre for a second class taking shape. This time around, instead of a final parachute qualification tacked on the end, the contingent was to be put through the paces of a more ambitious commando course.

The trouble was that Indonesia did not have any commando instructors. Brainstorming possibilities, Djanbi's dossier was dusted off and given to Sugiyanto with the idea of enticing the Dutch expatriate into imparting his skills.

Traveling to Bandung, the young lieutenant located Djanbi's farm and found the former captain tending to his tulips. Briefed on the intended commando syllabus, the Dutchman was so intrigued that Sugiyanto ended up spending three days fleshing out the details. In the end, Djanbi agreed to work as a civilian consultant for the duration of a single training session. The class was to be taught in a mix of Indonesian and Dutch, with an emphasis on the former.

Already, the second Combat Intelligence class, this time sixty strong, had been attending several weeks of classroom sessions. During the third quarter of the year, they were then turned over to Djanbi to learn the basics of being a commando.

As it turned out, Djanbi's primer ended up being long in enthusiasm and short on substance. Without any weapons or proper training facilities, the students were given what amounted to a strenuous regimen of running and calisthenics around the countryside south of Jakarta. This over, they were sent to Surabaya for a month of maritime operations under the auspices of Indonesian marine instructors.

By the close of 1951, the second class finished its paces. Again pleased with the results, the army looked to formalize the ad hoc course by establishing a fulltime intelligence school. And because Djanbi's commando instruction had been well received, he was invited to teach subsequent cycles. This initially appealed to him, but he quickly soured upon hearing that the Dutch government had agreed to dispatch military instructors to teach other courses at the same school. Stung by earlier charges that he was a traitor for taking Indonesian citizenship—and uncomfortable that he carried no rank as a civilian—Djanbi wanted no part of a program set to receive Dutch military assistance. Reluctantly, he returned to his tulips.[7]

The intelligence school's loss was Kawilarang's gain. Hearing that Djanbi was again a gentleman farmer near Bandung, he dispatched a staff member in February 1952 to make a pitch for his help in forming a commando outfit directly under the Siliwangi division. Thinking in modest terms, the unit was initially to total just one combat company.

Arriving at Kawilarang's office in khaki drill, Djanbi looked eager to get back into soldiering. But conscious that he carried insufficient weight as a civilian, he had one demand: he wanted to officially join the Indonesian army with the rank of major. This was a tall order. Accepting Europeans into their military—even those that had taken Indonesian citizenship—was a sensitive issue. Moreover, in the deflated rank structure of the Indonesian military at that time, majors carried considerable weight; the chief-of-staff for the entire armed forces was only a colonel.

The Indonesians, however, were not in a position to bargain. With the DI problem in need of resolution and Djanbi possessing vital skill sets, Kawilarang expedited the request to Jakarta with a favorable recommendation. An answer quickly came back to Bandung: the former Dutch captain was now an Indonesian major.

Sporting his new commission, Djanbi spent March assembling an instructor cadre. Because he had already put sixty students through commando qualification during the second Combat Intelligence course, he requested six of the best from that cycle. The army headquarters was lukewarm to this, allowing only half that number—two lieutenants and a sergeant major—to make the transfer.[8]

Looking elsewhere, Djanbi went to the Siliwangi division's non-commissioned officer (NCO) school and battalion recruitment center. Coming away with fifteen volunteers, he put them through a tough two-month course to learn the basics of commando tactics. In the end, just eight passed. Still short of what he deemed the minimum required number of instructors, Djanbi networked among the former KNIL paratroopers he had once trained. Half a dozen ex-sergeants, nearly all from eastern Indonesia, answered his call.

As Djanbi was busy organizing trainers, Kawilarang pushed through the paperwork to formally authorize his commandos. On 16 April, Kesko (*Kesatuan Komando*, or Commando Unit) was officially created within his Siliwangi division.[9] A further order on 28 May added four more sergeants to the burgeoning Kesko cadre, plus another twenty-five civilians to serve in administrative slots.

To that time, Djanbi was operating out of an austere two-room building in downtown Bandung containing nothing more than two tables and a typewriter. In need of a more permanent home close to the provincial capital, he scouted for options. Though it held negative undertones because it once hosted the infamous KNIL Special Troop Regiment, he viewed Batu Jajar with an approving eye. Encountering no resistance from Kawilarang, he promptly claimed the deserted post for the commandos.

By then already mid-year, Djanbi was ready to initiate training for Kesko's combat company. Just as with the Combat Intelligence class he trained the previous year, his instruction was to be heavy on physical fitness. Because it was a fair bet that many—if not most—would not go the duration, he requested four hundred students to allow for attrition. As the commandos were subordinate to the Siliwangi division, recruitment was limited to volunteers from within the West Java military region.

On 1 July, the requisite number of candidates assembled at a marshalling site near Cimahi, a small village neighboring Bandung. Among the four hundred were two captains, including one who had arrived with his entire infantry company in tow. Aside from a platoon of former KNIL troops originally from eastern Indonesia (including five paratroopers that had received airborne instruction from Djanbi himself), the majority were ethnic Sundanese.[10]

Physically, the candidates were a mixed lot. Looking to weed out non-commando material, Djanbi put them through a grueling five months of exercise, commando basics, and jungle and mountain warfare tactics. During the last week came a long march across West Java that took them through DI-infested territory. Still without proper equipment and facilities, much of the training was little different from an infantry course—though the intensity was ratcheted up several notches. Instead of a twenty-kilometer forced march, for example, they marched for sixty kilometers with little food. Before it was over, he had them quitting by the dozens.

On 6 December, Djanbi and his instructors reviewed their handiwork. Of the original 400 students, 242 remained. Though he had yet to put them through a further phase focusing on maritime operations, Djanbi had them turn out in parade formation. Satisfied they were steeled to a sufficient level, he presented each with a triangular green shoulder patch featuring an upright dagger; above it, an arc bore a single word: Komando.

While Djanbi had been putting his students through the paces, the army headquarters had watched enviously from the sidelines. On 14 January 1953, with Kesko barely a month old and yet to see its first deployment, Jakarta weighed in and determined that the commandos should come under its direct control. With this decision, Kesko was wrested from Kawilarang and placed under the army chief-of-staff. A month later, commando training was transferred from the Siliwangi division to the army's training and education inspectorate. Reflecting these shifts, on 18 March the unit was relabeled as the Army Commando Corps (*Korps Komando Angkatan Darat*, or KKAD).

Though Kawilarang was not overly pleased with Jakarta hijacking his pet project, the change was largely semantic. The KKAD base remained at Batu Jajar and, since the DI threat had not abated, West Java was still their likely proving ground.

Before the KKAD could have its baptism by fire, however, Djanbi was anxious to initiate the maritime phase of training. This primarily revolved around use of inflatable rubber boats in riverine and coastal conditions. But since these boats were to be produced by Indonesia's national rubber industry, and the local factory was slow in delivery, the fledgling commandos were forced to wait until 30 August before taking to the waterways and beaches around West Java.

Two months later, the KKAD students finished their maritime tutorial. Attrition had taken a further toll, reducing the corps to slightly less than two hundred men. Djanbi retained twin hats as both KKAD commander and chief instructor. Apart from his cadre of trainers, those that finished both the commando and maritime phases were grouped into a single combat company—appropriately dubbed Company A—under the command of Supomo, a bright and innovative captain who had arrived with his entire infantry company the previous July. At long last, the commandos were ready for battle.[11]

Even before Company A had started its maritime training, army headquarters was already contemplating an expansion of the KKAD. This time recruitment would be open to volunteers from across the archipelago, not just West Java. In anticipation of this widened training, headquarters issued an order on 21 July for the commandos to enlarge their instructor cadre.

This put Djanbi in a quandary. Finding good instructor material in the young Indonesian armed forces, he knew, was easier said than done. Qualified personnel were at a premium; those that showed potential were jealously hoarded by training centers that had sprung up in each of the military regions.

One possible source was graduates from the Infantry Instructor School in Bandung. Near the end of 1953, recruitment notices were posted by the

KKAD to the school's recent alumni. Among those that answered the call were several former student militiamen that fought in Central Java during the independence struggle.

These student-soldiers had been a disciplinary headache for years. Many had been yanked from high school (and in some cases, junior high school) well before graduation and, once the Dutch departed, were either too old or too ill disciplined to return to the classroom. Maladjusted to peacetime society, they were unruly at best and deadly at worst.

In an attempt to properly integrate some of these young combatants into the post-independence armed forces, four hundred of the most promising teenagers had been enticed into joining a cadet training program in Bandung beginning in January 1951. Because Holland was looking to mend bilateral ties after the war, the Dutch military was quick to offer advisors to run the course.

It was to prove a mistake. Sitting in front of their former enemies, the students—young, idealistic, overly confident, and rabidly anti-Dutch—were an educational nightmare. Baiting the Europeans, they continuously taunted the instructors or boycotted their classes. At one point, they staged a noisy sit-in when their stipend was late. Only a quarter of the class ultimately passed.

Among the graduates was a quiet, driven Central Java native named Leonardus Benjamin "Benny" Moerdani. One of thirteen children, Moerdani had been raised a Catholic and was fluent in Dutch—both on account of his mother being part Dutch. Though among the youngest in the Bandung cadet class, his intense persona and keen intellect made him a natural leader among his peers.

Without pause, Moerdani and forty-one fellow cadets were ushered across town into a further course at the newly-established Infantry Instructor School. When they finally emerged in mid-1952, they were now properly recognized as second lieutenants in the Indonesian army. Most were soon dispersed to regional training centers around the country, though Moerdani remained in Bandung.[12]

Hearing of the KKAD invitation for commando instructors, Moerdani was interested. Along with four of his fellow lieutenants—all former student troops from Central Java—he showed up at Batu Jajar in January 1954. By the following month, over eighty instructor candidates had been assembled.

Living up to their reputation, the former student-soldiers suffered frequent lapses in discipline. Moerdani, then only twenty-one years old, balked at being subordinate to Dutch expatriate Djanbi. In a bit of a stretch, he and his peers darkly hinted that Djanbi was a spy by noting that the major's initials—MID—were the same as the Dutch term for Military Intelligence Detachment (*Militaire Inlichtingen Dienst*). Djanbi did not exactly help his own cause by being an aloof disciplinarian.[13]

Incredibly, the railing by the instructor candidates had an effect. With their complaints striking a chord with some of the more xenophobic members of the army leadership, orders were prepared to drum Djanbi out of the commandos and into a less sensitive training slot. His replacement was to be the recently appointed KKAD chief-of-staff, Alex Prawira, an infantry captain who had yet to undergo the rites of commando training.

Hearing of the impending move, the original cast of KKAD instructors protested. Led by Lieutenant Marzoeki Soelaiman, the senior Indonesian trainer, they persuasively argued that it was far too premature to replace Djanbi and lose his expertise.

Eventually a compromise was reached. Djanbi could remain at the helm of the KKAD, but he was to begin preening an eventual successor. As Alex Prawira had suffered a loss of face following his aborted promotion, he took this as his cue to permanently leave the corps. His replacement, and Djanbi's new heir apparent, was Major R.E. Djaelani. An ethnic Sundanese, Djaelani had spent the independence struggle fighting along the west coast of Java, then served a tour with a Siliwangi battalion dispatched to southern Kalimantan. Like Prawira, Djaelani was not commando qualified. To rectify this shortcoming, Djanbi oversaw a special three-month course to bring his new chief-of-staff up to speed.[14]

Meantime, Benny and his class of future instructors completed their initiation course on 19 July. Just over half—forty-four candidates—successfully graduated the commando phase of training and were awarded shoulder insignia. Added to the previous cadre of trainers, the commandos were now poised to begin churning out more combat troops.

In mid-March 1954, the KKAD's combat company moved closer to its first taste of battlefield action. Marching his men out of Batu Jajar, Captain Supomo steered them toward the West Java district capital of Garut. The next town of note southeast of Bandung, Garut was home to a major textile factory that coincidentally produced army fatigues. Its surrounding countryside also happened to be a hotbed of DI activity.

On paper, the DI had been going from strength to strength. Spreading into Central Java, they held sway over the western periphery of that province. They had also moved beyond Java in September 1953 after militant Acehnese in northernmost Sumatra declared their simmering anti-secular struggle was DI's western chapter.

Under the surface, however, the DI was shaping up to be more a nuisance than a genuine threat. Even in its West Java stronghold, the Islamic guerrillas were poorly tutored in tactics and rarely coordinated activities between villages. Moreover, its diverse mix of weaponry—some turned over by the Japanese, much more of it stolen from the Indonesian military—was an armorer's nightmare. And even though the vast majority of Indonesians were Muslims, most adhered to a tolerant, flexible strain that often absorbed traditional mysticism; those fighting on Java were finding militant Islam a tough rallying call among the peasantry.

Still, defeating the DI guerrillas was proving a study in frustration for the Indonesian military. Playing off their village contacts and superior knowledge of the local terrain, the extremists would invariably melt into the jungle just ahead of patrolling troops. "Whenever we arrived on the scene," said one Siliwangi company commander, "we were always one step behind."[15]

Now it was the KKAD's turn to try their hand at counterinsurgency. On 5 May, they experienced their first contact with the elusive DI. For the next week, minor engagements continued. When it was over, the commandos emerged with a few bruises but no fatalities; DI casualties, though unconfirmed, were thought to be about the same.

Hearing of the skirmishes, Siliwangi commander Kawilarang was not overly impressed. Without proper gear—especially radios—he realized the KKAD was unable to conduct extended patrols, which had been his *raison d'être* for creating Kesko in the first place. "What was the difference between the infantry and the commandos?" he sniffed rhetorically. "Not much."[16]

The KKAD troops returned to Batu Jajar with newfound confidence. Not around long enough to share in the glow was Captain Supomo, who took his leave of Company A to attend staff college. His replacement was Lieutenant R.A. Fadillah, a former student-soldier from Central Java who had been in the instructor candidate class that graduated in July. Three months later, it was Fadillah who led the commandos through downtown Jakarta during the annual 5 October Armed Forces Day parade.

More than ever before, the parading commandos exuded a striking first impression. At the front of the marching column, Fadillah wielded a Dutch-style saber designed the previous century during the bloody colonial campaign against Acehnese rebels. On his hip was a Fairbairn-Sykes commando dagger, a British knife first issued in 1940 to elite Allied formations. Reflecting his British training during World War II, Djanbi had selected the Fairbairn-Sykes as the KKAD standard; a Fairbairn-Sykes was also featured on the KKAD shoulder patch.

Setting the KKAD apart, too, was the beret worn by Fadillah and his men. Back in September 1953, the army headquarters had authorized the commandos to wear distinctive headgear. Only two other formations received similar permission: the artillery corps, which wore olive berets, and cavalry troops, who used black. Recalling his Dutch service, Djanbi wanted to use red headgear like that issued by his airborne training school. The only ones available from the Indonesian quartermaster, however, were black. Attempting to improvise, the commandos soaked their issued items in tea. The result was a less than flattering chocolate shade.

In need of a beret badge to go along with the beret, Djanbi turned toward artists within his ranks. One particularly gifted lieutenant produced a winning sketch combining a saber (symbolizing land operations), anchor (maritime ability), and wings (fast mobility).[17]

Finally, all of the commandos were outfitted in one-piece camouflage coveralls. These uniforms had an interesting lineage. Originally produced in large numbers for U.S. Marines during World War II, they were theoretically reversible: a brown-dominant camouflage pattern was printed on one side (for use when storming beaches) and a green-dominant pattern on the other (for jungle operations). In practice, the marines found it impractical to reverse their uniforms in the heat of battle; in addition, they found the one-piece construction unwieldy when relieving the bowels—especially during bouts of diarrhea common in the tropics. Following the war, many of these coveralls had been donated by the U.S. to the Royal Dutch military. The Dutch, in turn, provided bolts of this reversible cloth to the Indonesian armed forces. Indonesia had then fashioned their own coveralls and provided the first lot to the commandos.

The KKAD might not have been fully versed in the ways of being a commando, but—between the uniforms and the accoutrements—at least they were starting to look the part.

1   The official name of the nationalist armed forces changed numerous times during the war of independence and its immediate aftermath. In August 1950, following the declaration of a republic, its title was *Angkatan Perang Republik Indonesia* (APRI, or Republic of Indonesia War Forces).

2   *Sejarah TNI*, Jilid II, p. 82.

3   Kawilarang interview.

4   Ibid., p. 5.

5   Interview with Jan Linzel, 5 March 1999.

6   Trisnoyuwono, "Terjun Payung di Indonesia," *25 Tahun AVES Sport Parachute* *Club*, (club magazine published in 1994), p. 6.

7   Sugiyanto interview; interview with Marzoeki Soelaiman, 20 May 1999.

8   Soelaiman interview.

9   This date, 16 April 1952, is celebrated as the founding day of the Indonesian army special forces.

10   Interview with Wenno A.L., 5 March 1999.

11   Interview with Soebari, 6 March 1999.

12   Following the Dutch system, graduates of the Infantry Instructor School were initially labeled as reserve lieutenants. In March 1953, this designation was changed to second lieutenant.

13   Soelaiman interview.

14   Soelaiman interview; Kawilarang interview.

15   Interview with H.H. Djajadiningrat, 5 September 2001.

16   Kawilarang interview.

17   Soelaiman interview; Sugiyanto interview.

CHAPTER THREE

POLITICAL INTRIGUE

Liking what it saw, the army headquarters wanted more. On 25 July 1955, Vice President Mohamad Hatta presided over an official ceremony at Batu Jajar upgrading Djanbi's KKAD into an Army Commando Force Regiment (*Resimen Pasukan Komando Angkatan Darat*, or RPKAD). To mark the occasion, the troops soaked their mud-colored headgear in scarlet dye. More in line with the color traditionally favored by airborne troops in Europe, the commandos from that point forward standardized to a red beret.

The changes extended beyond their name and head gear. As a single combat company was considered too small for a regiment, the RPKAD the following week began recruiting for a new training cycle. Of 332 candidates that answered the call, roughly half were volunteers from West Java and the other half from Central Java.

Once assembled, they were ushered before the RPKAD's training section at Batu Jajar. In line with its new regimental status, this section had been given the more formal title of Army Commando Force School (*Sekolah Pasukan Commando Angkatan Darat*, or SPKAD). Major Djaelani, the RPKAD chief-of-staff, was dual-hatted as the SPKAD commander; he was assisted by Lieutenant Benny Moerdani.

Despite the lessons learned from earlier cycles, the SPKAD's approach to training was still less than systematic. For nine months, this latest batch of candidates was put through a halting mix of exercise and commando basics. After that, they were taken on a month of patrols through jungles and over mountainous terrain. Most of the material was still new to the instructors, who had yet to perfect many of the nuances of commando operations. For budgetary reasons, most of the class was not given the amphibious portion of training.[1]

By May 1956, only 126 students remained. Among those that did not complete the instruction was the entire contingent from Central Java, which had grown disillusioned and returned to their home province en masse. The remaining graduates—all from West Java—were gathered into the RPKAD's second combat company, dubbed Company B.

With their combat capability effectively doubled, many of the RPKAD's senior cadre were now convinced they were ready to place the unit fully in the hands of indigenous officers. This meant finding a way to ease out Major Djanbi. Unfortunately, they were lacking in tact when they abruptly offered him a less visible position within the army's training command. Reading this as a snub, the major resigned in anger and took a position at a British plantation in West Java.[2]

In as the new regimental commander was Major Djaelani. As an alum of the Siliwangi division, a lineage shared by the vast majority of his troops, he had better rapport with the commandos than the often stiff Djanbi from the outset. He was also a pronounced disciplinarian and identified an immediate need to fine-tune commando training. Mandated to do this was his successor as head of the SPKAD, Captain Wiyogo Atmodarminto. Just back from the U.S.—where he had been the first Indonesian graduate of ranger training at Fort Benning, Georgia—Wiyogo's first step was to rationalize the training curriculum into an intensive three-month course divided evenly between basic commando, jungle/mountain warfare, and amphibious warfare phases. "I made departments for each of the three," he recalled, "with their own dedicated training teams."[3]

Wiyogo also scouted out better training venues. For mountain training, good rocky walls were identified near Lembang, a village near Bandung where Major Djanbi once tilled his tulips. For amphibious exercises, an initial site was chosen on the southern coast of Java near Cilacap, then moved to a beach on the western extreme of the island near Merak.

Wiyogo also oversaw plans to begin converting the regiment to airborne status. For Indonesia, military parachuting made tactical sense. As a nation of seventeen thousand islands covering a distance equivalent to that between New York and Los Angeles, getting troops from one part of the country to the other was a difficult logistical proposition. Much as the French had discovered in Indochina, parachutes were often the only viable means of rapid deployment over rugged terrain with few runways and even fewer helicopters.

The Dutch had quickly come to realize the utility of parachuting in Indonesia, and had performed a handful of combat jumps in the final years of the colonial era. Their opponents, the Indonesian nationalists, had also flirted with parachutes. In 1946, while still in the midst of the independence struggle, officers from Indonesia's fledgling air force had found some old chutes left by the Imperial Japanese. These were used that same year for practice jumps from biplanes near the nationalist stronghold at Yogyakarta.

The following year, the Indonesians planned for something far more ambitious. Recognizing that their independence struggle was stagnating on some of the outer islands, the revolutionary leaders on Java looked to jumpstart anti-colonial zeal on Kalimantan by dropping in a team of seasoned guerrillas. To do this, the air force trained a class of airborne candidates, most of whom were originally from Kalimantan.

That August, fourteen of the novice paratroopers were selected, put aboard a C-47 (flown by an American mercenary pilot) at Yogyakarta, and dropped over the jungles of Kalimantan. As soon as they landed, they found the population less than receptive. Dutch informants brought a swift colonial response, resulting in the capture or death of all the guerrillas in a matter of days.[4]

From this shaky start, the Indonesian air force maintained its small cadre of airborne instructors. In 1950, during the months immediately after independence, this cadre shifted to Andir Airbase in Bandung. Late that same year, it was this group of instructors that began training members of the first Combat Intelligence class. Though this class was comprised entirely of army officers and non-commissioned officers, the air force added on a few of its own students for the segment on airborne instruction.

One of the latter was Captain A. Wiriadinata, commander of the air force's airbase defense troops. Wiriadinata soon became smitten by parachutes, leading him in February 1952 to convert one of his airbase defense companies into an airborne-qualified Quick Reaction Force (*Pasukan Gerak Tjepat*, or PGT). As the nation's first parachute formation, the PGT was theoretically mandated with reinforcing airbases under siege and other contingencies that required an immediate introduction of government forces.

In late 1953, the air force's modest airborne school shifted across town to Bandung's second runway at Margahayu airbase. With them went the PGT, which eventually doubled in strength over the next three years.

Eyeing the benchmark set by the PGT, the RPKAD felt a tinge of inter-service rivalry. As the army's commando reserve, they saw themselves as the military's elite. But the air force's PGT had not only grown to about the same size, but also had bragging rights as the only formation capable of airborne operations. To even the score, the RPKAD successfully lobbied to put half of its combat element—Company A—through the air force's parachute school at Margahayu. Training for the first 62 members of the company was set to start on 16 November 1956.

It was not to be.

Since its inception, the Indonesian military saw itself as a revolutionary force that was one with society. Not surprisingly, some of its officers became heavily politicized, exposing themselves to the intrigues never far from the surface among Indonesia's top civilian leaders.

Perhaps none attracted more controversy than the army chief, Colonel Abdul Nasution. Given the unenviable task of rationalizing the structure of the post-independence army, Nasution had to balance the expectations of hundreds of thousands of militiamen (who sought slots in the military) with the realities of a limited budget. He saw little choice but to make sharp cuts, an unpopular decision that earned him enemies by the score.

At the same time, many officers in the armed forces were rubbed raw by Sukarno's fiery brand of populism. Emotions peaked in October 1952, when a putsch against the president was stillborn in its earliest hours. Sukarno responded by sacking many top commanders, including Nasution. Out of uniform, the colonel spent the next four years writing a couple of military treatises and dabbled in politics (he won, though never occupied, a seat in the national assembly). Nasution also kept his channels open to the president, patiently lobbying to one day go back to active military duty.

Seeing this, Nasution's detractors in the army moved decisively to prevent his return to uniform. In 1955, the top brass held a key meeting in which they voted on a series of decrees specifically targeted against the colonel. No officer could directly participate in a political party, they decided, and no officer could return to his post after a hiatus of more than three years. Nasution violated both stipulations.

Sukarno heard of these decisions, and decided to ignore them. Feeling that Nasution was sufficiently rehabilitated—and looking to send a bold signal to the military about his supreme authority—the president chose to reinstate him at his old position as army chief. Furthermore, the colonel was to get a double promotion to major general. All of this was set to take effect on 7 November 1956.

Nasution's critics were livid but not surprised. Since August, opposition within the army had been mounting behind the scenes. One group of dissenters was Sundanese officers from the Siliwangi division, including the Jakarta garrison commander. A second group consisted of young officers from across the army who resented the fall of liberal values under Sukarno. Both were united in their aversion to the president.

Acting as link between the two groups was Colonel Zulkifli Lubis. Though he was Nasution's own cousin, Lubis was a longtime rival whose distaste for Nasution had gotten personal. Rising to the post of deputy army chief, he saw himself as a contender for the top slot. But in early August, with Nasution's return already widely rumored, Lubis was informed of his imminent transfer to Medan as the regional commander for North Sumatra. This was part of a larger shakeup among the army's top officers, focusing on several who had transformed far-flung seats into virtual warlord posts.

As the order had the backing of the president, Lubis complied—but only to a degree. On 20 August, he stepped down from his position as deputy chief but refused to move to Medan. Preferring instead to stay close to the center of power, the colonel went underground in West Java. Stealing up to Bandung, he began conspiring with the restive Siliwangi officers.

Shortly before month's end, Captain Marzoeki Soelaiman, the longtime commando instructor who had gotten a recent promotion to RPKAD chief-of-staff, received an unexpected call from Junus Djohor. Junus commanded an infantry battalion commander in Bandung; he was also Marzoeki's brother-in-law. As the two got into a familial huddle, Junus spoke of Lubis and hinted at Siliwangi members taking matters into their own hands.

Listening intensely, Marzoeki took the message back to Major Djaelani at Batu Jajar. Thus began three months of clandestine meetings with a wide range of dissenting officers across West Java. From the RPKAD, knowledge of the brewing conspiracy was limited to Marzoeki, Djaelani and Sugiyanto, the same lieutenant who had first broached commando training with Djanbi in 1951 and had since transferred to the RPKAD as its intelligence officer.

As the months progressed, plans among the conspirators grew more grandiose. Several regiments of the Siliwangi division were to move into Jakarta and seize key points of control, the plotters agreed.[5] If possible, Nasution and other key leaders were to be kidnapped. If possible, too, Sukarno was to be pressured into dismissing the cabinet. The RPKAD was to merely lend moral support, marching through the capital in a final show of force after the Siliwangi infantrymen had secured their objectives.

The devil to all this was in the details—or lack thereof. For all their clandestine trysts during September and October, few specifics were ever finalized. In addition, the conspirators leaked like a sieve; though the top rebels did not know it, Nasution loyalists had gotten word of their scheming and passed the information to the general.

Pressing ahead, the dissidents continued meeting through the second week of November. The Siliwangi officers were still professing commitment, but had taken a hit when their sympathetic commander, Colonel Kawilarang, was abruptly stripped of his command and dispatched to the U.S. in September as the new defense attaché in Washington. Nasution's hand was seen behind this transfer.

On 15 November, Lieutenant Sugiyanto attended what would prove the final planning session of the conspirators. Gathering with Siliwangi members, they agreed to begin moving units into position that evening, with the march into Jakarta set to start during the pre-dawn hours of the following morning.

Reporting this news back to Djaelani, the major was in a quandary. He did not like the eleventh hour decree to get into position that same night. But after further consideration, he relented. "We are commandos," he offered. "It might be too late, but we must follow orders."[6]

Resigned to participate, Djaelani rushed to assemble reliable troops. He looked to Company A, which was slated to send the first half of its men for airborne training the next day. Command of that company had gone four months earlier to Lieutenant Benny Moerdani, Djaelani's former deputy at the SPKAD. But Benny had gotten serious food poisoning and had been convalescing in the hospital for a month. Sick, too, was Captain Marzoeki, who had collapsed from exhaustion at Batu Jajar after the previous week of late night coup planning.

Without a company commander, Djaelani took part of Company A under his wing and loaded them aboard civilian vehicles. Driving through the night, they arrived just outside the southeast edge of Jakarta. Because the RPKAD base at Batu Jajar did not have a sufficiently large radio, he remained in touch with his headquarters via a radio relay link (manned by a loyal lieutenant) at Bandung.

With the bulk of the RPKAD unit remaining outside Jakarta, Lieutenant Sugiyanto and two others stole up to the city limits. There they waited for word of the Siliwangi troops marching triumphantly through the capital. What they did not know was that Nasution, in a beautifully timed spoiling effort, had loyalists make sweeping arrests of most of the dissident officers across West Java.

None the wiser, Sugiyanto retreated back to Djaelani's position at noon. While they deliberated, a rebel emissary arrived at 1330 hours with new orders for the RPKAD to replace the Siliwangi infantrymen that were supposed to spearhead the march into Jakarta.

Looking back at his understrength company, Djaelani scoffed at the revised plan. Incensed that he had been left exposed and vulnerable, he told his men to eat and then get back aboard their vehicles for immediate return to Batu Jajar. And in a noble move, he vowed that he alone would take the fall for the regiment.[7]

That night, Djaelani arrived back at base. Incredibly, he and the remaining coup plotters ignored the earlier arrests and continued with their scheming at daybreak. Three days later, Colonel Lubis himself secretly arrived at Batu Jajar and agreed with the RPKAD commander to restart their attempt to overthrow the government.

If there was any remaining operational security, it was dashed the following morning when Djaelani opted to brief his regiment. Calling together key officers, he told them they had two days to decide if they wanted to participate.

The reaction from the unit was less than positive. On the morning of 21 November, the sound of gunfire reverberated across the barracks. Several sergeants from the untested Company B were firing their weapons into the air, roughing up officers and vowing to arrest Djaelani—who was attending a military ceremony in Bandung—for betraying the regiment.

Adding muscle to the sergeants was a tank that arrived at the gates of the compound. Standing on the turret was Captain Supomo, the same officer who had been the first commander of Company A. Claiming the moral high ground—some RPKAD members later suspected he personally incited the sergeants to rebel—he ordered the arrest of all officers connected to the stillborn putsch. Only Marzoeki, sick in bed, was found after a search of quarters. Placing him in shackles, Supomo retreated back toward Bandung.[8]

With the arrest of Marzoeki, the RPKAD maintained a low profile for the remainder of the month. Lubis had since disappeared from sight, leaving the last remaining coup plotters confused as to the status of plans. To get more details, Lieutenant Sugiyanto took a train down to Jakarta in early December. As he got off the train, he found a group of military officers waiting to place him under arrest. Two weeks later, Nasution finally got around to placing Djaelani in prison. In all, nine RPKAD officers spent the next six months in jail, then another two years under house arrest. Upon release, a disgusted Djaelani burned his military papers to erase all traces of his past service.

1   Djajadiningrat interview; interview with Wiyogo Atmodarminto, 12 April 1999.

2   There was a silver lining to Djanbi's transfer. When the Indonesian government began nationalizing foreign companies in late 1956, Djanbi—who carried Indonesian citizenship—was able to assume a senior managerial role at the plantation. He also remained on active duty; in 1969, at a moving ceremony during RPKAD anniversary celebrations, he was belatedly promoted to the rank of lieutenant colonel.

3   Wiyogo interview.

4   Only thirteen of the fourteen parachutists actually jumped; the fourteenth balked and returned aboard the plane to Java.

5   In 1952, the Siliwangi's brigades were reorganized into regiments, each of up to six battalions.

6   Marzoeki interview.

7   Sugiyanto interview.

8   Marzoeki interview.

CHAPTER FOUR

SECESSION

The intrigue of November 1956—in what became known as the Lubis Affair—was only the tip of the iceberg. On 1 December, Vice President Hatta resigned from office. Unlike the impulsive, philandering Sukarno, Hatta was practical and reasoned. And coming from Sumatra, he helped balance the Javanese chauvinism rife among Indonesia's top leaders.

The resignation of Hatta had a ripple effect across Indonesia's outer islands. Already, many regional army commanders were dissatisfied with the ineffectual political leadership in Jakarta. Compounding matters, they bristled at the stifling economic domination of the central government. And still others were sore at Nasution, who had returned with a vengeance to his earlier campaign of painful troop cuts.

Nowhere was dissatisfaction more pronounced than in the northern half of Sumatra. The forty-year old commander for that region, Colonel Maludin Simbolon, was one of the most prominent, and promising, among the army's first generation of officers. An ethnic Batak Christian, he had taken over the command from the equally impressive Alex Kawilarang back in 1952. Over the ensuing four years, he had grown powerful—militarily, politically and economically—from his seat in Medan.[1]

Simbolon had personal reasons for opposing Nasution. In an effort to rid the capital of the antagonistic Lubis, Nasution had pushed for his problematic cousin to replace Simbolon in distant Medan. Simbolon, in turn, was to receive the largely hollow title of army inspector general. In response to the proposed shuffle, Lubis had tried to topple the government. Though

Simbolon had similar inclinations, he reluctantly agreed to vacate his seat by year's end.

He never had the chance. On 16 December, officers from across northern Sumatra converged on his Medan headquarters to vent frustrations about developments in Jakarta. By meeting's end, forty-eight of the officers signed a petition indicating their serious dissatisfaction with the central authorities. Emerging as most outspoken was the regimental commander from Padang, Lieutenant Colonel Achmad Husein, who had long been stewing over Nasution's sharp cuts among local militiamen.

For Husein, the petition was only the beginning. Four days later, after returning to his Padang home base, he took to the airwaves and announced the overthrow of the Jakarta-appointed governor for central Sumatra.

Hearing of the move, Simbolon was in a fix. Though he had pledged to leave his Medan post within a week, Husein's move put the onus on him to match it with similar tough talk. On 22 December, the colonel rose to the occasion and announced he was no longer taking orders from Jakarta. Half of Sumatra was now in open defiance.

Worse for Jakarta, Sumatra was not alone. To the northeast on the island of Sulawesi, whispers about regional autonomy were fast growing louder. Encouraged by events on Sumatra, military officers from across Sulawesi met on several occasions during January and February 1957 to push for greater economic and political freedoms. They codified these demands in an ultimatum to the central government with a 1 March deadline. When the deadline expired without a response, they promptly declared a Charter of Inclusive Struggle (*Piagam Perjuangan Semesta Alam*, or Permesta) that said they were taking political and economic matters into their own hands without actually declaring independence. Going into spring, the central government faced fires on two fronts.

With the delicate ethnic patchwork of eighty million people in danger of unraveling, Jakarta realized it needed to respond decisively to the challenges from the outer islands. Trouble was, they had few troops available for rapid deployment. As an interim measure, they fired Simbolon from his territorial command and promoted his more pliable deputy. As the troops in Medan were uncertain who to back, Jakarta looked to tip the balance by dropping several planeloads of elite PGT commandos over the city to bolster the grip of the new commander. The resultant drop on 28 December—Indonesia's first combat jump after independence—was a fiasco. Leaving the plane from too low an altitude, the parachutists took heavy casualties (at least one fatality and fourteen with broken legs) as they impacted on the airport runway.[2]

Casualties aside, the jump had the intended psychological impact. Deciding it was best to fight another day, Simbolon fled into the countryside with hundreds of loyal Christian troops, later to reappear in Padang alongside fellow rebel Husein.

While all this had been transpiring, the acting commander for southern Sumatra, Lieutenant Colonel Barlian, was straddling the fence. Not until January 1957 did he jump on the rebel bandwagon and announce formation of a local council based in the city of Palembang. Like the other dissenting colonels, Barlian's council made noises about greater political and economic autonomy. But as he stopped well short of a full split, Jakarta chose to look the other way.

Over the next two months, this non-situation in Palembang persisted. But after the declaration of Permesta in Sulawesi, Barlian decided to push harder. On 9 March, he ousted the governor for southern Sumatra and took the reins himself. Toward this, Jakarta felt it could not afford to turn a blind eye. Establishing contact with one of the senior Javanese officers in Palembang, the central authorities looked to rush in reinforcements like they had done in Medan.

This time, it was the RPKAD that got the call.

In the aftermath of the Lubis Affair, the RPKAD had little time to lick its wounds. With Djaelani sacked and in prison, Jakarta appointed Major Kaharudin Nasution as the new head of the regiment. As a former Siliwangi company commander during the war of independence, he had the same lineage as most of the commandos. Perhaps more important in light of the scheming by Djaelani, he was from the same ethnic clan as the army chief.

With Kaharudin fresh at the helm, the unit had been tasked with a quick deployment out of Java. On the island of Ambon, where government troops had been overseeing the peace after crushing the RMS rebels earlier in the decade, one of the garrisons—disgruntled because of its isolated posting—was threatening to mutiny.

Loading a platoon of RPKAD commandos into a Dakota, they made their way to Ambon in order to confront their restive compatriots. The resultant confrontation was anti-climactic. "We found a company of frustrated troops," said one of the commandos. "We eased the tension through talk and came home."[3]

The deployment to Palembang was not unlike the Ambon mission, only with far higher stakes. Strung around Palembang were a number of lucrative oil refineries, the revenues from which were still going into Jakarta's coffers. The central government could ill afford to jeopardize this income, which meant walking a fine line between carrot and stick.

The stick was to be provided by Lieutenant Benny's Company A. Although most of the company had graduated from airborne training at Margahayu on 13 February, there was no desire to risk a repeat of the problems encountered by the PGT during its jump over Medan. Instead, the army commandos intended to airland directly on the Palembang airfield.

On 13 March, four days after Barlian ousted the governor, Benny placed twenty of his men in each of five Dakotas. With a total of one hundred troops, they made the short hop to Palembang. Representatives from each of the planes then disembarked and met with Barlian loyalists near the tarmac. Bluffing, they claimed that each plane had one hundred commandos.[4]

The feint worked, at least temporarily. Retreating back to Palembang city, the dissidents gave the commandos a wide berth as the latter set up tents at the end of the runway. But once he realized the modest number of government reinforcements, Barlian rose to the challenge. Threatening to blow up Palembang's refineries, he asked Padang's Husein for help and got a tentative pledge of twelve hundred troops. In the subsequent standoff, Jakarta blinked first. Realizing it could not jeopardize the revenue from Palembang's oil, Nasution withdrew the RPKAD company after three weeks. With the central government looking more impotent than ever, Barlian quietly consolidated his grip over the region. Aside from the small oasis in Medan, rebel forces now controlled all of Sumatra.

For the remainder of the year, a standoff ensued. For the most part, the battle between the dissidents and central government was being fought as a war of words. The country's air carrier, Garuda Airlines, still flew scheduled flights to rebel provinces. Most of the rebel and government leaders, too, had family and relatives that regularly crossed the lines. Harsh propaganda aside, neither side appeared particularly anxious about escalating their differences into armed conflict.

In all this, the U.S. government saw opportunity. President Eisenhower, and especially his puritanical Secretary of State John Foster Dulles, were never fans of Sukarno and his sharp anti-Western tongue. And now with major parts of Indonesia in rebellion, Washington in September authorized the U.S. Central Intelligence Agency (CIA) to devise a covert program to support the dissident colonels. Discrete contact was established the following month; in January 1958, the first covert delivery of weapons arrived at Padang.

Growing bold, top Sumatran rebels gathered on 10 February to discuss their next steps. What emerged from their tryst was an ultimatum to Jakarta demanding a new central government that included former Vice President Hatta. And in a calculated bow to Cold War politics, they also demanded that the Indonesian Communist Party (*Partai Komunis Indonesia*, or PKI) be declared illegal. The central government was given five days to respond.

On 15 February, the deadline expired. Jakarta, calling the rebels' bluff, failed to answer with a counteroffer. Backed into a corner, Padang made a fateful decision. After more than a year of threats, the dissidents passed the point of no return and declared formation of the Revolutionary Government of the Republic of Indonesia (*Permerintah Revolusioner Republik Indonesia*, or PRRI).

The scope of the PRRI quickly expanded. Secessionist rebels active in Aceh, as well as a pocket of Islamic guerrillas battling in the jungles of southern Sulawesi, offered their strong support to the newly-proclaimed rebel government.[5] Much more significant was the embrace offered by Permesta. By that time, the central government had managed to win back the loyalty of army officers in the southern part of Sulawesi, leaving only the northern reaches—a Christian-dominated area known as Minahasa—in the Permesta camp. Leading Permesta was Lt. Colonel Herman "Ventje" Sumual, a polished officer whose gripe with Jakarta was mainly over bad economic policies. His senior deputies were fellow Christian officers, many of whom had fallen afoul of the central authorities over barter trading from northern Sulawesi. Joining Sumual, too, was Col. Alex Kawilarang—a Minahasan by birth and the godfather of the RPKAD—who went absent from his Washington attaché post in March and returned to Asia to support the Permesta cause.

Shortly after the declaration of the PRRI, CIA paramilitary assistance to the rebels increased. On 22 February, the first airdrop of weapons occurred at Padang. By March, CIA advisors were posted to both Padang and the Permesta stronghold at the northern Sulawesi city of Manado.

By that point, Jakarta realized it could no longer delay in launching a forceful military response. Because of logistical constraints, the central government decided to focus its initial effort against Sumatra. There, the obvious target was the PRRI power base in Padang. But since this contained the bulk of rebel troops—estimated at several battalions of tough local fighters—the generals in Jakarta decided to seize an interim target beforehand.

Weighing options, they eventually settled on Pekanbaru, a central Sumatran town that was home to a large expatriate population servicing the nearby oil fields. Not only would Pekanbaru be good for psychological reasons—demonstrating that the central government could impose its control over an area with foreign workers—but it was believed to be only lightly defended by the PRRI.

For the retaking of Pekanbaru, Jakarta cobbled together a fleet of navy and merchant marine ships. Aboard these went the most reliable units from across Java: a company of marines, a company of infantry from East Java, a full battalion of infantry from Central Java, and two companies of PGT. From the RPKAD, the airborne-qualified Company A was slated to participate. The codename for the entire operation was Tegas, Indonesian for "resolute." RPKAD commander Kaharudin, freshly promoted to lieutenant colonel, was named the overall operational commander. Lieutenant Colonel Wiriadinata, head of the PGT, was named his deputy.

Though not the largest operation ever mounted in terms of numbers, Tegas promised to be the most complex. It was penned as an ambitious pincer, with a seaborne contingent making its way upriver from the east Sumatran coast and a second task force jumping directly on the airfield fifteen kilometers south of the town. Once the runway was secured, the Central Java infantry battalion would be flown in, link up with the paratroopers, and work their way into town.

On 4 March, the Tegas fleet set sail from Jakarta. Their destination was Bintan Island, twenty kilometers from the Malay mainland and almost within sight of Singapore. One week later, after a forty-eight hour delay due to a last-minute glitch in coordination, the operation was set to begin. The first wave—the two companies of PGT and the RPKAD's Company A—were set to parachute onto the Pekanbaru runway at first light on 12 March.

All of this was not exactly a surprise to the PRRI. The government had been telegraphing its build-up at Bintan Island, and had even told U.S. Embassy officials to evacuate its nationals from Pekanbaru. This information had been passed to the CIA, which scrambled to make an eleventh-hour airdrop of supplies to the small rebel contingent holding the town.

Shortly after midnight on 12 March, a U.S.-piloted C-54 transport overflew the Pekanbaru airstrip and dropped several tons of supplies. The PRRI defenders, who had lit bonfires to mark the dropzone, watched as the bundles rained across the tarmac and into the nearby teak forest. Most of the pallets were loaded into a line of half a dozen waiting trucks; for those caught high in the adjoining jungle canopy, the rebels decided to wait until daybreak before completing the retrieval.

They never had the chance. Just before sunrise, the Tegas airborne task force departed Bintan Island in a cluster of Dakota transports. Storm clouds littered the path, rocking the aircraft and setting nerves on edge. "We debated whether to continue," said Lieutenant Dading Kalbuadi, one of the RPKAD officers, "but decided to persist."[6]

Approaching the dropzone, black smoke from the PRRI bonfires still hung in the air. Aboard the lead transport was the company commander, Lieutenant Benny. As he had still been recuperating from illness when Company A rotated through Margahayu for jump training, this was to be his first leap from an aircraft. "If I hesitate at the aircraft door," he told the next paratrooper in line, "push me from behind."

Below, PRRI soldiers heard the approaching aircraft and assumed it was another aerial supply delivery. When they instead saw paratroopers emerge from the line of planes, they panicked and scattered. Seconds later, Indonesian troops touched earth. The majority drifted wide of their mark, snaring themselves in the branches of the nearby teak trees.

Forty minutes later, most of the paratroopers managed to free themselves and converge on the airstrip. They had been completely unopposed, without a single shot being fired by the PRRI. As they assembled on the tarmac, they spied the line of trucks. "We saw crates in the back," said Dading, "and thought it was canned milk."

Together with a fellow officer, Dading went toward the vehicles to fetch a drink. When he opened a crate, he was dumbfounded to see a bundle of rupiah notes. The other boxes held grenades, food, ammunition, and heavy arms. This included recoilless rifles and bazookas that were more sophisticated than anything in the Indonesian inventory. The RPKAD commandos, who had recently been equipped with Belgian FN semi-automatic rifles, were thoroughly outclassed by the PRRI weaponry.[7]

Encountering no opposition, the paratroopers radioed back an all-clear signal to Bintan Island. At 1200 hours, the infantry battalion airlanded at the runway without incident. Before it arrived, Lieutenant Benny and four of his men took a jeep into Pekanbaru and met no opposition.

Similar news was coming from the seaborne task force. Part of this force—consisting of the infantry company from East Java—paused on the coast to seize the docks used by foreign oil companies. The other part of the force, comprised of the marines, stayed on their boats and worked their way inland along the Siak River. No PRRI were encountered en route, allowing the military to complete its opening phase against the rebels with greater ease than could ever have been imagined.

Bolstered by its success at Pekanbaru, Jakarta set its sights on Padang. Before they could move, however, the Sumatran dissidents suddenly developed some backbone. Doing the unexpected, rebellious troops in Medan spread through the city shortly before dawn on 16 March. At the cost of just two wounded, they pushed out the pro-Jakarta commander and let him retreat unmolested toward Belawan, the port sixteen kilometers to the north.

Though a propaganda coup, the rebel victory proved short-lived. Their Medan offensive was originally supposed to be part of a coordinated push across northern Sumatra. But the other prongs, including one from sympathetic Acehnese rebels, failed to materialize. Worse, General Nasution, shocked by the sudden loss of his Medan foothold, was determined to retake the town in decisive fashion. Looking for troops to spare, he remembered that a fresh infantry battalion had just steamed north from Java to reinforce the Pekanbaru front. Keeping these troops on their ship, he ordered that they sail through the night toward Belawan harbor.

Besides infantry, Nasution also wanted some of his paratroopers to drop into Belawan ahead of time. This posed problems because the military had used all of its parachutes during the Tegas jump and the chutes were still sitting in piles on the side of the Pekanbaru airfield. With little time to spare, they were loaded on a Garuda Airlines Dakota and flown back to Java for repacking.

As the sun broke the horizon on 17 March, a pack of Mustang P-51 fighters and B-25 bombers arrived over Medan. As they began strafing the rebel headquarters, a formation of nine Dakotas approached Belawan to the north. Inside the transports, the RPKAD's Company A and another company of PGT filed toward the doors. For both units, it was to be the second combat jump in five days.

Without complications, the paratroopers floated down toward the Belawan drop zone. Assembling on the ground, Lieutenant Benny marched his men in the direction of several buildings along the waterfront. There he found dozens of civilians, including several expatriates, looking to evacuate aboard commercial vessels.[8]

No sooner had the paratroopers landed than the Javanese infantry battalion arrived by boat and began to disembark at the Belawan docks. Linking up with airborne forces, they commandeered vehicles and headed south toward Medan. If they expected opposition, there was none to be found. Aside from the looted office of the central bank branch, there was little indication of the brief rebel occupation. The dissidents, it turned out, had already taken a convoy of trucks and fled inland for a rendezvous with Simbolon.

While Company A was sweeping the area around Medan, the other half of the RPKAD—Company B—was about to get its first taste of combat. The company was headed by Lieutenant H. Djajadiningrat, Indonesia's first post-independence graduate of the Royal Military Academy in the Netherlands. The son of a famed linguist from West Java, he had commanded a platoon in the Siliwangi division before volunteering for RPKAD training in 1956.

Company B was assigned with expanding the Tegas foothold from Pekanbaru southeast toward the towns along the Indragiri River. Joining them would be a company of Banteng Raiders, the nickname for a tough infantry formation from Central Java.[9] Helping coordinate the thrust was Captain Fadillah. Previously the commander of Company A, Fadillah had taken leave of the regiment to attend a course in Bandung. He remained interested in his old unit, however, and had quietly returned to Batu Jajar in late 1956 to participate on the periphery of the abortive Lubis putsch. Managing to escape recriminations for this, he had rushed to Sumatra to rejoin his fellow Red Berets during the march toward the Indragiri.

By that time, the monsoon season had run its course. Much of the terrain remained inundated with water, however, and the waterways were swollen wide. Complicating movement was a small number of tenacious PRRI defenders moving through the jungle. As the combined government force approached the Indragiri on 3 April, shots from one such rebel group rang out from the opposite bank. Taking charge, Fadillah split the commandos and had them cross to either side of the suspected PRRI position. Djajadiningrat, with just a single RPKAD platoon, was to dig in as a blocking force to the north. Fadillah, with the rest of the company, would sweep them toward the ambush.

At that point, the PRRI troops did the unexpected. Rather than retreating north as planned, they rushed south with guns blazing. Surprised by the rebel onslaught, the RPKAD commandos faltered. One of their machine-gunners took a bullet to the neck and bled to death. Leaving cover to rally his men, Fadillah was cut down by a shot to the abdomen; he died two hours later. The PRRI force—its size was never determined—quietly melted into the bush.

Despite the setback suffered along the Indragiri, by early April the Indonesian military felt ready to press its attack against Padang. Heading the operation was thirty-six year old Colonel Ahmad Yani. Born in Central Java, Yani had received his early military training in Tokyo during the Japanese occupation. In 1955, he had been among the first Indonesian officers selected for training in the U.S. For nine months, he attended the Command and General Staff course at Fort Leavenworth, Kansas. After that, he went to England for a two-month primer on special warfare. Returning to Jakarta, he put his experience to good use in his new job as Nasution's chief of operations, then as his deputy for intelligence. In the latter role, he had gone to Eastern Europe in

January 1958 to canvass the communist bloc for weaponry ahead of the anticipated anti-rebel campaign (the U.S., covertly supporting the dissidents, had slashed military assistance to Indonesia).

Returning from Europe, Yani had been selected in the first week of April to orchestrate the retaking of Padang. His invasion plan bore more than a passing resemblance to the Tegas operation. Just as at Pekanbaru, this attack would include an airdrop of one RPKAD and two PGT companies to seize Padang's airfield. There would also be a simultaneous seaborne landing by more than five battalions, with the amphibious column and paratroopers linking up before marching into town. Taking a patriotic theme, Yani dubbed his campaign "17 Agustus"—the seventeenth of August—Indonesia's independence day.

For Benny's Company A, the Padang blitz followed the same script as Pekanbaru and Belawan. At 0630 on 17 April, the three RPKAD and PGT companies leapt from their C-47 transports over the town's airfield. Landing on the pitted runway, they missed a series of bamboo spikes that had been erected in the surrounding fields with the intent to impale paratroopers. The PRRI defenders, who could have inflicted heavy casualties on the descending government troops, had already fled their machine-gun nests.

Within Padang town, the rebel troops, along with a handful of CIA paramilitary advisors, could see the Dakotas making passes over the airfield. Thinking the planes were ejecting dummy paratroopers as part of a diversionary drop, they discounted the threat and instead focused on the sizable seaborne invasion fleet massing off the coast.

In the end, a battle for Padang never took place. Electing to fight another day, the vast bulk of PRRI combatants fled the city before firing any shots. Realizing they were hopelessly outnumbered, the CIA officers took the small remaining group of defenders and headed into the hills. When government troops arrived that afternoon, the PRRI was nowhere to be found.[10]

With the retaking of Padang, the fate of half of the PRRI appeared sealed. The Sumatran dissidents on the run, the government now looked to deal decisively with the Permesta rebellion in distant Sulawesi. This promised to be far more of a challenge, both because of the vast distances involved and because the Sulawesi rebels were a far more cohesive bunch than their Sumatran counterparts.

For the RPKAD, there were few assets to spare for the Sulawesi campaign. Company A was still committed to the Padang front, while Company B was busy pushing through the jungles and swamps southeast of Pekanbaru. And the RPKAD commander, Lieutenant Colonel Kaharudin, was given double-duty as head of an ad hoc infantry regiment slogging across Sumatra's interior.

Still, the RPKAD was being pressed for a contribution. Digging deep, Benny took fifteen men from his company—dubbed Team A—and readied it for operations against Permesta. Similarly, Company B released fifteen of its men—called Team B—and the RPKAD headquarters at Batu Jajar began piecing together the upper-echelon commandos into a third unit, Team C.[11]

Even before the RPKAD teams left for the new front, their Pemesta opponents suffered a pivotal setback. Prior to mid-May, the CIA had provided the Sulawesi rebels with a handful of Mustang fighters and B-26 bombers, as well as the American and Filipino pilots to fly them. Based at Mapanget airfield near Manado, this small number of airframes had inflicted heavy losses on the government and literally kept Jakarta at bay. Recognizing that any counter-offensive hinged on grounding this rebel air force, the government on 15 May staged a surprise morning bombing raid against Mapanget that destroyed most of the Permesta fleet on the ground.

Three days later, Permesta was hit by further misfortune. During a bombing run against a troop-laden government ship convoy near the island of Ambon, one of the CIA-supplied B-26 bombers was shot down and its American pilot captured. Its hand exposed, Washington on 20 May ordered its CIA paramilitary advisors and aviators at Manado to pack their bags and exfiltrate to the Philippines. For Permesta, this was a crushing blow. With no air support to keep Jakarta at a distance, the door was open to an amphibious landing campaign by government forces. Which is exactly what happened. On 20 May, the same day CIA advisors were abandoning Sulawesi, Jakarta dropped two PGT companies onto the small island of Morotai in the northern Maluku chain. Used by General Douglas Macarthur as a key staging base during his Pacific campaign, Morotai sported several vintage runways and docks. Infantry troops and marines converged at these facilities during the first week of June; close to midnight on 15 June, they reboarded ships for the short trip across the Maluku Sea toward the Sulawesi coast.[12]

Among those launching from Morotai were two of the three RPKAD teams. Lieutenant Benny had taken leave of Sumatra to personally lead

Team A. Lieutenant Sigarlaki, a Christian from Manado, was heading Team B. They were to conduct a clandestine infiltration along the beach twelve kilometers north of Manado. A second landing, totaling one marine and two Javanese infantry battalions, would be conducted thirty kilometers southeast of Manado on the opposite side of the peninsula.

On the morning of 16 June, the first wave of marines hit the beach. Permesta troops tried to make a stand, but soon lost ground due to heavy mortar and gunfire. The Permesta chief, Colonel Sumual, moved forward in a desperate attempt to steel his lines. Slammed by the concussion of an incoming round, he was forced to retreat back to Manado.

North of Manado, meanwhile, the two commando teams had spent the night steaming close to shore under cover of a moonless night. Getting within a hundred meters of the beach, half of Team B edged over the side into the surf. The water came up to their necks, forcing them to hold their FN rifles over their heads and wade toward the sand at a glacial pace. The second half of the team, struggling with a heavy mortar tube and base plate, took even longer. Half of Team A came next, but by then the surf was growing rough and dawn was about to break. Having run out of time, the remainder of Team A, including commander Benny, was forced to sail out to sea and wait over the horizon.

Resting on the beach until 0600 hours, the commandos headed inland. They walked until noon, taking pains to avoid being seen. Spying a lone hut, they determined the occupant was a Muslim by his attire. Approaching cautiously with their berets reversed to reveal the black insides, they pressed him to allow them to rest. Far from offering resistance, he prepared coffee for all the troops.

An hour later, they were again on the move toward their final target, Mapanget airbase. Though the CIA had already removed its air support, Jakarta did not know this and wanted the RPKAD teams to destroy any aircraft and pit the runway. At 2100 hours, they paused for a final briefing by Lieutenant Sigarlaki. They would resume their march at first light, he said, with the twenty-five commandos splitting in two and approaching the airbase from both flanks. The promise of combat held dour emotional overtones for the RPKAD. Not only would they be fighting their erstwhile countrymen, but— since sixteen commandos of northern Sulawesi origin had deserted Batu Jajar and joined the Permesta ranks earlier in the year—there was a good chance the commandos would be confronting former members of their own unit.

Pressing ahead, the RPKAD troops woke before dawn and made progress until 0800 hours. As forward elements reached the airbase perimeter, the battle began with no quarter given by either side. In the end, the Indonesians claimed to have killed thirty-two rebels and destroyed at least five machine guns. But it came at a cost. The Permesta base commander ordered his gunners to lower their .50-caliber antiaircraft mounts and blast the approaching commandos, forcing the raiders to leave behind two dead as they beat a fast retreat toward the beach.

Two others were seriously wounded. One of them, Sergeant Tahril, had set up a mortar and fired a single round when the firefight started. Shot under the left shoulder near his armpit, he remained near his heavy weapon until a second bullet passed through his right cheek, smashing the teeth on that side of his mouth.

Bleeding profusely, Tahril sought out his team's medic. Given a bandage, he stuffed it in his mouth and stumbled through the jungle. He did not get far before a third shot—this time to his left knee—left him crippled on the ground. Fading in and out of consciousness due to blood loss, he briefly woke to see Sigarlaki examining his wounds. He pleaded with the lieutenant to shoot him, then fainted.

When Tahril woke, he heard nothing but the normal background chorus of jungle noises. After six days with no food and only rainwater to drink, a patrol of Permesta troops chanced upon him. Taking him to the nearest village, they cleaned the maggots from his injuries and plied him with food. Ironically, he had been captured by Permesta's RPKAD defectors. Tahril's former instructor—now sporting the Permesta rank of lieutenant—recognized his old student. Unit camaraderie counted for little, however. Marched south through a series of Permesta camps, he was to face the next eighteen months in captivity.

Although most of the Permesta top brass lauded their defenders at Mapanget, a different reaction was offered by Alex Kawilarang. He had been walking a delicate tightrope since spring. Though he had deserted his post in Washington, Jakarta notably refrained from discharging the colonel, thereby leaving the door open for him to return to the fold. Kawilarang had no such intention, but at the same time, his embrace of the rebels was less than complete. While he supported most of Permesta's agenda for northern Sulawesi, he opposed the PRRI's links to religious extremists in southern Sulawesi and in Aceh. His years in West Java, after all, were largely spent in combat against similar fundamentalists.

The bloody engagement at Mapanget served only to compound Kawilarang's misgivings. As founder of the commando forerunner to the RPKAD, most of the regiment's original cadre were his comrades. As he inspected nameplates taken off the Mapanget casualties, one of those killed stood out. "I knew Sergeant Major Tugiman well," he said. "We had been on extended patrols together in Java looking for Muslim extremists." For Kawilarang, the realities of civil war had struck home.

1   Kawilarang did not technically hand over his command directly to Simbolon—a temporary commander served for a month in between.

2   Audrey R. Kahin and George McT. Kahin, *Subversion as Foreign Policy* (Seattle: University of Washington Press, 1995), p. 60.

3   Interview with Sumardji, 12 August 1999.

4   Ibid.

5   In 1953, the Muslim separatist movement in Aceh proclaimed it was part of the Darul Islam umbrella. In 1957, a pocket of Muslim extremists in southern Sulawesi also declared their membership in Darul Islam. Such professed membership was largely symbolic: Darul Islam never had a true unified command for its chapters in Aceh, Sulawesi, and Java.

6   Interview with Dading Kalbuadi, 29 May 1998.

7   At the airfield, the RPKAD troops encountered a single expatriate who claimed to be an employee from Caltex, the oil company operating the nearby fields. In reality, he was CIA case officer Fravel Brown, who had rushed to Pekanbaru to coordinate the airdrop of supplies earlier that morning.

8   Looking over the expatriates gathered at Belawan, Benny was shocked to see Fravel Brown, the same CIA case officer he had encountered at Pekanbaru. Still believing that Brown was an employee of Caltex, he made no attempt to block his departure.

9   The Banteng Raiders were conceived in 1952 as an elite infantry unit to spearhead the campaign against Darul Islam pockets operating in Central Java. Two companies were trained by mid-year, then quickly expanded into a full battalion. By 1958, Central Java fielded two Banteng Raider battalions. There was a certain amount of professional rivalry between the Banteng Raiders and RPKAD, each laying claim to the title of army's most elite.

10   The CIA officers evaded south and later rendezvoused with a submarine for a successful clandestine exfiltration.

11   The commander of Team C, Lieutenant Achmad Kodim, had briefly commanded Company B at its inception before Lieutenant Djajadiningrat.

12   Several boatloads of Permesta troops staging from Sulawesi had earlier seized Morotai on 27 April.

CHAPTER FIVE

MERDEKA

The campaign to retake North Sulawesi—codenamed Merdeka, Indonesian for "independence"—was supposed to be simple. The three seaborne battalions landing on the east would secure their beachhead, then plunge south toward the key Permesta-held towns of Tomohon and Tondano. At the same time, the two RPKAD teams, regrouping on the beach after having been rebuffed at Mapanget, were to be augmented by a Javanese infantry battalion before heading for Manado. If Padang was any indication, the city would fall before the troops could work up a sweat.

Initially, the game plan worked. To the east, the inexperience of the Permesta line was plainly evident as the rebels suffered early reversals. But very quickly, the government's advance slowed to a crawl. When Permesta brought forth some of its .50-caliber machine guns and British-made scout cars, the Javanese halted in their tracks.

North of Manado, the combined task force of commandos and infantry had also run into stiff resistance. Their assault stagnating, the government's senior staff gathered on 24 June and issued a new plan. Putting the stab toward Tondano and Tomohon on hold, both prongs were to focus their energies against Manado.

Inside Manado, the rebels paused to consider their next move. They had been holding their own for a week, but they realized the numbers were not in their favor. Looking to fight another day, they quietly packed their weapons on 24 June and stole south. Two days later, advance marine elements entered the city. They faced no opposition, the rebels having already completed an orderly tactical retreat down to Tomohon.

Permesta's shift was smart on two counts. First, the fertile fields around Tomohon were rich in rice. Second, a relatively high population density around the same area made it Permesta's sympathetic Christian heartland. The government realized this, and was intent to rob them of both the harvest and recruitment base. Set to spearhead their thrust into the area was an ad hoc regimental combat team (*Resimen Team Pertempuran*, or RTP) consisting of infantry, armor, combat engineers, and the three RPKAD teams (Team C had recently arrived in North Sulawesi).

Leading the RTP would be Lieutenant Colonel Mung Parhadimuljo. An ethnic Sundanese, Mung and RPKAD commander Kaharudin had military careers that read like the same script. Both had commanded Siliwangi companies alongside each other during the independence struggle. Both, too, had commanded Siliwangi infantry battalions earlier in the decade.

In terms of personality, the two were worlds apart. Unlike the colorless and conventional Kaharudin, Mung was famed for taking bravery to extremes. He had once wrestled a crocodile in Kalimantan to prove his mettle, and on another occasion had refused medical attention for a gunshot wound. Moving beyond bravery, some of Mung's idiosyncrasies bordered on the eccentric. He forbade his troops from drinking milk, for example, because he declared it too elitist. When subordinates bought a simple platter of traditional food for the unit's anniversary—almost compulsory practice in Indonesia—he chided them for wasting funds. And in an army where officers normally got a car, he took the bus.

Not exactly endearing himself with his men, Mung suitably impressed the army's senior staff. Electing to bring Kaharudin's tenure as RPKAD commander to an abrupt close, on 3 August they named Mung as the RPKAD's fourth commander. Wearing two hats, he immediately led his regimental combat team into the Permesta heartland. With commandos in the forefront, by mid-month all major rebel-held towns were easily retaken. Like its PRRI comrades on Sumatra, Permesta very much looked like a spent force.

For the next two years, Mung would spend the majority of his time in North Sulawesi pursuing elusive Permesta remnants through the bush. His other job—managing the RPKAD at Batu Jajar—was accomplished from afar. Normally, an elite unit would have withered from such neglect. But on account of a strong chief-of-staff, the RPKAD underwent substantial quantitative and qualitative growth.

That chief-of-staff, Major Widjojo Soejono, was a habitual over-achiever. A native of East Java, he was only sixteen (he falsely claimed he was eighteen) when he entered officer training in 1944 under the auspices of the Japanese occupation army. When the Japanese were vanquished, he rose swiftly through the ranks of the revolutionary forces in his native East Java. By 1953, he got his first battalion command at age twenty-five, leading them into combat against Darul Islam. Sent to Bandung for command and general staff school in 1957, he graduated first in his class and spent the next year as an instructor for the course.

When he was named RPKAD chief-of-staff in early 1959, Major Widjojo anticipated it would be his hardest role to date. By reputation, he knew Mung was hard to deal with. "He was very puritan," he recalls. "Very Spartan."[1]

Mung was only part of the problem. By the time of his arrival, Widjojo found the commandos suffering from collective exhaustion. In continuous action for over a year, Benny's Company A had shifted in its entirety up to North Sulawesi and was not expected to return until July. Company B had recently returned to Batu Jajar after a trying deployment in the jungles of central Sumatra. Attrition had hit both companies hard, with real troop strengths far below authorized levels.

Even before Widjojo's arrival, the regiment had recognized the need to bring in replacement personnel and to enhance its skill sets. To train replacements, a new class of two hundred candidates was recruited in October 1958. For the first time, they were recruited directly from among the general public; previously, all RPKAD candidates were solicited from other army units.

To enhance the RPKAD's skill sets, the Indonesian military found England willing to help. On the diplomatic front, ties between Jakarta and London had long been frosty, if not hostile. For its part, London was not enamored by Indonesia's declared expansion of its territorial waters to twelve miles, impinging on neighboring Malaya. Although England had recently granted independence to Malaya, it was still very much concerned about the defense of its former colony. And for its part, Jakarta correctly suspected that England had backed America's covert support of the PRRI and Permesta.

But following the rapid collapse of the rebels on Sumatra and Sulawesi, England (and the United States) was seeking to mend fences with Indonesia and the mercurial Sukarno. This included a pragmatic offer of military assistance, some of which was extended to the RPKAD. As a start, a single RPKAD lieutenant was accepted in late 1958 into a three-month jungle warfare course at the British Far East Land Forces Training Center near Johor Bahru, Malaya. In 1959, two more RPKAD officers (including the recently promoted Captain Achmad Kodim, a former company commander), were invited to the same course.[2]

More British assistance came in June 1959. During that month, two RPKAD lieutenants departed for jumpmaster training at the Royal Air Force Parachute Training School at Abingdon. When they came back after nearly five months, the RPKAD was set for a major change. While still able to keep the same initials, on 26 October the RPKAD officially became known as the *Resimen Para Komando Angkatan Darat* (Army Para-Commando Regiment). Also retaining the same initials, the SPKAD became the *Sekolah Para Komando Angkatan Darat* (Army Para-Commando School).

The nuance was significant. From that point forward, airborne training was to be a requirement for all RPKAD troops. The two Abingdon graduates—Lieutenants Gunawan Wibisono and Djajadiningrat—were named the commander and deputy commander, respectively, of the SPKAD's new parachute course. The ground phase of airborne training would take place at Batu Jajar, while actual jumps—for the time being—would be staged from the PGT facilities at Margahayu.

More changes followed. In mid-November, Major Widjojo was beckoned by Colonel Achmad Yani, the army's deputy chief-of-staff who had headed the operation to retake Padang. The SPKAD commander, said Yani, should be replaced by Major Sarwo Edhie Wibowo. The request reeked of nepotism. Both Yani and Sarwo Edhie hailed from the same district in Central Java. Both had served together since the Japanese occupation in 1943. And in 1948, Sarwo Edhie had commanded a battalion in Yani's brigade.

Widjojo resisted. Wiyogo was still highly effective, he argued in defense of the current SPKAD commander and Fort Benning graduate.

Yani refused to budge. "Sarwo Edhie is stubborn," he said of his pick, "but you can rely on him."[3]

Shortly before year's end, the RPKAD experienced yet another major change. While the SPKAD would remain at Batu Jajar, the regimental headquarters and its combat companies were to shift ten kilometers south of Jakarta near the village of Cijantung. Hearing of this, Major Widjojo again balked. "It is not good having a special force so close to the political center," he insisted. This was especially true with the prevailing political turmoil in the capital: Sukarno had dissolved the legislative assembly in July, consolidating power under the guise of "Guided Democracy." As a compromise, Widjojo offered an alternative site midway between Batu Jajar and Jakarta.

Once more, he was overruled. On 21 December, the regiment's shift to Cijantung was finalized.[4]

As these changes were taking place, Lieutenant Colonel Mung had been patiently mopping up diehard Permesta holdouts in North Sulawesi. He argued for a greater RPKAD presence in the campaign, but his commandos could not seem to break the glass ceiling of two combat companies. As of January 1960, neither of these were available: Company A had been whisked to Aceh for a show of strength, while Company B was in the midst of airborne training.[5]

To get around the problem of troop shortages, Mung presented an unconventional solution. He would create a new battalion of commandos— but give them training in reverse. Rather than taking experienced troops and offering them commando instruction, he would recruit civilians, offer them basic infantry instruction from an RPKAD cadre, then send them to North Sulawesi for extended training. For those that survived the ordeal, they could come back to Batu Jajar for commando and airborne classes.

Heading the project to create a battalion from scratch was Major Widjojo. Sending out notices around the country, he was deluged by five thousand applicants. From these, psychological, physical, and educational tests weeded out all but six hundred. This reduced number was then ushered to a vacant battalion-sized training facility in Jombang, East Java.

Taking along a handful of instructors from the SPKAD, Widjojo on 7 January 1960 began six months of basic training. "We had them crawling on their stomach from the first day," he recalled.[6] The recruits proved up to the challenge. By the sixth month, they shifted to West Java for brief skirmishes against a residual pocket of Darul Islam guerrillas. With just eight dropouts, the remaining 592 members were declared ready for operations in North Sulawesi.

Before heading for the front, the unit—dubbed Battalion 2—was given a leader. Major Seno Hartono, a former military academy instructor and Siliwangi company commander, had transferred to the RPKAD the previous year. Heading to Jombang in early September, he spent the next three months putting the battalion through final fitting before loading them into a vessel for the ride to Sulawesi.

Upon arrival, the battalion found the rebels defeating themselves. Over on Sumatra, serious cracks began to emerge in the spring of 1960 when civilian rebel leaders cemented an official merger with Darul Islam. For many PRRI military officers—who saw themselves as standard-bearers of the army's secular tradition—such a tight relationship with Islamic extremists did not sit well. Darul Islam, moreover, was an unreliable ally, with its armed elements in Aceh and southern Sulawesi already starting to rally to the government.

Bristling from this marriage, top PRRI officers began to negotiate terms of surrender with local army commanders in the spring of 1961. By July, all had come in from the bush. The flame of rebellion on Sumatra had burned itself out.

In North Sulawesi, several top Permesta commanders were also negotiating a ceasefire by the time Battalion 2 arrived. More so than in Sumatra, however, a small percentage of rebel units appeared intent on continuing their battle against Jakarta. Focusing their attention against two such dissident battalions—including one headed by a former RPKAD officer—Battalion 2 began seven months of training under fire.

For Private Yusman Yutam, Permesta proved a determined opponent. Wearing a steel helmet with the letters "RPKAD" painted on the front, his company, as well as the three others in the battalion, were led by five commando veterans. Making slow progress, they were under constant fire from a .50 caliber nest as they approached some strategic highground. Using a 60mm mortar for suppressive fire, his company attempted to flank the rebels. But as two scouts moved ahead, a Permesta guerrilla emerged from a spider hole and opened fire into their backs. One of the scouts collapsed with a fatal round entering his buttocks and exiting his groin.

Despite such stubborn resistance, Permesta was on its last legs. By July 1961, just as Battalion 2 finished its tour, most senior rebel officers were setting down their weapons. Three months later, the last holdouts had rallied to the central government.

Even before Battalion 2 returned to Batu Jajar for six months of commando and airborne training, the regiment had been undergoing yet another wave of upgrades. Figuring that a decent interval had passed since its disastrous policy of aiding the PRRI and Permesta rebels, the United States resumed offering military assistance to Indonesia.

The RPKAD was among the units benefiting from the new round of American largesse.[7] In 1959, the SPKAD deputy commander, Captain Prijo Pranoto, was sent for advanced officer training at Fort Benning. Remaining at Fort Benning through the following June, he then became the second RPKAD officer to graduate from ranger training.

Others followed in the second half of 1960. One member of the SPKAD's parachute instructor cadre was sent to the U.S. for six months of rigger training. And in April 1961, Captain Benny Moerdani, the former commander of Company A, became the first Indonesian to graduate from the twelve-week special warfare officer's course at Fort Bragg, North Carolina.

By the time Moerdani returned to Indonesia in mid-1961, he found the regiment in the midst of rapid expansion. There was a tangible urgency in the air. Judging from the fiery rhetoric of Sukarno, Indonesia was gearing up for a new war.

1   Interview with Widjojo Soejono, 1 September 1997.

2   Interview with Sumardji, 12 August 1999.

3   Widjojo interview.

4   Even before the decision was made to transfer the RPKAD headquarters to Cijantung, Moerdani's Company A had already been transferred to that base as of August 1959. The reason: after President Sukarno dissolved parliament in July, the commandos were tasked with bolstering security at his palace in nearby Bogor. On the same date that the RPKAD headquarters was shifted to Cijantung, 21 December, the SPKAD was subordinated to the Army Training and Education Command (*Komando Pendidikan dan Latihan Angkatan Darat*, or Koplat). The rest of the RPKAD continued to answer directly to the army chief-of-staff.

5   The Aceh deployment, which lasted less than a month, was meant as a show of force against resurgent Acehnese rebels.

6   Widjojo interview.

7   The RPKAD was not the only elite unit benefiting from U.S. assistance during this period. In January 1959, eight Indonesian police officers went to Okinawa for an eight-week ranger course under the auspices of the U.S. Army's 1 Special Forces Group. A ranger company within the Indonesian police was formed that September. In the first half of 1960, a second contingent of Indonesian police received ranger training on Okinawa. Atim Supomo and Djumarwan, *Pelopor* (Jakarta: Pusdik Brimob Watukosek Indonesia, 1998), p. 41.

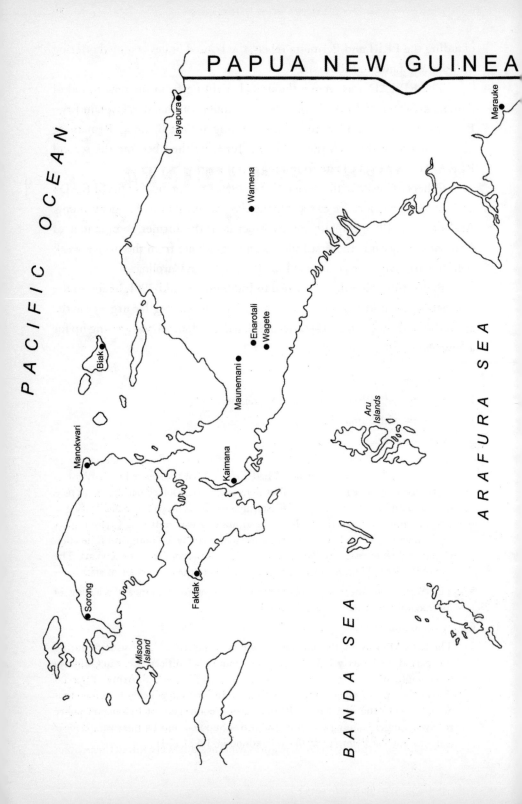

CHAPTER SIX

WEST NEW GUINEA

The hot, humid island of New Guinea is best described by superlatives. With nearly a thousand distinct tribal cultures and languages—a fifth of the world's total—most of these tribes live in isolation from each other. The reason is grounded in geography. Covered by thick rain forests (much of it unexplored) and towering peaks (including Asia's only tropical glacier), the island has been segregated by topography into cultural and linguistic pockets.

None of this made New Guinea particularly appealing to the European powers of the nineteenth century. Between its harsh climate, wealth of tropical diseases, and impenetrable jungles, the island ranked low as a colonial target. This was compounded by the reputation of the island's often hostile ethnic Melanesian population, many of whom had their feet firmly planted in the Stone Age. Tales of ritual cannibalism, though perhaps exaggerated in terms of frequency, had a basis in fact.

Not until 1848 did the Europeans, carried away by the momentum of carving up Asian empires, get around to staking claims on New Guinea. Britain, Germany, and Holland each took sections in theory—though none actually saw fit to dispatch administrators to the island. Not until two years short of the end of the century did the Dutch establish coastal outposts along its western half.

Aside from a brief interlude during the Japanese occupation in World War Two, the Dutch retained their presence in West New Guinea through the Indonesian war of independence. But when it came time to grant sovereignty to Indonesia in 1949, Holland was reluctant to include its New Guinea holding. Arguing that the island's Melanesians were kin to the peoples of the southernmost Pacific, not the ethnic Malay that predominated the rest of the Indonesian archipelago, the Dutch insisted that West New Guinea was not part of the package. The young Indonesian leadership bristled at this, insisting that all Dutch-controlled territories comprised a unitary Indonesia.

In the end, the question over West New Guinea remained unresolved. Both sides agreed to an ambiguous promise that the status quo (ongoing Dutch control) would be maintained for the time, but that West New Guinea's future status would be determined through negotiations within a year.

Neither side ever got around to seriously pursuing those negotiations. For President Sukarno, West New Guinea immediately became a symbol of Indonesia's incomplete nationhood. Using the issue to stoke crowds as early as 1950, it became his favorite nationalistic theme when urging the country to continue its revolutionary struggle.

Sukarno did not limit his campaign to words. In January 1952, the Indonesian government attempted to dispatch twenty-eight pro-Indonesian natives by boat to Gag Island, located off New Guinea's western coast. It was an amateurish affair, with the infiltrators arrested in days. A year later, a similar foray near the coastal town of Kaimana ended in fast arrests. A slightly more ambitious 1954 attempt by forty-two men, some of whom were armed, led to a swift Dutch response; eleven were killed, the remainder imprisoned for four years before being repatriated to Indonesia via Singapore.

Putting further infiltrations on hold, Sukarno looked instead to make gains in diplomatic circles. In 1957, he attempted to get international organizations involved in the issue. The United Nations, however, showed little interest. At the same time, the International Court of Law refused to entertain Indonesia's case, saying Jakarta had no legal claim to any part of New Guinea.

For Sukarno, the failure at the United Nations made him look again at a more forceful approach. In early 1958, he had his government create a National Front for the Liberation of West Irian, using Indonesia's preferred name for West New Guinea. At the same time, the Indonesian army created a special working group under Colonel Magenda, an assistant chief-of-staff with experience in intelligence operations. Magenda's working group was to brainstorm ways of making guerrilla pockets in West Irian (called Operation A), and to prepare for a conventional military invasion if necessary (Operation B).

Before much headway could be made, the PRRI and Permesta rebellions put West Irian on the backburner. Not until early 1960, with the Sumatran and Sulawesi uprisings largely quelled, could West Irian again receive top attention. Sukarno focused on the subject with a passion, in part because such an external confrontation provided a useful diversion to a faltering economy hobbled by his quasi-socialist precepts.

Into this mix came Soviet Premier Nikita Khrushchev for a state visit in February 1960. By all accounts, Khrushchev scored major diplomatic points by played to Sukarno's enormous ego and promising full support to Indonesia's claim over West Irian. Equally important, he promised to set aside upwards of US$500 million for economic and military aid.

Even before this Soviet assistance began to flow, Sukarno pressed his military to ratchet up the campaign to wrest control of West Irian. As of 1960, however, the working group's Operation A had little to show for its efforts. Just one company of ethnic Irianese had been assembled in West Java, where they were being readied in a secret camp prior to infiltration back to their home island. With no clear operations plan, and only vague instructions to land along the southern coast of West New Guinea and link up with sympathizers, a third of these partisans were dispatched east in early August. Known as Guerrilla Force 100 (*Pasukan Gerilya* 100, or PG 100), the unit was led by an Irianese lieutenant named Henkie Antaribaba. Over half of his men were members of the failed 1954 foray, each having served four-year prison terms before being expelled.

Arriving at a launchsite in the Aru Islands, a small cluster of Indonesian-controlled atolls and islets about one hundred kilometers off the southern coast of West Irian, PG 100 was plagued by trouble from the start. First, faulty boat engines caused a month's delay while replacements were sent from Java. Next, ten of its members had a change of heart and deserted.

Not until 9 November did the guerrillas—now reduced to twenty-three members—depart over the Aru Sea for West Irian. Three days later, Dutch authorities were receiving reports of armed interlopers in green fatigues moving along an isolated southern beach. Dispatching two platoons of marines to root them out, they spent the next four months chasing PG 100 through the jungle. In the end, seven of the infiltrators were shot dead and the remaining sixteen captured alive.

With the failure of PG 100, Colonel Magenda's Operation A had yet to establish any guerrilla pockets on West Irian. Looking instead toward Operation B—a conventional invasion of the island—army chief Nasution led a delegation to the Soviet Union in December 1960 to call in the February promises made by Khrushchev. Joined by a number of officers from all the services—including SPKAD commander Sarwo Edhie—the deal signed on 6 January 1961 focused almost exclusively on hardware for the navy and air force.

With the Soviet Union suddenly becoming a major sponsor of the Indonesian military, Washington took note. A new administration under John Kennedy assumed office that month, and America's youthful president was being hit by conflicting advice on how to deal with Jakarta. Kennedy's predecessor, Dwight Eisenhower, had long opposed Indonesia's left-leaning foreign policy—going as far as sponsoring rebellions to break apart the republic. Though some steps had been taken to improve ties over the previous two years—including the provision of ten C-130 Hercules aircraft—top policy makers in the State Department and CIA remained wary of, if not hostile toward, Sukarno's government.[1]

Kennedy was also getting a harsh anti-Indonesia spin from Dutch and Australian diplomats. The Dutch had reached a low point in relations with its former colony, breaking off diplomatic ties in August 1960. The Australians, who administered the eastern half of New Guinea as a trust territory, did not relish the idea of the Indonesian government moving onto the island.

But Kennedy was getting different advice from a handful of self-assured foreign policy advisors he had installed on his National Security Council. Afraid of Soviet gains in Southeast Asia, especially with conflicts in South Vietnam and Laos escalating, they argued that Washington could gain in Sukarno's eyes by assisting with a negotiated settlement over West Irian.

Before any changes in U.S. foreign policy were forthcoming, General Nasution departed in June 1961 for a second trip to Moscow in less than six months. This time he successfully cemented a deal for army gear, including parachutes and AK-47 assault rifles.

Although the Indonesian government was making clear gains in procuring equipment for an invasion of West Irian, Jakarta was concerned over developments on other fronts. Most troubling were moves by the Dutch in the first half of 1961 to promote political development in what they were now calling West Papua. With a view toward making an independent state by 1970, the Dutch allowed locals to vote for a new Papua council in February 1961, giving them the first taste of political representation. By April, the first two platoons of an armed Papuan battalion were formed, a national anthem composed, and a flag designed—all of which drove Indonesia beyond frustration.

With these Dutch initiatives as backdrop, Sukarno looked toward the United Nations. Despite his best efforts, the United Nations thus far had refused to take up the issue of West Irian. Because that body's annual General Assembly session was set to open on 20 September—and Sukarno himself was scheduled to attend—the Indonesian president wanted to grab their attention with a spectacle on the island.

Despite its lack of success to date, Colonel Magenda's Operation A got the assignment. As before, his infiltrators would come from the Irianese company secretly training in West Java. This time, the RPKAD was asked to lend a single officer that would help steel the resolve of the guerrillas. Selected for the assignment was a young Sumatran lieutenant named Djamaludin Nasution, who linked up with thirty-five Irianese—now going by the name PG 200—shortly before departing Jakarta in late August.

Like the foray during the previous year, PG 200 was plagued with problems from the outset. Initially allocated four motorboats, the engines proved highly temperamental. With just two boats in operational condition and an eye on the calendar, thirty-two men crammed aboard the pair and on 14 September departed from Indonesia's Gebe Island. Plans called for them to conduct sabotage missions (they were armed with a mortar, grenades, and Lee Enfield rifles) around the town of Sorong when the General Assembly convened in a week's time.

They never had the chance. Almost as soon as they set foot on West Irian soil, PG 200 was detected by locals. Although the guerrillas had been told the Irianese would welcome their arrival, the natives instead informed the Dutch. Scrambling through the jungle, the last two PG 200 holdouts were captured on 13 December. Of its thirty-two members, twenty-nine were captured, two were shot dead, and one was believed eaten by crocodiles.

All of which did little to assuage the impatient Sukarno. Still under pressure to show gains inside West Irian, Operation A had one last shot. This time, the RPKAD would play its greatest role to date. In October 1961, two sergeants from the regiment were sent to Bogor, where they linked up with 111 Irianese guerrillas in the restocked company maintained by Colonel Magenda. Two more RPKAD non-commissioned officers arrived soon after, with one commando assigned as company commander and the three others as platoon leaders.

More so than before, the Indonesian armed forces were stepping forward to offer help with infiltration. The air force was willing to lend three of its U.S.-made C-130 transports to carry the guerrillas and seven tons of equipment toward the front. The navy offered four of its West German Jaguar-class motor torpedo boats, each of which would take the guerrillas close to the West Irian coast. And the army, besides seconding the RPKAD cadre, loaned four motorized rubber boats and crewmen that would shuttle the insurgents from the torpedo boats to shore.

On 9 January 1962, preparations to dispatch the guerrillas—going by the codename PG 300—were underway. All four of the torpedo boats left Jakarta that day on their way to the Aru Islands. Three days later, the C-130 transports departed the capital for a rendezvous at the launchsite. By noon on 15 January, the men and three boats (one had developed engine trouble en route) were ready to head for West Irian later that night.

As scheduled, PG 300 departed the Aru Islands at 1700 hours. Like the guerrilla group of the previous year, they were mandated with conducting sabotage attacks, this time against the town of Kaimana. Given the large size of the team, and the fact that some of Indonesia's newest military hardware was being used, several senior intelligence and naval officers had elected to ride aboard the torpedo boats to witness the infiltration.

Unfortunately for PG 300, its impending mission was hardly a secret from the Dutch. The previous month, Dutch intelligence had received word of a possible infiltration along the southern coast of West Irian, prompting them to send reinforcements to towns along that coast and step up aerial patrolling by Neptune P-2 surveillance planes. Approaching Aru, one of the Neptunes had spotted the three torpedo boats soon after their arrival; with a rubber boat lashed to the top of each, it did not take much imagination to guess Jakarta's intentions.

By the time PG 300 headed across the Aru Sea, two Dutch destroyers were waiting in ambush just over the horizon. Halfway to their target, the Indonesian boat crews spotted them on radar and attempted evasive maneuvers at 31 knots. Closing on the lead vessel, the Dutch concentrated fire and hit its engine room. After burning for twenty minutes, the boat sank under the waves. Commodore Yos Sudarso, the deputy chief of naval operations, went down with the ship. Fifty-one others, including an RPKAD platoon commander, were plucked from the water and sent on their way to a Dutch prison.[2]

The fiasco on the Aru Sea made the limitations of guerrilla infiltration painfully evident. While still maintaining Colonel Magenda's Operation A as a sideshow, Operation B—involving Indonesia's conventional armed forces—from that point forward became the focus of efforts to expel the Dutch.

Talk along these lines was not new. Ever since December 1960, the army had been contemplating the formation of a strategic corps as the backbone for Operation B. On paper, this proposed corps went through numerous and confusing recalculations through the spring of 1961, each slightly smaller than the last as the generals wrestled with budgetary and manpower limitations. By March, a modified plan envisioned the formation of three (eventually reduced to two) airborne-qualified brigades and an infantry division. All of these would be formed from existing battalions in the Indonesian order-of-battle.

Looking to make use of the army's fledgling strategic corps, General Nasution in April instructed his top officers to come up with a menu of military options for seizing West Irian. Making little progress, an expanded working group was convened in June, with members now given just a month to finalize their recommendations.

Mindful of their deadline, Indonesia's top brass produced a vague plan by the opening of July. Rather than a single course of action, they subdivided Operation B into three divergent options. The first, dubbed B-1, called for a blitz to seize all of West Irian. The second option, B-2, had the Indonesian military seizing and defending only a section of West Irian, then using this as bargaining leverage for the rest of the territory. The last option, B-3, called for increased infiltrations to make guerrilla pockets.

None of these was a perfect solution. B-1, though offering the desired results in the fastest time, was not viable because Indonesia did not yet have sufficient troops and assets to seize all of West Irian. B-2, also judged beyond Indonesia's current abilities, was not fully desirable because it allowed the Dutch to bring in reinforcements and attack their lines of supply. Moreover, the results of seizing a portion of West Irian did not necessarily mean full victory. The last option, B-3, was within Indonesia's existing abilities. However, such infiltrations could spark a war for which Indonesia was not yet ready; moreover, the initiative remained in the hands of the Dutch.

In the end, Nasution recommended a blend of the options. B-2 would be Indonesia's eventual course of action, but the military would be allowed to prepare itself through the end of 1962. While the army finalized these preparations, the interim time would be spent creating resistance pockets as outlined in B-3.

For all the options under Operation B, the RPKAD factored heavily. In some cases, the role was indirect. For example, the army's proposed strategic corps envisioned two airborne brigades; the RPKAD's tireless chief-of-staff, the newly-promoted Lieutenant Colonel Widjojo Soejono, took leave of the regiment to form one of them.

Taking along a selection of RPKAD veterans as his staff, Widjojo scoured the army for three suitable battalions for his new brigade. The choice was limited by political and practical considerations. As there were as yet no airborne infantry battalions in Indonesia's order-of-battle, he wanted battalions of proven mettle that could be upgraded. And since airborne status would be a prized qualification, it was felt that he should divide the spoils by taking one battalion apiece from the military commands in West, Central, and East Java.[3]

Based on this narrower field, Widjojo named his preferences. All three of his chosen battalions were previously trained as raiders, an advanced infantry qualification first conjured by Brigadier General Yani. From East Java, the 530 Raider Battalion got the nod. From Central Java, the choice went to the 454 "Banteng Raider II" Battalion. And from West Java, the 330 Raider Battalion—recently returned from United Nations peacekeeping duties in the Congo—completed the selection. On 18 October, orders were cut for all three—grouped under what was now being called 3 Parachute Brigade—to get airborne qualified as soon as training slots became available.[4]

For the second airborne brigade in the strategic reserve, RPKAD chief Mung Parhadimuljo—freshly promoted to full colonel—was instructed to take the brigade command as his second hat. Looking for appropriate subordinate units, Mung quickly chose Major Seno's Battalion 2, which in July had emerged from its extended trial by fire in North Sulawesi. Sent to Batu Jajar, they were immediately ushered through three months of commando training. After that, they were retained for another three months of airborne instruction, which for the first time was being fully conducted under SPKAD auspices at Batu Jajar.

Battalion 2 was not alone at Batu Jajar. Back in April 1961, anticipating the need to expand the regiment for West Irian operations, a contingent of 587 enlisted personnel had been recruited from across the army and sent to the SPKAD. As they were already qualified as infantrymen, they went directly to commando and airborne instruction.

When this latest class graduated in late 1961, the RPKAD now had sufficient men to make three new companies. Just short of a battalion, Colonel Mung gave them the lesser administrative designation of detachment (*detasemen* in Indonesian). Maintaining numerical consistency with Battalion 2, the new unit became Detachment 3. Captain Kodim, the graduate of British jungle warfare training, was named its commander.

Detachment 3 proved short-lived. With West Irian operations looming, Mung in early 1962 sorted through the men of Battalion 2 and Detachment 3. Retaining only the best from both, the resultant four companies kept the designation Battalion 2. Seno Hartono remained battalion commander, while Kodim became his deputy.[5]

Unaffected by the formation of the two airborne brigades was the RPKAD's original two combat units, Company A and B. Both became the basis for a novel experiment by Captain Benny Moerdani. Upon his return in mid-1961 from special warfare training in the U.S., Benny was motivated to duplicate what he had learned. "The RPKAD was meant to hit in the rear like rangers," he later said. "I wanted to copy the U.S. Army Special Forces."[6]

The difference was significant. Rangers were effectively light infantrymen who packed a strong punch and excelled in seizing targets like airfields. But they required considerable logistical support and could not be expected to sustain a prolonged conventional battle. By contrast, the Special Forces were self-sustained units that performed unconventional tasks for long periods far behind enemy lines. According to U.S. Army doctrine of the time, U.S. Army Special Forces detachments in Europe and Asia would operate alongside friendly indigenous guerrillas in the likely event Chinese and Soviet juggernauts overran pro-Western governments along the periphery of the communist bloc.

Given this mission, Special Forces were structured unlike anything else in the military. Intended to win the hearts and minds of their targeted populous, the fundamental unit of the Special Forces—the twelve-man Operational Detachment—often included members who spoke the local language. These detachments always included medics that could offer assistance to villagers. Training and leading large contingents of local guerrillas, these twelve men offered a significant multiplier effect against a numerically superior foe.

Smitten by the Special Forces concept, Benny saw applicability in the West Irian setting. Given the long distance to the island, he realized that resupply missions would be difficult; the Special Forces, who were supposed to be self-sufficient, sidestepped this problem. And since it appeared like the Irianese needed some persuasion to rise up against the Dutch, the civic aid angle to the Special Forces would help build pro-Indonesia sympathies.

Winning support from his army superiors, Benny looked to realize his Special Forces project by piecing together a program of unconventional instruction. He scoured a series of manuals he had brought back from the U.S., but found them too general. Relying instead on his own imagination—and help from Captain Abdul Ramly, a colleague who had completed the six-week psychological operations course at Fort Bragg—he penned a most unorthodox training schedule.

On 23 July 1961, the first class commenced. Drawing on members of Benny's old Company A, the commandos were simply told to individually make their way from Cijantung across Java to the island of Bali. None were allowed to carry identification or weapons. Relying only on their wits, they were each given a list of targets that they needed to covertly observe en route within a specific deadline. At various checkpoints along the way, Benny would meet them and verify their information. "He would give us a little money," said one of the students, "but not enough for food or transportation."[7]

Apart from this cross-Java trek, a splash of lectures, and some parachute refresher jumps, that was the extent of Benny's ad hoc Special Forces curriculum. After a second training class near year's end—which was opened to members of Company B—the captain was left with 150 operators who passed muster. To this, four combat engineers were added to assist with demolitions.

And though a civic action program was never clearly defined, he was allocated two doctors, two social scientists, and an economist.[8] Together going by the name Special Forces Detachment (*Detasemen Pasukan Chusus*, or DPC), Benny and his men set themselves apart from their RPKAD mother unit by changing the black leather background on their beret badges to green.

Before the DPC or either of the airborne brigades had a chance to see action, officials in Jakarta turned up the heat against the Dutch. On 14 December, a High Command for the Liberation of West Irian was formed within the armed forces. Charged with crafting grand military and diplomatic strategy, Brigadier General Yani was named chief-of-staff of the command. Five days later, the ornery Sukarno took to the podium with his most fiery comments to date. Making reference to Three People's Commands—abbreviated in Indonesian as Trikora—he issued a trio of promises. First, he vowed to crush the elected councils the Dutch had formed in West Irian earlier that year. Second, he pledged to plant the Indonesian flag in the Dutch colony. Third, he promised to stage a general mobilization of the population to gain control of the territory.

Moving beyond rhetoric, a theater command to control operations against West Irian was created on the last day of the year. Formalized in an order dated 2 January 1962, the so-called Mandala Command was headed by Brigadier General Suharto. A mild-mannered Javanese, Suharto, who received his major general's star on 13 January, had been involved the previous year with helping map out the army's strategic reserve corps.

Despite this flurry of declarations and new commands, Indonesia was still far from ready to launch operations against West Irian. With most of its units still at just sixty percent strength, the generals now conservatively estimated that the fastest they could stage their campaign to expel the Dutch was the following year. But in the wake of the Aru disaster on 15 January, there was added pressure to show results for all the effort to date.

Combining the need for expediency with the realities of troops at hand, Suharto's Mandala Command configured the West Irian campaign into three phases. The first—an invigorated infiltration phase—would begin in early 1962 with a target of ten companies inserted into the territory by year's end. Next, an exploitation phase—involving a partial seizure of West Irian as outlined in B-2—would commence in early 1963. This would be followed by a consolidation phase, combining military and diplomatic efforts to win control over the entire territory.

Focusing on the infiltration phase, the Mandala Command began operations in March 1962. The country's various armed services offered elements of their best units for the campaign. From the RPKAD came Benny's DPC, now sporting AK-47 automatic rifles courtesy of General Nasution's July 1961 shopping trip to the Soviet Union. The air force extended its PGT, which had just expanded into a two-battalion regiment. In anticipation of this mission, the PGT commandos had been freshly outfitted with Heckler & Koch G-3 automatic rifles, Hong Kong-made camouflage jumpsuits, and Czechoslovakian jump boots. The marines made available a composite company drawn from their landing battalions. And the police dispatched a detachment from their ranger regiment, an elite formation created that March from a cadre trained by the U.S. Army Special Forces and equipped with the U.S. AR-15 automatic rifle.[9]

The Mandala Command also took control over Colonel Magenda's Operation A, which included the guerrilla remnants that survived the Aru incident. Still going by the name PG 300, these guerillas had been built back up to a 151-man company. Dividing this company into two groups of two platoons—each led by an RPKAD commando—the entire force was shifted to the Indonesian island of Gebe. For several reasons—calm seas, relatively short distance, and plenty of islets to hide among—Gebe was considered an optimal launchsite. Leaving this island during the third week of March, the first half of PG 300 departed for West New Guinea. Using motorized canoes, they barely made any headway before being spotted by Neptune surveillance aircraft. Diving for cover on Dutch-held Gag Island, they were quickly surrounded and captured.

The second half of PG 300 fared little better. En route to the Dutch-occupied island of Waigeo, they were forced to take shelter on an adjacent atoll to escape Neptune overflights. Under heavy fire and losing their canoes, they forged rafts in an attempt to leapfrog between islands back to Indonesia. They did not get far before one of the guerrillas was eaten by sharks and the rest were captured.

Unable to even reach the West New Guinea mainland, the Mandala Command decided to shift from maritime infiltrations to airborne insertions. In preparation for this, Benny had been fine-tuning his DPC. As of early March, he had subdivided his detachment into four teams. The first, Team I, were undergoing specialist training to become the first Indonesian freefall parachutists. Showing camaraderie among left-leaning non-aligned nations, Yugoslavia had rushed to Jakarta a three-man team of seasoned freefall instructors to serve as advisors. Using both Soviet D-1 and Yugoslavian PKT-3 chutes, jumps started on 13 March; Captain Gunawan Wibisono, the original chief of the SPKAD parachute cadre, was the first Indonesian out the aircraft door.[10] On 24 March, twenty-six members of the DPC, including fourteen from Team I, entered an abbreviated two-week course.[11]

The second DPC contingent, Team II, was slated for a wholly different kind of infiltration: from submarines. In 1959, a pair of Soviet Whiskey-class subs had been sold to Indonesia. As part of Nasution's January 1961 arms deal with Moscow, he had received permission to procure another ten. Four of the ten had arrived in January 1962, along with a contingent of Indonesian submariners who had completed six months of training in Vladivostok. Using these subs as launch platforms, Team II was scheduled to practice landings from rubber boats stored on their decks.

The remaining two teams in the DPC were available for immediate deployment. When the order came on 11 April to dispatch the first wave of paratroopers to West Irian, Benny put both on notice. The first of these, the thirty-strong Team III, was led by Lieutenant Agus Hernoto; a former sergeant major in the RPKAD transport section, Agus had been among the non-commissioned officers who mutinied at Batu Jajar in the wake of the failed 1956 Lubis Affair. Team IV, totaling 23 members, was headed by Heru Sisnodo, a diehard if somewhat idealistic young lieutenant. Both units had an assigned army engineer.

As neither of these teams was considered to have sufficient critical mass, an eleventh-hour call went out to the PGT for reinforcements. Ten air force commandos would go with Team III, nine with Team IV. This was probably for political as well as tactical reasons: the air force, competing for a tight budget and the favor of President Sukarno, wanted to showcase their elite force on the initial airborne operation against West Irian. Whatever the reason, the DPC commandos—who shared a healthy sense of competition with their air force counterparts—protested at having to share the limelight, especially with troops that had not trained alongside them as a cohesive whole.[12]

Despite such complaints, the mission went ahead. Just before dawn on 26 April, the flightline on Ambon island was packed with idling transport and fighter aircraft. Preceded by a series of diversionary flights, two groups of Dakotas took off at low level. Aboard the first group, Agus Hernoto's Team III flew toward the town of Fak-Fak. The second group carried Heru Sisnodo's Team IV toward Kaimana.

Flying in good weather, the Dakotas came upon their targets within two hours. Team III exited into the slipstream and quickly assembled in the jungle. Two factors immediately began working against them. First, the Dutch had brought marine reinforcements to Fak-Fak two weeks earlier. Second, the local population was decidedly hostile. When one DPC commando, who had drifted far from the others, attempted to seek help from an Irianese tribesman on a canoe, he was instead delivered to a police outpost.[13]

Following the arrest of this commando, the Dutch marines pushed into the jungle outside Fak-Fak. Between relentless Dutch patrols and the unreceptive local population, Team III was on the run from the start. Worse, they had failed to locate all their supply bundles and due to the threat of marauding Dutch fighter aircraft, resupply airdrops were out of the question. "We could find boars but could not light fires to cook the pork," said one member. "We only thought of food, not the enemy."[14]

Over the next three months, the emaciated members of Team III progressively fell victim to Dutch ambushes. Among the last holdouts was Agus Hernoto, who tenaciously fought to the end. Shot in both legs, the lieutenant would later lose a limb to Dutch surgeons.

Team IV fared better, but just. Landing in the jungle outside Kaimana, they also encountered Dutch patrols and an unsympathetic population. Still, Lieutenant Heru, the idealistic team leader, managed to keep most of his men one step ahead of the Dutch for almost three months. On 2 July, his bivouac site was overrun and personal diary captured. Entries from the journal revealed Heru's frustrations. Among them:

I am disillusioned because we do not have planes. I am disillusioned because we do not have maps that are good. I am disillusioned because I did not select these [PGT] that face this tough operation and I cry because the Papuans do not support us. They do not give us food: we must look for our own food or barter with our valuable equipment. They report on our movements to the Dutch.[15]

Back in Indonesia, the Mandala Command correctly interpreted the radio silence from the two airborne groups as a sign they were experiencing severe difficulties. But electing to forge ahead according to the same flawed script, on 13 May an order went out for a trio of new insertions. Again stepping forward was the PGT, which offered several of its platoons. The police, too, deployed their ranger detachment to a forward launchsite at Geser Island, where they awaited word to depart aboard speedboats.

As part of the political balancing act among the services, the army did not want to be left out of this wave of insertions. Because the two remaining DPC teams were still training on submarines and in freefall parachute techniques, alternatives were sought outside the detachment. Turning to the 3 Parachute Brigade, Lieutenant Colonel Widjojo made available elements of the 454 Airborne Battalion (earlier known as the 454 "Banteng Raider II" Battalion).

Beginning on 15 May and extending sporadically over the next ten days, infiltrations commenced at three locales. From the air, PGT commandos and army paratroopers jumped near Fak-Fak. Coinciding with this, a team of twenty police rangers approached the same coastline on speedboats. At Kaimana, a second group of PGT and army paratroopers descended over the jungle. Rounding out the blitz, PGT commandos jumped near the town of Sorong. This last drop was timed to coincide with a landing by guerrillas from PG 400, a partisan group comprised of the hardluck combatants who had been plucked from the sea during the Aru Sea incident in January. Detained in Dutch jail cells until March, they had been repatriated via Singapore, where Colonel Magenda wasted no time retraining them on Java and dispatching them back to the front.

The result of all this infiltration activity was under-whelming. The police rangers were arrested before even reaching the beach. And aside from a short-lived occupation of a village near Sorong—where the PGT was able to briefly raise the Indonesian flag—the elite parachutists were either captured or quickly on the run. None of the drops appeared particularly problematic for the Dutch, who were able to effectively give chase with relatively small patrols. And far from being swayed in Jakarta's favor, none of the local tribes were throwing out the welcome mat for their self-proclaimed liberators.

All of which had Brigadier General Yani steaming. As chief-of-staff for the office charged with forging a grand strategy for West Irian, he held a restricted session at army headquarters in mid-May to review the non-results to date. Arguing that the infiltrations were having absolutely no effect on the Dutch, he wanted to try again with a sufficiently large force that would have a better chance of capturing attention, if not territory.

Chosen as leader of this force was Benny Moerdani. On 4 June, an order was issued for his DPC to stage the next round of airborne jumps. Because Team II was still preparing for a submarine infiltration, Team I got the assignment. Although the team had been trained as freefallers, it was decided to insert them via static-line drop. Benny himself, along with a four-man command staff, would join them for the mission.

Between Team I and Benny's staff, the RPKAD contingent totaled fifty-six commandos. Still deemed short of Yani's "sufficiently large force," the DPC was forced to look for outside reinforcements. Again turning to the 3 Parachute Brigade, a 160-man company was taken from its 530 Airborne Battalion (previously known as the 530 Raider Battalion). This combined force of commandos and army paratroopers was codenamed Naga, Indonesian for "dragon."

Weighing a suitable target for Naga, the choice fell on the town of Merauke. Tucked away in the extreme southeastern corner of West Irian, Merauke was advantageous for several counts. First, it was believed defended by just two hundred troops—smaller even than the Naga contingent. Second, it hosted upwards of two thousand dependents, which Benny pragmatically calculated could be used as hostages if events turned sour. Third, Merauke was surrounded by several villages populated by the descendants of Javanese exiles; it was hoped these people might have more affinity toward the commandos than the ethnic Irianese. Lastly Merauke figured prominently in Sukarno's revolutionary call to arms. There was even a famous song, "From Sabang to Merauke," that captured in verse how the president's version of the Indonesian nation spanned from Sabang in the far west to Merauke in the east.

On the morning of 23 June, Benny and Team I were issued parachutes and boarded a C-130 Hercules transport for a flight to the East Java town of Madiun. There, for the first time, they linked up with the airborne company that constituted the rest of Naga. This was a far from perfect arrangement, with Benny dissatisfied not only with the lack of cross-training between the two units, but also by the fact that the men from the 530 Airborne Battalion would be making their first night jump on the day of their mission. During the preceding weeks, by contrast, the DPC had practiced numerous jumps after sundown.

Divided among three Hercules transports, Naga continued to South Sulawesi for an inspection by the Mandala commander, Major General Suharto. Reboarding, they headed east to the island of Seram. There, at an airstrip constructed near the village of Amahai, the men rested for the remainder of the afternoon.

For Benny, rest was an impossibility. Attending a final briefing, he was told to expect sixty percent casualties. Compounding his concern, when he called for Naga to reboard the planes at last light, there was general confusion from the paratroopers of the 530 Airborne Battalion. Uncertain which aircraft to board, they mixed their sticks without regard to earlier plans.

The situation got worse. Taking off from Seram that night with a decoy flight of Indonesian bombers, the three Hercules transports headed for Merauke. But with no detailed maps of West Irian, the pilot and navigator got in an argument over their correct location. Hearing the bickering from the cockpit, the Naga commandos grew anxious.

At long last, the red light in the cabin turned to green. From the rear of the three aircraft, Soviet D-1 parachutes blossomed in their wake. In the full moon, the commandos tried to stay close to fellow team members as they descended toward the jungle canopy. But with the limited maneuverability of the bulky D-1, there was little chance of maintaining a tight formation. In addition, three members of Team I balked at the last minute and flew back to Amahai.[16]

Crashing through the upper layer of branches, the Naga commandos lowered themselves by ropes to the jungle floor. It was not until first light that they realized they were victims of a major navigational error. Plans had called for them to land between the Merauke and Koembe Rivers. All of the commandos had been instructed to make their way to the southern bank of the Koembe, regroup there, then march west toward the beach.

But consulting their maps at dawn, they realized that finding each other would be more difficult than anticipated. Over a third of the assault force, including Benny, had landed 50 kilometers northeast of Merauke along the banks of the Merauke River. The second group, also more than a third of the total, landed on the opposite side of the rain-swollen Merauke. The remainder had been separated in small pockets up to 40 kilometers north of Benny on the far side of the Koembe River. Given that mangrove swamps dominated the terrain in between, there was little chance of linking up.[17]

The bad news did not stop there. Eight paratroopers had landed in the water and drowned, probably because they got confused between their parachute harness release and life preserver toggle. And in a familiar refrain, Naga was beset by food shortages and a local population that was indifferent at best, deadly at worst. One member of Team I poisoned himself to death by eating fern; another member was beheaded by a villager while foraging for coconuts.

On top of these challenges, a patrol of Dutch marines motored their way upriver. Four days after Naga's arrival, shots rang out across the jungle. Eight commandos, including the team's doctor, attempted to evade through the mangroves. One member was captured; three others ran east and did not stop until crossing the frontier into the Australian-controlled half of the island.

Encountering the Dutch, too, was Benny's sub-unit. Thinking they had lost their pursuers, the commandos rested. On 6 July, however, the Dutch launched a renewed attack on Benny's bivouac site, scattering the Indonesians. Propaganda leaflets were left behind, each bearing simple drawings to show the Indonesian troops how to surrender. "Remember your wife and children," the leaflet intoned.

With the Merauke force on the run, the B-3 airborne infiltration campaign was a bust. Aside from a single drop on the last day of July (performed by elements of the 328 Raider Battalion at Kaimana), the Mandala Command changed tack and again tried to gain access by sea.[18] A new guerrilla group—codenamed PG 500—used motorized canoes to go island-hopping among the atolls off the West Irian mainland.[19] And in a publicity stunt that played to the president's inflated libido, an attractive female media personality by the name of Herlina took up the partisan mantle and attempted to steal into West Irian by maritime means. Far from seriously threatening the Dutch hold on the territory, the guerrillas quickly had survival as their chief concern. Herlina, spotted by a Neptune when she tried to dry her wardrobe in a field, barely escaped with her life.[20]

After sacrificing some of its best soldiers with virtually no gains to show, the Indonesians called a temporary halt to their infiltration phase. While not questioning the competence of the individual commandos and guerrillas, the concept of deploying them across great distances among an unfriendly population with little prospect of resupply had proven sheer folly. Victory in West Irian would have to come via other means.[21]

1   It was an open secret that the provision of C-130 aircraft had been done in large part to win the release of a CIA pilot captured by Indonesia during the Permesta uprising. That pilot, Allen Pope, was eventually released in 1962.

2   *Cahaya Chandraca, edisi 1995* (Jakarta: Departemen Penerangan Republik Indonesia, 1995), p. 22. The 51 prisoners were repatriated to Jakarta in March. See *Foreign Broadcast Information Service* [hereafter FBIS], East Asia edition, 8 March 1962, p. RRR8.

3   In August 1958, the army revised the administrative structure for its territorial commands. Under the new system, there were sixteen Military Region Commands (*Komando Daerah Militer*, or Kodam) numbered between one and sixteen. These retained the names of the earlier regional divisions; for example, the Siliwangi division in West Java was now Kodam VI/Siliwangi.

4   *Kostrad* (Jakarta: Panitya Penyusun Sejarah Kostrad, 1972), p. 106.

5   When it was deployed to North Sulawesi, Battalion 2 fielded combat companies F, G, H, and I. Detachment 3 had companies C, D, and E. When the two units merged, the new Battalion 2 retained four combat companies numbered 1, 2, 3, and 4.

6   Interview with L.B. Moerdani, 20 January 1997.

7   Interview with Bambang Sutopo, 31 May 1999.

8   *Tri Komando Rakyat* (Jakarta: Pusat Sejarah dan Tradisis ABRI, 1991), p. 218.

9   The ranger cadre was trained by the U.S. Army Special Forces 1 Group on Okinawa. In a fit of linguistic nationalism, Sukarno later insisted that the police drop the ranger designation and adopt the closest Indonesian equivalent, *pelopor*.

10   The Yugoslavian freefall training team was comprised of Major Stoyan Jovic, Lieutenant Mladen "Mica" Milicevic, and civilian Dobel "Stani" Stanej. During 1968, Stoyan Jovic, by then a colonel, was named commander of Yugoslavia's airborne brigade.

11   On 15 April, an expanded class of nearly four dozen RPKAD students, along with two PGT commandos, began the first of fifty jumps on the way toward proper freefall qualification.

12   Poengky Poernomo Djati, *Perjuangan AURI dalam Trikora* (Jakarta: Sub Direktorat Sejarah Ditwatpersau, 1996), p. 101.

13   R.E. van Holst Pellekaan, I.C. de Regt, and J.F. Bastiaans, *Patroulilleren voor de Papoea's, 1960-1962* (Amsterdam: De Bataafsche Leeuw, 1990), p. 126.

14   Interview with Hans Salomon, 26 April 2000.

15   R.E. van Holst Pellekaan, *Patroulilleren*, p. 146.

16   Of the three who balked, one opened his reserve chute inside the cabin, one feigned sickness, and one simply refused to approach the door.

17   The author is grateful to Soedarto, the commander of Team I, who generously provided numerous original documents relating to the Merauke operation.

18   The 328 Raider Battalion was a second battalion from the West Java military region that was rushed through airborne training for the West Irian campaign. For reasons of unit pride, the battalion insisted on keeping the "raider" rather than "airborne" designation.

19   PG 500, numbering 89 guerrillas, consisted of the last band of diehard Permesta rebels to rally to the government in January 1962. To prove their loyalty to Jakarta, they were loaded aboard four motorized canoes in July and targeted against Sorong. Part of the force was interdicted en route, but a third was able to reach the mainland by mid-month. Interview with Johnky Robertus Kumontoy, 12 September 1997.

20   Herlina, with 35 guerrilla escorts, had attempted to piggyback on the PG 500 infiltration. The PG 500 commander, Johnky Kumontoy, was livid after her clothes were spotted from the air and their cover was blown. Johnky interview.

21   The only unit to benefit from a resupply drop was Naga; on 30 July, a Hercules parachuted rations to Benny's position.

CHAPTER SEVEN

GLORIOUS VICTORY

While coming up short on the West Irian battlefield, Indonesia was more than holding its own in the diplomatic arena. This was largely by default. Due to a Machiavellian calculation by the Kennedy administration, Washington by late 1961 had decided to frustrate Soviet inroads with Jakarta by promoting Indonesia's aspirations in a West Irian settlement. This meant accommodating Sukarno—despite his frequent baiting of the West—at the expense of America's Dutch ally.

With a resultant pro-Indonesia bias, Washington in March 1962 began brokering secret talks in the Virginia countryside between Dutch and Indonesian delegates. Ambassador Ellsworth Bunker, a respected and senior U.S. diplomat, acted as mediator while proposals and counter-proposals passed between negotiators for the next four months. By that time, pronounced diplomatic strong-arming was having an effect: the days of the last Dutch colonial outpost in Southeast Asia appeared clearly numbered.

Despite this almost certain outcome—or perhaps because of it—the Mandala Command ditched its earlier measured schedule and fast-forwarded the timetable for a major invasion of West Irian. Talks along these lines actually started on 25 June, but did not gather serious momentum until mid-July. Codenamed Djayawidjaya—"Glorious Victory"—the proposed campaign hedged by outlining four options. Djayawidjaya 1, which approximated the earlier B-1 plan, called for a simultaneous assault against five West Irian towns. Djayawidjaya 2, which more closely resembled B-2, was a more focused assault against Biak, a satellite island north of the West Irian mainland. Djayawidjaya

3 and 4 were attacks against Hollandia, differing only in timetables and allocated forces. Of these, the Mandala Command elected to go forward with Djayawidjaya 2.

While targeted only against Biak, the Djayawidjaya 2 campaign was still an exercise in hyperbole. Several orders in magnitude greater in scale than anything previously attempted by the Indonesian armed forces, it was virtually more ambitious than anything seen since World War II. It was to involve nearly twenty thousand combatants, with a successful outcome—the seizure of Biak—realized within just a week.

The plan hinged on unprecedented cooperation between the Indonesian armed services. It also hinged on total familiarity with all of its weapons systems—even those which had been delivered from the Soviet bloc just months earlier and never been combat-tested by their Indonesian crews. In both these areas, there was reason to doubt the Indonesian military could deliver.

Case in point was Indonesia's new Soviet-made air fleet. All of Indonesia's massive Tu-16 heavy bombers and Il-28 medium bombers were supposed to rain iron on key Dutch installations over the forty-eight hours prior to D-Day. While doing so, MiG jet fighters were supposed to keep more than a squadron of Dutch fighters at bay. This was doubtful at best, especially since the Dutch would likely have some forewarning from their radar sites at Biak, Kaimana, and Sorong.

Similarly, Indonesian sailors and submariners, also manning new and largely unfamiliar vessels, would be expected to have their first encounter with a capable foe during the opening hours of Djayawidjaya. Again, they would be going up against a robust flotilla of Dutch destroyers and submarines that had already proven highly effective in detecting the earlier Indonesian infiltration forays.

The backbone of Djayawidjaya was a major airborne assault against Biak on D-Day. This would be spearheaded by Colonel Mung's airborne brigade, codenamed Task Force Seno. Once Mung established a foothold, Lieutenant Colonel Widjojo's 3 Parachute Brigade, codenamed Task Force Gatotkaca, would jump into the same town as reinforcements.[1] The Mandala Command predicted each of these 3,660-man brigades would suffer 26 percent casualties. This was probably on the conservative side given that Indonesia—whose largest combat jump to date consisted of just three companies—was now contemplating the largest drop by any nation since World War II.[2]

Even more fantastic, the operation envisioned several infantry brigades arriving in rapid succession to build on the paratrooper's foothold, further augmented by an amphibious landing of marines. This amphibious assault would be supported by the clandestine introduction of marine reconnaissance troops (known as Kipam) and combat swimmers (called Kopaska), neither of which had ever been used in combat.[3]

The RPKAD's role in Djayawidjaya was to be prominent. Task Force Seno, built around the RPKAD Battalion 2 commanded by Major Seno, had spent the second quarter of 1962 making occasional practice parachute jumps into the rubber plantations near Jakarta's Halim airbase. Displaying characteristic bravado, Mung himself had been among the first Indonesians to jump from a C-130 Hercules at night.[4]

But with just one battalion, Mung's brigade was a bit anemic. Seeking further units to flesh out his task force, the colonel was seconded the 436 Airborne Battalion, a raider unit hurriedly upgraded to airborne status in July.[5] Seconded, too, was the 330 Raider Battalion, which was originally allocated to the 3 Parachute Brigade.[6]

The story was much the same for the 3 Parachute Brigade. Both the 454 and 530 Airborne Battalions had been initially allocated to this brigade, but each was understrength because they had been pressed to release paratroopers during the pre-July airborne infiltration phase. In addition, the 330 Raider Battalion had been shifted to Mung's Task Force Seno. In dire need of augmentation, Lieutenant Colonel Widjojo had been temporarily seconded a PGT battalion. In addition, he was assigned the 328 Raider Battalion, which was just concluding operations against the final pocket of Darul Islam guerrilla in West Java.

During this period, the SPKAD at Batu Jajar was a hive of activity. Besides continuing with freefall training for select RPKAD members, most of the airborne cadre was busy giving static-line instruction to several raider battalions.[7] In the past, airborne classes were limited to a company of students and took up to three months of ground exercises before conducting seven static-line jumps (including one at night and one into the jungle). But given the current urgency to churn out paratroopers, this schedule was shelved. Told to jump-qualify 1,000 soldiers a month, the SPKAD reduced the number of mandatory jumps from seven down to three; the requirement for a night and jungle jump was dropped. The time spent on ground training was also sharply reduced, in some cases down to just four days.[8]

The SPKAD was also dogged by equipment problems. Prior to 1961, the commandos had used the British Irvin chute. But with the Soviet Union supplanting the West as the primary sponsor of the Indonesian military, vast quantities of the D-1 chute had been delivered to Batu Jajar. Bulky yet functional, the cotton D-1 was far more rugged than the Irvin; it could even be dried in the sun.

The D-1, however, had a major drawback. Unlike the Irvin, it used a pilot chute deployed by two pieces of bent metal that acted as a spring. This was well suited for the high-speed exits from the Antonov transports used by the Soviets. The SPKAD, however, was using the slower C-47 Dakota as its jump platform. Almost immediately, the pilot chutes began to malfunction. Although the SPKAD cadre appealed to Jakarta for permission to modify the spring, the high command would not authorize any changes. Four student deaths were blamed on this shortcoming.[9]

Parachuting was not the only qualification being taught to the RPKAD. In early 1962, Captain Gunawan Wibisono, the original airborne cadre commander, was tasked with forming a combat swimmer unit that would support West Irian operations. The Indonesian navy had already flirted with this concept, putting together a fifteen-man cadre and penning procedures for amphibious reconnaissance and amphibious raids.[10] In March, Captain Gunawan approached the navy's cadre with the requirement to train a company of RPKAD candidates in combat swimmer techniques. Intensive instruction using Soviet diving equipment immediately commenced along the Jakarta waterfront. By the beginning of July, attrition left the RPKAD with two platoons.

From Jakarta, these novice combat swimmers shifted to Surabaya. With the fifteen navy instructors now formally attached to the RPKAD, the unit was given the literal, though somewhat unmartial, title of Frog Force Command (*Komando Pasukan Katak*, or Kopaska). In support of these troops, the national shipyard at Surabaya was given instructions to build a speedboat specially packed with explosives. The intention was to use Kopaska for suicide ramming attacks against Dutch warships. Experimentation over the course of a month went nowhere—allegedly because the shipyards could not source sufficiently fast engines, though more likely because suicide is a bit extreme for Indonesian military tastes. The human torpedo angle shelved, Kopaska was instead given a vague mission of raiding Biak ahead of the planned Djayawidjaya amphibious landing.[11]

Despite the lack of detail in the Kopaska mission brief, the Mandala Command appeared intent on pushing ahead with Djayawidjaya. According to their campaign plan, D-Day was tentatively set for 12 August. Because Task Force Seno would be the first Indonesian troops to set foot on Biak, parts of the brigade were deployed to forward launchsites as of late July. The bulk of Major Seno's 2 Battalion went to the Amahai airfield on Seram; a company was detached to an airstrip on the nearly Kei islands. Also at Kei was the 436 Airborne Battalion. The 330 Raider Battalion, which was waiting in queue for airborne instruction, did not leave West Java.

The 3 Parachute Brigade, too, moved toward the front. With the exception of the 328 Raider Battalion—most of which remained behind on Java while completing airborne instruction—the rest of the brigade was sent forward to launchsites in the Malukus. The campaign's infantry brigades, meanwhile, were shifted to Sulawesi where they awaited orders to move east.

It never came to that, however. Even as the Mandala forces were inching toward West Irian, continued American diplomatic pressure had browbeat the Dutch into accepting a face-saving formula whereby a ceasefire would be called and the United Nations would ostensibly relieve Holland of its colony. In reality, this would provide Indonesia with a figleaf to move in and seize control. All that was required was for delegates to sign an agreement at the United Nations headquarters in New York; this was expected on or about 15 August.

With a ceasefire all but certain, the Mandala Command shifted gears in the opening days of August. Drawing on the remaining B-3 infiltrators still waiting at launchsites near West Irian, dozens were piled aboard boats and sent forth. On 7 August, a handful of police rangers managed to reach the beach near Fak-Fak. On the same day, a final guerrilla group—PG 600—got as far as Misool Island.[12]

The following week, the infiltration rate reached its peak. On 14 August, a company of PGT commandos was dropped near Sorong, another PGT company landed close to Merauke, and a company from the 454 Airborne Battalion floated down into the jungles adjacent to Kaimana. The battalion's charismatic deputy, Major Untung, led this last company.

The introduction of these troops at the eleventh hour was of little comfort to the Indonesian soldiers that had been inside West Irian for weeks. At Sorong,

51 of the previous infiltrators were in captivity; another 63 were killed in action. At Kaimana, Major Untung found only nine holdouts from the DPC's Team IV under Heru Sisnodo.

The situation was equally grave at Merauke. Under the command of Benny Moerdani—who had been promoted to major at the opening of August—Naga force had been under constant pressure for seven weeks. The Dutch killed nineteen of its members; another thirteen were captured.[13]

Just about out of time, the DPC was called upon for one final mission. The detachment's last sub-unit, Team II, had been patiently training aboard Soviet Whiskey-class submarines through July. Totaling forty-five members—including a combat engineer, a sociologist, an economist, and a medical doctor—the team was given an extremely ambitious dual mission. In the event that the ceasefire did not materialize, two-thirds of its men were to conduct diversionary sabotage missions in Hollandia in support of Djayawidjaya. If the ceasefire did go into effect, the final third of the team—which included the doctor, sociologist, and economist—was to conduct civic action activities to win support from locals around Hollandia prior to the arrival of Indonesian government functionaries.

Not willing to let their specialized training go to waste, Team II was to approach the West Irian coast in a trio of submarines. With fifteen members per sub, they were to surface near the beach, inflate three rubber boats on deck, and ride them to shore.

As planned, the DPC commandos on 15 August headed for Dutch-controlled waters. Though riding submerged under radio silence, the Dutch navy detected the subs and began dropping depth charges. One of the three Indonesian vessels suffered a damaged stabilizer, forcing it to retreat.

Running the Dutch gauntlet, the two remaining subs—the Tjandrasa and the Trisula—neared the coast. Cautiously, the crew of the Trisula surfaced to periscope depth. Spotting an approaching Dutch vessel and a patrolling Neptune, the submarine crew aborted the mission and retreated toward Indonesian territorial waters.[14]

Alone, the Tjandrasa pushed closer to the beach. As it surfaced after last light, the DPC commandos scrambled to inflate the rubber boats strapped to the deck. But after just one was partially filled with air, a Dutch Neptune equipped with a spotlight materialized in the distance. Panicking, the submariners called the commandos inside and settled their ship onto the bottom.

For several tense hours, the DPC and navy officers debated whether to proceed. Fearing that the inflated rubber boat had been lost—or worse, spotted by the Neptune—there was concern they could not fit into the remaining boats.

Still uncertain, they tentatively elected to proceed the following night. Rising back to the surface, they peered onto the deck—and were surprised to see the partially inflated rubber boat still strapped to the top. Inflating the rest, all fifteen team members floated toward shore.

One of the commandos, Bambang Sutopo, paddled furiously for the next twenty minutes. Peering into the night sky, he steered toward a section of thick jungle and cliffs. Upon reaching the base of the cliffs, he and his teammates deflated their rubber boat and were instantly swallowed by the flora.

Reviewing their situation at sunrise, Bambang was confused. His remaining ten teammates had landed at a different section of beach and were nowhere to be found. Of those in his rubber boat, he and three commandos were armed with AK-47 rifles and a mortar. Their fifth member was the team's social scientist. Not knowing if the ceasefire was yet in effect, he was not sure if they should attack a Dutch settlement or instead have the sociologist make contact with the local Irianese community.

They never had a chance to decide. Wandering through the jungle without encountering any inhabitants, they were startled on the fourth night by shouts from Dutch soldiers and Irianese auxiliaries. Surrounded, they put down their AK-47 rifles and were led to the local jail. Approached by the warden, they were told their confinement would be temporary. The ceasefire, said the Dutchman, had already gone into effect.[15]

1   Task Force Seno was also known as Task Force 1; Task Force Gatotkaca went by the second name of Task Force 2.

2   *Komando Mandala Pembebasan Irian Barat*, Laporan Komando, Angkatan Darat Mandala, Laporan Operasi Bantuan Logistiek dari pada Operasi Milier Irian Barat, dated 1 April 1963, p. 8. The largest post-World War II drop until that time was 4,525 men, conducted by the French in November 1953 when they established their Indochina base at Dien Bien Phu. Unlike the French, who were jumping into a valley against (as yet) no opposition, the Indonesians intended to jump against a well-defended town.

3   The company-sized marine reconnaissance unit (*Kesatuan Intai Para Amfibi*, or Kipam) was created in March 1961, but had not been used in combat prior to the West Irian campaign. Its original cadre included two members who received British Marine Commando training in Malaya, one who was trained by the U.S. Marine Corps, and a large number of sergeants who were given combat swimmer instruction in Poland. The navy's combat swimmer unit (*Komando Pasukan Katak*, or Kopaska) had been officially raised on 31 March 1962 and was still in training through early July.

4   Looking to put his personal stamp on the regiment, Colonel Mung on 16 June 1962 kept the RPKAD's name but reworked its official abbreviation to Menparkoad (*Resimen Para Komando Angkatan Darat*). In practice, this new abbreviation was rarely used.

5   FBIS, East Asia edition, 25 July 1962, p. RRR5.

6   *Komando Mandala Pembebasan Irian Barat*, Laporan Komando, Angkatan Darat Mandala, Pctundjuk, No. 002/p/8/1962, dated 17 August 1962. p. 3.

7   The freefall class included two students from the PGT, including one sergeant who died in September on his thirty-fifth jump when his D-1 chute did not properly deploy.

8   Soebari interview.

9   Soebari interview; interview with H. Karlin, 21 May 2000.

10 *Angkatan Bersenjata*, 31 March 1997, p 8.

11 *Tri Komando Rakyat*, pp. 220-221.

12 PG 600 consisted of a company from an army raider unit recruited from across the Malukus.

13 R.E. van Holst Pellekaan, *Patroulilleren*, p. 149. Of the DPC's Team I, two were captured after sustaining injuries, three fled to Australia's half of the island and were arrested, and four died (including one who ate poisonous flora).

14 *Tri Komando Rakyat*, p. 301.

15 Bambang Sutopo interview; FBIS, East Asia edition, 27 August 1962, p. RRR3.

BRUNEI

SABAH

Kabu • • Kalabakan

•Lumbis

Pa Fani
•

Long Bawan
•

SARAWAK

Long
Jawai
•

•Tarakan

Kuching

Serian

Gumbang •
Tebedu

Mapu
•

•Nangabadan

Gunung
Entitik

Balai Karangan

•Pontianak

KALIMANTAN

MAKASSAR STRAIT

SULAWESI

JAVA SEA

CHAPTER EIGHT

LESSONS NOT LEARNED

O n 15 August 1962, Indonesian and Dutch delegates came together in New York to sign an agreement outlining the future of West Irian. Three days later, a local ceasefire went into effect. By 1 October, a temporary United Nations administration was to be charged with running the territory through the following May. The Indonesians would then take full control, though they were obliged to conduct a referendum on Irian self-determination before the end of the decade.

With the ceasefire canceling out the need for an invasion, Djayawidjaya was officially suspended on 29 August. The campaign's intended spearhead, Colonel Mung's ad hoc airborne brigade, was summarily dissolved and its subordinate battalions repatriated to Java. Among them, the RPKAD's Battalion 2 returned to new barracks at Cijantung. Mung himself went back to being the RPKAD commander.[1]

The DPC, which remained in West Irian for half of the United Nations transition period, did not get back to Cijantung until January 1963. The four teams in the detachment left behind twenty-six fallen commandos, representing a quarter of the army's dead or missing during the final five months of fighting.[2] The detachment had never been called upon to serve in its intended civic action role, aside from a pair of circumcisions performed by the doctor attached to Team I.[3]

In hindsight, Indonesia had lost all the battles in West Irian—but still won the war. The Dutch, after all, had suffered only nine deaths and had decisively countered every Indonesian foray. Of the Indonesians that were parachuted into the territory, by contrast, 216 were killed or missing and nearly 300 captured.[4] Rather than military prowess, the reason for Jakarta's victory was grounded primarily in diplomatic bluff and the intense Cold War competition between the superpowers. In this, Jakarta deserved credit for alternately milking Washington and Moscow to its advantage without alienating either.

But the Indonesian armed forces, and Sukarno himself, preferred not to see it that way. Preferring to heap credit on the military—rather than any foreign helping hand—the president fawned over his returning troops.[5] A dramatic display of this came on 19 February 1963, when Sukarno held a flashy celebration on the lawn of the State Palace in front of the diplomatic corps and senior government officials. Smartly outfitted in British-style Denison camouflage smocks and armed with U.S. M3A1 greaseguns, a contingent from the RPKAD was among the hundreds of troops that filed in front of Sukarno's reviewing stand. Singled out for praise was Major Benny Moerdani, who had the *Bintang Sakti*—Indonesia's highest military award—pinned to his chest.[6]

Heroes' welcome aside, the army saw little need to retain the special forces skills in Benny's DPC. Exactly one month after the State Palace parade, the detachment was disbanded. In its place, most of the former DPC members became the core of the RPKAD's newly-formed Battalion 1. Benny, named its commander, would spend much of the year bringing his battalion to authorized strength. This left Battalion 2 as the only combat-ready unit in the RPKAD, and it was this battalion which was called to participate in Indonesia's next foreign adventure.

On 27 May 1961, while Indonesia was still fully preoccupied with West Irian, Malayan and British government leaders first floated the proposal to form a wider Malaysian federation. The concept envisioned a union of Malaya, the adjoining city-state of Singapore, and the three British colonies—Sarawak, Sabah, and Brunei—in northern Borneo. The plan would enable Britain to grant independence to these remaining states, but was still obliged by treaty to shield them under the Commonwealth defensive umbrella.

Geography dictated that Indonesia take an interest in the proposal. Britain's Borneo holdings encompassed a relatively narrow strip along the northern coast of that island; the other two-thirds were governed by Indonesia as part of what Jakarta called Kalimantan. Sabah and Sarawak were contiguous, with Sabah lying to the northeast and Sarawak to the southwest. Together they shared an extremely rugged 1,750-kilometer border with Indonesia's Kalimantan, most of which was unexplored and never properly surveyed. The indigenous people along the border had traditionally moved freely between Indonesia and the British states.

For more than a year, Indonesia appeared mildly supportive of the Malaysia concept. To dispel fears that a post-West Irian Indonesia had its eye bent on territorial expansion, Soebandrio—Sukarno's influential lieutenant who served as both foreign minister and chief of the intelligence service— underscored in October 1962 that Jakarta had no claims over Borneo.[7]

Within Borneo itself, however, the Malaysian federation had serious detractors. This sentiment was spearheaded by A.M. Azahari bin Sheikh Mahmud, a charismatic politician from Brunei. Though not necessarily opposed to Malaysia, Azahari feared being overwhelmed by the more populous peninsular territories. To improve leverage, his priority was to push for a united Borneo entity—rather than three states—with the sultan of Brunei as titular head.

Though a politician, Azahari was also once a revolutionary and had crossed borders to fight in the Indonesian war of independence. Figuring that he might have to back his plans with military might rather than rely on the ballot box, for years he had been quietly sounding out the Indonesians on the possibility of providing military training to Borneo recruits. The first time he did this in 1959, the idea went nowhere. Two years later, after the Malaysia concept was tabled, he again approached the Indonesians. This time he managed to extract moral support from General Nasution. Intelligence chief Soebandrio, who shared Azahari's leftist inclinations, hinted at more substantial aid, though none was immediately forthcoming.[8]

Forging ahead on his own, Azahari quietly assembled a small rebel band in the Sarawak jungles outside of Brunei. The majority were ethnic Malay, who comprised half of Brunei's 84,000 residents. Armed with a mix of antiquated rifles and having virtually no proper training, Azahari's so-called North Kalimantan National Army (*Tentara Nasional Kalimantan Utara*, or TNKU) would theoretically jumpstart his plan of uniting Borneo by seizing Brunei in a lightning raid before the British could react.

When the TNKU finally set their plan into action on 8 December 1962, it was an amateurish affair. Azahari was himself on a diplomatic tour at the time, leaving the rebels without his leadership on the ground. Although they occupied several key facilities in Brunei Town, they failed to locate the sultan and secure his support. Denouncing the revolt, the sultan then called on British reinforcements from Malaya. Within a week, the affair was put down and the TNKU remnants were on the run.

Though Azahari had been decisively defeated, his attempted putsch had a curious effect in Jakarta. While Indonesia had previously hinted support for the Malaysian federation, within a month after the Brunei rebellion Sukarno did a complete reversal. Perhaps overly confident after the West Irian victory, or perhaps in need of a new foreign distraction from Indonesia's domestic economic woes, he devised the policy of Confrontation (*Konfrontasi* in Indonesian) toward Malaysia and its Commonwealth patrons.

From the start, Confrontation was far less specific than Indonesia's West Irian campaign. Whereas the Mandala Command had been charged with the military conquest of Dutch-controlled territory, Jakarta did not talk in terms of annexing Borneo. Still, the Indonesians immediately began to implement the combination of military bluff and diplomatic bluster so successful in West Irian. As a first step, this involved forging guerrilla units from among the Borneo residents that had taken refuge in Kalimantan. Among the most promising were hundreds of ethnic Chinese that had spilled across the border in the immediate aftermath of the British operation in Brunei. Chinese comprised over 30 percent of Sarawak's 818,000-strong population, plus another 23 percent of Sabah's 507,000 locals. Many of them, especially in Sarawak, belonged to communist political parties. While not specifically targeted after the Brunei revolt, they felt sufficiently threatened by the British crackdown to head for Kalimantan.

Eyeing this pool of Chinese recruits, both Nasution and Soebandrio began to map out separate programs of assistance. Because the Chinese were communists—and Soebandrio entertained leftist sympathies—the intelligence chief took ten of the more promising political leaders and brought them to Bogor, a town just south of Jakarta, for political and paramilitary instruction.[9]

Nasution's helping hand was equally limited. Turning to the RPKAD, he authorized three trainers from Battalion 2 to deploy to the West Kalimantan border. Given the lack of roads in the area, they boarded a C-130 at Jakarta, then flew direct to the village of Nangabadan near the Sarawak frontier. Armed with AK-47 rifles and a pallet of supplies, they parachuted out the rear doors. One of the three, Untung Suroso, remembers:

> We took lots of candies as gifts. The kids came out to greet us first; the parents followed later. They were mostly Sarawak Chinese, with a few indigenous tribesmen. There was a language problem, as some of them did not speak Indonesian very well.[10]

For the next three months, the three RPKAD instructors coached three hundred subjects in the basics of guerrilla warfare. No guns were issued; sticks doubled for firearms. At the end of that period, two young army lieutenants and a load of rifles were dispatched to Nangabadan. The first, Kentot Harseno, was a 1961 graduate of Indonesia's military academy. The second, Mulyono Soerjowardojo, had ironically attended the British jungle warfare course in Malaya.[11]

Splitting the three hundred novice guerrillas into two groups, Kentot and Mulyono directed a pair of cross-border forays to test British reaction. On 12 April, one column edged into Sarawak and attacked a police post at Tebedu, a village south of Kuching; a second party hit the village of Gumbang near month's end. Although the Tebedu strike resulted in one British fatality and some weapons taken, the Chinese guerrillas were hardly proving their mettle. "Only half returned to Kalimantan," recalls Kentot.[12]

For the next five months, the Chinese insurgents periodically returned to Borneo for further raids. One of them, a September attack directed by Mulyono against an isolated outpost at Long Jawi, resulted in five British deaths. Still, this did not prevent the official creation of Malaysia on 16 September. One day later, the new state severed diplomatic relations with Indonesia.

Incensed, these moves led Indonesia to ratchet up the Confrontation a notch. Sticking with the West Irian formula, an order was given to deploy elite military units to the Kalimantan border. Targeting the extreme east along the Sabah frontier, the Indonesian marines were authorized on 21 September to prepare a platoon for special operations. Arriving at the island of Tarakan early the following month, the marines readied themselves for their first incursion. They would not be going alone. Since the December 1962 Brunei revolt, about one hundred members of the defeated TNKU had sought refuge in Kalimantan. While Azahari's movement had effectively ceased to exist, Indonesia chose to maintain the fiction of the TNKU and use these remnants of this force as a fig leaf during future cross-border forays.

On 17 October, five marines and one TNKU volunteer—all dressed in civilian clothes—edged into Sabah. At the cost of one marine lieutenant shot dead, the team was able to burn down a village and rush back to the sanctuary of East Kalimantan. Two months later, a 47-man mixed platoon—11 of them marines—attacked the town of Kalabakan. Though eight of the marines were killed, they inflicted greater losses on a resident Malaysian paramilitary unit.[13]

With the marines handling Sabah, the army was given jurisdiction along the border with Sarawak. In mid-September, the RPKAD's Battalion 2 was alerted to prepare two companies for deployment to West Kalimantan. By that time, the battalion had a new commander. Despite the growing friction between Jakarta and the British Commonwealth, the U.S. was still providing limited military instruction for Indonesian officers. Among them was Major Seno Hartono, who departed in mid-1963 for ranger, airborne, and jumpmaster training at Fort Benning. Assuming his position as battalion commander was Major Kodim, the British jungle warfare graduate.

Selecting two of his four companies, Kodim loaded them aboard a pair of C-130 Hercules transports. With one company squeezed into each plane, the commandos were forced to stand for the entire trip. Wearing heavy main and reserve chutes, they were exhausted by the time they reached their dropzones at first light. One of the companies jumped at Nangabadan, the same village where the Chinese guerrillas had been tutored. The second, including Kodim and a small command detachment, landed to the west near Senaning. Except for Kodim, who had a parachute malfunction and broke both legs upon landing, the rest of the troops assembled on the ground without complications.[14]

With Kodim evacuated back to Jakarta for medical treatment, the RPKAD companies dug into their respective positions. They were scheduled to patrol the border for six months; cross-border missions were not part of their mandate. For the latter assignment, the 328 Raider Battalion, most of which had been airborne-qualified for the West Irian campaign, was sent to West Kalimantan in October for the purpose of staging Sarawak raids. Like the marines in Sabah, they were to team up with a handful of TNKU remnants and disguise their campaign behind the TNKU banner.[15]

In November, the 328 Raiders began their first shallow incursions into Sarawak. Both the weak scope and pace of the forays barely grabbed anybody's attention, however, leading to calls from Jakarta for a more ambitious infiltration near year's end. Given the assignment this time was yet another company from the RPKAD's Battalion 2, which boarded Dakotas for Pontianak in mid-December.

Upon landing, the commandos were given rudimentary disguises for their upcoming operation behind Commonwealth lines. Taking the TNKU ruse a bit further, all were issued "TNKU" military uniforms that lacked manufacturer's labels and were a lighter shade of green than normally worn by the Indonesian military. To further conceal their nationality, they borrowed U.S.-made AR-15 automatic rifles from the police rangers. For more punch, each platoon was issued one Yugoslavian 90mm rocket launcher capable of accurately sending a shaped-charge warhead across six hundred meters.

The target of the RPKAD company was the town of Kuching. With a population of fifty thousand, Kuching was the largest urban center in western Sarawak. It also had the largest airfield in the area, which the RPKAD commandos intended to be the focus of their attack.

Setting out for Borneo a week before year's end, they did not get far. Marching under heavy rains, they found the Seluas River near flood stage. Exhausted and disheartened, most of the commandos dragged their feet at the border, leaving just twenty men to cautiously shift into Sarawak.

Shortly before 1600 hours on 1 January 1964, the lead elements of the RPKAD column ran headlong into a British-led patrol. For many of the commandos, it was a brief but brutal initation. Private Ashadi took a round just below his eye socket. Nearby, Private Marjo collapsed with a sucking chest wound; though his teammates saw him attempting to form words, they were fixated on the arterial spurt from his shirt.

The British had also suffered a casualty. Creeping forward, the Indonesians encountered the lifeless body of a Royal Marine Commando. Rifling through his pockets, they found the identification for Corporal Michael Marriott. Placing a grenade with the pin removed under Marriott's torso, they reversed course and ran the short distance back to the border.[16]

Though they had inflicted a British fatality, it did little to camouflage the overall failure of the RPKAD's incursion. Ordering the entire company back to Java, Colonel Mung was livid. Unlike the marines—who had grabbed

headlines with their flashy raid against Kalabakan—the commandos had
proven so timid that the British were not even aware Kuching was threatened.
"Better to die in the field than fail," Mung intoned as he stripped the company's
officers of government-issue watches (a perk with the rank) for their abysmal
performance.[17]

Following the abortive Kuching raid by Battalion 2, it was deemed time to
give Benny's untested Battalion 1 a chance. On 2 February 1964, at a time most
Indonesians were returning to their home villages to celebrate the end of the
Islamic fasting month, three of the battalion's companies were told to prepare
for immediate deployment to East Kalimantan. Just as with West Kalimantan,
the lack of roads in the province made parachutes the only viable alternative
for fast entry. Company A was to jump near the small border village of Lumbis;
Companies B and C would parachute near the equally small village of Long
Bawan. Each company would be packed into a single C-130, making for a
another standing-room-only journey from Jakarta.

After three hours, the Hercules carrying Company A closed on Lumbis
near first light. "We were so tired from standing," recalls one company member,
"we could not wait to get out the door."[18]

Once on the ground, the commandos regrouped without complications.
They had landed along the bank of the Salilir River about half a day's walk
from Lumbis. This placed them nearly on the Sabah border, across from which
was a small Commonwealth outpost. For the first few weeks, the company
built their encampment. A crusty sub-district chief—he had fought alongside
Australian commandos during World War II—made the hike from Lumbis
to greet them. He reported the area sparsely populated by only a handful of
Dayak tribesmen—and for good reason. The surrounding jungle was
impossibly dense and perpetually damp. Although some fish could be caught
in the Salilir, the local bushes and trees were surprisingly devoid of edible
fruits. Resupply, as a result, became a major concern. Sensing an opportunity,
a lone Chinese entrepreneur soon set up shop on the edge of the RPKAD
camp and began plying foodstuffs and other wares.

Once properly settled, the company was given two missions. The first
was to begin training civilian volunteers; to add depth to the TNKU fig leaf,

Jakarta had decided to actively add members into the rebel force. These recruits were primarily locals from East Kalimantan; most were ethnic Malay out of the coastal towns rather than Dayak from the Lumbis vicinity. Training was extremely rudimentary, with no weapons issued; the initial plan was for the Lumbis contingent to act as porters rather than actual combatants.

The RPKAD's second mission was cross-border raids under the TNKU banner. Much like the commandos who performed the short-lived incursion toward Kuching, they were issued a light green uniform. TNKU insignia—including a flag ostensibly designed by the rebel group—were conspicuously sewn to shoulders and caps. Boots imported from Czechoslovakia were worn in order to leave treadmarks not readily linked to Indonesia. Jakarta even went as far as issuing fake TNKU identification cards listing bogus places of birth in Kalimantan or the Philippines.[19]

Not until June 1964 did Company A launch its first raid. Their target was a Commonwealth outpost at the village of Kabu, thought to host a small number of British, Gurkha, and Malaysian troops. Kabu was located along the same tributary of the Salilir, which theoretically made for a relatively easy hike from Lumbis. But because there was at least one Malaysian village closer to the border, and because Kabu reportedly had a helicopter presence in the daylight hours, it was decided to make a large counterclockwise arc and approach the target from an unlikely northeastern direction.

During the second week of the month, six RPKAD commandos departed on their foray. One carried a Yugoslavian 90mm rocket launcher; another pair slung a small mortar. The last three were armed with the BM 59 semi-automatic rifle, a magazine-fed modification of the M1 Garand that Italian arms maker Beretta license-produced in Indonesia. After the Belgian FN semi-automatic, the Soviet AK-47, and the U.S. greasegun, the BM 59 was the fourth rifle supplied to the regiment in the past six years. The commandos took an immediate dislike to the weapon, criticizing both its heavy weight and propensity to malfunction.[20]

For the next week, the six worked their way through the jungle. Upon their final advance on Kabu, however, they found the Salilir swelled with monsoon rains. Unable to conjure a means of crossing—and more, importantly, recrossing after they struck—the team decided to abort the mission and come home.

Rather than retracing their steps, the commandos took a more direct southern path toward their home camp. After reaching what they determined was the Indonesian border, they came across a small clearing and a Dayak longhouse. A quick check showed the quarters to be deserted, possibly because the occupants were off on a hunt. Not wanting to miss the opportunity, one of the team members, an Acehnese named Amin, stripped off his uniform and began scooping water from an urn. Dressing after the quick bath, he saw a lone dog nosing through the longhouse. As many Indonesians are sensitive toward canines—citing religious reasons for not keeping them as pets—the commando kicked the animal to scare it away.

The dog ran into the bush—and immediately started barking. Amin looked toward the commotion and froze. Staring out from the jungle's edge was a set of human eyes. Recognizing Asian features, Amin initially thought it might be a Dayak returning home. But when he lowered his glance and saw a rifle, he bolted in the opposite direction as bullets began to fly over his head. The remaining five members of the team—who had been resting in the longhouse—leapt out the far end of the structure.

What happened next was apparently a case of faulty communication. Pausing to scoop up their weapons, the RPKAD members had barely gotten into the treeline when they looked back and saw the Asian soldier—a Gurkha employed by the British Army—entering the clearing and peering into the longhouse. The Gurkha then fired three shots into the air, drawing more Asian soldiers into the clearing. The shots, however, must have been misinterpreted as a signal for heavy weapons, because seconds later artillery shells began to rain down on the site.

The RPKAD team fled from the scene, not stopping until they reached Lumbis. Dayak villagers, later returning to their flattened longhouse, reportedly found a severed foot in a jungle boot.[21]

The failed raid at Kabu brought a premature end to further RPKAD incursions from Lumbis. For the remainder of the year, Company A focused on training TNKU volunteers. The quality of the recruits varied considerably, with a small number of Dayaks proving the most loyal and capable. By the end of 1964, the company gladly turned over its BM 59 to their guerrilla students (the commandos received the AK-47 in its place). Forming mixed ten-man teams, with two RPKAD commandos for every eight TNKU civilians, they initiated patrols along their sector of the frontier. More ambitious raids into Sabah, however, remained off the schedule until their one-year tour was complete in February 1965. Walking south to the Mantarang River—a grueling jungle trek that took two weeks—the company boarded boats for the coast, then transferred to planes for Cijantung. No further RPKAD contingents were posted to Lumbis.[22]

On the same morning Company A had deployed to Lumbis in February 1964, Company C—nicknamed Company "Cobra"—approached Long Bawan.[23] In light rains, the Hercules circled over a fallow field. The commandos leapt from the back doors, landing in the clearing without casualties. As soon as they arrived, however, the skies turned dark and the cloudbank grew solid. By the time their sister Company B arrived overhead, the dropzone could not be identified. Aborting the jump, the second company eventually came back to Jakarta. Company Cobra, it was subsequently decided, would handle the Long Bawan assignment on its own.

Just like at Lumbis, the local sub-district chief arrived to welcome the RPKAD. A handful of TNKU guerrillas—veterans of the Brunei revolt— were camped in a nearby village.[24] A short hike to their immediate west was Sarawak, with British anti-aircraft weapons positioned along the border to fire on Indonesian resupply aircraft.

Once settled, the company members questioned their commander, Captain Alex Setiabudi, about their mission. "We were not told if we were supposed to conduct commando raids or train guerrillas," remembers one sergeant.[25]

Before any clear answer was forthcoming, Alex took his five-man company staff and attached it to a ten-man squad. Leaving the rest of the company behind, this augmented team then headed north to the village of Pa Fani. Without pause, they pressed north and crossed into Sabah during early March. The vicinity, a particularly rugged section of the border, was a hostile mix of rocky faces, fast mountain streams, and triple canopy.

After walking for two days, Alex called a halt. Their mission, he now revealed to the smaller group, was to establish at that location a permanent guerrilla base inside Malaysian territory. This was not welcome news to his men, each of whom had carried rice tubes with only enough of the staple to last three days. A quick search of the area showed few edible fruits, and the commandos were afraid of hunting game because rifle shots would alert Commonwealth patrols. Worse, Jakarta was unwilling to risk a supply airdrop.

After the complaints from his hungry commandos grew more shrill over the course of a week, Alex finally gave permission for the team to temporarily return to Indonesian territory to gather more rations. On 13 March, Corporal Ismael departed south with his ten-man squad. The remaining five, including Alex, followed an hour later.

By late the following afternoon, the lead commandos had reached what they assumed was Indonesian territory. Their exact location was difficult to determine. "Our maps were pathetic," said company member Bambang Sutopo. "We were given a single black-and-white sheet for all of Kalimantan; it had been torn from a school textbook."[26]

Conspiring against them, too, was the weather. At 1600 hours, the sky turned a deep purple. Between the massing rainclouds and the late hour, visibility was nil. Sounds, however, traveled far. From the nearby jungle, the RPKAD commandos heard the distinctive noise of wood being chopped. Thinking that it might be a TNKU camp, they vectored toward the sound in the hope of getting a meal.

With Corporal Ismael at point, the famished team advanced. But rather than encountering TNKU guerrillas, Ismael was shocked to stumble upon a shirtless Caucasian. Reeling backward in surprise, the Indonesian corporal narrowly avoided a bullet. He instinctively brought forward his BM 59 and returned fire. His fellow RPKAD commandos attempted to join their squad leader, but in the failing light could not distinguish between friend and foe.[27]

After fifteen minutes, the sound of gunfire ceased. In pouring rain, the RPKAD members froze uncomfortably in their respective positions to wait for morning. At first light, they regrouped and approached the scene of the previous night's firefight. Underneath an unfinished lean-to, they saw a British soldier sitting upright in a shallow depression. His dead eyes were unfocused and mouth partially open. The night's rain had filled the depression with water, which had turned a scarlet red from blood leaking out of a hole in his lower left abdomen. The commandos pulled the body from the water and stripped the corpse of his boots and rucksack. They also took his rifle and radio before covering him with leaves and soil.[28]

Upon returning to Pa Fani, Captain Alex decided not to press their luck by returning to the earlier guerrilla base inside Sabah. Instead, he ordered his company to begin training TNKU recruits at a series of satellite camps near Long Bawan. Two companies of volunteers were assembled by mid-year; as was the case at Lumbis, most were Indonesians from coastal Kalimantan. There was also a scattering of Brunei veterans as well as several dozen from North Sulawesi, the latter former Permesta rebels challenged to prove their loyalty to the central government.[29]

Once training concluded in the third quarter of the year, the RPKAD initiated cross-border raids with mixed teams. Without exception, the results were minimal. Most patrols barely entered Malaysian territory; of those that did, there were no confirmed casualties or damage inflicted on Commonwealth targets. In return, four RPKAD commandos and ten TNKU guerrillas were killed-in-action by the time Company Cobra was ordered home in February 1965. Just as in West Irian, Indonesia's infiltration campaign by elite troops was falling short of expectations.[30]

During the time Battalion 1's companies were deployed to Lumbis and Long Bawan, major changes were underway within the RPKAD. In large part because Battalion 2 had come up painfully short at Kuching, Colonel Mung was sufficiently concerned with the quality of the battalion to order it deactivated in April 1964. As of 18 May, its personnel were transferred to flesh out five companies in Battalion 1. Once more, this left the regiment with just a single combat battalion.

The downsizing did not last long. This was prompted by Lieutenant Colonel Sarwo Edhie, the Batu Jajar school commander who in July 1963 had been promoted to RPKAD chief-of-staff. A favorite of General Yani—who in 1962 had displaced Nasution as the army chief—Sarwo Edhie wielded considerable clout. Reflecting this, in late 1963 he successfully pushed plans to take two Banteng Raider battalions from Central Java and convert them into para-commando battalions under the RPKAD. There was a bit of nepotism in the decision: both Sarwo Edhie and Yani hailed from Central Java—and Yani himself had been the father of the Banteng Raider concept.

The first unit chosen for conversion was the 441 "Banteng Raider III" Battalion based at Semarang. Rotated through Batu Jajar one company at a time, they subsequently returned to Semarang redubbed as the RPKAD's Battalion 3. In the third quarter of 1964, the second unit chosen for conversion, the 436 "Banteng Raider I" Airborne Battalion based at Magelang, started a similar upgrade. This battalion had been briefly placed under Mung's airborne brigade during the West Irian operation. By the time it returned to Magelang during the second quarter of 1965, it filled the numerical gap in the RPKAD order-of-battle by becoming the regiment's new Battalion 2.[31]

Now three battalions strong, it was decided that a composite RPKAD unit would be sent to West Kalimantan. Set at three companies, two would come from Semarang; the third would be Battalion 1's Company B, which had tried—and failed—to parachute into East Kalimantan in February 1964. Heading the composite formation was Major Sri Tamigen, the commander of Battalion 3 in Semarang.

Landing at Pontianak in February 1965, the three companies walked directly northeast to the border, then shifted east along the frontier to the village of Balai Karangan. A section of East Java infantrymen was already deployed in the vicinity; they reported the area generally quiet.

The tranquility was not to last. Just 1,090 meters across the border was a British outpost near the village of Mapu. Hosting a company from the 2 Parachute Battalion, Mapu was situated on a small hill in a valley, exposing it to observation from the ridgeline along the border. Even worse for the British defenders, their sister airborne companies were in bases 32 kilometers away; though they could call in heliborne reinforcements during the daylight, chopper support would be unavailable during the night hours.

Sizing up Mapu's vulnerability, the Indonesians decided the target was too good to ignore. Over the next two months, select members from the three RPKAD companies began a series of reconnaissance forays to map out the base's layout. To disguise their affiliation from prying eyes while at Balai Karangan, all of the commandos wore shoulder insignia used by the army's combat engineers.[32]

On 25 April, final preparations were underway for the raid on Mapu. All three platoons from Company B—nicknamed Company "Ben Hur" after the popular 1959 film—were to participate in the actual mission; the two Central Java companies would remain just inside Indonesian territory as a reserve.

The raiders were heavily armed for the occasion. Most were equipped with the AK-47 assault rifle (the RPKAD had fully purged the unwelcome BM 59). Each platoon had three British-made Bren light machine guns; every squad had a Yugoslavian rocket launcher. And in a first for the RPKAD, they had been given two Bangalore torpedoes—an explosive-filled tube used for breaching minefields and barbed wire.

Crossing the border after last light, Company Ben Hur moved at a glacial pace. Resting during the day, they did not come within sight of Mapu until 0200 hours on 27 April. Stealing past Mapu village—which consisted of just five huts—they crept toward the adjacent British base. The outpost was circular and divided into wedge-shaped sectors, each wedge featuring a machine gun nest. The outer perimeter was protected by barbed wire, punji stakes, and claymore mines.[33]

In pouring rain—which helped disguise the sound of their movement— the commandos split in three directions. The center platoon, with its Bren guns trained on the high point with lights, was set to initiate the assault. The two other platoons circled to the sides and began snaking their Bangalore torpedoes through the outer wire.

At 0430 hours, the Brens kicked off the attack. Seconds later, each of the Bangalore torpedoes sliced through the barbed wire on the flanks. The defenders were at a major disadvantage: not only were they caught by surprise, but nearly all of the paratroopers assigned to the base were off on patrol. What remained was an understrength platoon of fresh British recruits, numbering just 34 men in total.

Rushing to man their machine guns, the British put up a spirited fight. One RPKAD private, a Catholic named Sunadi, received a fatal chest wound on the left flank. Another private was felled on the right.

But the RPKAD gave as good as it got. Over the next two hours, a withering amount of rockets and bullets all but razed the Mapu outpost. Two British paratroopers were killed, another seven seriously wounded.[34]

Withdrawing back into West Kalimantan, Company Ben Hur was greeted at Balai Karangan by the RPKAD's seniormost officers. In what would be the largest single battle in the entire Confrontation, they were hailed as victors. Most of the company's platoon leaders were given field promotions. Even more welcome, the company was allowed to cut its tour short and return to Jakarta, where they marched before President Sukarno at the front of the 17 August Independence Day parade.[35]

1   Interview with Seno Hartono, 18 October 1997.

2   Among army units, the 454 Airborne Battalion suffered the greatest number of killed-in-action (31). Within the entire military, the air force's PGT sustained the largest number of deaths (94).

3   The circumcisions were performed on Javanese settlers near Merauke, not ethnic Irianese.

4   Peter Dennis and Jeffrey Grey, *Emergency and Confrontation* (St. Leonard, New South Wales: Allen & Unwin, 1996), p. 173.

5   General Suharto, the Mandala commander, was convinced his military maneuvers were key to liberating West Irian: "Some people are still claiming that [West Irian] was won through diplomacy. Sure they can make that claim…But the fact is that eleven years of diplomatic struggle did not bear fruit. It was after…the military operation that diplomacy finally brought Irian Jaya into the fold of the Indonesian Republic…Washington then realized the strength of the Indonesian military and put pressure on The Hague to relent rather than risk a full-scale war." Paul F. Gardner, *Shared Hopes, Separate Fears* (Boulder, Colorado: WestView Press, 1997), p. 178.

6   Julius Pour, *Benny Moerdani, Profile of a Soldier Statesman* (Jakarta: Yayasan Kejuangan Panglima Besar Sudirman, 1993), p. 191; Central Intelligence Agency Research Study, *Indonesia—1965, The Coup That Backfired* (December 1968), p. 109. A Dutch arms merchant named DeLeon was contracted to import Irvin parachutes, British paratrooper helmets, and Denison camouflage smocks for the RPKAD. The original contract called for DeLeon to provide original Denison smocks from England, but he had maximized his profits by instead substituting a cheaper imitation—nicknamed the "Depison" smock—made in Hong Kong. When RPKAD officers complained of the switch, DeLeon belatedly provided a handful of authentic Denisons along with the Depisons.

7   FBIS, East Asia edition, 4 October 1962, p. RRR5.

8   Greg Poulgrain, *The Genesis of Konfrontasi* (Bathurst, New South Wales: Crawford Publishing House, 1998), p. 255.

9   Drs. Soemadi, *Peranan Kalimantan Barat Dalam Menghadapi* (Pontiankak: Yayasan Tanjungpura, 1973), p. 56.

10 Interview with Untung Suroso, 15 May 2000.

11 In 1965, Major Muljono was implicated in the abortive communist coup and executed.

12 Interview with Kentot Harseno, 6 May 2000.

13 *Korps Komando AL., Dari Tahun Ketahun* (Jakarta: Bagian Sedjarah KKO AL, 1971), p. 279.

14 Interview with Tata Loekita, 17 March 1999; interview with Darwin Nasution, 15 July 1999.

15 During the height of the Darul Islam uprising, the 328 Battalion had been the second battalion from West Java to get raider training. But because of an existing army regulation limiting the number of official raider battalions to no more than one per military region, they had been forced to wear a dark brown beret instead of the green shade adopted by the raiders (and later paratroopers). Even after the battalion was jump-qualified during the West Irian campaign, members of the battalion refused to part with their brown berets.

16 Interview with Kusnadi, 18 March 2000.

17 Ibid.

18 Interview with Subagyo, 21 August 2000.

19 Subagyo interview; interview with Agus S., 4 April 2000. Some of the TNKU identification cards listed birthplaces in the Philippines because that nation had a historical claim over Sabah.

20 Agus S. interview; Bambang Sutopo interview.

21 Subagyo interview.

22 An outpost of West Java infantrymen was established near the former RPKAD camp at Lumbis. This infantry position was razed by Gurkhas and the Australian Special Air Service in June 1965.

23 Company A was nicknamed Company "Ampera," a contraction for the popular Sukarno slogan "Message of the People's Suffering."

24 Mention of the TNKU presence is found in *Declassified Documents Reference System* [hereafter DDRS], Retrospective Collection, Department of State document from USARMA Singapore, dated 14 December 1963.

25 Interview with Kusno, 21 July 2000.

26 Bambang Sutopo interview.

27 The British patrol had strayed across the ill-defined border by accident. Not until June 1964 were elite Commonwealth units given secret authorization to make shallow penetrations (dubbed "Claret" missions) into Kalimantan.

28 Kusno interview. The British fatality was radioman James "Paddy" Condon, part of a four-man Special Air Service reconnaissance patrol that had strayed into Indonesian territory. Several British histories, citing hearsay, falsely claim Condon was captured alive and tortured to death by the RPKAD during interrogation. See Peter Dickens, *SAS, The Jungle Frontier* (London: Arms and Armour Press, 1983), p. 127.

29 Kusno interview.

30 Kusno interview; Bambang Sutopo interview.

31 Interview with Djasmin, 12 June 1999.

32 Interview with Mataksan, 16 August 2000; Bambang Sutopo interview; Untung Suroso interview.

33 Peter Harclerode, *Para! Fifty Years of the Parachute Regiment* (London: Arms and Armour Press, 1992), p. 261.

34 In an attempt to put a better spin on their loss, the British claimed to have inflicted 300 casualties on the RPKAD raiders. In reality, there were only two Indonesians killed and five wounded. See Harclerode, *Para!*, p. 265.

35 Untung Suroso interview; Mataksan interview.

CHAPTER NINE

STORMCLOUDS

W hile fighting was taking place along the Kalimantan frontier, the hottest battlefield in Indonesia was arguably in Jakarta. It was there in the capital where the armed forces were pitted in a heated struggle for political influence. Their opponent: the resurgent Indonesian Communist Party, the PKI, which had gone from strength to strength in the polls for over a decade. Prior to 1962, President Sukarno had meandered between supporting them and the military in a delicate balancing act. But after 1962, Sukarno seemed to throw in his lot with the PKI by favoring their political aims through both sins of omission and commission. Ties between the president and his armed forces, as a result, noticeably cooled.

Complicating matters, the military did not speak with one voice. The marines were diehard supporters of the president, which by association made them appear soft on communism. And the air force, led by Air Commodore Omar Dani—a *bon vivant* that looked like the Indonesian version of Errol Flynn—generally followed Sukarno's lead without question.

But the army, which was the true powerhouse among the services, bristled at the rise of the PKI. This was not because of any reflective opposition to communism (the army, after all, had greatly benefited from Soviet bloc largesse), but rather because of its perceived loss of clout to the only domestic organization that rivaled it in terms of organization and influence.

Fallout from this struggle was reflected in the Confrontation with Malaysia. The PKI strongly opposed the Malaysian federation—arguing it was a form of neo-colonialism—and proposed raising a fifteen million-strong armed militia that could take the battle across the border. Reflecting their unwavering support for Sukarno, the marines and air force, too, maintained leading roles in the simmering conflict against Malaysia.

The army's General Yani, by contrast, sought to shield his service from Sukarno's latest foreign adventure. "He was told to commit forty-seven battalions," said former RPKAD chief-of-staff Widjoyo Soejono, "but he said this was irresponsible because it would strip Java bare."[1] Responding in letter but not in spirit, Yani intentionally refrained from deploying many of his best battalions to the border. He also looked to minimize losses by not condoning major cross-border operations aside from those conducting by the RPKAD and a handful of other small units.

Sukarno recognized this disparity in support—and responded in kind. Back in June 1962, he had authorized creation of a presidential guard unit known as the Tjakrabirawa Regiment. As the regiment took shape over the following year, it grouped together four of the best battalions available: one from the marines, another from the air force's PGT, a third from the police, and the last from the army. In a telling decision, the army's contribution was not taken from the RPKAD, but rather from the Central Java military region, where a number of mid-ranking officers had shown sympathy for the PKI.

For many members of the RPKAD, the creation of the Tjakrabirawa Regiment was a source of bitterness. Declaring themselves the most elite formation in Indonesia, Tjakrabirawa members adopted a red beret like the RPKAD (though they wore it slanting to the left). And when the entire unit was slated to become airborne-qualified in mid-1963, they chose the PGT facilities at Margahayu over the RPKAD's Batu Jajar training center.[2]

Though the RPKAD was being bested by its service rivals, Colonel Mung did not seem to notice. More than ever, he had turned inward and busied himself fine-tuning his regiment's capabilities. Many of his ideas came from ranger training received at Fort Benning during 1963. Greatly influenced by this, when he returned to Cijantung that September he began to push advanced mountaineering at Batu Jajar. Carried over from Fort Benning, too, was the practice of rappelling from helicopters. This was showcased during a demonstration for visiting North Korean General O Zin Woo in November 1964. Watching the RPKAD commandos descend from a hovering chopper, the Korean turned to Mung and asked why they did not use a ladder. True to his Spartan image, the quirky colonel responded: "My wife's children use a rope ladder; my men use rope."[3]

A second source of inspiration for Mung was North Vietnam. In August 1964, the RPKAD commander visited that communist nation for a twenty-day training primer. As both Hanoi and Jakarta were the only Southeast Asian nations who had persevered in a revolutionary struggle against colonialism, there was an undercurrent of warm ties between their respective militaries. The North Vietnamese army, moreover, was renowned for its innovation against better-equipped French and American opponents. Among the topics shared with Mung were methods of makeshift boobytrapping, survival foods, firing a mortar without a baseplate, and modifying a mortar into a direct-fire anti-tank weapon. All of these were soon incorporated into the RPKAD repertoire of skills.[4]

When not experimenting with new tactics, Mung was especially hard on his officers. "He thought the regiment was unfit—especially the younger officers," recalls the Battalion 1 deputy, Captain Sumardji.[5] This attitude was readily apparent in June 1964 when fifteen new lieutenants transferred to the commandos; nearly all were recent graduates from the National Military Academy at Magelang, and only three had previous field experience. Mung personally greeted them upon arrival at Cijantung and led them through three grueling weeks of physical conditioning. Though thirty-nine years old—a full generation older than the lieutenants—he outstripped their stamina.

Once conditioning was concluded, the lieutenants were theoretically to proceed to Batu Jajar for commando induction. For the three with field experience, they were allowed to go. For the twelve untested lieutenants, however, Mung insisted that they first head to Sulawesi for half a year of combat.[6]

The security situation in South and Central Sulawesi had long been a festering sore for the central government. Back in 1950, Kahar Muzakkar, a former revolutionary leader, had entered the jungle near the South Sulawesi capital of Makassar in an attempt to mediate a settlement with local guerrillas irate at not having been integrated into the national army. Instead of making peace, Muzakkar himself joined the rebels as their commander. By 1953, his budding resistance movement took on an Islamic flavor, leading him to announce an alliance with the Darul Islam insurgents fighting in Java and Aceh.

To confront this challenge, Jakarta dispatched several battalions of Javanese infantry. But rather than root out Muzakkar, their heavy-handed tactics only served to alienate the Sulawesi population, which in turn helped give rise to the Permesta movement. Permesta and the PRRI went on to declare a separate state, forcing the central government to temporarily focus against those threats instead of Muzakkar's Darul Islam wing. Muzakkar won an additional reprieve during the West Irian campaign, which had left Jakarta with insufficient troops to spare for counterinsurgency efforts in Sulawesi.

As of 1963, Muzakkar showed no signs of abandoning his quixotic quest to found an Islamic state. Even though the Java core of Darul Islam had been soundly defeated, and the Aceh chapter had come to a truce with the government, Sulawesi's religious warriors persisted in their small but embarrassing affront to Jakarta. By 1964, the government felt it could no longer afford to turn its back. Two additional factors had brought them to this conclusion. First, Muzakkar had entered into a loose alliance with an ex-army officer named Andi Selle operating near the South Sulawesi town of Parepare. Selle was the latest in a string of former Sulawesi officers who had fallen foul of Jakarta. Selle, however, was several degrees of magnitude more serious than his predecessors; a virtual warlord, he exhibited a seething personal vendetta against the provincial military commander.

Second, there were growing signs that Muzakkar and Selle were both starting to receive covert foreign assistance. Looking to draw Indonesian military units away from the Borneo frontier, there was evidence that British intelligence by 1964 had opened a small clandestine pipeline of training and supplies to the Sulawesi rebels. In addition, they discretely sponsored a black radio station urging creation of a federal state in Sulawesi.[7]

Looking to crush the Muzakkar and Selle rebellions, a major sweeping operation spearheaded by Javanese infantry was underway by mid-1964. Most of the task force was initially focused against warlord Selle. With the prospective RPKAD lieutenants matched up with infantry battalions, they inundated the area around Parepare. By September, they had cornered the warlord and shot him dead.

Shifting into Central Sulawesi, the lieutenants were thrown into an even larger ongoing operation against Muzakkar. Among the main participants in this sweep were the 330 Airborne Battalion and a group of raiders from the local province. There were also two RPKAD companies: one from Battalion 1 in Cijantung and the other from Battalion 3 in Semarang.[8]

Assigned to these various units, the novice lieutenants were exposed to several months of running gun battles against Muzakkar's final diehard band of followers. Some of the heaviest fighting was experienced by the RPKAD company from Battalion 3, which had patrolled across a mountain and found a recently abandoned rebel bivouac site. Other RPKAD elements captured documents in January 1965 that showed Muzakkar was in the same vicinity. Although the para-commandos were the closest unit to stage a final attack, army politics dictated that they stand fast while the 330 Airborne Battalion was allowed to conduct an air assault from Soviet-made helicopters. On the morning of 3 February, the paratroopers raided their target; when Muzakkar's body was recovered, it had five bullets in it. Without its leader, the last pocket of Darul Islam was fully mopped up by year's end.[9]

As operations in Sulawesi wound down, the twelve lieutenants returned to Java and were belatedly allowed to proceed to commando training at Batu Jajar. Ironically, Colonel Mung was no longer with the regiment. His exit had come about following a long simmering dispute with the commander of Battalion 1, Major Benny Moerdani. At the core of their feud, Benny had taken issue over Mung's propensity to get consumed with the accoutrements of an elite unit. Mung, for example, had spent an inordinate amount of time testing new rifles and designing a jungle blade and flashy throwing axes. Dissatisfied with the Soviet D-1 parachute, the colonel had micromanaged the debate over alternative chutes.[10] He had also called for a new camouflage suit to replace the Depison smocks; he eventually approved a unique vertical stripe design, used on both uniforms and a bush hat, that debuted during the October 1964 Armed Forces Day parade.[11]

But it was money issues that eventually brought their conflict to a head. Famous for his modest lifestyle and intolerance of fiscal waste, Mung had earlier complained when General Yani provided Benny with Dutch currency for use by his DPC teams in the West Irian campaign. Again during Confrontation, Benny's Battalion 1 had been issued U.S. dollars for potential use while on cross-border missions into Borneo. When Mung demanded control over the foreign cash, Benny refused.

Benny, too, had amassed a small chit fund to compensate those killed or incapacitated on missions. One recipient was Agus Hernoto, the DPC team leader who had lost a leg in West Irian. Though handicapped, Agus was given an administrative job with Battalion 1.

Eyeing Benny's monetary intransigence, Mung struck back. During a regimental meeting in mid-December 1964, he demanded that all handicapped soldiers be axed from the roster. Agus Hernoto, for whom Benny felt personally responsible, was the obvious target. Venting his emotions, Benny openly criticized the colonel's decision in stark terms. Mung stoically took the heat without response.[12]

Following the terse meeting, Benny left Jakarta for a honeymoon with his new bride. Mung was seething but offered no sanctions against the feisty major. But the RPKAD's chief of staff, Lieutenant Colonel Sarwo Edhie, was not so willing to let the case drop. Drawing on his close personal ties with the army chief, he met Yani and recounted the clash in detail.

Hearing of the testy exchange, Yani was torn. Benny had already privately complained to him about Mung's fascination with accoutrements at the expense of developing the corps. By comparison, the marines had not raised their first battalion until 1960; two years later, that number had increased to six. For the army chief, the charge that Mung was allowing the para-commandos to be eclipsed by a competing service was damning. Still, Benny's insubordination could not be condoned.

Seeing little choice, Yani decided to expel both officers from the regiment. During the first week of January 1965, Mung was relieved of his RPKAD command and sent to East Kalimantan as the new head of that military region. Benny was shifted to the Army Strategic Reserve Command (*Komando Cadangan Strategis Angkatan Darat*, or Kostrad), a direct descendent of the strategic reserve concept developed for the West Irian campaign. Headquartered in Jakarta, Kostrad held loose administrative control over the 3 Parachute Brigade (another holdover from West Irian) and a selection of other Java-based infantry and cavalry units. It was headed by the former Mandala commander, Major General Suharto. As a second hat, Suharto also controlled a small cell for special Confrontation operations, and it was there that Benny was assigned and immediately dispatched to Thailand to brainstorm clandestine third-country methods of striking Malaysia.[13]

The winner in the shakeup was Sarwo Edhie. Promoted to full colonel, he was Yani's quick choice as the new RPKAD commander. Lieutenant Colonel Prijo Pranoto, a 1960 Fort Benning ranger graduate who had been heading the Batu Jajar training center, was elevated to chief-of-staff.

Sarwo Edhie's rise had come at a cost. Through force of personality, Benny had nurtured a sizeable contingent of supporters among the RPKAD officer cadre; most of this crowd was now sour toward the new RPKAD commander on account they saw him as profiting from Benny's expulsion. There were also comments about nepotism from Yani, as well as barbs about Edhie's lack of commando training. The colonel, after all, had never partaken in the Batu Jajar course or a foreign equivalent; his only overseas stint was to army staff college in Australia. "Many within the regiment saw him as only a transitional leader," said one RPKAD officer.[14]

Events in late September 1965 would dictate otherwise.

While Cijantung was wracked by internal disputes, Confrontation raged on. At the opening of September, Battalion 1 was put on alert to dispatch troops back to East Kalimantan. Since the first quarter of the year, the two RPKAD companies in that province had been replaced by infantrymen from East Java. The infantry had proven themselves an ineffectual lot: at Lumbis they had been run out of their outpost during a Gurkha cross-border raid; at Long Bawan they had refused to conduct aggressive patrols, allowing the British to place a 105mm pack howitzer on the high terrain overlooking the post. This artillery piece regularly shelled Long Bawan, keeping the East Javanese troops hunkered inside their bunkers.

To rectify the latter situation, it was decided to dispatch Company Cobra back to Long Bawan for a second tour. The company commander had changed in the interim, with Alex Setiabudi taking leave for a staff course. Filling his slot was Lieutenant Kentot Harseno, the same officer who had worked with the Chinese guerrillas along the West Kalimantan frontier. Having just completed training at Batu Jajar, this was his first RPKAD posting.

Prior to deployment, Kentot was given a briefing on the disposition of the British gun overlooking Long Bawan. Because the army command wanted this neutralized at all costs, a plan was developed for the lieutenant to parachute with a reinforced platoon near the top of the ridge and carry out an immediate raid on the artillery emplacement. The rest of Company Cobra would join them once the gun was destroyed.

On the afternoon of 26 September, an RPKAD jumpmaster briefed Kentot's men before boarding a single C-130. Unlike previous Kalimantan jumps, the Hercules was not grossly overloaded; this allowed the fifty-seven commandos to sit without wearing parachutes for most of the journey.

As they neared their target toward last light, the pilot notified the paratroopers to don their chutes. Once suited, Kentot—who had gotten married just three days earlier—reflectively glanced out the window before moving toward the rear. Despite not having heard or felt anything unusual, he was shocked to see the right wing engulfed in flames. Panic immediately swept through the cabin as black smoke entered the open rear door.[15]

Seconds later, the voice of Captain Suhardjo, the plane's pilot, came over the intercom. He instructed the paratroopers to immediately push out the cargo before jumping themselves; once the cabin was clear, he would attempt to make an emergency landing in the Long Bawan valley. Needing little prompting, the commandos surged out the back. Suhardjo then steered his burning aircraft toward a small clearing. Bellying into a field, the crew and jumpmasters sprinted from the plane just as the right wing fell off. This forced the plane to lurch to the left, splashing JP-4 aviation fuel across the airframe and causing an enormous fireball. Although there was no loss of life, the Indonesian order-of-battle was less one Hercules.[16]

For Kentot and his commandos, they had rained down across the jungle far from their intended target. In fading light, they regrouped and attempted to get their bearings. Fearful they had landed in Sarawak, they eventually came across a Dayak villager and confirmed they were inside Indonesian territory.

By the following day, they had managed to find Long Bawan and were met by Colonel Mung, the former RPKAD commander now in charge of East Kalimantan. Seeing the smoldering Hercules wreck, they learned it was victim of friendly fire. During the afternoon of their jump, the British howitzer had heavily shelled the Javanese infantrymen at Long Bawan. Often after such shellings, there was a resupply drop along the ridgeline by a British DHC-4 Caribou aircraft. This had prompted the Indonesians to bring in an anti-aircraft gun to harass the Caribou from a distance. Unfortunately, when the Hercules had come overhead in low light, its silhouette resembled a Caribou from below. The Indonesian gunners, as a result, had opened fire and shot it down.

Because the commandos had not landed on the ridge itself, they had lost the element of surprise and needed to develop a new plan to neutralize the howitzer. Lieutenant Kentot still wanted to storm the mountain, but he felt it necessary to have mortar support. The resident Javanese infantry had a pair of large mortars, but moving them through the jungle promised to be a challenge. The damp jungle floor, too, posed a major problem. "We experimented with placing the baseplate on canvas sacks," said one of the commandos. "But the backblast from the first round caused the mortar to begin imbedding itself into the ground."[17]

Finally, a week after their arrival a Soviet-made Mi-6 helicopter materialized over the camp. Assuming it had come to help lift the mortars closer to the ridge, the RPKAD commandos ran out to the landing zone. As soon as the chopper settled, however, a crew member handed Kentot an radiogram from Jakarta. "It said there was an emergency in the capital," said Kentot. "I was to return to Java immediately."[18]

On the eastern extreme of the Indonesian archipelago, things in West Irian were not going as planned. After Jakarta assumed full control of the territory from the United Nations in 1963, it expected the Irianese population would show gratitude for throwing off the shackles of Dutch colonialism.

This is not what happened. Far from seeing the 1962 Indonesian campaign as a struggle for their liberation, locals were more taken by the eleventh-hour Dutch concessions that allowed for their own flag, anthem, and representative council. They also were mindful about the promise for a vote on self-determination before the close of the decade.

Aside from the self-determination vote, Jakarta was in little mood to honor the Dutch promises. The flag, anthem, and council, as a result, were immediately abolished. There were even hints they did not see the self-determination referendum as necessary. In the eyes of many Irianese, such moves made Indonesian rule appear far less tolerant than its European predecessor.

Taking greatest umbrage at the Indonesians were residents from the town of Manokwari. Located on the eastern coast of what the Dutch called

Vogelkop—the "Bird's Head," a peninsula jutting off the western end of New Guinea island—Manokwari was home to the twenty thousand-strong Arfak tribe. When the Dutch had started forming an armed Papuan auxiliary corps in 1961, the volatile Arfak had constituted the backbone. In a last act of defiance before turning over control to the United Nations, the Dutch had encouraged these trained Arfak troops to fight a guerrilla war around Manokwari to keep Irian in the world spotlight—and reminded them of the location of Allied weapons caches left over from World War II.[19]

For over a year under Indonesian rule, the Arfak were relatively tranquil. Some of the ex-auxiliary members, in fact, were absorbed into the Indonesian military. But in late 1964, others from within the tribe were edging toward open revolt. Citing a lack of jobs and food shortages, dozens of Arfak tribesmen started leaving Manokwari in mid-1965 for the mountainous interior of the peninsula.

On 26 July, the tribesmen in Manokwari reached their flashpoint. Incensed during an oath of loyalty ceremony, some of the four hundred locals in attendance turned on government representatives with a mix of machetes and spears; three Indonesians were killed and eight weapons stolen. One day later, key Arfak tribal leaders slipped into the jungle; another day after that, guerrillas staged a pre-dawn raid against an infantry barracks in Manokwari. Calling themselves the Free Papua Organization (*Organisasi Papua Merdeka*, or OPM), the rebels killed three Indonesian troops and stole two more rifles. A second outpost was hit the same morning, resulting in yet another soldier's death.

Jakarta was fast to react. By 4 August, they had penned plans for Operation Sadar ("aware"). Focused around the immediate vicinity of Manokwari, Sadar called for two RPKAD companies to lead a joint task force of police, marines, infantry, and PGT commandos in a sweep aimed at capturing the top OPM leaders—dead or alive. In a rather ambitious schedule, they were to get results by the country's twentieth anniversary on 17 August 1965.[20]

By 10 August, the RPKAD contribution to Sadar was in West Irian. One of the two companies—Company A from Battalion 1—was under the new leadership of Lieutenant Edy Sudrajat; the second was from Battalion 2 at Magelang. Major Soegiarto, the Battalion 2 commander, was placed in overall charge of the RPKAD contingent.

As soon as the commandos fanned out from Manokwari, they were struck by the inhospitable terrain. The jungle was so thick that the government troops were largely confined to existing paths. And in a strange dichotomy, the jungle was incredibly lush while at the same time revealing little edible flora or fauna. "In East Kalimantan, we could find water and a bit of food," complained one Company A member, "but in Irian it was almost impossible to live off the land."[21]

Absent, too, was any sign of the OPM. With the Sadar task force channeled along known trails, the jungle-wise Irianese guerrillas easily kept out of sight. Missing the government's self-imposed 17 August deadline, the troops barely registered any contact with the insurgents—much less capture or kill their leaders. The only casualty suffered by the RPKAD was when one commando was accidentally shot dead by a marine.[22]

For another month, the two RPKAD companies—operating as separate platoons to increase their coverage—patrolled across the Bird's Head to little effect. While a pair of key Arfak tribal leaders chose to rally to the government, the bulk of the nascent OPM was successfully holding out in the jungle.[23]

Although the operation's objectives were still far from realized, the RPKAD contingent was not going to see their mission to its conclusion. During the first week of October, they received orders to cut their tour short and immediately march back to Manokwari. Waiting for them were two Hercules transports. Just as had been the case with Kentot in East Kalimantan, the commandos were told there was a problem in the capital. Remembers one member: "We were to get back as soon as possible."[24]

At Batu Jajar, the RPKAD training center had spent the previous year enhancing its airborne course. This had been complicated by a diversity of foreign equipment; the Indonesian parachute inventory, for example, included U.S., British, Soviet, and Yugoslavian models. Most prevalent was the Soviet-made D-1 chute, which was roundly disliked by the Indonesians for its bulk and bad safety record. Colonel Mung had favored the U.S. T-10 as an alternative—only to find out that the sale of American parachutes was embargoed because of Confrontation.

To bust U.S. sanctions, the Indonesians turned to West German parachute manufacturer Bruggmann & Brand. Using the T-10 as a basis, the RPKAD parachute cadre asked that the chute diameter be reduced by two feet and two gores added to each side for added maneuverability. Dubbed the RI T-10

("RI" for "Republic of Indonesia"), it was to become Indonesia's standard army canopy for the next two decades.[25]

The U.S. embargo had an effect on something else. With spare parts not being sold by Washington, the Indonesian Air Force had cut back use of its U.S.-made C-130 fleet to a bare minimum. To pick up the slack, Moscow had offered the Antonov An-12B transport; two sets of Indonesian crews ventured to the Soviet Union for An-12 training in 1964, and a second set of four crews went there in 1965.

The Hercules and the An-12 differed in several key respects. In particular, the Antonov cruised at 320 knots, slowing to 160 knots to drop paratroopers. By contrast, the C-130 cruised at a slower 300 knots, dropping paratroopers at 130 knots. For jumpers, the 30-knot difference was significant. When the first Indonesian tried to jump off the Antonov's ramp with a T-10, the shock from deploying the chute at higher speed nearly knocked him unconscious. Experiments with the British Irvin chute were equally painful and dangerous.[26]

Hearing the RPKAD complaints, the Soviet Union offered help. A handful of specialized high-speed chutes, known as the D-1-8, were sent to Batu Jajar for trials with the An-12. Tests by Indonesian parachutists in September 1965 were successful.[27]

Also in September, a group of ten army parachutists were sent to the Soviet Union for six months of advanced jump and rigger training using the D-1-8 and An-12 combination. Arriving at the Ryazan Higher Airborne Military College, the Indonesians found themselves amid a mix of Afghans, Indians, and other foreign nationals. "It was the first time I ever saw snow," recalled RPKAD Lieutenant Soerjo Handjono, "but the Soviets assured us it was good for jumping because it was soft."[28]

The introduction of new equipment was not the only concern among the Batu Jajar staff. Earlier, the training center had started to feel the intrusion of politics. The first instance of this came with a 1964 headquarters proposal to present Sukarno with a set of army parachute wings. Though he never had a reputation for physical courage, the president enjoyed adorning his uniform with honorary military badges. As a sop to him, the army placed an order with a Bangkok jeweler to manufacture a special set of gold jump wings framed by five stars. The plan was to award these during a ceremony at Batu Jajar.[29]

Hearing of this, Colonel Mung displayed an uncharacteristic burst of emotion. "Let him jump first," the colonel sniffed.[30] To sidestep his protest, the RPKAD's senior freefall instructor skydived into a ceremony at the National Military Academy at Magelang and handed over the five-star wing. Beaming, Sukarno was subsequently rarely seen in uniform without it.[31]

Shortly thereafter, Batu Jajar received a classified assignment linked to Confrontation. Although General Yani was looking to keep his distance from some of the more outlandish cross-border plans against the Commonwealth, the air force was sparing no effort in spearheading the campaign. Back in April 1964, the PGT had dispatched two companies to Sumatra to expand the war into peninsular Malaysia. To coincide with Indonesia's independence day on 17 August, two platoons were dispatched by motorboat within a day of that anniversary; neither fared well, with most of the members quickly incarcerated before inflicting any damage.[32]

Unfazed, the PGT had plans for a far more ambitious operation against the mainland. Convinced that the population of peninsular Malaysia was ripe for revolution, the air force commandos intended to drop three platoons for a long-term mission in Johor near Singapore. To help them operate among the locals, they were to be joined by ten ethnic Chinese communists that had exfiltrated from mainland Malaysia to Indonesia; among them were two females.

Because the Chinese were expected to parachute into Johor alongside the PGT, they needed basic jump training. To give it a share of the project, the RPKAD was ordered to take the ten recruits to Batu Jajar and give them discreet instruction at the center. This was completed by the close of August, marking the first time that foreign students had been trained at the RPKAD's school.[33]

Batu Jajar got its next chance to tutor foreigners in 1965. This followed from a new doctrine foisted upon the army in April 1965—known as *Tri Ubaya Sakti*—that stated Indonesia's enemy was not communism, but rather Western imperialism championed by the United States. Increasingly in close step with the PKI, Sukarno had pushed this policy on the army leadership despite protests from much of the top brass.

During that same month, Indonesia began to take greater interest in the Kingdom of Laos. In arguably the most complex standoff in Southeast Asia, control over Laos was divided among three fractions—each with its own armed forces and foreign sponsorship. On the left was the Pathet Lao, which received military support from North Vietnam, China, and the Soviet Union. On the right were the Royalists, backed primarily by the U.S. In the middle were the

Neutralists—led by an energetic but naïve paratroop officer named Kong Le—which at one time were close to the Pathet Lao but had since veered more toward the Royalists.

Indonesia's treatment of the three factions was telling. When Lao Prime Minister Souvanna Phouma—who headed the Royalist government—arrived for a state visit, he was largely snubbed. By contrast, when Prince Soupannavong, a leading Pathet Lao officer, came to Jakarta, he was feted by the PKI and government.

When Kong Le made a trip to Jakarta in late April, his treatment was more akin to the Pathet Lao than the Royalists. As a special guest of the Indonesian military, his escort officer was the former RPKAD chief of staff, Colonel Widjojo Soejono. Having returned from staff college at Fort Leavenworth, Kansas, the previous year, the colonel was given simple instructions from General Yani for dealing with the Lao officer. Said Yani: "We want to make him our friend."[34]

For a month, Widjojo escorted Kong Le around Java. The centerpiece of their trip was an extended visit to Batu Jajar. As a paratrooper, the Lao leader was smitten by the commando and airborne courses. By the end of the meeting, he agreed to gather a contingent of his men for training in Indonesia.[35]

On 21 August, an Indonesian Air Force C-130 landed at Wattay Airport outside the Lao capital of Vientiane. To avoid a possible shoot-down by British jets while near Malaysian airspace, it had been forced to perform a wide clockwise arc across Sumatra to southern Thailand, much of it below radar. As part of an operation codenamed Ubaya (Sanskrit for "promise"), the plane carried seven tons of non-lethal equipment—uniforms, boots, medicine—which was quickly offloaded into a waiting convoy of Neutralist trucks. Coming aboard the plane were sixty-eight Lao men and officers. A second C-130 arrived two days later, delivering supplies and backloading another sixty-one prospective students.[36]

Taken directly to Bandung, the Neutralist contingent was given a month of basic Indonesian language instruction before heading to Batu Jajar near the close of September. The previous RPKAD class had graduated on 20 September, and the Lao were told to expect a short lull before the next group of students had fully assembled. Things were especially quiet because the bulk of instructors had been rushed down to Jakarta to march in the upcoming twentieth anniversary of the founding of the armed forces.

On the morning of 1 October, the Lao students heard a commotion outside their barracks. Going out to investigate, they were shocked to find the Batu Jajar staff wielding weapons. "We were herded back into our quarters and detained there," recalls one of the Lao officers. "We were told there had been some kind of big problem in Jakarta."[37]

1   Widjoyo Soejono interview.

2   There was some preliminary discussion of RPKAD assistance to the Tjakrabirawa Regiment. In January 1963, for example, there was talk of offering Tjakrabirawa members commando and freefall instruction at Batu Jajar later that calendar year. Commando instruction was again proposed in March 1965. In the end, however, none of these plans came to fruition. Mention of proposed RPKAD assistance is found in *Tjakrabirawa Dirgayu Satyawira* [the official Tjakrabirawa magazine], March-May 1963 edition (p. 27) and March 1965 edition (p. 30).

3   Interview with Gunawan, 27 March 2000.

4   Soebari interview; Djasmin interview.

5   Sumardji interview.

6   The three with previous combat experience included Edy Sudjajat, a 1960 academy graduate who had fought in the Malukus, 1961 graduate Feisal Tanjung, who was also a Maluku veteran, and 1961 graduate Kentot Harseno, who had operated with Chinese guerrillas on the West Kalimantan frontier.

7   *Korps Komando AL.*, pp. 281, 293; Dr. A.H. Nasution, *Memenuhi Panggilan Tugas*, Vol. 6 (Jakarta: Yayasan Masagung, 1986), p. 410; DDRS, Retrospective Collection, #26C, CIA Intelligence Report, dated 2 March 1965.

8   The 330 Raider Battalion, which participated in the West Irian campaign, was officially redesignated as the 330 Airborne Battalion on 26 October 1962.

9   Interview with Sintong Pandjaitan, 19 November 1999; interview with Soekarno, 12 September 1999.

10 One of Mung's pet projects was to parachute RPKAD commandos into Sarawak from the belly of a fast-moving B-26 bomber. The plan was never implemented.

11 RPKAD Captain Djajadiningrat drew the initial concept for the new camouflage design. Based on the brushstrokes of the Denison/Depison smock, he envisioned a vertical stroke running down the entire length of shirt and pants. But when his drawing was taken to a local Bandung textile company, the brushstrokes were

misinterpreted as a more solid vertical stripe. The incorrect striped version was delivered to the regiment and subsequently approved by Mung. Djajadiningrat interview.

12 Soedarto interview; Djajadiningrat interview; Djasmin interview.

13 Benny operated from Bangkok, Thailand, under the guise of a Garuda airline representative. His attempts to infiltrate agents via Thailand into northern Malaysia bore minimal results. In a story that has become cliché, British historians writing about their Special Air Service (SAS) claim that SAS operatives nearly shot Colonel [sic] Benny dead while traveling in a "luxury motor yacht" along the Koemba River in West Kalimantan. Benny, who was supposedly traveling with a "raven haired girl in a daring white dress," was allegedly identified by a personalized banner on the bow of the yacht. A British SAS commando has claimed Benny was in his sights, but refrained from firing at the last moment. Benny, it is said, learned of the incident while visiting England in 1976 and thanked the British soldier for sparing his life. (See Dickens, p. 277.) Even discounting hyperbole ("luxury motor yacht," "raven haired beauty"), the facts of this story do not hold up to scrutiny. In an interview with the author, Benny confirms that the British told him the boat tale in 1976, but he was led to believe the alleged ambush was while he was traveling in a native canoe in East Kalimantan (where his Battalion 1 was deployed). Benny, a major at the time, had no reason to ply any rivers in West Kalimantan, much less in a "yacht" with a personalized banner. Even more damning, Benny was gone from the RPKAD and deployed to Thailand during the time the incident allegedly took place.

14 Djajadiningrat interview. To help rectify his lack of commando training, Sarwo Edhie ventured to Batu Jajar in August 1965 and underwent an abbreviated course.

15 Kentot Harseno interview.

16 Interview with Suhardjo, 10 August 1999.

17 Mataksan interview.

18 Kentot interview.

19 Robin Osborne, *Indonesia's Secret War* (Sydney: Allen & Unwin, 1985), p. 35.

20 *Irian Barat Dari Masa Ke Masa*, p. 130.

21 Agus S. interview.

22 Ibid.

23 *Irian Barat Dari Masa Ke Masa*, p. 132.

24 Subagyo interview.

25 Soebari interview.

26 Ibid; interview with Herman Soediro, 9 August 1999. The first jumps at Batu Jajar with an RI T-10 took place in November 1964.

27 Entry in jump log of Tata Loekita.

28 Interview with Soerjo Handjono, 2 August 1999.

29 In 1964, the Indonesian army approved three classes of airborne wings to denote the number of parachute jumps performed. A wing surmounted by a single star was for 30 jumps, a wing surmounted by a single star within a wreath was for 60 jumps, and a wing surmounted by two stars within a wreath was for more than 100 jumps. A half-wreath below the wing denoted jumpmasters. Red stars on the wings or canopy were for combat jumps. This system of classification remains in effect to this day. The gold wing with five stars was a fictitious class meant only for Sukarno; a second set was later made for President Suharto. Although Indonesian wings surmounted by three, four, and five stars have appeared in militaria collections, these are not recognized classifications. Djajadiningrat interview; Soebari interview; Herman Soediro interview.

30 Herman Soediro interview.

31 Soebari interview.

32 *Baret Jingga* (Jakarta: PT Gramedia Pustaka Utama, 1999), p. 307.

33 Soebari interview; interview with Anda, 29 May 1999. Anda was an officer at the Batu Jajar commando course.

34 Widjojo Soejono interview.

35 DDRS, Retrospective Collection, #27A, CIA Memorandum entitled "Indonesian Aid to Kong Le," dated 23 August 1965.

36 Herman Soediro interview.

37 Inteview with Chomsavanh Panyanouvong, 26 July 1999.

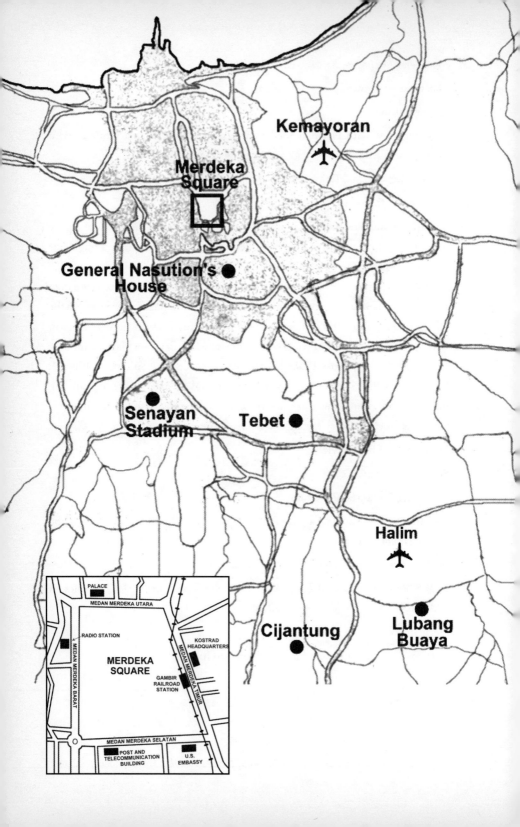

Kemayoran

Merdeka
Square

General Nasution's
House

Senayan
Stadium

Tebet

Halim

Cijantung

Lubang
Buaya

PALACE

MEDAN MERDEKA UTARA

RADIO STATION

MERDEKA
SQUARE

MEDAN MERDEKA BARAT

KOSTRAD
HEADQUARTERS

MEDAN MERDEKA TIMUR

GAMBIR
RAILROAD
STATION

MEDAN MERDEKA SELATAN

POST AND
TELECOMMUNICATION
BUILDING

U.S.
EMBASSY

CHAPTER TEN

BLACK SEPTEMBER

Red-eyed and still dressed in pajamas, Sarwo Edhie greeted the pair of army officers—both adjutants to General Yani—standing nervously in his front guest room. It was close to 0530 hours on the morning of Friday, 1 October, and his wife had jarred the colonel from his sleep after the officers said they came with urgent matters.

Digesting their story, Edhie quickly came to share their alarm. One of the pair, Major Subardi, related how he was woken by Yani's maid at 0430 with news that the general was shot and abducted by unknown persons earlier that morning. Along with the second adjutant, Major Sudarto, they had immediately gone to the house of General Siswondo Parman, the army's intelligence chief. But Parman, they discovered, had also been kidnapped during the night.

By 0500, the two had reached the house of Major General Umar Wirahadikusumah, commander of the Jakarta military region. Not knowing the fate of Yani, Subardi suggested that the RPKAD block all of the major roads leading to and from the capital. Umar agreed and dispatched them to Sarwo Edhie's house in Cijantung.[1]

As they relayed the request to the RPKAD chief, Edhie walked to the nearby cabinet and picked up a framed photograph of him posing with Yani and President Sukarno. Yani had long been Edhie's mentor, and his RPKAD position was owed in no small part to the general's unyielding support. Instinctively, the colonel suspected that the PKI was behind the abduction: Yani was the *bête noire* of Indonesia's communist party, and the feeling was mutual.

Going to the telephone, Edhie placed a quick call to Major Chalimi Imam Santosa. Hailing from the same batch of student-*cum*-soldiers as Benny Moerdani, Santosa had astutely avoided the earlier personality clashes within the regiment and managed to remain on good terms with Colonel Mung, Benny, and Edhie. When the first two had been expelled from the unit, Santosa was chosen as the new commander of Battalion 1.

Finding Santosa at his home a few blocks away, Edhie asked him about the disposition of his battalion. Some of his men were camping at the Senayan parking lot, said Santosa, where they were scheduled to practice in the shadow of the national stadium during the final days before the 5 October Armed Forces Day parade. It was the twentieth anniversary celebration for the Indonesian military, and the RPKAD was slated to have a prominent role; Santosa himself was chosen as ceremonial commander. Though the commandos at Senayan were all armed with rifles, none had been issued bullets.[2]

Edhie realized he needed all the commandos back at Cijantung—and quickly. On his orders, Santosa raced through the quiet morning streets and was at Senayan by 0600. Gathering his men, the major ordered them to board trucks and immediately head back to their regimental headquarters. This prompted a navy admiral, assigned with coordinating the parade practice, to rush out to the lot and start berating Santosa for disrupting that morning's pending schedule. The battalion commander politely ignored the senior officer and kept piling his men atop vehicles.

Heading east, the RPKAD commandos had not gotten far before a truck materialized in the opposite direction. As an afterthought, Sarwo Edhie had decided to rush ammunition toward Senayan to get his men armed as quickly as possible. Stopping in the middle of the road, Santosa broke open the boxes and had the bullets distributed among the commandos.[3]

Once back at Cijantung, all available RPKAD troops were ordered to the lawn in front of the headquarters building. From Santosa's own Battalion 1 were two full companies: Company Ben Hur, which had been practicing at Senayan, and Company D (nicknamed Company "Dracula"), which was preparing for a possible Confrontation deployment on the Malaysian mainland. Also present from Battalion 1 was half of Company Cobra, which was on the verge of joining Captain Kentot in East Kalimantan, and the understrength Company E, whose commander was on sick leave.[4]

Two other RPKAD companies were on hand at Cijantung. Company I from Battalion 3 in Central Java had arrived there a couple of weeks earlier. Scheduled for a Confrontation deployment along the West Kalimantan border, they had been delayed in Jakarta at the eleventh hour because of a lack of transport aircraft. Also present was an ad hoc company of instructors from Batu Jajar, who had been among the commandos grouped at Senayan for the 5 October parade.

Eyeing the assembled mass, Santosa issued a simple directive: "Nobody is allowed to move without orders. If you move, I will shoot you."[5]

Sarwo Edhie, having exchanged his pajamas for a military uniform, next stepped forward with words of warning. He told his men that some generals had been abducted, to where and by whom nobody knew. It was not yet clear who was friend or foe. "We must be cautious," he warned.[6]

Returning to his house for additional consultations with his officers, the colonel was startled by the sound of an approaching armored car on his residential street. From the vehicle came Herman Soediro, a lieutenant colonel who General Yani had earlier placed in charge of logistics for the army's airborne units. Edhie did not know Herman well, though some of the other officers present vouched for his credentials.

Seeing the *panser* parked in front of his house, Edhie could not help but feel suspicious toward the lieutenant colonel. The feeling was mutual. Having had numerous opportunities to visit Batu Jajar, Herman knew the RPKAD training base had its share of PKI sympathizers among the instructor cadre; several were known to attend classes in Marxism. Spotting the commando officers huddled with Edhie, Herman did not know if any PKI were among them.[7]

Despite his doubts, Herman plunged into a description of his activities earlier that morning. After hearing a report that yet another general—Donald Pandjaitan, the army's logistical chief—was missing, he had driven to the Kostrad office on the eastern side of Merdeka Square in the center of Jakarta. Already present was Major General Suharto, the Kostrad chief, who had arrived shortly before 0700 alongside Major General Umar.

An unassuming, apolitical general, Suharto was easy to underestimate. Though he had fared well during the Irian Jaya operation—when he was theater commander for the Mandala campaign—his current position as chief of Kostrad was a largely hollow posting. A holdover from the Djayawidjaya preparations, Kostrad was supposedly the army's strategic reserve in control of some of Java's best cavalry, infantry, and paratroop units.

In reality, Kostrad commanded little. All of the units it purported to oversee were firmly under the thumb of military region commanders who had no intention of ceding control to a Jakarta-based paper organization. Case in point was the 3 Parachute Brigade. First raised during the Irian operation, it had remained on the army's books and was ostensibly Kostrad's spearhead. But while there was a tiny brigade staff that reported to Suharto, its three airborne-qualified battalions—the 328 Raiders from West Java, the 454 from Central Java, and the 530 from East Java—remained within their respective provinces and had never once exercised—much less deployed—as a coherent whole. In fact, the first time that the brigade had come together was earlier that week when the three battalions arrived in Jakarta to practice for the 5 October parade.

On the previous day—Thursday, 30 September—Suharto had himself ventured to Senayan to review the airborne battalions theoretically under his command. They were again scheduled to practice on the morning of 1 October, and it was to Suharto's surprise—and deep concern—that he spotted armed Kostrad paratroopers deployed around Merdeka Square.

Seeing the Kostrad troops posted within sight of his office, Suharto was momentarily at a loss. He was not yet sure how many generals were missing, or who was behind the abductions. Shortly after 0700, however, the fog started to lift. From the Radio Republik Indonesia (RRI) building on the opposite side of Merdeka Square, the first of several rebel radio broadcasts hit the airwaves.

The broadcast was nothing short of explosive. Allegedly the words of Lieutenant Colonel Untung Sjamsuri speaking on behalf of a "30 September Movement," it stated that their action had been done in opposition to a so-called General's Council that was planning to seize power during the 5 October parade. It further stated that President Sukarno was safe in their custody.

The apparent power behind the movement—Untung—had been known to Suharto for years. A short, charismatic, and somewhat naïve officer, Untung had participated in an ill-fated 1948 communist uprising against the nationalist guerrilla movement fighting the Dutch. Though he also had a foot in the nationalist camp—and had actually been a member of the Solo-based regiment headed by Suharto—his leftist transgression was not forgotten and for many years his military career was in a rut. But paralleling the improving electoral fortunes of the PKI, and especially its meteoric increase in Central and East

Java, his star had sufficiently risen for a promotion to deputy commander of the 454 Airborne Battalion—based in the city of Semarang—by the time of the 1962 Irian campaign. With the rank of major, he had been the seniormost army officer to parachute into that theater.

Sukarno had duly taken note of Untung's Irian performance. During the February 1963 parade honoring Irian veterans, the major was singled out for praise by the president. Untung returned the favor, growing outspoken in his support for the country's leader. Suddenly on the fast track, in early 1965 he was selected for the prestigious post of commander of the army battalion within the Tjakrabirawa Regiment; not coincidentally, that battalion consisted of raider-qualified troops from Untung's native Central Java.[8]

Suharto was also well aware of the General's Council that Untung was allegedly confronting. Established by General Yani earlier that year, the council was an informal clique of less than ten like-minded senior generals united in their opposition to the PKI. (Suharto—whose relationship with Yani was more like a distant competitor than supporter—had not been a member.) Far from contemplating a putsch against Sukarno, the council had merely been a way for Yani to brainstorm ways of shielding the army from the political onslaught of the president and PKI.

Following Untung's initial radio broadcast, Suharto was able to make several assumptions. Because Untung was involved, it was likely the Tjakrabirawa Regiment had its hand in the disappearance of the generals. And seeing the Kostrad paratroopers across Merdeka Square, it was a given they were subverted. Though suspicion had to also fall on the PKI because of its tense political standoff with the army, this was unconfirmed. Also unconfirmed was the location of the president.

While Suharto felt compelled to act against Untung and whoever else was behind the 30 September Movement, the reality was that he had no troops. His own Kostrad airborne soldiers were obviously operating outside of his control. In addition, Major General Umar, who was at his side and theoretically could call on his Jakarta garrison, was having trouble marshalling loyalists.

With few other alternatives, Suharto decided to turn toward the RPKAD at Cijantung. Penning a message to Sarwo Edhie on Kostrad letterhead, he gave it to Lieutenant Colonel Herman and urged him to bring back the colonel.

Now looking at Suharto's letter, Sarwo Edhie faced a hard decision. Suharto, who was not his direct superior, was asking that Edhie report with his unit even though the RPKAD was not a part of Kostrad. But given that his mentor Yani was missing, and Suharto seemed willing to mobilize a response against those that were his abductors, Edhie saw the Kostrad chief as a tactical ally. He nodded his willingness to head downtown.

"Do you want to ride in the armored car or your own vehicle?" asked Herman.

Edhie laughed. "The *panser*."

By the time Sarwo Edhie pulled into the Kostrad office, it was shortly after noon. Behind him was a colorful convoy of jeeps, sedans, and trucks—all brimming with RPKAD commandos. Suharto, visibly pleased with their arrival, immediately launched into a briefing about the confused situation. He cut his comments short when RRI relayed a second and third rebel broadcast in rapid succession.

In the first of the new airings, the 30 September Movement revealed far more details about itself and its intent. First, the movement again repeated that it had acted against members of the General's Council. Suharto by that time knew six generals were missing; a seventh, army patriarch Nasution, had narrowly eluded capture by jumping over the back wall of his house.

Second, the movement said it was controlled by a Revolutionary Council at the national level. Under this council, it called on further councils to be formed at the provincial, district, sub-district, and village levels.

Third, the movement revealed its commander and four deputies. Lieutenant Colonel Untung, who had signed off on the initial radio broadcast, was named commander. Brigadier General Supardjo—one of Suharto's staff members in Kostrad—was his ranking deputy.

This last bit of news came as a shock to Suharto. Supardjo was the senior Kostrad officer assigned to West Kalimantan, where he held one of the many overlapping commands created to manage the Confrontation against Malaysia. Not by coincidence, Supardjo had sent an unusual radiogram to Sarwo Edhie in late August asking that the RPKAD's entire Battalion 1 be sent to West Kalimantan. As the request seemed somewhat excessive, Edhie dispatched Major Santosa to determine Supardjo's requirements.

For the next month, Santosa traveled the breath of the West Kalimantan border. Given the existing coverage along the frontier (and the fact that the

RPKAD's Company I from Battalion 3 was soon slated to arrive), Santosa came to the determination that Battalion 1 was not needed. He reported this assessment to Supardjo on 27 September, then prepared to return to Cijantung the following morning. To his surprise, Supardjo met him at the airport and took a seat on the same flight. The general claimed to have received a special order to return to the capital, though Santosa noted nobody met him at the tarmac in Jakarta.[9]

The third radio broadcast appeared designed to sow confusion. Again signed by Untung, it listed forty-five members who allegedly comprised the Revolutionary Council at the national level. Although the majority hailed from the military services and police, it also included some politicians, senior civil servants, students, and even reporters. They spanned the political spectrum: a handful were committed communists, but many more were ardent Sukarno supporters of no clear ideological persuasion. The vast majority had no idea they were being named on the council; this included General Umar, who was standing at Suharto's side when the list was announced.

After listening to the broadcasts, Suharto turned to Sarwo Edhie. To deprive the 30 September Movement of its soapbox, he realized the need to eject them from the RRI facility and the nearby telecommunications building. He also knew that resistance could be expected from the 454 and 530 Airborne Battalions, which were deployed across Merdeka Square and had already rebuffed two requests from Suharto for them to revert to Kostrad control. The RPKAD, Suharto told Edhie, would need to confront the numerically stronger paratroopers and seize the two targets. Agreeing to the order, the colonel headed back to Cijantung to plan the assault.

During the pre-dawn hours of 1 October, the conspirators that comprised the core of the 30 September Movement—less than a dozen persons in all—had assembled in and around Halim airbase south of Jakarta. Nearly all were from Central or East Java, all were sympathetic to the PKI, and all were united in their willingness to support violent revolutionary change in Indonesia.

Of the movement's members, perhaps none were more influential than the two hailing from the PKI. Known by their aliases Sjam and Pono, they were from a secret five-man party cell known as the Special Bureau. For years, the pair had acted as handlers for several of the military members of the movement: Omar Dani, the air force chief; Supardjo, the Kostrad general; Untung, commander of the army battalion within the Tjakrabirawa Regiment; Colonel Abdul Latief, head the strategic 1 Infantry Brigade from the Jakarta garrison; and Major Soejono, commander of air defense troops at Halim.

On ten occasions since August, a quorum of these members had gathered for secret planning sessions in Jakarta. Each time, they added more details to a bold scheme to eliminate the army leadership and seize control of the country. Time was of the essence, they believed. Part of this was because the political situation in the region was uniquely favorable: with communism apparently making fast inroads across Indochina, PKI leaders saw a window of opportunity to match this in insular Southeast Asia. Part of this, too, was because President Sukarno, who shielded the PKI from army opposition, was ill; most recently, he had collapsed at a public ceremony in early August. Should Sukarno pass away, there was a very real chance of serious military retribution.

There was also the matter of the 5 October parade in Jakarta. According to rumors spread by the PKI hierarchy, the General's Council was planning to use that event to stage a coup. In mid-August, top communist party officials told Sukarno as much; on 20 September, PKI officials even briefed the president that the generals planned to issue parade units with double ammunition.[10]

In fact, the opposite was true. Since late August, the conspirators had worked hard to ensure the cooperation of key units that would be in the capital during 5 October. Through Untung, sympathy from his Tjakrabirawa battalion was assured. Similarly, Colonel Latief had the loyalty of elements of his 1 Infantry Brigade, while Major Soejono delivered the support of his air defense troops. Through discreet lobbying from Untung and Supardjo—both of whom had personal links to the Kostrad paratroop commanders in Central and East Java—they had been able to get pledges of support from the 454 and 530 Airborne Battalions. To add even more muscle, they were fairly certain of receiving help from a Kostrad cavalry unit that was expected to be present in Jakarta for the parade. The conspirators were equally confident of signing on the PGT battalion within the Tjakrabirawa Regiment, whose deputy commander had just returned from training in Yugoslavia.[11] The next closest units that might intervene—from the Siliwangi division in West Java—were led by Ibrahim Adjie, an anti-PKI general but avowed Sukarnoist rated as unlikely to act decisively in support of his fellow top brass.[12]

All of which left the RPKAD as one of the few other units with a combat-ready force in Jakarta. To eliminate resistance from this quarter, the rebels had taken the precautionary step of having General Supardjo issue his request for the RPKAD deployment to West Kalimantan.

On the morning of 29 September, the conspirators gathered for a final planning session. The venue was just south of the Halim perimeter at a hamlet known as Lubang Buaya. There, in the midst of an abandoned rubber plantation, they did a final tally of their impending strike force. Not all of the news was good. General Supardjo, who had arrived the previous day from Kalimantan, reported his failure to get the RPKAD dispatched from the capital. Worse, the deputy commander of the PGT battalion in the Tjakrabirawa Regiment had kept the conspirators at arm's length, as had the Kostrad cavalry commander.

While registering slight concern, the conspirators went ahead with configuring their available loyalists into three task forces. The first, consisting of select members from the Tjakrabirawa Regiment, the Kostrad paratroop battalions, and the 1 Infantry Brigade, would abduct seven generals from their homes and bring them to Lubang Buaya. The second, comprised of the bulk of the two paratroop battalions and a small detachment from the 1 Infantry Brigade, would seize key facilities at Merdeka Square: the palace, the RRI studio, and the telecommunications building. The last task force, which included air defense troops and communist militiamen, would guard rear bases at Halim and Lubang Buaya.[13] They would put their plan into action, said Colonel Latief, on the following night.[14]

Not wavering from this schedule, the plotters were back at Lubang Buaya at 0230, 1 October. There they reviewed members of the three task forces that had assembled earlier in the night. One hour later, the squads assigned to seize the generals departed for their targets. Another convoy of air force trucks took the second task force to Merdeka Square.

Within an hour, the rebel troops had completed what appeared to be a flawless operation. Without complications, the 454 Airborne Battalion had occupied the north end of Merdeka Square closest to the palace, the 530 Airborne Battalion had taken the south side near the telecommunications building, and a detachment from the 1 Infantry Brigade moved into the RRI studio. A copy of the first radio broadcast—which had been pre-scripted by the PKI members from the Special Bureau cell—was rushed to the radio station.

Elsewhere in town, the seven teams of kidnappers had approached the generals' homes under cover of darkness. In the course of the abductions, three of the senior officers were fatally shot; another four were bundled unharmed into trucks and rushed back to Lubang Buaya. Once there, the four living victims (including an adjutant that was mistakenly kidnapped at Nasution's house in lieu of his boss) were executed. All seven corpses were stuffed into a twelve-meter dried well, the top of which was camouflaged with dirt, leaves, and discarded food that had been stockpiled in an adjacent house.

At the same time, General Supardjo, along with the commanders of the 454 and 530 Airborne Battalions, had departed Halim with a small team meant to intercept Sukarno at the palace. They had good reason to believe they would be welcomed by the country's top executive. The president had been generally aware of the plotting over the previous weeks; on the previous day, in a conversation with his long-time military aide, he had made little secret that he knew the PKI was planning an imminent putsch. But in vintage form, the cagey Sukarno had retained buffers between himself and the conspirators in the hope of remaining above the fray if the plan went sour.[15]

The plan, it turned out, did quickly sour. The first flaw to emerge was the failure of the conspirators to abduct General Nasution. As the one military leader with national influence almost on par with Sukarno, his survival was potentially a crippling blow to the plotters. Learning that Nasution was alive while en route to his palace that morning, Sukarno stopped short of Merdeka Square and instead ordered his chauffeur to proceed directly to Halim.

Pulling into the airbase, the president was warmly embraced by Air Marshal Dani. Sukarno, however, brushed off the welcome and instead brooded over the holes emerging in the conspiracy. It was by then apparent that Nasution, who broke a leg and lost his young daughter during the abduction attempt, had linked up with Suharto at the Kostrad office. Sukarno was also irate to learn that RPKAD commandos were in town and reinforcing Suharto. Turning to Supardjo (who had returned to Halim from the palace), Sukarno tore into the general: "You told me the RPKAD would not be in Jakarta."[16]

Quickly losing heart, by noon the mercurial president told the plotters that he could not support their movement. Immediately thereafter, he couriered the first in a series of messages to the generals at the Kostrad office in an attempt to safeguard his own standing. Though the conspirators did not fully lose heart with the president's limp reversal—Air Marshal Dani, in fact, belatedly went public at 1300 hours with the air force's commitment to the movement—it was hard to see how they could regain momentum.

For Suharto, the president's messages from Halim were a turning point. Prior to that point, Sukarno's status was uncertain. But now that it was apparent that he was not a hostage at the air base, the Kostrad chief was emboldened to move decisively against the rebels.

Emboldening Suharto, too, was the success he was having in winning over his Kostrad airborne battalions. Earlier that morning, the third battalion in the 3 Parachute Brigade—the 328 Raiders from West Java—had ventured from the Senayan parade ground to pledge their loyalty to him. At 1400 hours, after persistent lobbying by Suharto, the ranking officers from the brigade's two other battalions also came to Suharto's office. Just over two hours later, the 530 Airborne Battalion pragmatically rallied. This left only the 454 Airborne Battalion under rebel control; tired and unfed, this last unit abandoned Merdeka Square near nightfall and retreated toward Halim.

Back at Cijantung, Sarwo Edhie had been consumed with preparations to seize the RRI and telecommunications buildings. Three companies were assigned to the task. Two of them, Company Dracula from Battalion 1 and Company I from Battalion 3, were designated with retaking the RRI studio. The latter company had been literally a day away from deploying to West Kalimantan, and had already been issued light green "TNKU" uniforms and AR-15 automatic rifles borrowed from the police (to give Indonesia plausible deniability during raids into Sarawak). But given their resultant foreign appearance, there were fears they might fall victim to friendly fire. To prevent this, they were hurriedly given red berets and the RPKAD's trademark camouflage jackets to help identify them from a distance.

Targeted against the telecommunications building was Company Ben Hur, the same unit that had conducted the much-lauded raid at Mapu.

Because there were few vehicles at Cijantung, Sarwo Edhie scrounged a fleet of civilian trucks from neighboring factories. At 1800, the three companies drove in an extended convoy toward the Kostrad office. Contacting Suharto, he had them momentarily pause. The general had scripted a speech, which he wanted read over RRI by the army spokesman. "How long do you think you will need?" he asked the RPKAD commander.

"Twenty-five minutes," promised Edhie.

At 1900, Company Ben Hur sprinted across Merdeka Square toward the telecommunications building. The 530 Airborne Battalion had already melted away, but a new set of armed rebels had suddenly materialized in their wake. These consisted of a couple dozen communist youth that had been hastily trained at Lubang Buaya during September. Growing desperate, the plotters at Halim had thrust automatic weapons into their hands and urged them to take up positions alongside the dissident paratroopers at Merdeka Square. By the time they arrived, however, the airborne troops were gone. Company Ben Hur took the militia's surrender without firing a shot; the telecommunications building was declared secure in less than twenty minutes.

On the western side of the square, Company I was the first to arrive at a deathly quiet RRI building. Like the paratroopers, the rebel detachment from the 1 Infantry Brigade had disappeared into the night. Bounding up the stairs, platoon commander Sintong Pandjaitan found the recording studio lit but empty. While he stood guard with his AR-15, the army spokesman took his position behind the microphone and began reading Suharto's statement.

With Merdeka Square secure, all eyes now turned on Halim. At 1900 hours, Suharto had dispatched a courier to the airbase urging Sukarno to leave because it was going to be hit by Kostrad troops. The president took the hint; four hours later, Suharto received confirmation that the country's leader was now at his alternate palace in Bogor.

With Sukarno gone, Suharto ordered the RPKAD to lead the charge to retake Halim.[17] When the request reached Sarwo Edhie at 0100, 2 October, he prepared his five available companies for the assignment: the three that had returned from Merdeka Square, the ad hoc company of instructors from Batu Jajar, and elements of Company Cobra and Company E that had been temporarily merged as one.[18] Supporting the commandos would be the 328 Raider Battalion and nearly two dozen tanks and armored vehicles that had been cobbled together by Suharto.

Two hours later, the combined task force was approaching Halim from the east in a ninety-vehicle convoy. That direction was chosen because it was relatively less populated, and because the RPKAD had once gone there for training and generally knew the area.

By that time, the commandos and raiders were thoroughly exhausted from a lack of sleep. There was also a problem with coordination: plans had been literally hatched on the run, and the RPKAD companies had never performed field exercises together. Despite these shortcomings, they dismounted from their vehicles and edged slowly toward the Halim perimeter. In the lead was the RPKAD's Company I, which at 0530 approached a guard booth along the fenceline. Inside were two PGT members—the RPKAD's counterparts from the air force—who exited the booth in the dim light to confront the approaching commandos. The RPKAD had no quarrel with the PGT; in fact, both units had shared close ties since inception. But because Marshal Dani had declared the air force's allegiance to the 30 September Movement the previous afternoon, all armed combatants at Halim were to be considered suspect.[19]

"The two PGT made the mistake of pulling their charging handles," remembers RPKAD Lieutenant Sintong Pandjaitan. Members of Sintong's platoon responded with a volley from their AR-15 rifles, leaving both air force commandos riddled with gunfire.

Spilling into Halim, the RPKAD by 0600 had fanned out to the administrative buildings. They found little evidence of the conspirators, who had all fled by foot or aircraft during the earlier morning hours.

Soon after passing word back to Sarwo Edhie—who remained outside the perimeter with the tank column—that the base was secure, a Cessna light aircraft materialized overhead. As it landed on the main airstrip and taxied toward a hanger, the RPKAD commandos moved forward with their weapons raised. From the Cessna emerged Air Commodore Ignatius Dewanto. Having gained hero status because of his involvement in the downing of a CIA aircraft (and capture of its American pilot) during the 1958 Permesta rebellion, Dewanto had rocketed to the top of the upper echelon of the air force.

For the RPKAD commandos that confronted him, Dewanto's past heroics counted for little. Summarily disarming the commodore's adjutant, they ordered all air force personnel to lay down their weapons. As the senior officer present, Dewanto attempted to maintain his personal dignity and that of his service by continuing to issue orders; in reality, the RPKAD detained them in the hanger as they swept the rest of the base.

Until that point, no resistance was encountered. Omar Dani had tactfully disappeared, and the remaining air force officers at Halim showed no hint of following his rebellious bent. It was air force sources, in fact, who told the RPKAD that the renegade 454 Airborne Battalion had retreated to the extreme south of the airbase near a parachute dropzone used by the PGT; further south of that was the village of Lubang Buaya.

Not wasting time, the RPKAD at 0700 hours closed on the dropzone. In the lead was the ad hoc company of Batu Jajar instructors under the command of Lieutenant Mochtar. Moving forward, the instructors walked into an ambush set by the rebel Kostrad paratroopers. With one RPKAD commando receiving a fatal gunshot, the rest of the commandos quickly pulled back.

Hearing about the loss of his man, Sarwo Edhie was livid. Orders were quickly passed for all available forces to mass for an assault on the paratroopers. At the same time, messages were couriered to the dissident battalion demanding their surrender. Realizing they were hopelessly outnumbered, they maintained a distant dialogue in an attempt to buy time while they contemplated an escape.

Before this situation was resolved, Sarwo Edhie entered Halim and headed for the main hanger. Under orders from Suharto, he was assigned as the first army commander to confront Sukarno at Bogor. With the air force now proving highly cooperative, at midday they flew the RPKAD commander by helicopter to see the elusive president. This set the stage for a meeting three hours later between Sukarno and Suharto.

By the time Sarwo Edhie returned late that afternoon, the situation at Halim was largely resolved. The 454 Airborne Battalion had effectively ceased to exist, with most of its members captured by an army dragnet as they attempted to flee the air base on foot. Its work done, the entire RPKAD contingent was recalled to Cijantung at 2200 hours for a much-needed rest.[20]

With armed resistance quelled inside Jakarta, the army was now able to focus on the unresolved fate of its six missing generals. Piecing together anecdotal evidence—most convincingly from a police officer who claimed to be a witness—there were hints by 3 October that a series of killings had taken place south of Halim at Lubang Buaya. Sent to investigate were two of the RPKAD companies that had retaken Merdeka Square: Company Ben Hur and Company I. Arriving that morning, they swept across the former rubber plantation until 1300 hours. By that time C.I. Santosa joined and the major ordered the men to rest during the stifling afternoon heat.

Seeking shade, several of the commandos veered toward the handful of small buildings and bamboo huts peppered across the plantation. One of these structures—a single empty room with concrete sides—was found to have revolutionary slogans painted across the walls; strewn across the surrounding grounds were empty bullet shells. Equally damning were bolts of red and green cloth found inside: the rebel paratroopers at Merdeka Square had been wearing scarves in those colors.

As the commandos were making these discoveries, an elderly local resident approached the group and volunteered information that a well once stood in front of the building. At the general location of the well, there was now only a slight depression filled with fresh dirt and leaves. Poking at the depression, one of the RPKAD members from Company Ben Hur was surprised to find discarded vegetables and a buried cluster of peanuts. Famished from their exhaustive schedule over the previous couple of days, he dusted off the nuts and started eating.[21]

The mood quickly darkened. Pulling up more vegetables and bananas from the emerging hole, they found the dirt suspiciously loose. "We continued digging for an hour," said Lieutenant Sintong, "but then a putrid smell began to seep from the ground."[22]

Reasoning that the smell would increase the deeper they dug, one of the RPKAD officers suggested using scuba tanks. Back during the Irian campaign, the commandos had jointly raised a combat swimmer unit—known as Kopaska—with the navy; one of the navy swimmers, in fact, was still stationed at Cijantung. But when they contacted him by radio, they found that the scuba tanks allocated to the RPKAD had since been sent to Batu Jajar.[23]

Shortly before last light, the commandos excavating the well abruptly paused. To their horror, they had uncovered a foot. News of this was reported to Sarwo Edhie, who in turn passed word to Suharto. The general ordered them to postpone digging until the next morning, at which time he would personally oversee the recovery effort. He also told them to guard the hole until that time.

Such precautions proved necessary. Near midnight, a second search team arrived at Lubang Buaya with spotlights. Consisting of officers from the air force and Tjakrabirawa Regiment, they claimed to be acting on orders of the president. Rising to the challenge, Major Santosa refused to yield ground to the new arrivals.[24]

By 0900, 4 October, Suharto was at Lubang Buaya. The marines, who had the only scuba tanks available in Jakarta, had dispatched a support team with the needed gear. But given the emerging friction between the marines and RPKAD—the former were considered suspect because of their coddling by the president—the team was forced to wait at a streetside coffee stall until Suharto belatedly granted them permission to enter the plantation.[25]

Making use of the marines and their scuba gear, bloated bodies were removed in the scorching heat. By mid-afternoon, seven corpses were unearthed. On the following day, when the military had been scheduled to celebrate its twentieth anniversary, Suharto, Nasution, and the remaining senior officers of the army instead presided over funerals. Members of the RPKAD, which had been the linchpin in defeating the 30 September Movement in Jakarta, served prominently as pallbearers and honor guards.

1   Amelia Yani, *Profil Seorang Prajurit TNI* (Jakarta: Pustaka Sinar Harapan, 1990), p. 222-223.

2   Several contemporary accounts claim that eleven RPKAD companies were at Senayan preparing for the 5 October parade. This is false. There were eleven companies in the entire RPKAD at that time, of which just two were at Senayan. The rest were at Cijantung, Semarang, Magelang, and on combat operations.

3   Aristides Katoppo et al, *Menyingkap Kabut Halim 1965* (Jakarta: Pustaka Sinar Harapan, 1999), p. 90.

4   Interview with Simungkaryo, 11 August 1999; interview with Atang Sanjaya, 9 August 1999.

5   "Sarwo di Saat Kudeta Komunis," *Editor* (No. 11, 18 November 1989), p. 17.

6   Ibid.

7   Drs. H. Herman S. Soediro, *Bhaktiku Padamu Indonesia Tercinta* (Jakarta: Yayasan Bina Wawasan Kebangsaan, 1995), p. 43.

8   Mention of the Banteng Raiders from Central Java entering Battalion 1 can be found in *Tjakrabirawa Dirgayu Satyawira* (June 1963), p. 51.

9   Aristides Katoppo, *Menyingkap*, p. 67.

10   Central Intelligence Agency Research Study, *Indonesia-1965, The Coup that Backfired*, dated December 1968, p. 239-240.

11   Aristides Katoppo, *Menyingkap*, p. 87.

12   The plotters correctly discounted the police, which were fractured and ineffectual. The marines had a large contingent within Jakarta, including one battalion within the Tjakrabirawa Regiment and two honor battalions that were to march in the 5 October parade. But the honor battalions had yet to receive combat training and, in any event, the marines were more loyal to Sukarno than the state—and were not expected to show resistance unless ordered by the president.

13   Using the Confrontation as pretext, the Communists had long been calling for the formation of a massive armed militia. Unlike his army counterparts—who were seething in their opposition—Air Marshal Omar Dani was warm to the concept, in large part because Sukarno had embraced the idea in May 1965. On 11 September, Major Soejono, the air defense commander at Halim, quietly began the first training session for communist militia candidates at Lubang Buaya. Five days later, Dani had flown to the People's Republic of China, where he received a pledge for 100,000 weapons to arm these volunteers. Several dozen graduates were ready by 30 September.

14   As this had been transpiring, and the conspiracy expanded to include military units across Java, it was only natural that hints of the plan leaked. On 14 September, army intelligence chief Parman informed Yani that the PKI was contemplating the assassination of key generals in four days. Precautions were taken, but the date came and went without event. On 30 September, reports of an imminent abduction of generals was raised at an army staff meeting; having already heard cries of wolf earlier in the month, the threat was discounted. *Indonesia-1965*, preface.

15   *Indonesia-1965*, p. 256. Sukarno had conveniently claimed illness late on 30 September, and had retreated to the homes of one of his wives—and out of contact with his minders—throughout that critical night.

16   *Indonesia-1965*, p. 35.

17   General Nasution, who remained alongside Suharto during this critical time, told

the RPKAD to seize Halim just like when they captured Mapanget airbase near Manado during the Permesta uprising. (Aristides Katoppo, *Menyingkap* p. 19). Permesta veterans have scoffed at this comparison, noting that the RPKAD failed to seize the airbase in the Mapanget example.

18   Simungkaryo interview.

19   Although an entire PGT battalion was assigned to Halim, only one company remained at that airbase as of 2 October 1965; the battalion's remaining companies were dispersed at other bases across Java. Aristides Katoppo, *Menyingkap*, p. 31.

20   The 454 Airborne Battalion was later purged of its PKI sympathizers and retained in the army's order-of-battle; to indicate a break from its rebellious past, it was redesignated as the 401 Airborne Battalion.

21   Untung Suroso interview.

22   Sintong Pandjaitan interview.

23   Ibid. Kopaska remained a joint unit under the RPKAD's administrative control at Batu Jajar until 1967, after which it was transferred to navy jurisdiction in Surabaya.

24   Hendro Subroto, *Perjalanan Seorang Wartawan Perang* (Jakarta: Pustaka Sinar Harapan, 1998), p. 196

25   *Korps Marinir* (Jakarta: PT Gramedia, 1996), p. 51.

CHAPTER ELEVEN

SPECIAL WARFARE

With the discovery that six of its senior generals were murdered, Suharto and the remaining army leadership scrambled for a response. Part of their wrath was directed against Sukarno; having apparently cooperated with the rebels through sins of omission—and probably commission—the president was displaying equal parts callousness and defiance over events earlier in the week. Part of their wrath, too, was focused against the chief plotters and, by association, the PKI, which in a bit of exceptionally poor timing had declared support for the 30 September Movement on the verge of its collapse in Jakarta.[1]

Most of the conspirators, it soon became apparent, had headed for Central Java. There was good reason for this. In centuries past, Central and East Java had been ruled under a system of de facto castes. Influenced by Hinduism, this form of stratified society had been continued under Islam with the religious elite holding great privileges over the vast Javanese peasantry. The resultant social inequalities led to simmering class conflicts, which in turn fed the popularity of the PKI.

Nowhere was this more apparent than in the Central Java port of Semarang. More than any other town, Semarang laid claim as birthplace of the PKI. Not surprisingly, when the 30 September Movement made its appeal over the airwaves on 1 October for revolutionary committees to be formed in the provinces, several pro-PKI military officers—including two colonels—organized the seizure of the Semarang radio station that afternoon and began issuing proclamations. By nightfall, the town was effectively in their hands.

Facing this challenge, the government was hard pressed to fight back. Semarang, they discovered, was all but stripped bare of troops. The 4 Infantry Brigade—which normally had elements stationed in the vicinity—was deployed to Sumatra for Confrontation contingencies. And the resident 454 Airborne Battalion—which had defected to the rebels—was in the capital. One of the few pro-government units on hand was the RPKAD's understrength Battalion 3, but it counted just two anemic companies (the battalion's third company—Company I—was in Jakarta).

Scrambling to piece together a counter-force, the commander of the Central Java military region hurriedly grouped some armored cars and combat engineers from the nearby town of Magelang. By the following morning, this column reached Semarang, linked up with RPKAD Battalion 3, and entered the town without firing a shot. Pro-PKI officers were nowhere to be found, having apparently fled inland.

While Semarang was tentatively back in government hands, Jakarta was rightfully concerned. The PKI had thousands of diehard party adherents around town ready to fight back. Top PKI leaders, including several that had fled Jakarta, were also organizing mini-uprisings in towns stretching across the eastern half of the province. A handful of mid-ranking officers were joining their cause; in the cultural capital of Yogyakarta, Major Mulyono, the same officer who had trained Chinese guerrillas in West Kalimantan in 1963, revealed himself as a prominent sympathizer.[2]

Watching this from Jakarta, General Suharto was torn. He realized the need to maintain critical mass in the capital during this sensitive period, especially with the unrepentant Sukarno still holding great sway over the masses. At the same time, he needed to bolster the army's foothold in Central Java (and to a lesser extent, East Java) before the PKI could get its second wind. And he needed to do both of these in short order with few loyal troops at hand.

Suharto's answer hinged on a multiplier effect. By the second week of October, the army began discreetly inciting Muslim crowds to rise up against the PKI.[3] This was particularly effective in East Java, where the Nahdlatul Ulama—a massive Islamic grassroots organization led by the local religious elite—had long bristled over the land reforms and social criticism championed by the atheistic PKI. With a modicum of prompting from the military, that organization directed its followers against the communists and threw the PKI on the defensive.

For Central Java, Suharto leaned on the RPKAD as a catalyst. With three commando companies retained in Jakarta as a reserve, three other companies—Company Ben Hur and Company E from Battalion 1, and Company I from Battalion 3—were readied for deployment to Semarang. Major Santosa was placed in overall command of the three.[4]

On 17 October, Santosa's task force departed Jakarta by road. On the next afternoon, after awaiting a handful of armored cars, the column pushed from the airport on the outskirts of Semarang into the town proper.

The PKI, they discovered, had prepared a rude welcome. Communist cadre organized an emotive anti-RPKAD demonstration on the following day, while another group of communists (including Pono, the secretive cadre member who had been a leader in the 30 September Movement) withdrew south to make a stand at the town of Salatiga. There they strung banners across the road reading "Make Salatiga a Grave for the RPKAD."[5]

Against this, the commandos looked to make an early example. Joining his men on 19 October, Colonel Sarwo Edhie initiated a show of force across Semarang that resulted in over a thousand arrests by nightfall. By the following day, the town was declared pacified.

Not willing to loose momentum, Edhie divided his force in two. Three of the companies—Company Ben Hur, along with two others from Battalion 3—remained behind in Semarang. The remainder—Company E and Company I—piled onto armored cars and drove southwest on 21 October toward Magelang. Arriving in the late afternoon, they linked up with their fellow commandos from the chronically undermanned Battalion 2 and did a quick tour of the town. No opposition was encountered.

Continuing his frantic pace, Edhie proceeded in multiple directions. The RPKAD element at Semarang was directed south across the island to Yogyakarta. Arriving in what was becoming standard fashion—piled atop *pansers*—they found the PKI leadership had fled. The task force at Magelang, meanwhile, turned east. With one RPKAD company remaining at the town of Boyolali, the other proceeded to Solo.

Far from resembling a military campaign, the RPKAD's trans-Java maneuvers bordered on the festive. Edhie had placed a loudspeaker on the lead vehicle, from which blared popular songs of the time. As rural crowds came out to investigate, the colonel offered up a remarkably simple message to his audience: "It's the intent of the PKI to stage a *coup d'état*, so we have to be vigilant."[6]

Upon reaching Solo on 22 October, the campaign took a dark turn. Greeted by a large anti-PKI demonstration, Edhie proceeded to the town's train station and fanned the flames with the same simple call to the masses. What happened next was remarkable for its speed and fury. Crowds that had once been generally supportive of the PKI turned against the communists with a vengeance. By month's end, a grassroots anti-PKI movement had spread across the province; reports of atrocities in the countryside soon began to filter back to Jakarta.

Encouraging this war by proxy, elements of the RPKAD in late October began offering rudimentary instruction to Muslim youth groups in Central Java.[7] Once trained, these vigilantes were incited to take up weapons (primarily knives and clubs) and run amok against the PKI. The resultant orgy of violence caused the deaths of at least tens of thousands—and possibly hundreds of thousands—across the Javanese heartland.

Other elements of the RPKAD, meanwhile, focused on tracking down the key plotters still at large. In this, they were assisted by the 4 Infantry Brigade, which in early November had been rushed back from its Confrontation vigil on Sumatra. Their combined efforts paid off, with the commandos able to capture fugitive Major Mulyono near Boyolali; he was later executed. The 4 Infantry Brigade, meanwhile, seized PKI chairman D.N. Aidit near Solo on 22 November; he was shot dead while allegedly trying to escape the following day.

By 1 December, only a handful of lead conspirators had eluded capture. Most of them, including a renegade army colonel, were believed hiding in the foothills of Mount Merbabu, a towering volcano midway between Magelang and Boyolali. Targeting these last holdouts, Sarwo Edhie launched Operation Merapi (named after a neighboring volcano). Using four RPKAD companies as the vanguard, the commandos pushed up Merbabu's slopes during the second week of the month. By 14 December, these last senior rebels had been flushed out and shot dead. With the PKI threat to Central Java all but gone, the RPKAD contingent from Battalion 1 was repatriated to Jakarta on 25 December.[8]

In contrast to Central Java, the post-30 September reaction on the island of Bali was even more spontaneous and violent. For several reasons, tensions were running high on the island. For one thing, the Balinese—a Hindu bastion in an otherwise Muslim nation of 105 million—deeply resented recent waves of migrants from over-populated Java. For another thing, they were soured over the fact that the PKI—which was closely identified with its power bases in Central and East Java—had monopolized top positions in the island's provincial government.

Simmering over this, the collapse of the 30 September Movement offered a pretext for locals to violently lash out at the interlopers. But preoccupied with Central Java, it was not until early December that Jakarta took serious note of reports that Bali was experiencing a full-blown pogrom. To gauge the excessive bloodshed, and to restore government control, Sarwo Edhie was instructed to dispatch a contingent from his stretched RPKAD. With few troops left to spare, the colonel redirected the two companies freshly returned from Central Java—Company Ben Hur and Company E—to board a trio of An-12 transports and rush east.

Landing at Denpasar, the commandos were horrified by what they found. "We saw heads on the side of the road," said Major Djasmin, the senior RPKAD officer overseeing the deployment. "There were kids doing many of the killings."[9]

As the RPKAD companies stood by, Balinese society continued its bloody convulsions. Unlike Central Java—where the commandos had made speeches to incite the crowds—on Bali they had to urge restraint. After two months, during which time untold thousands of Javanese and ethnic Chinese were killed across the southern half of the island—the RPKAD troops returned home.[10]

As significant as events in Central Java and Bali were, the most critical battlefield remained Jakarta's political arena. It was there that the army generals and President Sukarno maintained a tense standoff through the final months of 1965. Neither side was willing to blink first, yet neither appeared able to move decisively against the other.

Into this stepped the RPKAD. Falling back on the formula perfected in Central Java, the generals had the commandos parade through Jakarta on the last day of the year. Again on 4 January 1966, the RPKAD flexed its muscles at a parade near Senayan stadium. Even Sarwo Edhie's wife got into the act, marching at the head of a column of women paramilitary volunteers wearing distinctive commando camouflage jackets.[11]

Again parroting its Central Java formula, the RPKAD began to preen a proxy. Instead of Muslim youths, this time they worked with student activists. On 10 January, Edhie and his staff ventured to the medical school campus at the University of Indonesia. There they addressed leaders from the Indonesian Student Action Group (*Kesatuan Aksi Mahasiswa Indonesia*, or KAMI). For a variety of reasons—the natural inclination of students to rebel, Sukarno's mismanagement of the economy, distaste over the PKI's linkage to the murder of the generals, the perception that the military was the emergent winners—the RPKAD found a sympathetic ear.

The resultant synergy between the commandos and the students was potent. With Major Prijo Pranoto, the RPKAD chief of staff, acting as the main point of contact, KAMI activists showed aptitude in maintaining pressure—through street demonstrations—against the president and his dwindling sources of support. Sukarno hardly helped his own case, provocatively forming a new left-leaning cabinet on 21 February that all but invited a reprisal from the military.[12]

The generals did not disappoint. On the evening of 6 March, Suharto beckoned Sarwo Edhie and four other key officers. He noted that the marine contingent in the Tjakrabirawa Regiment had started reacting violently against student demonstrations; the presidential guards had even fired into the crowd two weeks earlier.[13] Seeing this as proof that the protests were having an unnerving effect, they were expanded in pace and scope. Venting especially hard against Soebandrio—the key Sukarno lieutenant who was simultaneously deputy prime minister, foreign minister and chief of intelligence—KAMI students (joined by a sister organization comprised of high school students) on 8 March marched on the Foreign Ministry building. Two days later, hundreds mobilized outside the gates of the Chinese embassy to condemn Beijing's earlier support for the PKI.

That evening, Sarwo Edhie huddled with his men. Sukarno still retained the loyalty of some military units in the capital—primarily from the Tjakrabirawa Regiment—and both sides seemed poised for a final bloody showdown. Already, there had been street fights between RPKAD commandos and the Tjakrabirawa marines. Fearing a surprise artillery attack against

Cijantung, Edhie had even taken the precaution of dispersing his commandos from their barracks.

Now the colonel was preparing to launch his own surprise. Taking aside fifteen select members from Company Ben Hur, he ordered them to mingle among a planned student demonstration outside the presidential Palace the following morning. Seven would remain near the palace gates, while the other five would position themselves at the street intersection west of the palace. All of them would wear civilian clothes and carry four concealed grenades apiece. They would be there mainly for psychological effect, though there remained the possibility of using the grenades against targets of opportunity.[14]

The Ben Hur commandos would not be alone. For the previous three days, Captain Kentot Harseno—the same officer who had parachuted from the ill-fated C-130 into East Kalimantan—had been assigned with tracking down and capturing Soebandrio. Dressed in green fatigues without any identifying insignia, he and fifteen of his men had run circles around the city in jeeps. Their efforts were in vain: the minister, perhaps sensing the endgame was near, was proving impossible to track down.

Now came word that Soebandrio would be attending a political meeting scheduled for the palace on the morning of 11 March. Racing there with his team, Kentot attempted to maneuver close to the gates for an ambush. Watching from a distance, Sarwo Edhie positioned himself atop the Bank Indonesia building and peered through a set of binoculars.[15]

On schedule, thousands of KAMI students began to gather in a rowdy mass across from the palace entrance. As they chanted for Sukarno to dissolve the leftist cabinet he had formed in February, the fifteen incognito members of Company Ben Hur took up their assigned positions. Kentot's team, in unmarked military uniforms and armed with AK-47 rifles, were overwhelmed by the same crowd.

Tense minutes passed as Kentot watched the gates. Several cars approached—the students parting to let them enter the palace—but none carried Soebandrio. At that point, the sound of rotors materialized overhead. A chopper passed low, then landed on the lawn within the palace grounds. From a distance, the RPKAD commandos watched their target emerge from the aircraft and take a car the short distance to the building.

Frustrated, Kentot pondered his next move. At least a battalion of Tjakrabirawa marines were positioned inside the gates, providing ample disincentive for him to cross the barrier. Reasoning that there might be a weak point in the rear, he beckoned his men and circled around the back. During an attempt to scale the wall, however, a Japanese photographer stepped forward and began taking pictures. Sprinting after him, the captain grabbed the camera and destroyed the film.

Unfortunately for Kentot, the scuffle caused a small crowd to gather. This in turn drew the attention of the Tjakrabirawa assistant for operations, Major M.I. Soetaryo. As a former RPKAD officer, Soetaryo instantly identified Kentot as a company commander in his old regiment. He immediately challenged the captain and asked why he was loitering in the rear of the palace.

Thinking fast, Kentot conjured an excuse. "I told him that we had been dispatched to the area to act as an outer ring of guards," he said. This was plausible, as Edhie had ordered some of his men over the previous weeks to stand vigil within sight of the Jakarta and Bogor palaces; the colonel had also made a recent pledge (of questionable sincerity) that the RPKAD stood ready to act at the disposal of the president. Suitably convinced, Soetaryo retreated from the scene.

Relieved but still frustrated, Kentot returned to the front of the palace. While he was gone, members of the Tjakrabirawa Regiment had taken note of the members of Company Ben Hur congregating near the entrance. The presidential guards did not know the parent unit of the commandos, nor did they know how many were present. Fearing the worst, they interrupted the political discussion inside the palace to inform Sukarno that unidentified troops were among the demonstrators.

The report had a profound effect among the attendees. Abruptly calling short the meeting, Sukarno, Soebandrio, and Soebandrio's deputy rushed to the door and piled into a car to whisk them to the waiting chopper.

By that time, Kentot and his men had worked up enough courage to move up to the palace gate opposite the helicopter. But as the presidential limousine approached, the captain panicked. "The Tjakrabirawa troops had the same weapons as us," he convinced himself. "If there was a firefight, we would not know who fired."[16]

At the last moment, Kentot stood at attention. As the car stopped and the president emerged to board the chopper, the RPKAD troops offered weak salutes. The aircraft quickly took to the sky and headed for the relative safety of Bogor.

Members of RPKAD's Company A graduate from basic airborne training at Margahayu, 13 February 1957. They are wearing an early reversible camouflage jumpsuit; the original design for this had been developed by the U.S. Marine Corps in World War II, then passed to the Dutch, who in turn gave samples to the Indonesians. (Courtesy Ippos)

Lieutenant Benny Moerdani (pictured right) assembles with his commandos at Manado after performing sweeps against Permesta, circa 1959. (Courtesy Ippos)

Kopaska combat swimmers during the Armed Forces Day parade, 5 October 1962. A hybrid unit between the navy and RPKAD, the members wear RPKAD berets. (Courtesy Ippos)

Yugoslavian instructors Mladen Milicevic, Stoyan Jovic, and Dobel Stanej at Bandung during the graduation of the first RPKAD freefall class, 26 October 1962. (Courtesy Ippos)

Members of the first RPKAD freefall class, 26 October 1962, receive a certificate and freefall qualification badge (which has been pinned upside-down in error). They wear so-called Depison smocks, a Hong Kong-made imitation of the British Denison smock. (courtesy Ippos)

President Sukarno reviews the 454 Airborne Battalion during a celebration in front of the State Palace for veterans of the West Irian campaign, 19 February 1963. Immediately behind the president is Major Untung (left), commander of the 454 Airborne Battalion, and General Suharto, head of the Mandala Command. Untung later led the abortive September 1965 coup; Suharto would become president for three decades. (Courtesy Ippos)

*President Sukarno at a February 1963 reception with Herlina,
the female guerrilla who was inserted into West Irian with PG 500. (Courtesy Ippos)*

*Major Untung, commander of the 454 Airborne Battalion, during a celebration at Tanjung Priok,
Jakarta, for veterans of the West Irian campaign, 26 February 1963. (Courtesy Ippos)*

An RPKAD company prepares for a parachute jump into East Kalimantan, February 1964. (Courtesy Hendro Subroto)

Members of the RPKAD parade near the Senayan stadium during Armed Forces Day celebrations, 5 October 1964. This was the first time they publicly wore the RPKAD's distinctive vertical stripe camouflage. The bush hat was briefly favored by RPKAD commander Mung, but was soon dropped for a return to the red beret. (Courtesy Ippos)

Colonel Sarwo Edhie participating in a show-of-force demonstration at the Senayan parking lot, 4 January 1966. He wears the newly-issued RPKAD qualification badge on his left breast. (Courtesy Ippos)

Brigadier General Widjono Soejono with President Suharto at RPKAD anniversary celebrations, April 1968. In the background are Colonel Djajadiningrat and Colonel Soeweno. (Courtesy Ippos)

RPKAD anniversary celebrations, 16 April 1968.
The commandos wear the modified beret badge for the first time. (Courtesy Ippos)

*Brigadier General Widjoyo Soejono (left) turns over command to
Brigadier General Witarmin, April 1970. (Courtesy Ippos)*

Cambodian troops undergoing commando training, circa early 1972.

General Benny Moerdani at Batugade with Umi commander Sofian Effendi (right) and Kogasgab staff member Darwin Nasution, circa September 1975.

Members of Susi's Prayudha 4 assemble at Balibo, circa 17 October 1975.

*Elements of Nanggala 13 and the Special Platoon (Ton Sus)
armed with G-3 and SP2 rifles at Soibada, circa November 1976.*

*Acehnese religious leader Daud Beureueh taken in a
helicopter by Kopassandha members, May 1978.*

Members of the task force that raided the Woyla pose with crew members on the flight home, 31 March 1981.

The body of Achmad Kirang, the only Kopassandha fatality in the Woyla raid, is returned to Jakarta, 2 April 1981. (Courtesy Ippos)

Beret badge, 1954-1968. The initial RPKAD beret badge, designed by Lieutenant Dodo Sukampto and first worn during the October 1954 armed forces day parade, incorporated a saber (to signify ground operations), an anchor (maritime ability), and wings (fast mobility).

Beret badge, 1968-present. In a slight reworking of the original design, the saber was slimmed down to a commando dagger, and the wings were given an extra layer of feathers to conform to the design of army parachute wings.

Army airborne wings.
The top wing, designed and issued by the air force PGT, was issued to army commandos who graduated from PGT jump training at Margahayu from 1957 to 1959; it differs from the air force wing in that the letters "RPKAD" are stamped on the reverse.

The center wing, designed by then Lieutenant Djajadiningrat and nicknamed the "moustache wing" (wing kumis), was briefly issued to graduates of the newly-formed SPKAD parachute course at Batu Jajar in 1960.

The bottom wing became the standardized army wing issued by Batu Jajar from 1961 to the present.

Chest qualification badge, 1966-present. Designed by then Major Djajadiningrat, this badge is worn by all graduates of the commando course at Batu Jajar.

RPKAD freefall wing, designed by H.H. Djudadiningrat and first issued in 1962, depicts a skydiver surmounted by a wreath comprised of small parachutes.

Shoulder insignia, 1952-1985. The green triangle with a dagger was first issued to commando graduates in December 1952. This design, surmounted by the para-commando arc, was issued to members of the RPKAD/Kopassandha from 1959 to 1985.

Shoulder insignia worn by Kopassus, 1985 through present.

Members of Group 4 during Kopassus anniversary celebrations, April 2000.

Retreating to the Bank Indonesia building, Kentot rendezvoused with his regimental commander. Though his mission appeared to have been a bust, the psychological pressure outside the palace gates set the stage for pivotal events that took place later that same afternoon. Driving to Bogor, an army delegation sent by Suharto presented Sukarno with a decree that shifted de facto power to the general. More of an ultimatum than a choice, the president signed the document and effectively ceded authority.

The next day, the RPKAD joined fellow army units in a major show of force on Jakarta's streets. The students, in a valedictory performance, sacked the headquarters of Soebandrio's intelligence agency. Though Sukarno was still the president on paper, the baton had been passed to Suharto.

No military unit emerged from the upheavals of 1965 with a higher profile than the RPKAD. Within the regiment, however, there were a few loose ends that needed attending. Across the military, units had been busy purging themselves of PKI sympathizers. In one case, air force chief Omar Dani had fled for sanctuary in Cambodia. The generals saw it as imperative that Dani come back to Indonesia—both to stand trial over his own conduct, and to interrogate him over Sukarno's role in the failed putsch.

Unfortunately for Suharto and the generals, Cambodia had no intention of extraditing their guest. It was at that point that the top brass turned toward the RPKAD. Over the previous year, a handful of members of the regiment had been seconded to participate in a highly compartmentalized Confrontation operation to strike at Commonwealth targets from unexpected directions. Assisted by intelligence officers disguised as shipping agents and Garuda airlines representatives, they had experimented with infiltration routes through Cambodia, Hong Kong, and Thailand. Benny Moerdani, the former RPKAD battalion commander now acting as the Bangkok link under Garuda cover, had assisted one team of loaned RPKAD operatives in an abortive 1965 attempt to link up with Muslim Thai guerrillas on the southern border near Malaysia.[17]

In early 1966, five RPKAD members, disguised as crewmen for the Kie Hok shipping lines, used the Cambodian pipeline to steal into the port of Sihanoukville. Rather than fomenting Confrontation violence, however, their mission this time was to force Omar Dani to return home. Upon arrival, they passed messages through Cham (a Muslim minority in Cambodia) and ethnic Chinese intermediaries to the wayward air force officer. The gist of their communications—that Dani would be forcefully repatriated if he did not voluntarily return—had it desired effect: on 20 April, he came back to Jakarta to stand trial.

Looking inward, the RPKAD itself had not been immune to PKI encroachment. By far its most tainted element was the airborne and commando school at Batu Jajar, where more than twenty-four instructors had openly sided with the 30 September Movement on 1 October. All were subsequently expelled.

Among the regiment's three para-commando battalions, it came as little surprise that Battalion 3—garrisoned at the PKI stronghold of Semarang—had the largest number of party members. During the first half of 1966, these sympathizers were systematically weeded out and shifted to non-combat roles. A lesser number of PKI supporters in Battalion 2 were afforded similar treatment.

Battalion 1 at Cijantung had the fewest PKI adherents—though there were a couple of surprises. Captain Urip Sucipto—who had led Company Ben Hur with distinction at places like Mapu, the telecommunications building in Jakarta, and Central Java—was belatedly discovered to have been a PKI member during the revolution and participated in some post-war reunions. Despite his insistence that his contact with the communists had stopped years earlier, he was drummed out of the regiment.

More serious were the charges leveled against Captain Heru Sisnodo. As a team leader in the DPC, Heru had rubbed many of his fellow officers raw because of his pronounced ambitions. Still, he had performed well as commander of Company Dracula and appeared headed for better things within the regiment—until it was discovered he had been a member of a secret PKI cell. Though allowed to remain within the RPKAD after showing contrition, he was forever off the fast track.[18]

The monumental changes in Jakarta had not put a damper on the Confrontation against Malaysia. Some of the most audacious attacks in that simmering conflict, in fact, had taken place in the six months immediately before the 30 September Movement. In February 1965, President Sukarno had passed word to his military commanders that he desired a spectacular attack to coincide with two upcoming dates. The first was the tenth anniversary of the Afro-Asia Conference in April; that conference, hosted by Sukarno himself in Bandung in 1955, had given birth to the so-called Non-Aligned Movement. The second date was 29 June, when the second Afro-Asian Conference was scheduled to take place in Algeria. Sukarno thought it imperative to have a series of military operations in Sarawak and Sabah in the months up to the Algeria gathering to show the world the people of "North Kalimantan" were active.

Fast to answer the president's call were the ever-loyal marines, who obediently mapped out a schedule of operations to take place along the Sabah frontier. These operations included increased border patrols by its regular battalions, as well as shallow cross-border unconventional forays under the tired fiction of the TNKU.[19]

Not to be left out, the RPKAD also began preparing for a small but flashy cross-border event. Three companies had just deployed to West Kalimantan—two from Semarang's Battalion 3, as well as Company Ben Hur—and Sarwo Edhie personally ventured to these units to canvass them for volunteers to fill four seven-man teams. Two teams were ultimately drawn from Company Ben Hur—appropriately dubbed Ben Hur 1 and Ben Hur 2—and one apiece from the Semarang companies. The plan was for them to stage a series of bold raids against bridges, convoys, barracks, and airfields between the border and Kuching.

Although none of the teams received any specialized training, greatly assisting them in their venture would be leftist partisans from the Sarawak People's Guerrilla Force (*Pasukan Gerilya Rakyat Sarawak*, or PGRS). Tracing its origins back to 1963, the PGRS had sprung from over eight hundred ethnic Chinese communist sympathizers who had fled to West Kalimantan in the aftermath of the abortive Brunei Revolt. Fearing a British crackdown, these Sarawak émigrés had gotten such a sympathetic reception from Indonesian intelligence chief Soebandrio that he organized training for their leaders in Bogor, and arranged the dispatch of instructors (including three RPKAD commandos) to the West Kalimantan border to coach the remainder.[20]

Over the next two years, the PGRS ran infrequent raids into the westernmost corner of Sarawak. Much more of their time was spent returning to their homeland to preen pockets of sympathizers. With over thirty percent of that state consisting of ethnic Chinese (the highest percent among the three Borneo states), the narrow alluvial plains west of Kuching were particularly fertile grounds. Directing them in this effort was a 120-man contingent from Soebandrio's intelligence agency based near the West Kalimantan village of Batu Hitam. Added to this mix was a handful of cadre trained in the People's Republic of China and strong support from the PKI; spearheaded by Sofyan— an ethnic Arab revolutionary who was the most prominent PKI leader in West Kalimantan—the nexus between Soebandrio's intelligence agency, the PGRS, and the PKI grew strong.[21]

Given these links to Indonesia's political left, the PGRS had been kept at arm's length by General Yani and the army through early 1965. But with Sukarno's urgent call to grab headlines in Borneo, political infighting was temporarily set aside in order for the military to piggyback on the PGRS network inside Sarawak.

Because the PGRS would be assisting the RPKAD on this infiltration, the commandos for the first time planned for an extended mission to take advantage of food handouts from pro-PGRS locals. As they would not be carrying any radios, they would also depend on the PGRS for guides and couriers to coordinate their raids.

In mid-February, the four commando teams received a final briefing from Sarwo Edhie. One of the four, Ben Hur 1, then veered toward Gunung Entitik, a towering peak that straddled the frontier. There they received a rude welcome as Commonwealth forces coincidentally begin a major sweep— replete with heavy artillery shelling—around the mountain. The team's commander, Sergeant Matseh Pangma, was forced to delay movement for nearly a week until the opposing troops moved on.

Already behind schedule, Ben Hur 1 skirted the village of Tebedu in what they expected to be a five day hike to a secret PGRS camp. Conspiring against them this time was the terrain, with dozens of flooded rivers nearly doubling their time to the rendezvous point.

Bad luck continued to mount. Because of the swampy geography, trenchfoot had taken its toll. Forced to wait another ten days to rest and recuperate, Sergeant Matseh learned from PGRS couriers that the other three RPKAD teams were making no progress in their trek from the border.

Continuing alone, Ben Hur 1 slowly leapfrogged between pockets of PGRS sympathizers for the next two months. Not until mid-May did the seven commandos get near their goal, a Malaysian army barracks close to Kuching's airport. Members of the team would later claim they entered the barracks, detained the occupants at gunpoint, and scored three rocket hits against the structure. This account almost certainly contains more than a little embellishment: Commonwealth records indicate no significant Indonesian raids during that timeframe, much less a brazen strike just ten kilometers from Kuching.

Whatever the case, Ben Hur 1 began evading back to the border. To their credit, six of the seven Ben Hur 1 members managed to reach Gunung Entitik on 2 June; four days later, they arrived at an Indonesian government garrison to be greeted by Sarwo Edhie.[22]

The saga of Ben Hur 1 did not end there. One of its members, Corporal Malete Simon, had gotten separated from the team and failed to show at the border. Simon had been looking for redemption during this mission: as a member of the DPC in 1962, he had panicked and refused to exit his aircraft during the parachute drop at Merauke. Now on the run, he spent the next two months evading with PGRS partisans through the jungles of Sarawak. At one point using a bamboo tube to hide submerged among reeds during a close encounter with British troops, it was not until August that he made it back to Indonesian lines.

It would be the PGRS guerrillas themselves that inflicted the only confirmed damage in response to Sukarno's renewed call to arms. Operating without the RPKAD, Chinese guerrillas attacked a police station along the Kuching-Serian road on the night of 27 June, killing six civilians and stealing a quantity of weapons. The raid was noteworthy because it was one of the deepest armed penetrations by PGRS guerrillas during the entire conflict, and because the murder of the civilians was committed in particularly brutal fashion. As a consequence, Commonwealth security forces mounted a major sweep that netted fifty-seven suspects and saw most of the local Chinese population grouped into three secure hamlets.[23]

Ironically, the Afro-Asian Conference on 29 June—which was the *raison d'être* for the raids—never took place. On the eve of the event, a senior Algerian army officer overthrew leftist leader Ben Bella. With world leaders turned away from Algiers at the last minute, the meeting fell by the wayside.

Back in Jakarta, the exploits of Ben Hur 1 had captured General Yani's imagination. Rather than conducting a raid, however, he became fixated on the idea of capturing a live British prisoner.[24] Posing this challenge to Sarwo Edhie, the task was forwarded to Major Sumardji. A graduate of the British jungle warfare school in 1959, Sumardji had been slated to receive U.S. special forces training in 1963, only to have the offer revoked due to the outbreak of Confrontation. Instead, he had gone to West Germany as team leader for a military freefall competition (Yugoslavia, which had provided Indonesia with its first freefall instructors, sponsored the team). Upon return, he had been named deputy commander of Battalion 1 at Cijantung.[25]

With Yani's mandate for a prisoner snatch, Sumardji was given instructions to form a composite RPKAD battalion drawn from across the regiment. In late June, word was passed to each of the three para-commando battalions to release the equivalent of one company apiece for a special selection process. Because Batu Jajar was already full, this was to take place near the Battalion 2 barracks at Magelang. The new unit would be given the cover designation of Battalion 2C, with C standing for *chusus* (Indonesian for "special").[26]

As word of the special selection spread, company commanders vied to have their men go to Magelang. Heru Sisnodo, the ambitious captain at Cijantung, managed to have his company land many of the one hundred slots allocated to Battalion 1. No privates were allowed; the lowest acceptable rank was corporal.

Quickly reaching the three hundred man ceiling, ad hoc training commenced. Though the RPKAD had no clear syllabus for special warfare—much less for prisoner snatches—the instructor cadre used a regimen of tough physical drills that whittled the volunteers down to less than a third in four months. Those who did not pass muster returned to their original battalions.

Far short of authorized battalion strength, Sumardji's remaining company never saw action. No sooner had it finished the Magelang course, the 30 September Movement rocked Jakarta and the nation. With all eyes focused on Central Java, the Magelang graduates participated in Sarwo Edhie's anti-PKI maneuvers across Central Java during October and November.

Not until December, with the back of the PKI effectively broken, did Sumardji's special mission get revisited. But given the confusion over the previous months, the major could only muster sixty available men. During the final week of the year, half of these were sent to West Kalimantan under the codename Manjar, a species of weaver bird endemic to Kalimantan. The other half went to East Kalimantan under the name Beo, a Kalimantan myna bird.

Once in Kalimantan, the two thirty-man teams moved up to border staging areas in January 1966. Beo, it turned out, waffled over its mission and ultimately never saw action; those in West Kalimantan did. Remarkably, despite the anti-PKI massacres the army had been instigating across Java and the rest of the country, Manjar was ordered to again turn toward the leftist PGRS for support. Training alongside the Chinese guerrillas at a camp near Gunung Entitik, they were ready to infiltrate by month's end.

Unlike the previous year's Ben Hur 1, which was assigned a clear target and a specific deadline, Manjar had a rather nebulous mandate. With General Yani dead, the earlier call to capture a live British prisoner was forgotten. "We were told to go inside Sarawak midway between the border and Kuching," recalled one member, "and make guerrilla pockets."[27]

To do this, each member was given an AK-47 rifle, three hundred bullets, and dehydrated rations to cover their first ten days. They wore sterile green uniforms and, to disguise the origin of their shoeprints, civilian athletic shoes.

On the morning of 2 February, a dozen members of Manjar—dubbed Manjar 1—matched up with an equal number of PGRS guerrillas and moved directly up to the frontier. Waiting until nightfall, they slipped into Sarawak.

Their baptism by fire was not long in coming. One day into their mission, they had a fleeting encounter with a British patrol in the early afternoon. As shots rang out, one of the RPKAD commandos took a fatal round through the forehead. Two hours after that, a second contact sent the mixed team scattering in all directions. Although nine of the commandos eventually managed to regroup, they could find none of their Chinese counterparts. Worse, their team leader was among the two missing Indonesian members.

As the survivors huddled in the dark, they debated who would be their new team commander. Deciding to choose the most senior in age, thirty-year-old Sergeant Nur Salam got the nod. Their decision was then radioed back to a rear base monitoring their progress from West Kalimantan.

Under Nur Salam's direction, they pressed north toward Kuching. Concealing themselves during the day to avoid detection by helicopters, they anticipated their trek would take twelve days. While still en route, however, a third clash again sent the team racing in all directions. This time, their radioman went missing, meaning they had no way to communicate with their base.

Now reduced to eight, their unlucky streak continued. Running headlong into a patrol of Malaysian auxiliaries, one of the commandos was hit by a shotgun round as he ducked into the bush. Though foliage deflected most of the pellets, he had twenty-two holes in his back. Unable to proceed with the mission due to the pain, he split from the team and headed back toward Indonesia. He was fortunate: one other member was missing—and presumed dead—during the same encounter.

For the remaining six, they at long last reached their assigned rendezvous point twenty-one kilometers south of Kuching. There they managed to link up with ethnic Chinese sympathizers who would play their host for the next three months. "The local partisans were good," said one team member. "We initially bought food from them, but they later gave it for free."[28]

Although Manjar 1 had been assigned with forming guerrilla pockets, their ensuing longevity was precisely because they laid low and did little to attract the attention of the authorities. On one occasion when they did stray from their shelter, they got caught in a Commonwealth sweep that claimed the lives of three more RPKAD commandos.

In the meantime, the remaining members of Manjar, now called Manjar 2, had crossed the border in May. Like Manjar 1, they were matched up with a like number of PGRS partisans. Also like Manjar 1, the Chinese wafted away soon after crossing the frontier. Alone, the RPKAD commandos had trouble making their way toward their designated area of operations to the immediate west of Kuching.

From messages passed by PGRS couriers, the three remaining Manjar 1 members received news that Manjar 2 was on its way into Sarawak. The Chinese south of Kuching were proving reliable allies, shielding them from the Malaysian and Commonwealth authorities; they had even provided the Manjar 1 commandos with a small transistor radio. It was from this radio that the commandos heard a 3 June newscast out of Jakarta that Confrontation was over.

In fact, reports of Confrontation's demise were premature. It was true that secret peace talks had been taking place since March; with Suharto effectively assuming power that month, the general had quickly concluded Sukarno's quasi-war against Malaysia held few benefits for Indonesia. Making a pragmatic policy reversal, he ordered Benny Moerdani to drop his Garuda guise and act as one of the country's top negotiators with the Commonwealth. Though an armistice seemed likely, none had yet been signed as of June.

Such technicalities mattered little to the men of Manjar 1, who immediately left their bivouac and headed for home. All three made it across the border and were feted in Pontianak during the 17 August National Day celebrations. In October 1967, each were awarded the Bintang Sakti and given double promotions backdated to July 1966.[29]

For Manjar 2, the premature news of Confrontation's end came when they were only halfway to their target. Reversing direction during the second week of June, they had not gotten far before running into an Australian ambush. During the ensuing nocturnal firefight, two Indonesians and one Australian were killed. Two other RPKAD commandos were later captured; the rest slipped back across the border.[30]

Two months later, on 11 August, a Malaysian delegation ventured to Jakarta. In grand style and with smiles all around, a formal peace accord was signed. After over three years of clashes and harsh rhetoric, Confrontation was officially over.[31]

The RPKAD's experience in fielding special teams like Ben Hur and Manjar had been decidedly under-whelming. Training was haphazard, little was accomplished, and casualties were high. Yet compared with Indonesia's other elite units, the RPKAD's special warfare record looked enlightened. In August 1964, for example, the marines and air force PGT had cooperated to launch what they hoped would be a spectacular raid in peninsular Malaysia timed to coincide with Indonesia's National Day. Joined by two dozen communist Malaysian agents, over one hundred men infiltrated the mainland during a twenty-four hour period ahead of 17 August. They intended to stay as long as two months in order to establish Malaysian guerrilla pockets in the wake of their raid. But Commonwealth forces, who had increased patrols ahead of the date, rounded up nearly all of the commandos within two days.[32]

The following month, on 2 September, the PGT had parachuted three platoons onto the mainland in yet another attempt to create guerrilla pockets. Not only did one of three C-130 transports crash into the Malacca Straits while en route, but the parachutists from the other two planes were hopelessly spread out due to bad weather, high winds, and poor navigation. Of the 96 who jumped, 31 were killed and 59 captured in a matter of days.[33]

Yet despite such collective setbacks, Sarwo Edhie was determined to pursue unconventional capabilities. "He kept saying that the RPKAD was really not much different from the infantry raiders," recalls Major Sumardji. "He wanted a special warfare—or *sandhi yudha*—component."[34]

The basis for such a component within the RPKAD existed in the remnants of the Manjar and Beo teams already returned from Kalimantan. To build on this, Sumardji was instructed in mid-1966 to hold a second qualification course. Instead of Magelang, this time it would be at Batu Jajar. Sixty students were soon drawn from around the regiment, including four lieutenants.

Showing ingenuity, the Batu Jajar instructors this time had come up with a unique syllabus that actually reflected some unconventional thinking. Divided in four parts held over four months, it combined old and new material. Among the old was a demolitions tutorial and airborne refresher jumps; among the new were classes on intelligence and civic action. Several trainers were brought in from outside the army, including from the police.[35]

By the end of the fourth month, the class was divided into seven-man teams and deployed on a final field training exercise. Harkening back to the ad hoc DPC instruction of 1962, one of the teams was told to change into civilian clothes and go to Tegal, a town near the western border of Central Java. With PKI militants still said to be operating in the surrounding countryside, team members were told to reconnoiter the town's bridges and hypothetically determine locations for placing demolition charges—all without drawing the attention of local security forces.[36]

Of the fifty-eight students who eventually passed selection, they were merged with the Manjar and Beo veterans from the first class. Though still far short of authorized strength, Major Sumardji by year's end was officially named commander of the RPKAD's Special Warfare Battalion.[37]

---

1   The 2 October edition of the PKI's official daily newspaper—which was distributed that afternoon—had come out unequivocally in support of the 30 September Movement. Although this editorial would have been prepared in advance, its belated publication after the movement had collapsed in Jakarta served little purpose other than inciting the military to seek revenge.

2   Pusat Sejarah dan Tradisi ABRI, *Bahaya Laten Komunisme di Indonesia*, Volume IVA (Jakarta: Markas Besar ABRI, 1994), p. 210.

3   DDRS 0517-2000, White House memorandum, subj: The Week in Asia other than Vietnam, dated 14 October 1965.

4   The three companies retained in Jakarta were Company A (which had been whisked back from Irian Jaya), part of Company Cobra (repatriated from East Kalimantan), and Company Dracula. Kentot Harseno interview; interview with Talahatu, 31 August 2000.

5   *Gerakan 30 September Pemberontakan Partai Komunis Indonesia* (Jakarta: Sekratariat Negara Republik Indonesia, 1994), pp. 158-159.

6   *Editor*, p. 15.

7   FRUS, 1964-1968, Vol. XXVI, Embassy telegram to Department of State, dated 4 November 1965, p. 354.

8   Used in Operation Merapi were Company Ben Hur, Company E, and one company apiece from Battalion 2 and Battalion 3.

9   Djasmin interview.

10 Djasmin interview; Untung Suroso interview; FRUS, Vol. XXVI, Editorial Note, p. 340.

11 Sarwo Edhie's wife had formed the female volunteer corps in mid-1965. Known as *Kartika Chandra Kirana* (literally, "Beautiful Star and Moon"), the unit wore jackets and bush hats in the distinctive RPKAD camouflage. It was scheduled to march during the 5 October Armed Forces Day parade. *Dua Puluh Tahun ABRI* (Jakarta: Puspen AD, AL, AU, dan AK, 1965), p. 36.

12 *Editor*, p. 16.

13 *Kostrad, Darma Putra* (Jakarta: Panitya Penyusun Sejarah Kostrad, 1972), p. 74.

14 Ibid., p. 20.

15 Kentot Harseno interview.

16 Ibid.

17 Interview with Kusnadi, 11 March 2000; Pour, *Benny Moerdani*, p. 258.

18 Heru was fortunate compared with Supomo, the first company commander within the RPKAD. Peaking as the chief of staff for the military region encompassing West Irian, Colonel Supomo was discovered to have forged close ties with the PKI. In May 1966, he was discharged from the armed forces. Kaharudin Nasution, who had briefly served as the RPKAD's commander, was wrongly identified in one published history as a PKI sympathizer. (Poulgrain, *The Genesis of Konfrontasi*, p. 275).

19 *Korps Komando AL*, p. 299.

20 *Peranan Kalimantan Barat dalam Menghadapi* (Jakarta: Yayasan Tanjungpura, 1973), p. 56.

21 *Rumpun Diponegoro dan Pengabdiannya* (Surabaya: Percetakan Delta, 1977), p. 619; Poulgrain, *The Genesis of Konfrontasi*, p. 261.

22 For a highly sensational and disjointed account of Ben Hur 1, see the official Kopassus history: *Pengabdian Korps Baret Merah Abad XX* (Jakarta, 2000), pp. 169-170.

23 Peter Dennis and Jeffrey Grey, *Emergency and Confrontation* (St. Leonards, New South Wales: Allen & Unwin, 1996), p. 278.

24 Yani was furious when he heard that a British Special Air Service trooper had been killed, rather than captured alive, during the March 1964 firefight with RPKAD commandos in East Kalimantan.

25 Besides sponsoring the freefall team, Yugoslavian largesse toward the RPKAD was shown in one other way. In 1962, they presented each freefall graduate with a camouflage "skydiving" uniform. In actuality, the bulky suits were normally issued to Yugoslavian sniper teams and were hardly appropriate for parachuting. The Yugoslavians also gave their students padded military vests and gloves— good for Europe but inappropriate for the tropics.

26 Sumardji interview.

27 Interview with Ramedi, 26 August 2000.

28 Ibid.

29 Ibid.

30 Dennis and Grey, *Emergency and Confrontation*, p. 293; Ramedi interview.

31 The final Indonesian incursion into Borneo was conducted not by the RPKAD, but by a team from the 600 Raider Company based in East Kalimantan. Led by Lieutenant Sombi, yet another graduate of the British jungle warfare school, the raiders slipped into easternmost Sarawak in June. Their target was reportedly the oil installations in Brunei. Not detected until 29 July, the team was pursued for the next month; Sombi himself was not captured until 3 September. *Sejarah Singkat Kodam IX/Mulawarman* (Balikpapan: Dinas Sejarah Militer Kodam IX/ Mulawarman, 1973), p. p. 100.

32 *Korps Komando AL*, p. 331.

33 The three C-130 transports departed Halim airbase and were following a commercial airways flightpath in order to avoid detection. Dropping low under British radar, one of the aircraft hit the sea. The following day Jakarta issued a press statement falsely claiming the plane was flying seventy Cambodian dancers to Phnom Penh. DDRS 0625-1999, CIA Intelligence Information Cable, dated 12 September 1964; FBIS, East Asia edition, 3 September 1964, p. RRR3; Major General R. McAllister, *Bugle and Kukri*, Volume 2 (London: The Regiment Trust, 10th Princess Mary's Own Gurkha Rifles, 1984), p. 197.

34 Sumardji interview. Although *sandhi yudha* literally translates as "secret warfare," the Indonesians actually were trying to reflect the connotation of "special warfare," which was the nomenclature in use at the U.S. Army Special Warfare Center.

35 Interview with Dalio, 31 August 2000; interview with Sudjadi, 10 October 2000.

36 Sudjadi interview.

37 The Special Warfare Battalion, or *Yon Sandhi Yudha*, was often abbreviated as *Yon Sandha*.

CHAPTER TWELVE

THE GOLDEN BOYS

Despite a public enamored with its romanticized image, the RPKAD could not shake manpower problems. Among normal attrition, the post-30 September chaos, the purges of PKI sympathizers, and the personnel demands for creating Sumardji's Special Warfare Battalion, the regiment's three para-commando battalions remained chronically short-handed.

Compounding matters, Batu Jajar had been hard pressed to return to a normal training schedule. After an almost three month hiatus, they had finally reopened their gates to a new cycle in December 1965 that included the two hundred Lao students that had been held in virtual house arrest since 1 October. More than ever before, the trainees were squeezed by a lack of food rations. Remembers one:

> The economy was very bad, so the school could not give us enough food. For the Indonesian students, we could get a little bit of help from our families. The Lao students could not get any family help. We were all getting very gaunt toward the end of training.[1]

In April 1966, after abbreviating the course by two months, the cycle graduated. For the Lao, they returned home escorted by a six-man RPKAD training team.[2] The Indonesians, including ten fresh lieutenants, were primarily split between the two battalions in Central Java. Of these, Battalion 2 at Magelang had a headquarters company at full strength, but four combat companies were mere skeletons.[3]

The situation with Battalion 3 was even worse. A decision had earlier been made to shift the battalion headquarters from Semarang to more spacious facilities being built in Solo. The battalion headquarters and two companies moved into the unfinished Solo quarters in June, but the two remaining combat companies remained behind at Semarang. Not only was the battalion split between two locales, but all units were at a fraction of authorized strength.[4]

To make up for the shortfall, the RPKAD took drastic measures. Playing off their newfound popularity with the public, they pitched both civilians and fellow soldiers in June with a call to join the regiment. Hundreds responded, almost all of them from West Java. Sent to Magelang, they received three months of basic training under RPKAD auspices before continuing to Batu Jajar for the standard commando and airborne courses.[5]

At the end of 1966, a second recruitment drive brought hundreds more to Magelang. This time, nearly all were from Central Java. Training in the shadow of the majestic Borobudur temple, this contingent also continued on to Batu Jajar. Between the two cycles, the RPKAD gained nearly six hundred new members.[6]

As this had been taking place, Sarwo Edhie was slowly becoming a victim of his own success. For someone once derided as a temporary regimental commander, by mid-1966 he was one of the most recognized officers in the entire armed forces and was genuinely liked by university students.[7]

Suharto, who had been patiently building his power base over the course of 1966, remained more indebted to Edhie for his rise than perhaps any other officer. Returning the favor, he had boosted the RPKAD commander's slot to a brigadier; Edhie, as a result, was sporting his first star by the opening of 1967.

At the same time, however, Suharto did not appreciate competition from his fellow army brass—especially from a popular commander like Edhie. In mid-March 1967, after a provisional national assembly formally removed the last vestiges of power from Sukarno, rumors were rife that "Acting President" Suharto was preparing to cut the wings of Edhie and other politically-empowered officers.[8]

The rumors proved correct. On 16 April, during the RPKAD's founding day anniversary, it was announced that Edhie would be replaced by Brigadier General Widjojo Soejono. As the former RPKAD chief-of-staff who had left the regiment to form the 3 Parachute Brigade during the Irian campaign, much had happened to Widjojo in the interim. On 10 October 1965, he had rushed to West Kalimantan to fill the slot left by fugitive General Supardjo. Reviewing the troops strung on the border, he found the 5 Brigade from Central Java was rife with PKI sympathizers and itching to rebel. Sending the brigade back to Java by ship, the pro-PKI elements were sent packing to prison.

For the next year, Widjojo remained on the border to run the sputtering Confrontation campaign into Sarawak. But once peace accords were initialed in August 1966, the position became meaningless. In a sign of the times, he was invited to Kuching in early 1967 to meet his Malaysian counterparts.

On 27 May 1967, Widjojo formally took the reins of the RPKAD from Edhie. It was a very different regiment from the one he last remembered:

> The RPKAD was extremely popular at the time. They would get food for free, but the next week they would be expected to act as debt collectors. I once saw a Red Beret at the head of a Chinese funeral in downtown Jakarta. I stopped my jeep, put the soldier in back, and took him to a cell.[9]

The RPKAD had also become ensconced in politics like never before. On 7 July, the regional military commanders from Java began a series of monthly trysts to discuss broad security matters. Invited to the meetings were the heads of the RPKAD and Kostrad (command of which had passed from Suharto to General Kemal Idris). During the first session, the assembled officers signed a joint declaration that demanded harsh measures be taken against anybody wishing to restore powers to Sukarno. This came during a sensitive period when Sukarno had already been effectively stripped of the presidency, but heir apparent Suharto had yet to be formally elected to office.[10]

After three such meetings, the assembled generals agreed that the RPKAD—which occupied a sensitive post on the outskirts of the capital—should leave politics and focus on its mission. While Widjojo fully agreed with this sentiment, his chief-of-staff, Colonel Prijo Pranoto, resisted. A holdover from Sarwo Edhie's administration, Colonel Prijo had been the officer who handled most of the regiment's links to the student movement and was smitten by the RPKAD's extra-military role. After several months of tension, Prijo was eventually transferred out of the regiment to army headquarters.

Political diversions aside, Widjojo quickly earned the reputation as a conceptualist and it was soon after he took command that the RPKAD underwent a major reorganization. Copying U.S. Army Special Forces nomenclature, the regiment's three para-commando battalions were to be expanded into para-commando groups. Roughly analogous to a brigade, each group would consist of three combat detachments. Each detachment, in turn, would consist of three companies. Although the detachments would not have attached heavy weapons and only a small headquarters element, they would be analogous to a light battalion. All of this allowed for a significant boost in the RPKAD's allocated officer ranks, with each group theoretically to be commanded by a lieutenant colonel and detachments led by captains.[11]

There was a problem with these numbers, however. According to the new structure, the regiment would have twenty-seven para-commando companies in the nine detachments under the three para-commando groups. In actuality, the RPKAD in mid-1967 counted less than half that number of companies—and more than half of these were not fully operational.

Despite the massive shortfall, on 17 July the three groups became official. Much of the change was semantics. Battalion 1 at Cijantung became Group 1; the battalion's five companies were split up to partially fill Combat Detachments 11, 12, and 13.[12] Magelang's Battalion 2 became Group 2; because of its excessively thin roster, this group initially only counted Detachments 24 and 25. Battalion 3, split between Semarang and Solo, became Group 3; also because of chronic manpower shortages, this group listed only Detachments 36 and 37. The battalion commanders—all majors—were for the time being upgraded to group commanders without promotion to higher rank.[13]

Ten days later, Sumardji's Special Warfare Battalion was caught up in the reorganization. Now renamed Group 4, it was to be intentionally modeled after the U.S. Army Special Forces in both structure and unconventional warfare mandate. Overseeing this transformation was Group 4's newly designated commander, Major C.I. Santosa. Formerly the head of Battalion 1, Santosa was a good choice. During the first half of 1963, he had ventured to Fort Bragg for both the 12-week special forces course and 6-week psychological operations course.[14]

But even with Santosa's special warfare background, the challenges he faced with Group 4 were greater than those confronting the other three groups. For one thing, Group 4's manpower problems were the most serious in the regiment. Plans called for it to control three detachments; Santosa, however, inherited barely one hundred troops from the Special Warfare Battalion.[15]

Not only was this paltry sum insufficient, but it fell short in quality. Again looking at the U.S. Army Special Forces for a model, Widjojo wanted Group 4 to include only officers and non-commissioned officers. Moreover, he wanted them to include specialists in fields like medicine, combat engineering, and intelligence. As yet, Group 4 counted only a handful of members with such skills.

Finally, there was serious confusion over Group 4's true role. Brainstorming, Widjojo initially considered giving each of the group's three detachments a different focus: one would handle demolitions, another would be for psychological warfare, and the third would conduct civic action.[16] This was later dropped in favor of blending the various functions within each detachment. Still, Group 4 members were left scratching their heads as to their intended mission. "The mission for the para-commandos was clear, but not for *sandhi yudha*," said one officer present at the group's inception. "Was it more of an intelligence-type mission? For what ends?"[17]

In the midst of these changes, the RPKAD did not have the luxury of rest. Unlike never before, the Indonesian military was being whipsawed by brushfires across the archipelago. Shaping into a perennial headache was West Irian, where the OPM rebel band operating around the Bird's Head was still at large. Moreover, a second hotspot had emerged around Merauke in January 1967. This was the same border town where Benny Moerdani had parachuted with his DPC five years earlier. Worse for the government, according to agreements it made in 1962 there were only two years left before Indonesia was obliged to conduct an independence referendum in the territory.

With this deadline looming, the armed forces restarted its earlier Operation Sadar in June 1967. Similar to the previous effort, the RPKAD's contribution—totaling one company—focused on the area around Manokwari. Also like the previous effort, the commandos spent the year making minimal headway though the impossibly thick jungle against an elusive guerrilla foe.

Trouble for the government was also being experienced in Central Java. Having gone underground after the anti-communist massacres of 1965-66, neo-PKI bands had started to organize in the countryside for a partisan struggle. They were not alone: an undetermined number of servicemen had deserted with their weapons to join this leftist cause.

Most of those who broke ranks had come from the marines. Prior to October 1965, the marines had parlayed their close ties with Sukarno into a significant expansion in their numbers. Even in the months immediately after the failed putsch, the marines had still been able to keep momentum and add four more battalions to their roster during early 1966.

But now that the RPKAD had supplanted the marines as the military's golden boys, repercussions against the latter were in the making. In March 1966, Sukarno's Tjakrabirawa Regiment was disbanded; its marine battalion was removed from further presidential guard duties. Over the next year, rumors began to mount that Suharto was maneuvering to oust the marine commandant, General Hartono.[18] Combined with the slow but steady leaching of Sukarno's power, many marines grew disillusioned; taken to an extreme, some took to the jungle in support of PKI remnants.

The most threatening of these rebel bands was taking shape along the border of Central and East Java near the village of Nginggil. Led by a former village chieftain and black magician named Mbah Suro, Suharto was so concerned about this latest leftist threat that he called for a military sweep in early 1967.

Selected to spearhead this action was an RPKAD company from Battalion 3. Departing Semarang by truck on 5 March, they arrived in Nginggil and marched to the head of a column comprised of elements of three infantry battalions. Two days later, they walked straight into an ambush. In the ensuing half-hour firefight, three commandos were killed. Breaking contact, they called in the infantry and showed little quarter. Eighty-nine communist suspects were subsequently killed, including several ex-marines. The threat from Mbah Suro promptly subsided.[19]

During this same timeframe, reports of pro-PKI army deserters began to filter in from the easternmost extreme of Java near the town of Banyuwangi. This was soon after Group 4 had been officially formed, and it was this group that was called to dispatch *sandhi yudha* operatives to the scene.

While Group 4 was theoretically being molded on the U.S. Army Special Forces in terms of structure and function, the RPKAD had yet to work out the details. For the Banyuwangi deployment, they prepared an ad hoc 22-man team under the command of Lieutenant Feisal Tanjung. Previously with Battalion 3, Feisal had been head of the company that had distinguished itself during operations at the *Republik Radio Indonesia* building in Jakarta, Halim airbase, and across Central Java. In July 1967, he had joined Group 4 as one of its initial cast of officers.

Taking a train from Jakarta, Feisal's team crossed Java. Switching to a bus at Surabaya, they disembarked at Banyuwangi. All of the members wore civilian clothes and were armed with AK-47 rifles with folding stocks. For the next seven months, they roamed in and around the town to surreptitiously gather intelligence. The deployment proved somewhat anticlimactic, as just three deserters armed with pistols were ultimately apprehended.[20]

Immediately thereafter, yet another PKI pocket flared in East Java. This time, the guerrillas were active in southern Blitar district near the coast. This grabbed Jakarta's attention because Blitar was where Sukarno had spent his youth; there were fears that Sukarno's latent hometown support and communist militants could make a dangerous mix. To nix this, the armed forces in May 1968 penned plans for Operation Trisula ("trident"). Utilizing most of an airborne brigade for the sweep, the RPKAD was tasked with collecting battlefield intelligence. To do this, a mixed team of seven commando sergeants were dispatched (three from Group 2, four from Group 4) on a four-month tour. Passing on the information to the paratroopers, this final PKI remnant on Java soon became history.

Although Indonesia's generals were sensitive to PKI guerrillas close to home, the threats on Java paled in comparison to those on the island of Kalimantan. Here the headache was of Jakarta's own making. During the Sukarno regime, the government's intelligence agency had helped raise, shield, and arm the leftist PGRS guerrilla movement. Ostensibly created to liberate Sarawak from Malaysian rule, the PGRS increasingly spent as much time proselytizing with PKI cadres in West Kalimantan as it did running cross-border activities. The same was true of a smaller PGRS splinter faction known as the North Kalimantan People's Force (*Pasukan Rakyat Kalimantan Utara*, or Paraku), which was primarily active along the central border of West Kalimantan.

By the time of the October 1965 upheaval in Jakarta, the lines between the PGRS, Paraku, and PKI had almost fully blurred. Although the RPKAD cooperated with the PGRS as late as June 1966, there was a complete reversal of attitude by October. During that month, a small military task force pushed toward PGRS/Paraku border camps as part of Operation Tertib ("order"). Their message to the ethnic Chinese guerrillas was blunt: surrender or be killed.

The campaign was a resounding failure. Thumbing their collective noses at the government, less than one hundred rallied. More than seven times that amount took to the jungle with their weapons, including two hundred from Paraku and numerous senior PKI officials from West Kalimantan.

Trying again, the government launched Operation Sapu Bersih ("Clean Sweep") in March 1967. Poorly coordinated, this venture also made no gains. Worse, the PGRS was starting to retaliate with raids against army supply lines. Then on 16 July, Chinese partisans launched a surprise attack on an air force base north of Pontianak and made off with more than one hundred weapons.[21]

This last action brought about an immediate government response. Throwing together plans for Sapu Bersih II, the call went out to the RPKAD for an initial contribution to what would eventually become a four thousand-man task force. The request was passed to the newly formed Group 2 at Magelang, which dispatched its Detachment 24. That detachment was commanded by Captain Samsudin; a former combat engineer, Samsudin in 1965 had been one of six young officers who transferred from the engineers to the RPKAD in order to bolster the latter's expertise in demolitions.[22]

Arriving in Pontianak one week after the airbase attack, Samsudin steered his commandos toward the border. Although Detachment 24 was supposed to consist of three companies, its troop strength was actually one-third the authorized amount. Confronting them were four pockets of PGRS strung along the western third of the West Kalimantan frontier, plus a single Paraku pocket further east. One of the PGRS guerrilla bands was led by a China-trained commandant named Lai Pa Ka; another band was led by Sofyan, the PKI's ranking cadre member in West Kalimantan.

Significantly outnumbered by the communists, the RPKAD spent the first weeks waiting for reinforcements. These arrived in mid-August in the form of a company of air force commandos. Formerly called the PGT, they were now known by the slightly reworked acronym Kopasgat (*Komando Pasukan Gerak Tjepat*, or Quick Reaction Force Command). The reason for the new title was grounded in politics. Under the Sukarno regime, the PGT had attained a high profile and were arguably every bit the RPKAD's equal as an elite commando formation. But shortly before the chaos of October 1965, the PGT had been subordinated within an air force umbrella command alongside anti-aircraft troops and airbase defense forces. Because the airbase defense forces were subsequently involved in the 30 September Movement, the PGT had fallen under a cloud by association. To symbolize its break from this past, they had gotten their new name in May 1966.

After the arrival of the Kopasgat company, reinforcements from across the armed forces soon began to pour in. Surging into the PGRS sanctuaries in August and September, the troops began to inflict heavy guerrilla losses. In return, the first fatality on the government side was an RPKAD corporal.

Though finally making progress against the guerrillas, the military was growing impatient. Looking for an unconventional shortcut, the West Kalimantan regional command initiated a secret operation known as Mangkok Merah ("Red Bowl"). This term had significant cultural meaning among the Dayak tribes in the province: when they declare war on an enemy, the Dayak symbolically drink from a bowl filled with blood. If the Dayak could be convinced that the Chinese were their enemy, the PGRS/Paraku would be the toast of the Red Bowl.

This is exactly what happened in October. That month, several Dayak chieftains were mysteriously killed. When the PGRS was fingered, the Dayak predictably declared war. For the remainder of the year, the military sat back as the tribesmen unleashed their infamous fury. Hundreds of guerrillas were killed or captured; hundreds more, including Lai Pa Ka, surrendered.

There was a problem, however. Not limiting their attacks to guerrillas, the Dayak started terrorizing Chinese in general. By the time rioting subsided in early 1968, the local economy had been severely disrupted and some sixty thousand ethnic Chinese had fled to makeshift refugee camps near Pontianak. Worse from the government's perspective, Mangkok Merah had the counterproductive effect of stimulating guerrilla recruitment. Suddenly and inadvertently, the PGRS/Paraku movement had a new lease on life.[23]

On the other side of Kalimantan, problems were being encountered along the border with Sabah. Here, too, the issue was of the government's own making. During Confrontation, hundreds of Indonesian civilians had been loosely trained as part of the quasi-notional TNKU. Most were unemployed urban youth scrounged from cities in Kalimantan and Sulawesi. When Confrontation ended and the fiction of the TNKU was abandoned, they were left behind at their border camps.

Ex-TNKU members were not the only thing left behind. In its haste to leave, the government did not bother to disarm the volunteers. Moreover, the last infantrymen departing Long Bawan had not wanted to be inconvenienced with hauling out heavy machineguns and mortars. These weapons, too, had been abandoned in place.

Predictably, the ready supply of weapons and unemployed volunteers became a volatile combination. By late 1967, Jakarta had received reports that the former TNKU partisans were stealing food and raping women in the Long Bawan vicinity. Colonel Mung, the former RPKAD commander now serving as head of the military region, reported that the outgunned local government was screaming for help.

Jakarta was in a fix. For a sizable infantry unit to respond, it would take up to three weeks for them to make their way upriver from the Kalimantan coast. In need of a more rapid response, the RPKAD got the assignment. Scouring available resources, it was decided to dispatch an ad hoc detachment consisting of a para-commando company from Group 3 and a *sandhi yudha* team from Group 4. Significantly, the detachment commander, Captain Alex Setiabudi, and the officer leading the Group 4 contribution, Captain Kentot Harseno, had both previously served at Long Bawan.

During the first week of January 1968, the designated units assembled at Cijantung. Because of the lack of suitable runways, they would be making a combat jump into paddies a half-hour trek east of Long Bawan. Although they would be parachuting with their weapons—including two rocket launchers—they were correctly concerned about opposition they might face. The ex-volunteers, after all, were better armed and knew the lay of the land after living there for almost four years.

But rather than repeating the mistakes made in West Kalimantan— where military offensives had only served to harden PGRS resolve—Captain Kentot suggested a more nuanced approach. "It would be better not to go in with full force," he counseled, "but rather with gifts like food, writing pads, and clothes."[24]

Kentot's idea was adopted—with precautions. At 0200 hours on 10 January, a pair of Hercules transports departed Jakarta on what was codenamed Operation Linud X ("Airborne X"). Approaching Long Bawan just after first light, Captain Alex stood at the head of a ten-man pathfinder stick. He carried two flares: red if he encountered resistance on the ground, green if it was okay for the jump to continue.

Moments before reaching their target, one of the commandos got a case of the nerves and pulled his reserve chute inside the cabin. Jumpmasters descended on him, ordering him to remove the reserve and retake his place in the stick.

Coming over the dropzone, silk canopies mushroomed in the wake of the lead Hercules. Landing near a pig enclosure, Alex reached for his AK-47 and braced for possible resistance. With none forthcoming, he broke out the green flare.

As the remainder of the detachment jumped, their only opposition came from the terrain. The rice paddies were adjoined by a swamp, and several of the commandos drifted wide of their mark. Captain Kentot landed in mud up to his armpits and nearly drowned, while a pallet containing one of the rocket launchers knifed into the muck and disappeared.

Regrouping, the commandos pressed down the trail and arrived at Long Bawan village. The wreckage of the downed Hercules still stood where it crash-landed more than two years earlier. Waiting nearby was the village chief, who greeted Captain Alex like an old friend. Beckoning all available Dayak, the chief immediately tasked them with collecting weapons from nearby cache sites. The rebels proved to be extremely tame, taking kindly to the gifts and offering up their arms with no resistance. "It turned out to be a picnic," said Kentot.[25]

Four months later, with smiles all around, the RPKAD detachment packed to leave. With the air force's Soviet-made helicopter inventory now grounded due to a spare parts embargo from Moscow, the commandos were forced to hike to the nearest river landing. After a speedboat shuttle toward the coast, they were back on Java by June. For once, what had the potential for being another festering security challenge had been resolved without firing a shot.

1   Interview with Todo Sihombing, 8 September 1999. The Lao contingent was a constant disciplinary challenge. Judged to be of poor mental and physical aptitude, they had only five weeks of language training and had difficulty following instructions. Several balked during the final Long March—"in Laos, we use helicopters"—and many frustrated their instructors by their less-than-martial attitude. Said CIA Station Chief Hugh Tovar: "We got word that the Indonesians were complaining the Lao were contracting a lot of venereal diseases."

2   Lieutenant Sentot Sugiarto, who led the Commando Section at Batu Jajar, escorted a six-man RPKAD team to Laos for approximately two months. They remained at Kong Le's Vang Vieng garrison to oversee the formation of a new battalion—*Bataillon Volontaire 58*—that incorporated the Indonesian-trained students.

3   On 9 March 1966, Major Soeweno, a Fort Benning airborne graduate, became the new commander of Battalion 2. The previous Battalion 2 commander, Major Sugiarto, became the new commander of Battalion 3.

4   Soekarno interview.

5   In 1965, there was a short-lived attempt to merge the airborne training schools used by the PGT and RPKAD into a single Combined Airborne Training Command (*Komando Gabungan Pendidkan Para*). Staffed by a handful of army and air force personnel, the command theoretically intended to run all further parachute training only from Margahayu. In reality, however, the Batu Jajar school never ceased offering airborne instruction. Moreover, because the air force fell out of favor due to Omar Dani's support for the 30 September Movement, the idea of having the air force monopolize airborne training at Margahayu did not sit well with the army generals. As a result, the combined training command concept was quietly dropped in mid-1966.

6   Soekarno interview; Todo Sihombing interview.

7   Looking to put his personal imprint on the regiment, Edhie in February 1966 ditched the name of Menparkoad—which had been conjured by his predecessor, Mung—and instead officially renamed the RPKAD as the *Pusat Pasukan Khusus Angkatan Darat* ("Army Special Forces Center"). At the same time, the Batu Jajar school was renamed from Separkoad to *Pusat Pendidkan Pasukan Khusus Angkatan Darat* ("Army Special Forces Training Center"). In reality, the name "RPKAD" remained in common usage.

8   FRUS, 1964-68, Vol. XXVI, "Telegram from Embassy in Indonesia to Department of State," dated 15 March 1967, p. 497.

9   Widjojo Soejono interview.

10 O.G. Roeder, *The Smiling General* (Jakarta: Gunung Agung Ltd., 1969), p. 142.

11 Each of the groups was allowed to create rectangular ceremonial flags, which would indicate a brigade-sized unit (as opposed to triangular flags for battalions).

12 All existing companies were redesignated once the groups came into being. For example, Battalion 1's Company A became Company 111 under Detachment 11. The company's first two digits indicated its detachment affiliation.

13 Not only was Group 3 split between two locales, but even its detachments were bifurcated: Detachment 37 had one company at Semarang and two at Solo.

14 Santosa had been one of the last RPKAD officers to receive special forces training at Fort Bragg before Washington placed all courses related to guerrilla warfare off limits to Indonesians due to Confrontation. FRUS, 1964-68, Vol. XXVI, "Memorandum from Rusk to Johnson," dated 6 January 1964, p. 5.

15 To bolster Group 4, Batu Jajar conducted three more *sandhi yudha* cycles during 1967, resulting in 244 more members.

16 Soerjo Hanjono interview.

17 Kentot Harseno interview.

18 A relative by marriage to former intelligence chief Soebandrio, Hartono later committed suicide under mysterious circumstances.

19 *Bahaya Laten Komunisme di Indonesia*, p. 162; Soekarno interview.

20 Dalio interview.

21 CIA Intelligence Memorandum, "Security Problem in Indonesian Borneo," dated 20 March 1968, p. 4.

22 Interview with Samsudin, 30 September 1999.

23 CIA Intelligence Memorandum, "Security Problem in Indonesian Borneo," dated 20 March 1968, p. 5.

24 Kentot Harseno interview.

25 Kentot Harseno interview; Soekarno interview.

CHAPTER THIRTEEN

FREE CHOICE

In 1968, *The Green Berets* hit theaters worldwide. A John Wayne vehicle that updated the Western genre to the fast-escalating Vietnam War, the film exposed and glamorized the U.S. Army Special Forces like never before. In one particularly memorable scene, a twelve-man team of unconventional warfare operators was showcased at a press conference; displaying their ability to operate in foreign environments, members of the team gave a briefing in languages like German and Danish.

While the movie was widely panned for its wooden acting and blatant agitprop message, *The Green Berets* had a profound effect at an unlikely place: Cijantung. As Indonesian army students had been forbidden from attending courses at Fort Bragg for almost five years (due to restrictions imposed during Confrontation), the cinematic depiction of the U.S. Army Special Forces filled the gap and provided inspiration for the RPKAD's Group 4.

Until that time, the Indonesian take on special warfare had been ad hoc and confused. Although Group 4 was supposed to the equivalent of the Special Forces in mandate and structure—as opposed to the para-commandos, who approximated airborne rangers—the reality was that the group's training regimen had little focus. Its internal organization (broken into detachments) was nearly identical to its sister para-commando groups. Moreover, RPKAD commanders did not seem to appreciate how to best use *sandhi yudha* operatives. In places like East Java, they had been employed for combat intelligence collection; in East Kalimantan, they had been used interchangeably with para-commandos during the non-event at Long Bawan.

Deciding it liked Hollywood's model, Group 4 underwent a thorough reorganization in late 1968. Parroting the basic building block of the U.S. Army Special Forces—the twelve-man Operational Detachment, popularly known as an A-Team—Group 4 divided its members into nearly identical thirteen-man units known as *prayudha* (literally, "pre-war"). Led by a captain, each *prayudha* would include a deputy commander, two medics, an operations sergeant, two intelligence/territorial operations specialists, two communications specialists, two weapons specialists, a logistician, and a combat engineer/demolitions specialist.[1]

More important, the *prayudha* would have a true special forces role. Like the DPC of the Irian campaign, this entailed the ability to operate alone for extended periods in a hostile environment. It also meant working closely with rural populations, conducting civic action missions to win their support and, if needed, providing paramilitary training to raise local militias.

To do this effectively, *prayudha* members needed to be aware of cultural sensitivities in their areas of operation. They also needed to be able to communicate with their subjects, a challenge given that Indonesian was not fluently spoken in some far-flung parts of the archipelago; just like the Green Berets on film (and in reality), the special forces of Group 4 would have a multi-linguistic requirement.

Providing oversight for the *prayudha* was the *karsa yudha*. With *karsa* the Sanskrit term for "desire" or "willingness," the *karsa yudha*—so named because it targeted the enemy's desire to perpetrate a war—was directly analogous to the U.S. Special Forces B-Team. Led by a major, the *karsa yudha* would control a twenty-man headquarters staff and four *prayudha*. Taking the place of the existing detachments in Group 4, the *karsa yudha*—though numbering only seventy-two members—would be considered equivalent to a battalion. Long-term plans called for up to six *karsa yudha*, all of which answered to the Group 4 headquarters.

Following this blueprint, the group began reassigning its members and initiating new courses to raise necessary skill sets. By the opening of 1969, three understrength *karsa yudha* had roughly taken shape—though only one had the human resources that approximated those needed for an unconventional warfare mission. Showcasing this single *karsa yudha*, a demonstration was held at Cijantung for the army commander, General Maraden Panggabean. It was a scene—quite literally—from *The Green Berets*. Remembers RPKAD chief Widjojo:

One of the *prayudha* came to attention in front of Panggabean. The commander stepped forward and gave his job outline in Chinese. The deputy commander then stepped forward and spoke in Arabic.[2]

The reorganization of Group 4 came at an opportune time. In West Irian, where Indonesia was obliged to conduct an independence referendum before the end of the decade, OPM guerrillas were proving difficult to pacify. They were still primarily operating in the Bird's Head, with two Arfak concentrations near Manokwari and a smaller band taking shape near the town of Sorong.

Arriving in June 1968 to take control of the situation was the former RPKAD chief, Brigadier General Sarwo Edhie. In part because of his proven leadership ability, and in even larger part because Suharto wanted him far from Jakarta, Edhie had gotten the assignment as military commander of West Irian during the critical period before the referendum.

When Edhie arrived, he found the earlier Sadar campaign continuing with little direction or apparent success. Changing tack, he tried a softer approach than his predecessor by unilaterally releasing dozens of detainees. Then in early November he showered surrender leaflets over the Bird's Head in an attempt to woo ralliers.

Later that same month, he tried a more personal approach. During the 1962 Irian campaign, DPC team leader Heru Sisnodo had befriended several Irianese chieftains while evading through the jungle near Kaimana. Networking from these acquaintances, it was found that they were linked to the senior OPM commandant near Manokwari, Lodewijk Mandatjan.

Although a long shot, it was decided to send a team under Heru into the jungle near Manokwari to negotiate directly with Lodewijk. For Heru, this was a chance at redemption: with his previous PKI links exposed, he had been sidelined as a *sandhi yudha* instructor at Batu Jajar.

The gamble worked. On 23 December, Heru and his team made contact with senior Arfak rebels Lodewijk and Barens Mandatjan. Enticing them to surrender, they were escorted by Sarwo Edhie to Jakarta on 7 January 1969 as a belated New Year's present to the government. Both were given the honorary rank of major. Nearly 600 other rebels surrendered at the same time, bringing with them 106 antiquated weapons.

Though this represented a large percentage of the thin OPM ranks, Jakarta wanted the remaining pockets of guerrillas eliminated ahead of the referendum. Having exhausted the soft approach, Edhie got tough. In early February 1969, he finalized plans to resume combat operations across the territory. Unlike the halting Sadar campaign, the new effort—codenamed Wibawa, or "Authority"—would involve 6,220 men spread across the entire territory.

As the RPKAD's contribution for Wibawa, Group 4 was to field a *karsa yudha* for the first time. Because of the lack of qualified majors, chosen to head the unit was Captain Feisal Tanjung, the same officer who had led Group 4's first team deployment to East Java two years earlier. Feisal was permitted to form a composite *karsa yudha*, bringing together the best members from across the group to make four subordinate *prayudha*. Moreover, each *prayudha*—which, due to a dearth of qualified captains in Group 4, would be led by lieutenants—were to be temporarily augmented with extra support personnel, swelling them to twenty members apiece.

By the second week of February, Feisal had his *karsa yudha* chosen and ready for deployment. To give the unit wide coverage, he intended to deploy the *prayudha* to four different locations. The first, Prayudha 1 (abbreviated to PY 1) under Lieutenant Kuntara, was to operate on Biak island. Of partial Chinese descent, Kuntara had grown up exposed to Mandarin and was Group 4's foremost linguist in that tongue. PY 2, under Lieutenant Saparwadi, was responsible for the Fak-Fak sector.

Command of PY 3 was held by Lieutenant Sintong Pandjaitan. A Batak Christian from North Sumatra, Sintong had served as a platoon commander in Feisal's company in Battalion 3. During that time, he had personally led such operations as the retaking of the radio center at Merdeka Square in 1965. His *prayudha* would be responsible for the Manokwari sector, where Sintong had already served an RPKAD tour during 1967.

The last *prayudha*, PY 4, was commanded by Lieutenant Wismoyo Arisunandar. Though not the most academically gifted RPKAD officer—he had graduated seventy-third out of eighty infantry cadets at the military academy—Wismoyo was rated as an outstanding motivator of men. PY 4 would cover the southern border near Merauke.

On 18 February, the entire *karsa yudha* had transited through Biak airport and arrived at their four operating locales. At Merauke, Wismoyo's PY 4 was briefed by local security officials about the OPM threat. There were few guerrillas in the vicinity, they were told, and all were poorly armed. However, dozens of Javanese migrant families had been settled around the town; clearing away the jungle and planting crops, they were appealing targets for partisans in need of supplies. The RPKAD's mission was basically to wave the Indonesian flag: overtly patrol the vicinity, gather tactical intelligence about OPM movements, and strike at the guerrillas if the opportunity arose.

For PY 4's Sergeant Sunarya, it was a homecoming of sorts: he was part of the DPC team that jumped into Merauke seven years earlier. He immediately noticed a major difference between the two tours. To maximize its coverage, PY 4 had sub-divided into four-man teams. Each of these was matched up with Irianese porters, and together they marched out of town in all directions. For the most part, they mingled among Javanese farmers. "In the DPC days we stayed in the jungle," he recalled. "This time, we stayed in developed areas."[3]

On one occasion when PY 4 strayed from migrant settlements, West Irian proved deadly. On 4 April, two members of the *prayudha* and two Irianese porters walked east toward the border. Four days later, they were spending the night at a tribal hut when OPM guerrillas crept inside. Both Indonesians were slashed to death with knives and axes; a porter met the same fate. Grabbing an AK-47 and Thompson submachine gun from their victims, the guerrillas slipped across the border into the Australian trust territory on the eastern side of the island.

When word of the losses got back to Wismoyo, he was predictably enraged. Grabbing ten of his men, he raced to the scene. A river ran across the border in that area, and the RPKAD troops were able to see what looked like armed OPM combatants on the opposite shore. Without pause, the team crossed the frontier, settled the score, and returned. Verbally reprimanded for the border violation by his *karsa yudha* commander, Wismoyo was expressly forbidden from staging further incursions.

For the remainder of PY 4's tour—which lasted fourteen months—boredom was the chief opponent. Except for the 8 April ambush, no members of the *prayudha* ever experienced armed contact with the OPM. "We never actually saw them in the field," said Sunarya. "We only received information that they had passed through an area, and never in groups larger than seven men."[4]

Much the same story was being experienced by the other three *prayudha*. In Biak, Kuntara's men encountered fleeting opposition on only a single occasion when they attempted to pull down an OPM flag. In Fak-Fak, the sector was tranquil. Most surprising of all, Manokwari was also placid—

perhaps because most of the previous year's ralliers had come from that area, depleting the OPM's numbers from this traditional hotspot.[5]

Not all of West Irian was so peaceful. During March, over eighty armed Irianese police auxiliaries revolted in the Paniai Lakes district. Roughly centered in West Irian, the district was the most heavily populated and cultivated part of the island. Several small towns—Eranotali, Wagete, Maunemani—quickly fell to the dissidents. Emboldened, villagers soon began digging holes into five area airstrips to prevent government reinforcements from landing.

Taken by surprise, Sarwo Edhie overflew the region on 29 March. As he spotted the damage to the runways, shots rang up from below. Incensed, Edhie wanted the revolt quelled immediately. Getting there, however, posed a problem. Some of Irian's highest peaks surrounded the district, making overland travel from the coast a time-consuming venture. The sabotage to the airstrips, meanwhile, frustrated landings by fixed-wing aircraft. (Rotary-wing landings were also precluded because Indonesia's small helicopter fleet was almost fully grounded due to a spare parts embargo from the Soviet Union.) Yet again, parachutes were the only viable alternative.

Favoring his alma mater, Edhie turned to Feisal and requested an airborne task force to lead the campaign into the lakes district. Cognizant that civilian deaths might encourage sympathy for the OPM, he urged the RPKAD captain to limit Irianese casualties.

Canvassing across his *karsa yudha*, Feisal quickly selected nineteen members. Armed with AK-47 assault rifles, they strapped on chutes and boarded a C-130 transport at Biak on the morning of 4 May. Their target was Wagete, a lakeside settlement midway between the two other rebel-controlled towns. Leaping from the Hercules, the team landed near the shore of the lake and went into combat mode—only to find that the rebels had skipped town.[6]

Filling in the holes to the runway, the special forces were at the tarmac as Sarwo Edhie and Feisal landed. With a platoon of police rangers arriving soon afterward, Edhie ordered the RPKAD to scout ahead of the rangers toward Eranotali. This promised to be an exhausting hike along a mountainous trail, compounded by the possibility of encountering well-armed dissident police en route.[7]

Personally taking the lead with six of his men, Feisal kept a fast pace. Approaching Eranotali on 8 May, they split up to enter the town from three directions. One pair of commandos scaled the adjoining high ground, atop of which was the machine gun that fired on Edhie's plane. Finding the weapon abandoned, they picked up a discarded Indonesian flag and raised it on a pole to signal there was no resistance. As this was happening, a second RPKAD team marched from Wagete west to Maunemani and found a similar lack of resistance. The Paniai Lakes revolt was declared over, though the dissident police had fled to fight another day.

For the next two months, the *karsa yudha* saw almost no military action. The territory, however, was a hive of political activity as the much-heralded independence referendum—dubbed the "Act of Free Choice" by Indonesia—began in mid-July. Living up to the letter but perhaps not the spirit of its promise, Jakarta had chosen 1,025 village elders to cast their vote on behalf of West Irian's 800,000 residents. Indonesian officials oversaw the entire process, with foreign observers arriving only to see the last 200 votes. On 4 August, the unsurprising results—overwhelming support for integration with Indonesia—were announced and quickly accepted by the United Nations.

With the referendum labeled a resounding success by Jakarta, most of the Wibawa troops began returning home before the final quarter of the year. Part of the *karsa yudha* was among those leaving, though Captain Feisal retained fifteen of his men for an unusual assignment. A camera crew from the National Broadcasting Corporation in New York had received government approval to film a documentary at an unspoiled Irian village whose residents were still living in the Stone Age. Feisal's team was assigned to escort the cameramen during the month-long expedition.

On the morning of 2 October, after three weeks of delays due to tardy equipment shipments from Japan, the expedition members piled into a civilian DC-3 transport. Their targeted village—nicknamed Valley X—was centered along West Irian's eastern border.

Chosen as pathfinder was RPKAD Lieutenant Sintong Pandjaitan. Outfitted with a camera mounted on a helmet, he was to parachute into Valley X and make first contact with the villagers. The plan then called for the DC-3 to make a large orbit before returning for further drops.

Upon a signal from the cabin, Sintong exited the plane and descended into the valley. Landing in a tight muddy clearing that passed as the village square, he worked fast to strip off his chute and helmet. Just as he finished, Irianese wearing nothing more than penis gourds poured from their huts. All were carrying bows, and all were aiming their arrows at the lieutenant.

Recalling a briefing he had received from a Catholic missionary before departure, Sintong tried to adopt a non-threatening pose. Making a welcoming motion with open outstretched hands, his AK-47 slipped off his shoulder and fell to the ground. With his weapon out of immediate reach and the villagers still closing in with their arrows at the ready, Sintong suddenly felt extremely vulnerable.

Just then, the DC-3 came back overhead. Hearing the drone of the plane's props, the villagers fled back into their huts. Sintong used this as his cue to scoop up his rifle and sprint in the opposite direction.[8]

Seconds later, the second stick of paratroopers—including Feisal—landed at the same clearing. Growing more confident with their increased numbers, the RPKAD commandos beckoned the villagers. This time they came not bearing arrows, but a clump of cooked pork. Sintong took the porcine offering and took a bite. Seeing their gift was accepted, the villagers pantomimed a warm welcome to the visitors.

For the next four weeks, the RPKAD escorts remained at Valley X. Almost fully cut off from the outside world, the village was an anthropologist's dream. The cameramen shot numerous reels of film, after which the entire expedition boarded rubber boats and began a slow exfiltration to civilization.

Elsewhere in West Irian, the OPM threat had subsided to a handful of isolated pockets. Overseeing the government response was a new military region commander, Colonel Acub Zainal. Replacing Sarwo Edhie in January 1970, Acub favored using local Irianese troops and social programs—especially sports—to make inroads among the population. The strategy bore fruit. In late October, army intermediaries made contact with Ferry Awom, the last high-ranking OPM leader roaming the hills south of Manokwari. On 19 November, he accepted government amnesty and came in from the jungle. Wearing a necklace of crocodile teeth and a bush hat adorned with a piratical skull and crossbones, Ferry solemnly shook hands with Acub and signed a document pledging his loyalty to Jakarta.

The epithet to the secessionist struggle in West Irian, it seemed, was ready to be penned.

1   Although twelve men was the norm, U.S. Army Special Forces A-Teams were flexible; some, like those deployed to Laos in 1959, were pared down to eight members, while others, like many of those sent to South Vietnam, were expanded to fourteen. The structure of the *prayudha*, too, was somewhat flexible, with some early teams counting just twelve members.

2   Widjojo Soejono interview.

3   Interview with E. Sunarya, 5 August 2000.

4   Ibid.

5   Sintong Pandjaitan interview. Besides the fatalities suffered by PY 4, a communications officer attached to the *karsa yudha* staff, Lieutenant Hazmi, was killed in an OPM ambush on 28 June south of Jayapura (the post-1962 name for Hollandia).

6   Untung Suroso interview.

7   The police rangers—translated into Indonesian as *pelopor*—traced their origins to the police contingent trained by the U.S. Army Special Forces on Okinawa in 1959. By 1962, they had been expanded into a ranger battalion. Expanded yet again two years later into a regiment, its members infiltrated mainland Malaysia six times on sabotage missions during Confrontation. In the course of those missions, 33 policemen were killed and 76 captured. A detachment from the airborne-qualified regiment was deployed to West Irian during Operation Wibawa. Atim Supomo and Djumarwan, *Pelopor*, p. 110.

8   Sintong Pandjaitan interview.

CHAPTER FOURTEEN

FLAMBOYAN

The operations of the first *karsa yudha* in West Irian had hardly conformed to a true special forces model. After all, there had been little attempt by the four *prayudha* to perform civic action missions ("territorial" operations, in Indonesian parlance), much less raise tribal militias and conduct guerrilla warfare. Rather, they had yet again been channeled toward more conventional fare like small-unit patrolling and pathfinding for conventional assaults.

Still, the deployment had captured imaginations within the RPKAD and army hierarchy. Even though Group 4 had yet to meet its authorized strength, it was decided to upgrade a second formation—the para-commandos of Group 3—to special warfare status. Selecting its best members for the *sandhi yudha* course at Batu Jajar, the remainder were transferred to Groups 1 and 2. By mid-1970, Group 3 fielded five skeletal *karsa yudha*; three of them, and the headquarters, were based in Solo, while the other two were in Semarang.[1]

With this transformation, the RPKAD was evenly divided between two para-commando and two *sandhi yudha* groups. As the latter looked like the wave of the future, it was further decided to reflect the changing emphasis with a new name. On 17 February 1971, the regiment was redesignated as the Special Warfare Forces Command (*Komando Pasukan Sandhi Yudha*, or Kopassandha). At the same time, the Batu Jajar school became officially known as the Special Warfare and Airborne Center (*Pusat Sandhi Yudha dan Lintas Udara*). References to its original commando lineage had been struck from both titles.

Overseeing this transition was a new commander. Back on 16 April 1970, Brigadier General Widjojo had received reassignment as chief of the North

Sulawesi military region. Replacing him as the new head of the RPKAD was his handpicked deputy, Brigadier General Witarmin. Both hailing from East Java, Witarmin had served as a company commander in Widjojo's infantry battalion two decades earlier. Though not commando qualified, Witarmin was a paratrooper and had earned kudos for leading Operation Trisula against the PKI remnants in Blitar. Moreover, Witarmin was no newcomer to the RPKAD; in August 1969, Widjojo had secured his transfer to the regiment as his deputy, filling the long vacant slot left by the argumentative Prijo Pranoto.

The change from the RPKAD to Kopassandha proved a turning point in more ways than one. Although the regiment had experienced much growth during Widjojo's tenure, it had been a period of relative isolation. During the Sukarno era, the RPKAD had benefited from cross-fertilization with other elite units around the world: American, British, North Vietnamese, Yugoslavian. The regiment had even been able to impart its skills to others, notably the Lao.

But after October 1965, external contact had been almost fully curtailed. This partly stemmed from Suharto's more isolationist foreign policy, which was a stark reversal from the adventurism of Sukarno. Aside from a trio of Malaysian students who briefly visited Batu Jajar in 1968, no other foreigners were allowed to attend the school. The lack of contact, too, was partly a holdover from Confrontation, with both the U.S. and Britain still embargoing special warfare courses for Indonesian students.

Under Witarmin, Kopassandha started to come out of its shell. The testing ground was the Khmer Republic—formerly the Kingdom of Cambodia—where a non-communist government led by armed forces chief Lon Nol had come to power in March 1970. The similarities between Lon Nol and Suharto were striking. Both were soft-spoken, underestimated generals who deposed charismatic, left-leaning civilian leaders. Both, too, faced armed challenges from communist parties. In the case of Indonesia, Suharto had succeeded in wiping out the PKI. The Khmer Republic had a far tougher job, facing not only a formidable domestic leftist insurgency—the Khmer Rouge—but also tens of thousands of communist Vietnamese combatants that used the eastern third of Cambodia as a sanctuary.

Compounding Lon Nol's problem was the fact that his military had long been neglected during the royalist days. By the time he took power in March 1970, it numbered just 30,000 poorly trained and badly equipped members.

Desperate to exponentially expand that number, Lon Nol's top assistants wrote letters to regional non-communist nations to request military assistance. One of the very first such requests arrived in Jakarta on 14 April.[2]

Although the Indonesians were predisposed toward helping, there was debate over what it could, or should, offer. Several generals were reportedly in favor of sending Indonesian military units to defend Phnom Penh. But other key leaders, notably Foreign Minister Adam Malik, were not comfortable with any high-profile intervention in Indochina.

Avoiding any controversial decisions for the time being, the Indonesian military limited its assistance to material aid. Gathering all of the Soviet-made AK-47 rifles from the ranks of the RPKAD's Group 1, these were rushed to the Khmer army. This had been done with a wink and a nod from Washington, which arranged for the regiment to be the first Indonesian formation incrementally re-equipped with M-16 assault rifles.[3]

To explore other areas where it might help Cambodia, Colonel Seno Hartono was dispatched to Phnom Penh in September 1970 for an extended fact-finding mission. A graduate of U.S. ranger training, Seno had been commander of the Batu Jajar school for the past five years. Once in the Khmer Republic, he was provided a helicopter and given carte blanche to tour dozens of garrisons and battlefronts over nine months.[4]

From this exposure, it became apparent that the country had more than enough recruits—but was sorely lacking in training. Already, Thailand and the U.S. (from bases in South Vietnam) had initiated programs of instruction. On the basis of Seno's recommendation—strongly influenced by his own background—Indonesia agreed to put a sixty-man Cambodian contingent through airborne and commando courses.

In helping select the sixty, Seno looked for a combination of health and mental aptitude. He was limited to two pools of prospects. The first came from the 2 Airborne Battalion, considered one of the best in the Khmer army. And to show affinity with Indonesia's vast religious majority, the second was from the 5 Infantry Brigade; this brigade was the only Khmer unit composed of Cham, Cambodia's small Muslim minority. In the interests of parity, roughly half of the pupils would be paratroopers, and the other half Cham.[5]

In September 1971, Seno escorted the Khmer contingent back to Indonesia. For the next five weeks, they underwent a crash Indonesian language course. After that, they arrived at Batu Jajar. For the next nine months, the contingent went in quick succession through a basic infantry primer, then jump school, and finally the commando course.

Some of the school's cadre were less than impressed with the Khmer. "Becoming a commando is 50 percent mental, 30 percent physical, and 20 percent technical," said one trainer, "but the Cambodians did not seem to have the mental skills."[6] Those with institutional memory, however, saw reason for cheer. "They were a lot better than the Lao," said another commando instructor who had been present in 1965.[7]

In mid-1972, the contingent graduated. Each was issued a set of distinctive Kopassandha camouflage (the vertical stripe design was a holdover from the RPKAD days), army wings, and a red beret with the Indonesian para-commando badge. Flown home to the Khmer Republic, the Cham returned to their parent 5 Infantry Brigade. Those from the paratroop battalion were immediately sent to South Vietnam for an additional course in reconnaissance patrolling, then were used as the cadre for a new training center specializing in commando and reconnaissance tactics. Three years later, in the final desperate weeks of the dying republic, the bulk of the Indonesian graduates were rushed back to Phnom Penh and used as the core of a quickly assembled Para-Commando Battalion. Sent to guard the dikes north of the capital, they were overrun by the Khmer Rouge and slaughtered to the man.[8]

Cambodians were not the only foreigners passing through Batu Jajar in 1972. When the Khmer had reached the second semester of their commando training, a contingent of over 150 Malaysians arrived to take the same course. These students came from the Malaysian Special Service Regiment (MSSR), an airborne commando formation first raised with British marine assistance in March 1965. Between these Malaysians and the Cambodians, foreign pupils temporarily outnumbered Indonesian students at Batu Jajar by more than three to one.

Kopassandha's renewed contacts with the international special forces community was a two-way street. In 1972, two officers from the unit attended the Fifth Special Forces Commanders' Conference in South Korea, an annual gathering of senior commando and unconventional warfare officers from non-communist Southeast Asian and Pacific countries. And during the following November, Kopassandha headquarters at Cijantung was the venue for the sixth such gathering.

After a long hiatus, Kopassandha students began venturing overseas for specialized courses. In 1971, a pair of its officers received jungle warfare instruction in Australia. The following year, Captain Bambang Soembodo, an instructor from Batu Jajar, spent eleven months in the U.S. attending jumpmaster, pathfinder, ranger, and special forces courses. In 1973, Captain Yunus Yosfiah, a deputy *karsa yudha* commander from Group 4, was the next to arrive at Fort Bragg for the special forces course.[9]

Returning a favor, the Malaysians in July 1972 invited a thirty-eight-man Kopassandha contingent to its MSSR training center. Twenty-one of that number were from Group 4; the remainder were para-commandos. For the next three months, the Indonesians and Malaysians cross-trained as integrated patrols. Integration came easy: not only did they speak mutually intelligible languages, but most of the Malaysians were Batu Jajar graduates. In October, this Kopassandha contingent, matched with an equal number of MSSR commandos, flew to Kuching. Under the codename Rajawali ("Hawk"), they were each issued Malaysian army camouflage uniforms and divided into mixed six-man teams. In a stunning reversal from Confrontation, they shuttled by helicopter to the Sarawak frontier and for the next eight months jointly patrolled the border from the Malaysian side.[10]

Rajawali's focus was the diehard remnants of the PGRS and Paraku that were straddling the frontier. In what had become an embarrassment for Jakarta, the ethnic Chinese guerrilla pockets in West Kalimantan were showing remarkable resilience. Ever since 1967, the RPKAD had been rotating detachments to West Kalimantan on nine-month tours in an unsuccessful attempt to deliver a knockout blow to these revolutionaries. For the first three years, the detachments were wholly comprised of para-commandos; all were rated as only moderately successful.

Trying a new approach, the RPKAD detachments—those rotated from 1970 onwards—mixed one para-commando company with a *karsa yudha*. This was the first time such a pairing was attempted since the 1968 Long Bawan mission. The idea was to use the *sandhi yudha* operatives to operate among the locals and gather intelligence, which would then be exploited by para-commando raids.

Though good in theory, the bifurcated task forces did not live up to expectations. "We had a special warfare element," said the operations officer during the 1971 deployment, "but everybody was being used like para-commandos."[11]

During 1972, two combined Kopassandha detachments rotated through West Kalimantan. The second of these was Task Force 42 (so named because it mixed a *karsa yudha* from Group 4 and a para-commando company from Group 2) under the command of Major Sintong Pandjaitan. The same officer who had parachuted into West Irian's Valley X, Sintong was fixated on a particularly elusive Paraku commander. Through mid-1973, his task force tracked its target. In the end, however, they came up empty handed. "We thought we shot him," said one member, "but he managed to cross into Sarawak."[12]

Hearing this, the government was not impressed. Not only were the PGRS and Paraku an ongoing irritant, but Jakarta was fuming that PKI leader Sofyan was still roaming the same jungle and providing de facto leadership for the Chinese partisans. Determined to eliminate this last PKI holdout, Jakarta deployed a second Rajawali contingent (appropriately titled Rajawali 2) to block the Malaysian side of the border through the end of 1973.

At the same time, Brigadier General Seno Hartono was installed as the new West Kalimantan military region commander. Although he had a good reputation after eight years at Batu Jajar (and the interlude in the Khmer Republic), Seno in September 1973 was handed an almost impossible challenge. "I was given one hundred days to crush the PKI," he remembers, "and get Sofyan dead or alive."[13]

With an eye on the calendar, Seno turned to Kopassandha. Already in the province was Cijantung's latest deployment of para-commandos and special warfare troops, codenamed Task Force 31. Nearly doubling it in size, they became the spearhead for what Seno dubbed Operation Gawaru—the name for the fragrant, but rotting, core of a dead tropical tree.

Under the Gawaru plan, the *sandhi yudha* portion of Task Force 31—named Team Halilintar ("Thunderbolt")—moved with unprecedented urgency to surreptitiously gather tactical intelligence on suspected guerrilla-held villages. Armed only with pistols and daggers, they were decidedly vulnerable. When the team commander, Captain Hendropriyono, crept toward one village, Chinese guerrillas brandishing knives sprung an ambush. Hacked deep across the left arm and stomach, the badly wounded captain barely escaped with his life.

Despite such resistance, Halilintar was able to narrow its search for the PKI remnants to a relatively small stretch near the West Kalimantan coast. Passing on this intelligence, para-commandos raided a series of villages and made arrests. On 29 September, one of Sofyan's couriers was captured; under interrogation, he provided leads on his commander's recent movements. Closing the net, Sofyan's wife was captured on 4 October.

With blocking forces in position, a Kopassandha raid was conducted on 12 January 1974. When the dust settled, Sofyan's body was identified among the casualties. At 112 days, Seno had completed his assignment twelve days after the government's deadline. Grateful for closure, Jakarta was not complaining.[14]

Though it had won a symbolic victory in West Kalimantan, the central government had little time to celebrate. Three days after Sofyan's death, Jakarta exploded in an orgy of violence that came to be known as the Malari Affair. Allegedly a violent student reaction against Japan's resurgent economic prowess in Southeast Asia, dozens of civilians were killed and hundreds of Japanese-made vehicles burned.[15]

While true that there was a certain amount of public unease over Japan's economic relations with Indonesia, not all about the Malari Affair was as it seemed. Behind the scenes, a handful of key generals were vying for President Suharto's favor—or perhaps looking to position themselves as a successor. It was that internecine competition that resulted in the riots by student proxy.

Suharto wasted no time taking corrective measures. Much of his focus was on shuffling trusted lieutenants into key intelligence posts. General Yoga Sugomo, a long-time acquaintance who had earlier headed the country's civilian intelligence agency, was brought back to head that agency for a second time. And on 22 January, General Benny Moerdani was rushed home from his consultant general's posting in South Korea and named the highest intelligence official within the Ministry of Defense and Security.[16]

Benny was well preened for the job. For the past nine years, he had risen through the army ranks while serving overseas alternately as an intelligence officer and diplomat. Several of his assignments had been highly sensitive. In 1966, for example, Benny had been instrumental in progressing the negotiations that led to an end to Confrontation. Two years later, he made three discreet visits to South Vietnam in an unofficial capacity to review the U.S. counterinsurgency campaign.

These experiences had made Benny somewhat unique in the Indonesian defense establishment. His overseas exposure gave him an appreciation for the international dimension to security issues too often lacking in the Indonesian military. Moreover, his success as an able intelligence operative had quietly earned him the confidence of the president.

Three months later, the stage was set to put this confidence and experience to the test in a most unlikely proving ground. In distant Lisbon, a small group of disgruntled army officers overthrew Portugal's authoritarian government in a bloodless coup d'etat nicknamed the Carnation Revolution. They were motivated in large part by their bitter counter-insurgency experiences in Africa, where Lisbon had been combating leftist independence movements in its colonies of Angola, Guinea-Bissau, and Mozambique for a decade. Not surprisingly, the coup leaders gave priority to negotiating a commonwealth that would allow Portugal a de facto exit from Africa.

This sudden policy reversal had major implications for Portuguese Timor, the tiny colonial foothold that Lisbon retained amidst the Indonesian archipelago. Encompassing half the island of Timor (plus a couple of offshore islets and an enclave on the western side of the island), a more neglected backwater could hardly have been imagined. During five centuries of colonialism, Portugal had only laid thirty kilometers of asphalt road, given a quarter of one percent of the population a secondary education, and provided one doctor for every 27,000 locals. Not until the sixties had the capital of Dili been wired for electricity. And never once had a senior Portuguese cabinet member ever visited the territory.

For the Timorese themselves, such benign neglect suited them fine. Almost without exception, the Portuguese had not upset the traditional hierarchy and ruled indirectly through existing local chieftains. Moreover, they had not insisted on superimposing its culture or religion; only about a third of Portuguese Timor's 680,000 people thought of themselves as Catholics.

But within a month of the Carnation Revolution and the subsequent mad dash to arrange for a commonwealth, Timorese sentiment began to shift when Portuguese officials lifted restrictions on forming indigenous political parties. The three that quickly took shape reflected the options open to locals. The first of these, the Timorese Democratic Union (known by its Portuguese initials, UDT), initially consisted of two dozen privileged intellectuals and favored the commonwealth relationship proposed by Lisbon. UDT had its main appeal among the small, Portuguese-speaking middle class that ran the construction and coffee plantation sectors.

A second party was the Timorese Social Democratic Association, an umbrella for a disparate ensemble of civil servants and seminary graduates. In September 1974, following the return to Timor of five pro-communist student leaders heavily influenced by the left-leaning independence movements active in Africa, the association lurched to the left and changed its name to the Revolutionary Front for an Independent East Timor (known by its Portuguese acronym, Fretilin). As the name implied, the front supported a fast and complete split from Portugal.

Taking the opposite extreme was the Association for Indonesian Timor Integration, which called for merger with Indonesia. Founded on 27 May, it later toned down its name—but not its goal—to the Timorese Popular Democratic Association (known in Portuguese as Apodeti). Most of its support came from chieftains living along the border with Indonesian-controlled West Timor.

Since its independence, Indonesia had gone out of its way to emphasize it had no territorial ambitions over Portugal's half of Timor island.[17] But with Lisbon reassessing its links to the territory, Portuguese Timor was suddenly propelled to the top of Indonesia's security concerns. This was driven home in June, when most of the Apodeti leadership crossed the border to West Timor and sought an audience with Indonesia's top intelligence officials.

Taken to Jakarta, the group sat down with General Ali Murtopo. Long one of Suharto's closest personal advisors, Murtopo headed Operasi Khusus ("Special Operations", abbreviated as Opsus), the informal but highly influential troubleshooting body that since 1962 had handled covert military operations desired by General, later President, Suharto. Though he had been forced to take a lower profile in the wake of the Malari Affair, Murtopo was now looking to score points by overseeing Indonesia's clandestine response to Timor's decolonialization process.[18]

After receiving the Apodeti delegation, Murtopo dispatched one of his deputies to Dili on an initial fact-finding mission. Getting the assignment was Aloysius Sugiyanto, the Catholic army colonel who as a young RPKAD officer had gotten arrested in the aftermath of the 1956 Lubis Affair. Forbidden from rejoining the RPKAD upon his release, Sugiyanto had instead become one of Murtopo's top Opsus deputies and was heavily involved in the negotiations to end Confrontation.

In July 1974, Sugiyanto received a visa stamp from the Portuguese consulate in downtown Jakarta, then flew to Dili via a commercial flight from Darwin, Australia. He made the trip under the guise of a marketing officer for a fictitious trading house in Surabaya. Using this same business pretext, Sugiyanto went on to frequent the Portuguese colonial backwater on nearly a monthly basis. The real purpose of his travels was to gather general intelligence on the emerging Timorese political parties and their chief personalities. Though Indonesia had obvious common ground with Apodeti, he made a point of visiting each of them.[19] Said Sugiyanto:

> I would be met at the airport at Dili by representatives of Apodeti. After talking with them, I would go back to the hotel and see the UDT leaders for a coffee. Later that night, I would have dinner with Fretilin. It was like that on each trip.[20]

While Sugiyanto was busy visiting Dili, General Murtopo had established a wider strategic intelligence operation against Portuguese Timor during the third quarter of 1974. Known as Komodo—after the gargantuan monitor lizards that populate the Indonesian island of the same name—the operation was based in the West Timor capital of Kupang, with a forward post at the border town of Atambua. Modest in size, Komodo consisted of a dozen civilian intelligence officers and army personnel on secondment to Opsus. Included in the latter category were two Kopassandha officers; like Sugiyanto, both were Catholics.[21]

From intelligence gathered by Komodo, warning bells started sounding in Jakarta by year's end. Some of this was due to the leftist shift displayed by Fretilin beginning in September. While anecdotal, Sugiyanto noted with concern that the Fretilin office in Dili had a stack of Mao Tse-tung's red books on offer. In addition, officials at the Taiwanese consulate (one of the few foreign outposts in the Portuguese territory) darkly hinted at a nexus between Fretilin and Chinese communists operating from Portugal's other Asian foothold in Macao. Still sour over Beijing's support for the PKI, Indonesia was especially sensitive to charges of Chinese intervention.

Concerning Jakarta, too, were developments in Africa. In September 1974, a second wave of younger, more leftist army officers had taken control in Lisbon. Ditching the earlier proposal for a commonwealth with its colonies,

Portugal now wanted a faster, complete divorce. Following from this mindset, in January 1975 Lisbon reached agreement to grant independence to Angola before year's end. With Portugal all but certain to encourage a similar outcome in Timor, UDT ditched its earlier support for vestigial links to Lisbon and now entered into a coalition with Fretilin seeking full independence.

Eyeing these events, Suharto's key advisors were torn. Although fearful that Portuguese Timor might ultimately be handed over to anti-Indonesia parties—and especially communists—they were reluctant to intervene with an overt military force. Murtopo, for one, advocated clandestine means of swaying the Timorese population and lobbying support from Portuguese officials. Already, he was helping underwrite Apodeti and channeling limited financial incentives to key UDT leaders. In January, Komando expanded its operations to include pro-Indonesia radio broadcasts from Kupang in various Timorese dialects. Suharto himself was prone to agree with this indirect approach, in large part because he remained sensitive to Indonesia's international standing—especially in the U.S. and Australia—and did not want to be tarred with his predecessor's penchant for foreign adventurism.

Many of his generals, however, were more hawkish. As the senior intelligence officer in the Department of Defense and Security, Benny Moerdani felt it prudent to be prepared for any future military contingencies in Portuguese Timor. (In addition, given the overlapping mandates of Indonesia's multiple intelligence bodies, Murtopo—and, by extension, his Operation Komodo—was something of a competitor.) Picking up the phone, he dialed Colonel Dading Kalbuadi.

Two years Benny's senior, Dading was a friend and colleague from their days serving as student-soldiers in the independence struggle. Joining RPKAD together, they had both been on combat jumps into Sumatra during the PRRI uprising. But when Benny headed for Sulawesi to take on Permesta, Dading had stayed behind to mop up resistance near Padang. It nearly proved a fatal choice, with a bazooka shot impacting within meters of him and a piece of shrapnel lodging in his neck. Recovering for almost a year and sidelined to logistical slots as a result, he had spent the 1962 Irian operation traveling overseas to procure equipment for the commandos.

While Benny moved up the ranks and geared his RPKAD battalion for Confrontation, Dading had taken his leave of Indonesia in 1963 and ventured to the U.S. for instruction at Fort Benning. Returning the following year, he was placed in charge of logistics for all Soviet supplies used by the army. In this capacity, he led the contingent of RPKAD and Kostrad paratroopers that went to the Soviet Union for airborne and rigger training.

It was not until 1967 that Dading came back to the RPKAD as the regiment's chief of logistics. Then in 1972, after more than a decade handling supplies, he was named commander of Group 2 at Magelang. While still keeping this post, he was diverted to South Vietnam for eleven months of service with the Indonesian contingent monitoring the 1973 Paris Peace Accords.[22]

Fresh from South Vietnam and newly promoted to colonel, Dading was met with orders to report to army headquarters for a mundane assignment with the logistical section. It was at that point he received the phone call from Benny.

"I'm heading back to logistics," said Dading.

"Forget logistics," said Benny. "I've got something much better."

"What do you know about Portuguese Timor?" Benny asked the question, then sat back to let Dading talk.

The response was disappointing. "Just what I've read in the papers," answered the colonel truthfully.

The general then launched into a description of the ongoing Operation Komodo. While Murtopo's covert campaign was focused on providing strategic intelligence, Benny wanted the Department of Defense and Security to have its own tactical combat intelligence in the event of Indonesian military intervention. Said Benny: "I want you to start a Timor operation for me."[23]

Intrigued, Dading wasted no time sending letters and placing phone calls to a dozen Kopassandha officers who served under him in Group 2. "I merely told them I had a job that was very interesting," he recalls. "To the man, they all volunteered."[24]

With his team fast taking shape and an initial fact-finding mission scheduled to take place, Dading debated a codename for the new operation. "The *flamboyan* [poinciana tree] was just coming into beautiful bloom at the time, like the cherry blossoms in Washington," he remembers. "I saw our mission blossoming like a flower."[25]

Operation Flamboyan was about to be born.

1   Interview with Sofian Effendi, 1 July 1999; interview with Tarub, 22 July 1999; interview with Slamet Riyanto, 28 May 2000.

2   U.S. Department of Defense memorandum from Paul Kearney (Office of the Chairman of the Joint Chiefs of Staff) to Admiral McCain (Commander in Chief, Pacific), dated 14 April 1970. (On file at the U.S. Army Center for Military History)

3   Immediately after the failed October 1965 coup, Suharto had attempted to maintain cordial relations with the Soviet Union. For its part, the Soviets continued military aid deliveries through 1966. By later that decade, however, the Soviets had soured toward Suharto's increasingly pro-Western foreign policy and curtailed its earlier largesse. When Jakarta asked for AK-47 ammunition and spare parts, Moscow demanded cash payments—something that came hard for the cash-strapped Indonesian military. Although some units retained the AK-47 (such as the marines), the RPKAD led the way for a U.S.-sponsored transition to the M-16.

4   Seno Hartono interview.

5   Some Cham community leaders clung to an unrealistic hope that they could see the rebirth of Champa, a historical kingdom that comprised part of eastern Cambodia and southernmost Vietnam. The most senior Cham officer in the Khmer army, General Les Kosem, secretly supported this goal. "Before we left for Indonesia," said Cham student Sen Tith, "the general told me and the members from the 5 Brigade to train hard in order to continue the struggle for Champa." Interview with Sen Tith, 11 October 1990. ·

6   Tata Loekita interview.

7   Anda interview.

8   Interview with Chap Tony, 6 March 1995. A lieutenant in 1971, Chap Tony was the ranking airborne officer in the contingent sent to Batu Jajar. Due to a fortunate assignment near the Thai border in April 1975, he managed to flee the country and resettled in France for sixteen years. In 1991, he returned to Cambodia and was named a colonel in the resurrected Royal Cambodian Armed Forces. Ironically, when Indonesia once more agreed to give para-commando training to a Cambodian contingent in late 1994, Colonel Chap Tony went along as the senior liaison officer.

9   Interview with Bambang Soembodo, 3 February 2002.

10   Sudjadi interview; *Cahaya Chandraca*, No. 5/1973, p. 10.

11   Tarub interview.

12 Interview with Johannes Bambang, 3 May 1999.

13 Seno Hartono interview.

14 Upon Sofyan's death, there were no other key guerrilla leaders left along the West Kalimantan frontier. Although the leftist guerilla threat was all but gone, Kopassandha continued to occasionally deploy contingents to the area. These rotations were as much live-fire exercises as they were dictated by actual security considerations.

15 Kopassandha involvement in the military's efforts to restore order was minimal: a small detachment from Cijantung was rushed to stand guard at the National Monument in Merdeka Square.

16 Benny took on several intelligence hats in quick succession after returning from South Korea. Initially named commander of an Intelligence Task Force, he officially became the Chief of G-1/Intelligence on 3 August 1974, then Assistant for Intelligence in the Department of Defense and Security on 17 February 1975.

17 During the heyday of Sukarno's foreign policy adventurism, there was apparently one brief flirtation with intervention in Timor. In August 1963, a rebel "emergency government" of the "United Republic of Timor" issued a circular in Jakarta listing a 22-member cabinet and its intent to send envoys to the United Nations to oppose Portuguese imperialism. The Indonesian Foreign Ministry claimed it had no knowledge of the rebel government, and the group quickly grew dormant. FBIS, East Asia edition, 13 August 1963, p.3.

18 During this period, there were multiple intelligence organizations with much overlap in mandate. Murtopo's Opsus was an ad hoc body that specialized in engineering and financing covert paramilitary and political operations, like running the 1969 West Irian referendum. By contrast, General Yoga Sugomo's State Intelligence Coordination Agency, known by the Indonesian abbreviation Bakin, focused more on intelligence collection and analysis. A third intelligence body—the Intelligence Task Force found within the Command for the Restoration of Security and Order—had been under the control of General Soemitro; when his star dimmed after the Malari Affair, this task force was shifted under the control of Benny Moerdani. Further complicating matters, officers often held simultaneous seats in more than one of the above agencies.

19 The initial Opsus assistance provided to Apodeti was extremely modest. Besides offering verbal advice on how to organize a political party (drawing on previous

Opsus experience in establishing Golkar, Suharto's expansive political conglomerate that was effectively synonymous with the Indonesian government bureaucracy), Sugiyanto helped Apodeti leaders purchase a single motorcycle and typewriter. *Tempo*, 22 February 1999, p. 28.

20 Sugiyanto interview.

21 Besides being one of Suharto's closest confidantes, Murtopo was both head of Opsus and deputy chief of Bakin. For Operation Komando, which fell under his personal command, Murtopo was able to assemble a task force of operatives drawn from both Opsus and Bakin.

22 Indonesia deployed observers to South Vietnam from January 1973 until the fall of the Saigon government to communism in 1975. The contingents were primarily drawn from the army, though they contained a small number of marines and air force personnel. During the initial deployment—known as Garuda IV—twenty members of Kopassandha were included, the most senior of whom was Colonel C.I. Santosa.

23 Dading Kalbuadi interview.

24 Ibid.

25 Ibid.

CHAPTER FIFTEEN

WAVES IN A BACKWATER

By February 1975, Dading and an eight-man Flamboyan staff—all Kopassandha officers—had transited Kupang and arrived at the sleepy town of Atambua. Seventeen kilometers from the border with Portuguese Timor, Atambua had been host to Operation Komodo's forward outpost for the previous six months. Komodo's activities in the town were extremely limited: besides a debriefing point for a handful of cross-border agents, they had set up a physical fitness training course for several hundred recruits dispatched by Apodeti leaders.[1]

While his staff set up shop in an abandoned church, Dading, carrying cover documents as an immigration officer, spent the next few weeks on a reconnaissance trip to familiarize himself with the border region. As he was doing this, the situation in Portuguese Timor grew ever more confused. Jakarta was particularly alarmed by the January pact between UDT and Fretilin. Earlier, UDT leaders had assured Indonesia they were anti-communist; now they were in league with them—and together focusing their opposition against pro-Indonesia Apodeti.

Confusing signals were also coming from Portugal. In conversations with General Murtopo, some leaders in Lisbon had sympathized with Jakarta, and had even seemed to acquiesce to eventual Indonesian control over their colony. Other Portuguese leaders, however, spoke of Timor's eventual independence after proper preparation.

All of which was taking place as communism was on the ascendance in mainland Southeast Asia. Pro-Western governments in the Khmer Republic,

Laos, and South Vietnam were all in their final dying weeks. Reflecting Jakarta's sensitivity to this shift, propaganda broadcasts from Kupang grew more shrill, including apocryphal reports of Chinese communist advisors arriving in Dili. Further stoking Jakarta's paranoia was the arrival of three openly leftist Portuguese officers—two majors and a captain—to assist Timor's military governor.

Prompted by all these developments, Murtopo's Operation Komodo ratcheted up its activities in March. Part of this focused on channeling covert political support to Apodeti. At the same time, Sugiyanto ventured to Dili and looked to drive a wedge between the UDT and Fretilin coalition. This he did by playing favorites among the UDT leadership, with party chairman Francisco Xavier Lopes da Cruz, a customs officer and former Jesuit seminarian, becoming a target of Indonesian largesse.

Forging ahead on a parallel but separate track, Dading laid plans to assume control over the Apodeti training program at Atambua. Looking to expand the effort, trainers were to come from Kopassandha's Group 4. Over the previous two years, that group had been able to flesh out its six *karsa yudha*. In addition, the group had focused particular attention on honing its linguistic abilities. Select members were taking weekly lessons in tongues like Arabic, English, and Vietnamese. Two young Group 4 officers were even sent to Malaysia for a year to study Cantonese and Mandarin.[2]

Chosen as head of the Atambua training team was Yunus Yosfiah. A thirty-year-old captain from South Sulawesi, Yunus had been part of the Military Academy's massive Class of 1965 (the class included 225 infantry cadets, almost three times the number admitted the previous year). Like many of his classmates, he was drawn to the romantic allure of the high-profile RPKAD upon graduation and went through para-commando training. After several years with Group 2, where he eventually became a company commander, in 1973 he became the second Indonesian to attend the Special Forces Officers Course at Fort Bragg after post-Confrontation restrictions were lifted. Upon return, he was promoted to captain and took command of a Group 4 *karsa yudha*.

For the Timor assignment, the Kopassandha command fell back on the precedent set during the 1969 West Irian operation. Just as in Irian, Yunus was told to nearly double the authorized strength of his *karsa yudha* prior to deployment. To do this, his four *prayudha* commanders were ordered to canvass the group and expand their 12-man teams to twenty members. Once these augmentees were chosen, the heavy *karsa yudha*—given the feminine codename Susi—spent the next month training together near Cilongsi, a small town just south of Jakarta. A handful of members used the opportunity to take a crash course in Tetum, the lingua franca spoken by the majority of locals in Portuguese Timor. All Susi members also received a briefing on the situation inside Timor from the former RPKAD officer turned Opsus operative, Sugiyanto.[3]

On 29 April, Yunus and his men—each wearing civilian clothes—arrived at Atambua. There they were presented with 400 Apodeti recruits; many came courtesy of Guilherme Gonclaves, a top Apodeti patron and the wealthy chieftain from the coffee-growing mountain town of Atsabe. Guilherme's own son, Tomas, was among the pupils.

Initiating a simple regimen of paramilitary training (minus actual weapons instruction), the Susi instructors found the Timorese to be good subjects. Observed one of the trainers:

> It was different than Kalimantan, where the [TNKU] volunteers were mostly city dwellers and could not live outside a village. In Timor the terrain was much more open, and nearly all the Timorese knew how to live in this environment.[4]

Not all of the *karsa yudha* was devoted to training. In keeping with Benny's requirement to collect tactical intelligence, some of the members conducted reconnaissance patrols along the main border as well as along the frontier with Oecusse (a tiny Portuguese enclave along the northern coast of Indonesia's West Timor). A handful of operatives even entered the eastern part of the island incognito to get an understanding of its geography and society. One of them, *prayudha* commander Untung Suroso, made repeated forays over a period of four months. He remembers:

> I had taken the crash course in Tetum, and entered [Portuguese]Timor as a businessman doing barter trade. I bought in sugar and cloth, and brought back coffee. I was able to go as far as Dili; there were almost no travel restrictions.[5]

As this was taking place, the political landscape inside Timor was lurching in unpredictable directions. Part of this was of Operation Komodo's making. In mid-April, Murtopo had invited two top UDT leaders to Jakarta—including chairman Lopes da Cruz—where they were feted by Suharto himself. The result, from Jakarta's perspective, was a resounding success: on 27 May, UDT unilaterally withdrew from the pro-independence coalition with Fretilin.

By the following month, however, events were fast spinning out of Komodo's control. On 26 June, the three parties had been encouraged to attend negotiations in the Portuguese territory of Macao. But Fretilin boycotted the talks because of Apodeti's attendance, and UDT representatives, claiming they enjoyed support from eighty percent of the Timorese population, also shunned Apodeti.

No sooner had the ill-fated Macao talks concluded, Portugal made two surprise announcements. First, on 17 July they set elections in a year's time for a popular assembly that would determine Timor's future. Second, they called snap elections on 29 July for district councils. Hearing this, Komodo's Sugiyanto was irate. "Fretilin had gotten advance funding from Portuguese leftists to order hundreds of metal campaign buttons from Macao," he said. "We rushed to make shirts that Apodeti could give away as gifts."[6]

The results from Timor's first poll were telling. Among an electorate that was ninety percent illiterate, 55 percent voted for Fretilin's populist themes. The second largest bloc went to UDT; Apodeti got a single seat.

Even as the votes were being counted, Murtopo enticed a top UDT delegation back to Jakarta in late July. Compared with the successfully engineered outcome of the West Irian referendum, Opsus was finding Timor much more complex and volatile. Portugal was oscillating wildly between word and deed, the Timorese parties were bickering among themselves, and there was even strife within the parties. In many cases, there were intricate rivalries that cut across families and generations—rivalries that were more personal than ideological. Showing little appreciation for these nuances, it was ideology—specifically, the need to embrace anti-communism over Fretilin's radical socialism—that Indonesia's leaders stressed to their UDT guests.

The talk had an effect, though probably not the one Jakarta desired. On the night of 9 August, hundreds of UDT supporters fanned across Dili and occupied the radio station, airport, and police headquarters. Seizing rifles from the police armory, they staged a raucous anti-communist demonstration the following day. While this was obviously targeted against Fretilin, and was therefore reason for Jakarta to cheer, the UDT ringleaders then lashed out at

Apodeti. And in a striking display of party discord, one faction of UDT leaders placed chairman Lopes da Cruz, who had championed cooperation with Indonesia, under arrest.

Understandably concerned with the direction of the fast breaking events, Sugiyanto flew with a small Komodo team to Dili in an attempt to liaise with the UDT leadership. Stopped at the airport, he was told that Lopes da Cruz was unavailable for a meeting. With mortars flying overhead and with many of Dili's thirty-thousand residents fleeing toward the waterfront, the Opsus colonel soon retreated back to Kupang with more questions than answers.

The Portuguese, meanwhile, were refusing to take sides in the conflict. In fact, there were few Portuguese troops available for intervention. Unlike its African colonies, the benign security environment in Timor had allowed Lisbon to maintain a limited armed presence that was almost exclusively comprised of highly loyal Timorese recruits. Through the end of 1974, the backbone of Timor's 2,500-man colonial military had consisted of just six *cacadores* ("hunter") light infantry companies. Each of these companies counted 120 men armed with G-3 automatic rifles, some light machineguns, and a handful of mortars. There were also two cavalry squadrons—one at Atabae and one at Bobonaro—that rode on small but rugged Timorese ponies, a military police company, two artillery companies, a training center, and a maritime defense command with four ships. Besides this main force, there were also about 2,000 Timorese auxiliaries divided into militia (*segunda linha*, literally "second line") companies armed with antiquated rifles. Apart from the artillery and military police companies, all of these units were overwhelmingly manned by Timorese.

During the first quarter of 1975, this paltry force was pared down further. All three of the companies comprised of Europeans—the artillerymen and military police—were withdrawn to Portugal with their equipment. Two of the hunter companies—at Dili and Ossu—were disbanded, leaving one apiece at Baucau, Lospalos, Maubisse, and the Oecusse enclave. And both of the cavalry squadrons—at Atabae and Bobonaro—were consolidated and reduced into a single *agrupamento de cavalaria* (cavalry group) at Bobonaro.[7]

Belatedly realizing that this small number of troops could not keep the peace in the event of social unrest, Portugal had flown in a sixty-man detachment of paratroopers on 7 April. But as chaos spread across Dili in the wake of the UDT 9 August blitz, the Portuguese military governor ordered his European soldiers to withdraw to the piers and not take sides. After more than two weeks of non-action, the governor radioed Lisbon that he had lost control, then loaded all Portuguese on ships and retreated to Ilhe de Atauro—the Isle of Goats—sixteen kilometers to the north.

Although the Portuguese troops had refrained from intervention, they had left intact their Timorese-dominated military. These troops—four hunter companies, the cavalry group, training center, and militia—wavered at first. Two of the hunter companies—at Baucau and Lospalos—then leaned toward the UDT as of 15 August. But Fretilin soon proved more persuasive, aided in large part because the most senior Timorese officer, Lieutenant Rogerio Lobato, was the brother of ranking Fretilin officer Nicolau Lobato. At Rogerio's urging, the training center at the mountain town of Aileu on 17 August declared support for Fretilin. In fast succession, the remainder of the colonial army switched hats and instantly gave Fretilin its own trained, cohesive, and relatively well-armed military.

As Fretilin's newfound army marched into Dili, UDT's novice combatants tried to make a stand. With mortars again flying across the city, chaos ensued. Apodeti leaders, refusing an Indonesian offer to be evacuated, suddenly came under fire from UDT. There were also reports that UDT supporters had run Apodeti out of its strongholds at Atsabe and Balibo. In the interests of survival—and to maintain some political relevance—Apodeti took the surprise step of announcing an unlikely tactical alliance with Fretilin against UDT.

Fretilin hardly needed the help. By 20 August, they had pushed halfway across Dili. Three days later, the Indonesian and Taiwan consulates prepared for an evacuation as UDT started retreating west toward Liquisa district. By 29 August, with hundreds of bodies lying on the streets, Fretilin controlled Dili.

In Jakarta, Indonesia's leaders saw their worst fears unfolding in Portuguese Timor. During the days immediately after the UDT coup, Lisbon had hinted it might give a green light for Indonesian military intervention. They also acquiesced in allowing Indonesian assistance for the evacuation of foreign nationals out of Dili. This suited Suharto just fine, as he did not want a military invasion to cloud his upcoming trip to Washington, nor did he want Indonesia to be seen as an aggressor by the international community at large. Though his generals were lobbying for fast action, and had even started preparing an invasion plan during the second week of August, he repeatedly vetoed this course of action through month's end.[8]

But by the beginning of the fourth week of August, Portugal had still not given Indonesia its blessing to move in and restore order. Feeling compelled to respond, Jakarta authorized Operation Flamboyan to move beyond passive training and initiate limited covert cross-border paramilitary operations.

This expanded mandate came at a bad time for Colonel Dading. By coincidence, during the days immediately before the UDT move in Dili, Captain Yunus had pared down Susi to its normal *karsa yudha* complement; this left him with just four 13-man *prayudha*.

Apodeti, meanwhile, seemed unable to decisively act on its own. Although it counted four hundred Kopassandha-trained partisans at Atambua—and thought had been given to unleashing them on 15 August—these pro-Indonesia guerrillas had yet to move from their training site during the climactic battle to control Dili.

With little time to hammer out a detailed plan of action, Dading sent an emergency request back to Cijantung for additional personnel. Then on 22 August, he ordered Yunus to ready Susi for an imminent foray. Dading met resistance to the idea from within his own staff. "I thought it was a bad idea for Susi to infiltrate alone," said Major Yusman Yutam, Flamboyan's chief of logistics. "I said we should wait until the reinforcements come, so we could whipsaw the enemy."[9]

With time deemed of the essence, Yusman was overruled. Electing to dispatch Susi on its own, the *karsa yudha* members were to disguise their national origin in order to give Jakarta plausible deniability—and to avoid any protests from the U.S. for using American weapons. Already, they had gone four months without proper haircuts; as uniforms they wore blue jeans and civilian shirts. For weapons, Dading expedited a request to his former Group 2 at Magelang to dispatch a shipment of AK-47 assault rifles (Group 2 was one of the few RPKAD units that had yet to start transitioning to the U.S. M-16). Also rushed to Susi were some old stocks of 90mm Yugoslavian rocket launchers.[10]

The aim of Susi's mission was decidedly ambitious. Besides "gauging local conditions," the Indonesian commandos were to establish guerrilla bases for Apodeti and, when possible, conduct sabotage. To maximize their coverage, they were to split in half and proceed along two routes. Captain Yunus would take "Susi A," comprised of half of his *karsa yudha* staff and a pair of *prayudha*, east from Atambua toward the former Apodeti stronghold at Atsabe, then turn north to Aileu. His deputy, Captain Sunarto—nicknamed "Narto Coolie" because of his dark complexion—would take "Susi B," consisting of the remaining half of the *karsa yudha* staff and the other pair of *prayudha*, north to the town of Atabae, then cut east toward Ermera. Both components would have sixty Apodeti members acting as guides and porters; none of these partisans would yet be armed. Optimistic plans called for Susi A and B to push inland and link up near Dili.[11]

At the end of August, both Susi columns crossed the border. Almost immediately, they had trouble with navigation—no surprise given they were issued schoolbook maps that listed towns and villages but showed no terrain features. Even those that had surreptitiously crossed the border for bogus trade forays could not get their bearings. "I knew the roads during the day," said Lieutenant Untung, "but could not find my way after dark."[12]

Relying on their Apodeti guides, Yunus moved cautiously during the night and approached Atsabe through a vast coffee plantation. Pausing two days to observe movements in and out of the town, Susi A saw reason for concern. Once an Apodeti stronghold, pro-Indonesia supporters had been expelled by UDT, who in turn were evicted by Fretilin. "We could see the area filled with dozens of *tropas*," said Susi operations officer Gatot Purwanto, using the Portuguese term for the former colonial troops.[13]

Most of the *tropas* were gathered in the center of Atsabe near a unique Portuguese fort that had been constructed like steps along a hillside. A formidable target, the structure featured a mortar platform at the mid-level and firing slits cut into the stone walls up its entire length.

Despite the fort's visual deterrent value, Yunus decided to move into the town. As they only had AK-47 rifles and rocket launchers, he stressed the need to move quickly in order to prevent Fretilin from bringing their mortar into play.

Waiting until 0500 hours, the commandos sprang into action. Storming the base level of the fort, they peppered automatic fire up its walls. Waking fast, Fretilin sentries stuck their rifles out of the slits in the rock and returned fire. Realizing time was critical, *prayudha* commander Untung took a rocket launcher and circled around the side to look for a good angle. His first round hit its mark, killing three *tropas* and silencing their fire long enough for his teammates to enter the fort and quickly work their way up to its top.

Resting briefly, Yunus reviewed their status. Only two members were slightly wounded, and the rest were in good spirits following their fast victory. But they had expended more than half of their ammunition during the engagement, and Yunus calculated it would take at least a week before adequate reinforcements could reach them. Yunus also knew there were many more Fretilin in the vicinity than the three killed in the fort. Already he could hear bugles sounding in the surrounding bush, as well as the guttural rumble of a Mercedes Unimog—the Portuguese military transports inherited by Fretilin—floating in from the distance. All of these reasons were good incentive, Yunus felt, to vacate no later than noon.

But before departing, Susi A used the opportunity to proselytize to the masses. Near the top of the fort, dozens of ethnic Chinese operated small shops. Like most of the twelve thousand Chinese living in Portuguese Timor, they were actively courted by the Taiwan consulate in Dili; most held Taiwanese passports and several flags from the Republic of China fluttered along Atsabe's main road. Calling out these Chinese and dozens of Timorese residents, the commandos used a blend of Indonesian and broken Tetum to play up Jakarta and condemn Fretilin.

The pitch had an effect. A dozen Timorese volunteered to join the Apodeti porters carrying supplies. Taking them along, Yunus and his men melted into the bush.

As this was transpiring, Susi B had made good time marching in broad daylight toward Atabae. The decision to move during the day came from the team leader, the somewhat eccentric Narto Coolie. A firm believer in mysticism, Narto never went into battle without his kris, an Indonesian ceremonial dagger said to be endowed with magical powers. Blending bravado and supernatural protection offered by the kris, Narto openly moved Susi B through a number of villages en route to their target.[14]

By the time they arrived at Atabae, however, Narto pragmatically decided not to tempt fate. Peering through binoculars, they saw the town was packed with armed Fretilin troops. Outnumbered and outgunned, they instead tried to skirt Atabae and reach the coast. Before getting far, they had a brief encounter with Fretilin and tactfully retreated into a coffee plantation.

As they debated their next move, Susi B received a radio message from Captain Yunus. Both Susi contingents were now to rendezvous along the banks of the Ribeira Batuta, a narrow tributary fifteen kilometers east of Atabae. One day later, both halves of Susi linked as scheduled. Though they were able to find sanctuary in yet another coffee plantation, the *karsa yudha* was experiencing discord. For one thing, food was becoming scarce. Though their Apodeti porters were carrying food thought sufficient for fifteen days, they had nearly exhausted their supply four days early. In addition, they were forbidden from cooking, making for repeated and unappealing meals of dried noodles.

Of even greater concern was an emerging conflict between Yunus and his deputy, Narto. Whereas Yunus had insisted on conducting a covert operation, Narto wanted to make an overt show of force. Upon hearing that Susi B had marched during the day, Yunus was not amused.

While they spent the next two days cleaning weapons and letting tempers cool, two of the *prayudha* conducted security patrols and one went in search of food. The fourth, Prayudha 2 under the command of Lieutenant Suwarso, took a Yugoslavian rocket launcher and hiked three kilometers north to the village of Fatu Besi. Sighting a Fretilin jeep, they fired off two projectiles before withdrawing south with a flaming vehicle in their wake.

In its quest for food, half of Prayudha 1 exited the plantation and came upon a small village atop a neighboring hill. Leaving behind their weapons, two of the commandos emerged from the bush. A dozen locals congregating in the village square saw the interlopers and froze. The Kopassandha commandos now had a critical decision to make. Each of the main political parties had devised hand signals to identify their supporters: Fretilin had a clenched fist salute, UDT had an upright thumb, and Apodeti had a peace sign. Not knowing which to offer, the Susi members chose the peace sign. The villagers considered them for a moment, then gave the UDT thumbs up.

The pair of Indonesians now began to panic. Feeling naked without their weapons, they had revealed themselves to be supporters of a rival party; as of the previous week, UDT and Apodeti were bitter enemies. To their relief, however, the villagers were not heavily politicized and were amenable to selling a bag of rice, a goat, and two chickens.[15]

Though pleased that their foray had been a success, the six commandos knew that their food haul would not go far. Once back at base camp, they risked a brief campfire to cook the goat and set aside a few mouthfuls of meat for each team member.

Very quickly, food became the least of their concerns. On the following morning, three of the *prayudha* departed on perimeter patrols. Alone at the basecamp was the *karsa yudha* headquarters, Lieutenant Sihombing's Prayudha 1, and some Apodeti porters. An unseasonably heavy rain was falling, but it failed to drown out the screech of a parrot from the distant bush. Thinking the bird had been disturbed by one of the returning patrols, Yunus ordered the porters to watch for them from the high ground.

Seconds later, the telltale whistle of a mortar sent the commandos scurrying for cover. As the first round impacted, the Kopassandha members scattered from the camp in all directions. With almost a dozen more rounds falling all around, Sergeants Kusno and Said waded into the rain-swollen Ribeira Batuta. Both fled without taking weapons; Said, the Prayudha 1 communications sergeant, abandoned his radio set. Not until reaching the opposite bank did they look back to see a line of victorious Fretilin waving rifles in victory.

Lieutenant Untung Suroso, commander of Prayudha 4, had nearly ran headlong into the Fretilin mortar crew on its way toward Susi's base camp. Walking point and not carrying a radio, Untung tried doubling back in the driving rain in an attempt to rally his men, then get to their bivouac and warn his teammates. Coming upon his deputy, Sergeant Seno, the two promptly got into a heated dispute. Arguing it was foolhardy to go back to camp, Seno insisting they use the opportunity to return to Indonesia. In the end, Seno policed up half the *prayudha* and headed home; Untung and the other half rushed toward the bank of the Ribeira Batuta. Before getting there, they saw the Fretilin troop concentration near their apparently abandoned campsite. Circling wide, they caught up with Seno and continued southwest toward the border.[16]

Captain Yunus had not sprinted far into the bush before he tried regrouping his scattered *karsa yudha*. With his staff gathered round, he announced that they still had a mission to complete. Hearing this, Yunus nearly had a mutiny on his hands. Hungry and on the move for just short of two weeks, his men openly criticized their lack of clear objectives. Moreover, most of the *prayudha* members were not responding to radio contact—and one of the *karsa yudha*'s own radios had been riddled by bullets fired from suspiciously close range.

With seemingly little choice, Yunus relented and ordered a swift march back to Indonesia. After exactly fourteen days, they reassembled on the border. Sergeant Said, the radioman last seen on the bank of the Ribeira Batuta, did not make it to the rendezvous; his fate remains a mystery.[17]

Back in Cijantung, a new Kopassandha commander reviewed Dading's request for reinforcements. Back on 31 May, Brigadier General Witarmin had handed off his top post to Colonel Yogie Soewardi Memet. Born in West Java, Yogie had spent virtually his entire military career leading units from that province. Many had been paratroop formations, and it was Yogie that earned accolades for commanding the 330 Airborne Battalion when it killed rebel leader Kahar Muzakkar in South Sulawesi. Like Witarmin, he had not gone through Batu Jajar commando training but for the past two years had been serving as deputy Kopassandha commander.[18]

By the time Colonel Yogie took the helm at Cijantung in late May, Susi had already departed for Atambua on its training mission. Then in early August, he was asked to send another Group 4 *karsa yudha* to Irian Jaya (literally, "Victorious Irian," the new name for West Irian after 1973) following signs of renewed OPM activity. Looking to affix his personal stamp on the special forces, Yogie determined that all Kopassandha deployments during his watch be given the codename Nanggala, the name of a legendary Hindu spear with multiple deadly points. Accordingly, the *karsa yudha* to Irian Jaya became Nanggala 1 and Susi retroactively took the name Nanggala 2.

Seeing that Dading wanted more men—and he wanted them with combat operations in mind—Yogie made fast arrangements to assemble Nanggala 3 and 4. Unlike Susi, which was comprised of a complete *karsa yudha*, the two new units would each mix two *prayudha* and two para-commando platoons. This would offer the ability to liaise with Timorese partisans (a *sandhi yudha* specialty) and the added punch of the para-commandos. To ease administration, Yogie decided to use only the Cijantung-based Groups 1 and 4.

Selected as the commander of Nanggala 3 was Major Tarub. A long-time member of Group 3, he was a veteran of four tours in West Kalimantan. Having only recently transferred to Group 4, he was a *karsa yudha* commander at Cijantung for just a couple of months before getting this Timor assignment.

Command of Nanggala 4 went to Major Sofian Effendi. A native of Aceh, Sofian was also a long-time officer in Group 3. Following a tour with the Garuda observer contingent in South Vietnam, he had made the transfer to Group 4 on the eve of departure for Timor.

As the two majors selected troops, more AK-47 rifles and Yugoslavian rocket launchers were gathered for their use. Denim jeans and civilian shirts—and lots of black dye—were also quickly procured. Though consideration was given to finding a patch of savannah-like conditions in West Java where they could practice in terrain similar to Timor, orders came on 27 August for the assembled teams to take civilian flights to Kupang and make their way overland to Atambua.

As they got settled at Colonel Dading's Flamboyan headquarters, plans for their use were constantly being superceded by events inside Timor. When they lost the battle for Dili, the bulk of UDT had shifted west along the coast with Fretilin in close pursuit. Some of them—about two hundred men with no heavy weapons and no radios—stopped at the deserted village of Batugade, about two kilometers from the Indonesian border, to make a quixotic stand.

The remainder of UDT, including chairman Lopes da Cruz (who had been released from incarceration before Dili fell), crossed into Indonesia and were greeted by Komodo's Sugiyanto. Already sympathetic toward Indonesia, Lopes da Cruz on 1 September began talking in terms of Timor's possible integration. Four days later, the party openly called for a merger with Indonesia.[19]

With this statement, UDT and Apodeti were now allies. This did not concern Fretilin much: apart from Batugade, they effectively controlled the entire territory. On 8 September, they were sufficiently confident to declare victory in the short civil war. But sensing Indonesian opposition, Fretilin leaders dropped their earlier call for quick independence and instead began advocating gradual decolonialization.

In response, Jakarta offered its own double-speak. On the one hand, on 13 September Indonesia announced agreement in principle for negotiations between the Portuguese and three main Timorese factions to restart in a week's time in Macao. On the other hand, with Susi encountering tough times on the Ribeira Batuta, authorization was given for a new round of Flamboyan cross-border forays.

There were some obvious problems that first needed to be addressed. As Susi had painfully learned, Fretilin's troops were better than expected. Fighting on their home turf with good weapons and sufficiently large numbers, the *tropas* were more than a match for far smaller groups of Kopassandha commandos. Moreover, the element of surprise was gone after the Susi incursion.

Recognizing this, Dading did away with any thought of extended missions or seizing territory. Instead, the two new Nanggala teams were strictly mandated with hit-and-run raids of short duration. To add extra punch, Flamboyan's logistician, Major Yustam, modified bamboo and hard plastic pipes to hold propellant charges for extra 90mm rockets; porters were now able to carry two projectiles on each side of their backpack.[20]

Before crossing the border, the two teams picked radio callsigns. In keeping with the feminine precedent established by Susi, Nanggala 3 was dubbed Tuti (the name of Tarub's wife) and Nanggala 4 became Umi.

On 17 September, Umi slipped across the southern border of West Timor under cover of darkness. Helping them as guides and porters were two light companies of Timorese—one Apodeti, one UDT—which had been quickly assembled in Atambua. After making fast progress five kilometers inland, the column split in two. Half—one *prayudha* and a para-commando platoon—veered toward the interior village of Tilomar. The remainder pressed further up the coast toward the town of Suai.

In command of the Suai sub-team was Captain Sutiyoso. Born in Semarang, 31-year-old Sutiyoso had just started a combat intelligence course in Jakarta when he was yanked from the class and dispatched to Timor. For the next two days, he led his men at a slow, cautious pace across dried riverbeds, thorny scrub, and open savannah packed with razor-sharp elephant grass. Unlike the mountainous interior and northern sector, they found Timor's southern coast to be a parched environment unlike anything encountered by Kopassandha in Kalimantan or Irian Jaya.

Like Susi, the Umi commandos also had navigation difficulties. In the tall elephant grass, even Umi's Timorese guides were having trouble staying on the path to Suai. When they chanced upon two local hunters—a man and a boy—both had their hands bound and pressed into service steering them toward their target.

Coming across the sandy bed of the Ribeira Tafara—still a day of slow patrolling from Suai—they cut inland to approach their target from an unexpected northern direction. Peering down from high ground, they realized they had a tough order. On the northern edge of town was the regent's office, a concrete structure with a hint of Iberian influence. South of that were a cluster of whitewashed concrete buildings, one of which their UDT guides fingered as a barracks for *segunda linha* auxiliaries.

To get into range, Umi had to cross an open field of one hundred meters. Waiting until shortly after midnight, the commandos allowed Suai's lack of electrification to blanket the town in darkness. Then splitting in two, Sutiyoso took half his men in the direction of the barracks. Lieutenant Johannes Bambang, a *prayudha* commander, took the remainder toward the regent's office.

As they moved into concealed positions opposite their targets, the commandos readied their rocket launchers. Not heavily used since Confrontation, the Yugoslavian weapon was not the most popular system in the Indonesian arsenal. This was because the warhead and the propellant chamber had to be loaded separately into the rear of the launch tube. Not only was this a slow and unwieldy process, but the propellant was vulnerable to tropical humidity; instances of misfires abounded.

Taking their chances, the commandos took aim and waited for Sutiyoso's signal. At 0100 hours, a flare arced across the sky and the first wave of rockets flew into Suai. Barely able to see through the darkness and smoke, Umi unleashed a second round of projectiles.

The town of Suai did not take long to react. Dogs began barking, people were screaming, and, very soon, rifles began firing. Exiting through the rear of the barracks, the militia directed accurate shots toward the Indonesians. What ensued was a three-hour stalemate, broken only by the occasional staccato burst of an AK-47 or a rocket slamming into concrete.

Remarkably, the Portuguese architecture was proving almost impregnable to the 90mm rounds. "I fired nine rockets into the regent's house," said Lieutenant Bambang, "but it only left small cracks." Sutiyoso, too, could not get the barracks to burn.[21]

The assault left Umi with several casualties. Two serious injuries were caused when a pair of commandos accidentally strayed behind a rocket launcher and were hit by the backblast. A third member—a corporal named Suparman—had been running when his foot fell in a hole, causing it to snap in a compound fracture. A fourth commando had his thumb shot off.

With dawn about to break, Sutiyoso passed word to withdraw to a pre-agreed rendezvous point. Fellow commandos helped escort the two victims of the rocket backblast, both of whom could walk but were temporarily blinded. When they looked for Suparman, however, he was nowhere to be found; information later suggested he was captured by Fretilin and executed.

Back inside West Timor, an urgent radio message from Umi arrived at the Flamboyan headquarters. Three were wounded and one was missing went the message, and their slow pace might cause them to get overrun during exfiltration. Turning toward Major Yusman, Dading urged him to expedite a medical evacuation flight. The major rushed from the church, found an idle Bell-206 Jet Ranger (one of several Indonesia-registered civilian aircraft that had been chartered by Flamboyan) and pilot, then took to the sky.

Yusman faced a tough mission. The Jet Ranger had a small radio that could communicate with Atambua, but not with Umi. This meant that messages from Captain Sutiyoso had to be relayed via Atambua. Through this indirect link, they learned that Umi had made a direct withdrawal toward the dry Ribeira Tafara. Using this as a reference point, Yusman told them to light a pentagram of signal fires, then lay crossed panels in the middle.

Looking for the smoke from the signal fires, the chopper pilot was frustrated. The vicinity was extremely dry, and there was smoke from dozens of small fires filtering up from the scrub. Going as far as Suai without spotting the missing commandos, the Jet Ranger doubled back. With an eye on the fuel gauge, the pilot dropped down to treetop level at Yusman's request. At long last, the crossed panels came into view.[22]

Settling next to the markers, the pilot kept the engines running as the three injured were piled into the aircraft. As they lifted off, a Fretilin mortar round landed nearby. Realizing they may have betrayed the location of Umi, the Jet Ranger made two diversionary landings near the beach, then turned west for Indonesia.

No longer encumbered by the wounded, Sutiyoso increased his pace toward the border. Apart from one member—Lieutenant Johannes—who became separated for three days, they crossed the frontier without incident. There they learned that the other half of Umi had managed to get within range of Tilomar and fire off several rockets, destroying a water tower.

Taken together, Umi's performance had been mixed. Though they had been able to reach their targets and conduct raids, the damage inflicted had been minimal. Moreover, second-line Timorese militias had shown considerable fight, and had even been able to inflict losses on Indonesia's elite.

Much the same story was encountered by Tarub's Tuti. Focusing on the mountainous central sector of the border, Tuti entered Portuguese Timor on the same day as Umi and, like Umi, split to hit two separate targets. Half, under Tarub's personal command, focused on Bobonaro, the town fifteen kilometers from the border that hosted the colonial cavalry group. The other half, led by Captain Lubis, Tuti's deputy commander, went just five kilometers over the border to the town of Maliana.

As he reconnoitered Bobonaro, Tarub had a sinking feeling. Fretilin militiamen could be seen milling around the town, as well as what appeared to be a wheeled cannon. Pressing ahead, he launched a nighttime raid—only to be slammed hard by return mortar fire. Carrying their wounded back across the border, he learned that the Maliana column had been repulsed in similar decisive fashion. Flamboyan, it seemed, was in need of a new strategy.[23]

1   The Komodo training camp was established in late 1974, and was run by local army personnel dispatched from Kupang. Sugiyanto interview.

2   The Cantonese student, Dolfi Rondonuwu, had been slated to operate under diplomatic cover at the Indonesian Chamber of Commerce and Industry office in Hong Kong; these plans were cancelled, however, and Dolfi returned to Group 4. The Mandarin student, Agum Gumelar, began four years of intelligence work under diplomatic cover at the Indonesian Chamber of Commerce and Industry office in Taipei; he later returned to Kopassandha with the rank of major.

3   Sugiyanto interview; interview with Dolfi Rondonuwu, 5 June 1998.

4   Bambang Sutopo interview.

5   Untung Suroso interview.

6   Sugiyanto interview.

7   The author is indebted to Colonel Luis A.M. Grao for information on the Portuguese order-of-battle in Timor.

8   An outstanding compilation of CIA daily and weekly intelligence reports during this period is found in 30 May-5 June 1982 edition of Australia's *The National Times*.

9   Interview with Yusman Yutam, 2 August 1999.

10   Dading Kalbuadi interview.

11   In Indonesian military parlance, porters were dubbed TBO (*Tenaga Bantuan Operasi*, literally "manpower to support the operation").

12   Untung Suroso interview.

13   Interview with Gatot Purwanto, 3 June 1999.

14   Bambang Sutopo interview.

15   Kusno interview.

16   Untung Suroso interview.

17   On 26 September, Fretilin spokesmen claimed to have taken an Indonesian prisoner. As Flamboyan was a covert operation, Jakarta throughout that month repeatedly denied charges that it conducted an incursion (see, for example, FBIS, Asia-Pacific edition, 22 September 1975, p. N1). Fretilin never gave further details about their alleged captive and it remains unknown if they took Sergeant Said alive.

18   In February 1973, the Kopassandha deputy commander, Colonel Kodim, was implicated in a car smuggling scandal at the Jakarta waterfront. Transferred out of the regiment as punishment, Kodim was replaced by Yogie.

19   Mention of the merger can be found in FBIS, Asia-Pacific edition, 16 September 1975, p. N2.

20   Yusman Yutam interview.

21   Johannes Bambang interview.

22   Yusman Yutam interview.

23   Mention of the Bobonaro raid can be found in FBIS, Asia-Pacific edition, 22 September 1975, p. N1.

CHAPTER SIXTEEN

PHASE TWO

As Susi, Tuti, and Umi licked their wounds inside Indonesia, Fretilin took advantage of the temporary lull to expand its control. On the morning of 24 September, following a rather tame firefight, they pushed UDT out of its Batugade foothold. Several hundred UDT combatants and 2,500 refugees spilled into Indonesia, leaving Fretilin the undisputed master over the entire territory.[1]

Perhaps heady from their easy advance, Fretilin moved an 81mm mortar into Batugade fort and lobbed several rounds across the border toward the frontier town of Motaain the following day. Immediate retaliation was not possible: the Indonesians were afraid of being outranged with the 60mm mortar they had on hand.

While fuming, Jakarta was far from idle. Though still unwilling to authorize an all-out invasion, Suharto allowed Flamboyan to advance to what was euphemistically termed "Phase Two." Much more than the previous hit-and-run raids, Phase Two entailed the resolve to covertly move into Portuguese Timor and seize border enclaves in the name of the pro-integration Timorese parties.[2]

Flamboyan would not be conducting the new phase alone. To plan and implement the campaign, the Department of Defense and Security back on 31 August had approved creation of a Combined Task Force Command—*Komando Tugas Gabungan*, or Kogasgab—under Brigadier General Suweno. A long-time RPKAD veteran—his most recent post was as commander of the Batu Jajar school—Suweno hailed from the same student-soldier batch as Dading and Benny Moerdani. Kogasgab's existence was to remain a public secret; as cover, Suweno and seven staffers were supposedly organizing a military exercise in West Timor codenamed Wibawa VI-X.[3]

Now subordinated under Kogasgab, Flamboyan remained its combat intelligence spearhead for the upcoming Phase Two. They were soon joined by reinforcements from across the military. On 2 October, a battalion of marines from Surabaya—complete with ten Soviet-made amphibious tanks and seven BTR-50 armored personnel carriers—landed in West Timor to participate in the fictitious Wibawa maneuvers.[4] At the same time, Kopassandha expedited the dispatch of two companies of para-commandos from Dading's alma mater, Group 2 in Magelang. Dubbed Combat Detachment 2, both companies (unlike the para-commandos already with Tuti and Umi) carried their own light mortars for extra firepower.

Further Kogasgab support came from naval vessels—including an ex-Soviet submarine tender, the *Ratulangi*, that sported twenty guns—floating offshore. From the Indonesian air force were several helicopters (supplementing the civilian aircraft that had previously been chartered by Flamboyan) as well as a B-26 light bomber and two C-47 transports.[5] These two transports had been modified with U.S. assistance into AC-47 "Spooky" gunships, a weapons system that had performed to great effect during the Vietnam War. Instead of rotating gattling guns used on the Vietnam models, the Indonesian airframes had a trio of .50-caliber machineguns in fixed mounts firing out the left side of the plane; banking the plane, the pilot would steer the gunfire into the target. To maintain plausible deniability, the B-26 and gunships had their Indonesian national markings removed.[6]

Kogasgab could also count on armed support from Indonesia's Timorese allies. After being used solely as guides and porters during the August and September incursions, the decision had been made to arm eight companies as full-fledged partisans (this decision was made easier when the UDT garrison from Batugade crossed the border and had little intention of turning over their weapons).[7] Flamboyan's Dading had already arranged for hundreds of outdated rifles to be rushed in from Java, including Chinese-made carbines secretly sent to Indonesia in 1965 for the PKI's stillborn militia concept.[8]

Before Phase Two could kick off, Fretilin looked to draw first blood. Loading an 81mm mortar onto a landing craft (one of four vessels that had been in Portugal's Maritime Defense Command in Dili), they maneuvered the ship off the coast near Batugade and on 5 October lobbed a few more mortars toward Motaain. More puzzled than annoyed by the bizarre provocation, Dading, who remained the senior officer at the frontline, ordered one of the marine PT-76 tanks—which had moved to Motaain under the guise of the Wibawa exercise—to drive it off with a few rounds of its own.

Fretilin had probably resorted to this desperate measure because it had gotten wind of Kogasgab's buildup opposite Batugade. Besides the marine battalion, Flamboyan's Umi, elements of Combat Detachment 2, and several hundred partisans were massing at Motaain with obvious cross-border intent. None bore insignia or identification linking them to the Indonesian armed forces; in addition, pains were being taken to issue the Indonesians with non-U.S. weapons.

This latter requirement was proving a headache for Indonesia's quartermasters. Initially, Flamboyan had been able to borrow AK-47 rifles from within Kopassandha. But once this source had been exhausted, General Benny had scrambled for alternatives. From his days when he was posted as a diplomat in Kuala Lumpur, he recalled that Malaysia kept a stockpile of AK-47 rifles captured from the Indonesians during Confrontation. Making some quick calls in late September, he received Malaysia's promise to give back the captured weapons, which were then rushed to Dading.[9]

On the afternoon of 7 October, the motley assortment of commandos, marines, and Timorese at Motaain were itching to begin operations. The members of Flamboyan—with cowboy hats, jeans, and long hair—lacked any sense of conventional military demeanor. The Apodeti and UDT Timorese, dressed much the same way, toyed with their rifles and grenades; in a rather inauspicious start, one Mauser accidentally discharged and a grenade fumbled to the ground while Dading was giving a briefing.[10]

According to the Islamic calendar, most of the Indonesian troops would be celebrating Idul Fitri—the end of the Muslim fasting month—the next day. But despite the holiday, Dading received orders from Suweno to commence his move on Batugade. As instructed, the Motaain task force crossed the border that night. By the pre-dawn hours of 8 October, they had approached their target from three directions. Leaving behind a single dead comrade, as well as some 81mm mortar shells, Fretilin placed their heavy weapons on Unimogs and retreated inland after a little more than an hour. The official Indonesian news agency quickly released a cover story that the town had been taken by an Apodeti platoon.[11]

Pausing at Batugade, Dading considered his next move. Because he had received intelligence that the Fretilin leadership might have pooled near the southern Timorese town of Viqueque, he and his Flamboyan staff hatched plans for a daring special operation. Using rubber boats launched from a navy vessel, Umi would infiltrate into the mountains near Viqueque and make a guerrilla pocket that would be supplied by airdrops.[12]

Perhaps realizing the plan was too ambitious, the Viqueque plan was quietly shelved. Instead, Umi focused on partisan training. For the next week, its members ran a rudimentary weapons course to hone the firing skills of the Apodeti and UDT guerrillas. In the shadow of Batugade's sprawling stone fort—a nineteenth century structure that covered a full acre—the Timorese guerrillas familiarized themselves with automatic rifles, light machineguns and 60mm mortars.

The respite was not to last. By 11 October, Kogasgab had penned further Phase Two plans for a blitz against five more towns and villages near the border. Moving 8 kilometers north along a crude coastal road, the marine battalion at Batugade was to seize the village of Palaka. At the same time, Flamboyan's Tuti, along with a troupe of partisans, would hit Maliana (and the neighboring village of Memo) for the second time in as many months. Assisting them would be Company A from Combat Detachment 2, as well as elements of the 2 Infantry Brigade from East Java (a single battalion from this brigade landed in West Timor on 12 October). Once Maliana was taken, Tuti would theoretically lead the column east and take the town of Bobonaro. Finally, one of the companies from the 2 Infantry Brigade would be detached to strike at the village of Lebos, nineteen kilometers south of Maliana.[13]

Belatedly, Dading proposed an additional target. Between Maliana and Batugade stood the highland pass town of Balibo. Host to a historic stone fort, Balibo had a local populace that was initially sympathetic to Apodeti, subsequently evicted by UDT, and then occupied by Fretilin. Dading was convinced that the former Fretilin occupants of the Batugade fort fled there— along with the 81mm mortar they had used to strike Motaain. Although the mortar's range fell short of Batugade, it did not make good tactical sense to allow a Fretilin outpost with a heavy weapon—and especially one that occupied a commanding view—to go unchecked. When Dading asked for approval to strike Balibo as well, Suweno offered his consent.[14]

Chosen to capture Balibo was the convalescing Susi. Having been deployed to Timor longer than either of its two sister teams, and having taken casualties during its maiden foray, its members had been resting since their return from the field. During the pause, *prayudha* commander Untung Suroso had been stuck down with malaria. With his men also sitting out, the remaining three *prayudha*, as well as the karsa yudha staff under Captain Yunus, were chosen to spearhead the Balibo assault. A mixed force of partisans and porters would be joining them for support. And because Susi was comprised of lightly equipped *sandhi yudha* operatives, they would additionally be backed by the para-commandos of Company B from Combat Detachment 2.

On the evening of 15 October, all of the assigned units prepared for their respective strikes. At 0430 hours the next morning, the blitz began. Taking the lead on the Maliana front, Tuti unleashed its automatic rifles and rocket launchers just before the sun broke the horizon. Joining the battle, para-commandos from Company A sent in a volley of 60mm mortar rounds; sixty partisans and nearly a battalion from the 2 Infantry Brigade soon added to the onslaught.

Though outnumbered, Fretilin was not necessarily outgunned. Using its own 81mm mortar, they started a heavy weapons duel in which they held the edge. Almost immediately, Tuti took casualties. One of its members— Private Samsy—fell with fatal injuries, while the commander of one of its para-commando platoons, Lieutenant Istarto Subagio, received a serious bullet wound to his forearm.[15]

Back inside Indonesia, members of the Flamboyan staff followed the Maliana battle over the radio. When word came that Istarto was bleeding profusely and in danger of losing his arm, Dading once more turned to Major Yusman and ordered a heliborne evacuation. Boarding an air force chopper, Yusman crossed the border at low altitude and started looking for signal panels. Finally sighting some florescent strips, the pilot dipped lower.

Yusman immediately had a bad feeling. "Nobody could be seen on the ground," he recalled. "I thought it might be an ambush."[16]

Grabbing an AK-47, the major exited the helicopter with the intention of reconnoitering the edge of the clearing. "If there is any incoming fire," he yelled toward the pilot, "take off without me."[17]

It never came to that. After Yusman took just a few steps, members of Tuti came out of hiding. Istarto, weak from blood loss, was among them. Piling him aboard, the chopper took to the air and headed for a field hospital established inside the Batugade fort.[18]

Back at Maliana, meanwhile, Indonesia's numerical advantage ultimately proved decisive. By nightfall, Fretilin opted to fight another day. Withdrawing in good order, they retreated east and allowed the Kogasgab forces to move in and consolidate their hold over the smoldering town.

At Balibo, the battle began with a perfectly timed diversion. At 0430 hours on 16 October, Dading ordered four trucks at Batugade to turn on their headlights and drive in circles near the town's fort.[19] From high atop Balibo, the small Fretilin garrison gathered to watch. Joining them were five Australian and British journalists, all eagerly waiting to get video footage of Indonesian involvement in the escalating border conflict.

Fretilin knew a concerted defense of Balibo was all but impossible. In its favor was its commanding view of Batugade and the protection offered by the two-meter-tall external stone wall around the Balibo fort. In addition, vehicular traffic from Batugade was channeled along a single dirt road that wound up the steep hill from the coast; in theory, the Balibo defenders could use their single 81mm mortar and two Madsen machineguns to keep the path under fire.

But just as at Maliana, they were at a major quantitative disadvantage. Seeing the Indonesian military concentration at Batugade, and the Indonesian naval vessels multiplying offshore over the previous week, Fretilin's leadership knew their two dozen soldiers at Balibo would only pose a minor irritant in the face of a major offensive. If they came under heavy pressure, plans called for them to retreat toward the larger Fretilin garrisons at Atabae or Bobonaro. From there they would trade space for time: if they could hold through November, the onset of Timor's rainy season would complicate any further Indonesian ground advance until the monsoons subsided the following year.

As the sound of the Batugade trucks wafted up to Balibo, such an assault looked imminent. As had been intended, the gaze of the Fretilin defenders remained riveted in the direction of the coast.

Thirty minutes later, the vehicles at Batugade abruptly stopped circling. As the sky slowly turned a deep slate gray, quiet descended over the hilltop.

It was not to last. At 0600 hours, Susi launched a ground assault from the rear. Over the previous evening, they had quietly marched from the border to the southeastern edge of town. Dividing in two, Prayudha 2 and 3 skirted left of the town square and advanced on the fort; Prayudha 1 kept right and targeted Balibo's small barracks. The *karsa yudha* command staff, meanwhile, paused on the southern edge of town.

Hitting from this unexpected direction, the attack proved fast and decisive. Firing short bursts from their AK-47 assault rifles, the commandos swept through the square without encountering opposition. Almost no residents were to be seen; the town's few shops were shuttered.

Not until they approached the fort were Prayudha 2 and 3 met by a volley of Fretilin machinegun rounds. Bringing forward their 90mm rocket launchers, the commandos responded in kind—only to watch the rockets deflect off the masonry with almost no effect. In need of indirect fire that could come down over the wall, they radioed a request for mortar support back to the *karsa yudha* staff, which in turn relayed the message to the para-commandos of Company B. Still en route lugging their mortars, delays ensued as the company worked its way to the south of Balibo, erected a 60mm tube, and finally sent rounds arcing over the town.

The tardy mortars did the trick. As the fort drew silent thirty minutes into the operation, the two *prayudha* advanced. Inside they found two dead Fretilin combatants, an 81mm mortar, and bloodtrails leading over the eastern wall and into the forest. One round had punched a small hole in the roof of the regent's bungalow in the center of the fort; apart from that, there was little other visible damage inflicted to the immediate area.

The same was not true for the rest of Balibo. On the heels of the three *prayudha*, several hundred Timorese partisans and porters had poured into town. The vast majority were members of Apodeti; only a handful were UDT. Armed and deployed for the first time in such large numbers, they directed gunfire at the shuttered buildings. Some could not resist the opportunity to loot; others set fire to a row of gasoline drums near the town square. Black smoke began to mix with the morning fog, cutting down visibility to a minimum.

Forty-five minutes into the assault, Balibo was burning but otherwise quiet. Suddenly, sporadic gunshots crackled from a house near the road juncture toward Maliana. To that time, Fretilin resistance had been minimal; the attack force suffered just two casualties: one Susi member had taken a bullet to the hand, while another round had hit a partisan in the back. Reacting to this late outburst, twelve members of the closest *prayudha*—which had gathered at the square after finding the barracks empty—assessed the source. With whitewashed concrete walls and a tin roof, the unremarkable house had once belonged to Chinese traders. Ironically, the commandos later recognized its Chinese ownership for a different—albeit wrong—reason. Said one:

> The house had a flag with stars painted on the front wall. When we were in Atsabe, we remembered the Taiwan flags had stars on them, so we thought this was another Taiwan shop.[20]

In fact, the Chinese house bore a crude rendition of the Australian, not Taiwanese, flag. This had been painted by the five foreign journalists who had been waiting at Balibo for almost a week to get good newsreel footage of the fighting. Now huddled inside the house, they would not live to tell the tale. Rushing forward, the *prayudha* unleashed a withering amount of AK-47 fire through the windows; return fire ceased almost immediately.[21]

As was the case elsewhere in town, the Timorese partisans barely waited before descending on the Chinese house in search of loot. No sooner had they entered, one of the Apodeti guerrillas (who, like many of the others living along the border, spoke passable Indonesian) ran out screaming *"Bule! Bule!"*—"Caucasian! Caucasian!"

The Indonesian commandos quickly entered the house and looked over the white bodies. They also found several dead Timorese, as well as a single Carl Gustav "Swedish K" submachine gun. Assuming the foreigners were Portuguese, the deputy *karsa yudha* commander used a handheld radio to relay word of the incident to Yunus.[22] The captain, who had moved up to the fort in the interim, raised Colonel Dading on his larger tactical radio. Balibo, he simply reported, was under Indonesian control.

Down at Batugade, Dading had been watching events on the hilltop through a set of binoculars. As the partisans ran amok, he watched as black smoke started to curl into the sky. "It looked like a riot was taking place," he recalled.[23]

Once Yunus sent word that the town was secure, the colonel boarded a chopper for an inspection. Going with him was Tommy Martomo, a medical doctor assigned to Umi at Batugade. As they landed at Balibo's town square, they made their way past smoldering houses up to the fort. There they inspected the regent's bungalow, an elegant structure oddly out of place with its checkered tile floors and Western-style flush toilets.

As Dading toured the site, partisans continued to pick through the town. The colonel was informed of the Caucasian fatalities, though their nationalities were still not yet known. Like so many other structures in Balibo, the Chinese house was soon put to the torch. Four charred bodies were subsequently turned over to Australian authorities; a fifth decaying body was allegedly recovered the following week in the forest outside the town.

Elsewhere along the front, the news was mixed. Along the coast, the marine battalion had pushed eight kilometers into Palaka against limited resistance. But the single infantry company targeted against Lebos was having trouble consolidating its grip against an equal number of Fretilin. At Bobonaro, too, a combined force of Tuti and members of the 2 Infantry Brigade were making no headway in capturing this key Fretilin stronghold.

Strong Fretilin resistance was not Kogasgab's only problem. Some seventy percent of its mortar rounds were proving to be duds, prompting a request to Malaysia to provide an emergency mortar shipment. In addition, the rain was increasing in intensity and frequency, hailing the imminent onset of the rainy season; Indonesia's supply lines were already becoming mired.[24]

The result of all this was a stalemate. Aside from three sorties flown by the lone B-26, three strafing runs by AC-47 gunships, and a single barrage from the *Ratulangi*, over the ensuing five weeks few rounds were exchanged along the entire front.[25]

During the lull, Kogasgab rushed in reinforcements. By 15 November, the two remaining battalions from the 2 Infantry Brigade arrived in West Timor and shifted to the border. Maintaining its aversion to using U.S.-made weapons, Jakarta also sent along Yugoslavian mountain guns and Soviet-made mortars and multiple-barrel rocket launchers—so-called Stalin's Organs—all purchased during the 1962 Irian campaign.

Not until 21 November did the Indonesians restart their offensive. Their primary goal was now Atabae, the major Fretilin troop garrison and logistical center first reconnoitered by Susi in September. Given Atabae's size—and the stiff Fretilin resistance elsewhere along the border—Kogasgab planned to overwhelm the town with three separate columns. Coming from Palaka on the left flank would be the marine battalion and their armor. In the center would be the para-commandos of Combat Detachment 2, as well as Flamboyan's Umi with hundreds of Timorese partisans in tow. On the right was an infantry company marching north from Maliana. All three of the columns would be supported by aircraft and naval gunfire.

Kogasgab was under no illusion that the fight for Atabae would be easy. The terrain, while not particularly problematic for infantry, posed serious challenges for armor. Fraught with thick bamboo forests and narrow hill paths turned slick with the rains, this was certain to frustrate the PT-76 amphibious tanks and BTR-50 personnel carriers used by the marines. Still, General Suweno optimistically saw Atabae falling into their hands within three days.

Not surprisingly, this timetable was overly optimistic. One day into the operation, the column driving up the coast from Palaka came under mortar fire. Taking several casualties, the marines on foot immediately ground to a halt. Pushing onward, the tanks and personnel carriers turned inland—only to be reduced to a glacial pace as their treads and wheels spun on the muddy slopes.

Four days into the campaign and with limited progress to show, Flamboyan's Major Yusman arrived at the front in an attempt to regain momentum. By that time, Umi had worked its way immediately behind the marine armor. Imploring the commandos to advance in conjunction with the tanks, he coordinated naval gunfire on Atabae and its environs. As villagers fled the shelling, the Indonesian task force inched forward.

Not until the morning of 28 November, following a final heavy weapons barrage, did they belatedly take their target. Performing well in the light infantry role, the commandos of Umi entered Atabae to find its Fretilin defenders had already withdrawn into the surrounding hills. The team's assigned doctor, Tommy Martomo, recalls:

> The town was coated in mud, and malaria was soon rampant. We found some empty stables that had been used for the Portuguese cavalry unit. We also found a bathroom with a sitting toilet in the district officer's house; after two weeks in the field, this was like a throne.[26]

Umi had little time to enjoy Atabae's relative creature comforts. Though Suharto had been hovering just short of approving an open invasion of Portuguese Timor, two events in late November pushed Jakarta to the brink. On 24 November, Washington publicly revealed that a Cuban military task force had landed in Angola to fight in support of the nascent leftist guerrilla government that assumed power from Lisbon. For Indonesia's top brass, the parallels with Timor were obvious and disturbing.[27]

Four days later—at nearly the same time Kogasgab captured Atabae—Jakarta was rocked by something far more provocative. Burning its bridges, Fretilin leaders in Dili made a unilateral declaration of independence in a desperate attempt to garner international support. "This was the red line that was not supposed to be crossed," Major Yusman was later to comment. "This forced our hand."[28]

1 UDT took with them twenty-three Portuguese military prisoners captured during their earlier retreat toward Batugade; all of the Portuguese were eventually repatriated to Lisbon.

2 Yusman Yutam interview.

3 U.S. intelligence discounted the fiction of the military exercise and correctly saw it as a pretext for preparing an invasion. See 2 September 1975 entry in *The National Times* (30 May-5 June 1982), p. 36.

4 Hendro Subroto, *Eyewitness*, p. 114.

5 Though capable of dropping bombs, the Indonesian B-26 in Timor was outfitted only with rockets and machineguns.

6 During the waning years of the Vietnam War, the U.S. government helped modify C-47 transports into AC-47 gunships for the governments of Cambodian, Indonesia, Laos, South Vietnam, and Thailand. The Cambodian and Indonesian versions used machineguns; the others utilized multi-barrel miniguns. The Indonesian modifications were completed in July 1971, but had not been used in combat prior to October 1975.

7 Porters were paid a small daily stipend and a rice ration; the stipend paid to partisans was five times higher.

8 Yusman Yutam interview.

9 Benny Moerdani interview.

10   Hendro Subroto, *Eyewitness*, p. 60.

11   FBIS, Asia-Pacific edition, 8 October 1975, p. Q1.

12   Sofian Effendi interview; Johannes Bambang interview.

13   By 11 October, U.S. intelligence was reporting on the impending strike: "The first of the enclaves is to be established on October 14, when Indonesian units are to attack the town of Maliana." See 11 October 1975 entry in *The National Times* (6-12 June 1982), p. 16. The actual attack did not take place until 16 October.

14   Dading Kalbuadi interview.

15   Tarub interview.

16   Yusman Yutam interview.

17   Ibid.

18   Three doctors had been rushed to Batugade soon after it was retaken to establish a field hospital for Kogasgab. My mid-October, it included a surgeon, an anesthesiologist, a radiologist, a dentist, and a neurologist. Interview with Tommy Martomo, 8 June 1999.

19   Dading Kalbuadi interview.

20   Kusno interview.

21   The October assault on Balibo remains a highly emotive issue in Australia and has spawned a number of conspiracy theories. Among them: that the Balibo assault was specifically targeted against the journalists, and that the newsmen attempted to surrender but were executed by Susi members in cold blood. One melodramatic version allegedly has Captain Yunus on the scene personally ordering the execution, with one of his Susi members drawing a commando dagger to fatally stab a journalist in the back (see Desmond Ball and Hamish McDonald, *Death in Balibo, Lies in Canberra* (Sydney: Allen & Unwin, 2000), p. 106). Eight members of Susi were interviewed in the course of this research; six were in Balibo on 16 October. None of these sources denied the fact that Susi fired the fatal shots, nor did they offer apologies. They denied, however, having advance knowledge any foreigners were in the town; if Jakarta knew about the newsmen, which is not at all apparent, they apparently did not pass prior word to the Susi members in the field. Rather than assaulting Balibo to eliminate journalists, the Susi members more plausibly explained the assault as an effort to evict Fretilin in concert with the simultaneous attacks at Maliana and Palaka. They also insisted that the assault on the Chinese house was conducted by automatic weapons through the windows, that the

incident took place after the first wave of commandos had already moved up to the fort, and that they were drawn to the house after gunfire came from inside.

22 In the days immediately prior to the capture of Batugade on 8 October, Flamboyan members conducting a reconnaissance of the fort reported seeing what they believed were Portuguese military advisors among the Fretilin defenders. Given that Fretilin's ranks included many Timorese troops with mixed blood, and the fact that some wore distinctive Portuguese camouflage uniforms, it is not surprising that such mistaken sightings took place. It is also for this reason that Susi members assumed the dead foreigners at Balibo were Portuguese.

23 Dading Kalbuadi interview.

24 Hendro Subroto, *Saksi Mata Perjuangan Integrasi Timor Timur* (Jakarta: Pustaka Sinar Harapan, 1997), p. 60; 20 October entry in *The National Times* (6-12 June 1982), p. 16.

25 The AC-47 strikes were conducted on 17, 18, and 20 November near Atabae. During the last mission, the AC-47 received return ground fire.

26 Tommy Martomo interview.

27 Angola's emergent leftist government requested Cuban military assistance in July 1975, but it did not arrive until early October. The Cubans initiated military operations in Angola on 5 November, five days before the official departure of the Portuguese. David Deutchmann, ed., *Changing the History of Africa* (Melbourne: Ocean Press, 1989), p. 43.

28 Yusman Yutam interview.

CHAPTER SEVENTEEN

SEROJA

In October 1974, Captain Richard Meadows was a pioneer of sorts. A legend within the U.S. Army Special Forces—he had been among the initial American sergeants to lead reconnaissance teams along the Ho Chi Minh Trail during the Vietnam War, earning himself one of that conflict's first battlefield commissions—he was the first Green Beret officer permitted to visit Batu Jajar in order to assess Kopassandha's needs.

His visit came at a critical juncture. U.S. ground troops had already left Indochina, and it seemed only a matter of time before those governments fell to communism. The U.S. Congress, asserting itself in the wake of the Watergate scandal, appeared in no mood to authorize further assistance to its besieged allies. Not surprisingly, the other non-communist nations in the region had little confidence in Washington.

Looking to chip away at that sentiment, Meadows brainstormed possible avenues of assistance to his Indonesian counterparts. He immediately identified several glaring deficiencies in Kopassandha's tactics. For example, Batu Jajar had only a rudimentary pathfinder course based loosely on the experiences of two Indonesians who trained at Fort Benning in 1964. Their freefall techniques had not been updated since the brief encounter with the Yugoslavians in 1962, while their jumpmaster procedures, based on those brought back by the class that went to the Soviet Union in 1965, were largely inappropriate for the C-130.

With the concurrence of the training center's commander, General Suweno, Meadows drafted a proposal to deploy a limited number of U.S. Army Special Forces advisors to Batu Jajar. Ironically, the U.S. no longer had any

Green Berets readily available in Southeast Asia. Just three years earlier, thousands had been training and fighting across the battlefields of Indochina. But reeling from the setbacks in Vietnam, the Pentagon had ordered drastic cuts in the special warfare community. Four months earlier in June, the 1 Special Forces Group—whose area of responsibility covered Southeast Asia—was officially disbanded.

Sending his request for instructors all the way back to Fort Bragg, it landed at the 7 Special Forces Group. Though targeted for operations in Latin America, the group allocated two captains and four sergeants for immediate deployment to Indonesia. They were to be equally divided into two separate teams. The first, led by Captain Richard Sweezy, would coach the Indonesians in freefalling accuracy and midair maneuvering. The second, commanded by Captain Norman Bruneau, would instruct in jumpmaster techniques, pathfinding, and air-ground operations.

On 9 November, after a briefing from Meadows, the two teams accepted their first students.[1] They found the Indonesians apt learners, though initially somewhat inscrutable in their emotions. "One of them told me that they were learning English and Chinese, the languages spoken by their friends and enemies," said Sergeant Joe Garner. "I asked him which was the friend, and he smiled without comment."[2]

By the time they concluded their courses on 19 May 1975, the atmosphere had warmed considerably. Returning for the graduation, Captain Meadows took aside Captain Bambang Soembodo, the Batu Jajar operations assistant. "You could probably use additional instruction for operations in the east," said Meadows cryptically.

"You mean Irian Jaya?" said Bambang.

"No," replied Meadows. "Timor."[3]

Airborne operations, in fact, were to play a pivotal part in the invasion of Portuguese Timor. The Indonesian order-of-battle included two formations with this capability: Kopassandha and Kostrad. Though a large-scale parachute assault was more suitable for Kostrad, that unit was experiencing severe growing pains. Far more than the paper organization it had been in 1965, the reserve had been given administrative control over its subordinate units in 1969. This was a significant shift: military region commanders had previously retained control over the purse strings to the troops, undercutting the influence of the Kostrad chief.

But once Kostrad had gained complete sway over its allocated units, further problems became apparent. Influenced by European models, Indonesian battalions had traditionally followed an inflated "square" arrangement with up to 1,200 men in four, sometimes five, companies. Belatedly deciding this was too large and unwieldy for modern battlefields, Jakarta in 1973 decided to switch to a smaller, triangular arrangement like the U.S. This entailed paring down battalions to an authorized strength of 760 men, with actual strength usually hovering near 600.[4]

The pilot project for this reorganization was the East Java military region. Commanded by General Widjojo Soejono—the former RPKAD chief—he spent the next year streamlining the soldiers in his region into four brigades: two of these were for Kostrad, while the other two remained under the jurisdiction of his military region.

By early 1975, the Indonesian army had finished the process of converting to smaller battalions. Still, there were problems. "Nearly all of the officers lower than lieutenant colonel had no combat experience," said General Benny. "Most had never experienced shots fired in anger."[5]

Within Kostrad, theoretically the army's spearhead, the problem was particularly acute. Due to the expenses involved, Kostrad's two airborne brigades rarely had the opportunity to exercise as a coherent whole; rather, they were usually wielded as individual battalions.

In February 1975, Indonesia's top brass tried to address this shortcoming. During that month, the 17 Airborne Brigade was selected to parachute into southern Sumatra during a major combined arms maneuver codenamed Wibawa VII. By the time the exercise was finished, however, the foreign diplomatic corps—particularly the Australians—were crying foul. Fearing it was a direct prelude to an invasion of Timor, Canberra rushed a letter to Jakarta urging them to desist.

Feigning innocence, the Indonesians professed that Wibawa VII was not practice for Timor. This was true, at least in part. Though the Sumatra maneuvers were not specifically conducted with Timor in mind, the Indonesian military was concurrently penning preliminary plans for a full-scale invasion of that territory. Those plans centered not around Kostrad but rather Kopassandha, specifically its Group 1 at Cijantung.

The Group 1 commander at that time was Lieutenant Colonel Samsudin, the former engineering officer. Along with a small team from his headquarters staff, Samsudin in March was assigned with fleshing out details for an airborne assault on Dili using only his group. As part of this, he was to scour Java for suitable sites where practice jumps could be discreetly conducted. After a week, he found a quiet stretch along the island's southern coast. Said Samsudin: "It had seaside cliffs just like near Dili."[6]

Before plans could proceed far, politics intervened. President Suharto had just returned from a state visit to Australia in April; with bilateral relations bolstered in the aftermath, he did not want it spoiled by leaked word of Timorese preparations. Kopassandha, as a result, was ordered to put further practice on hold.[7]

Four months later, in the wake of UDT's abortive coup in Dili, Indonesia's generals revisited invasion plans with a vengeance. By month's end, they had sketched out a three-pronged assault across Portuguese Timor's northern coast. Foreshadowing things to come, one of the prongs would push east from Motaain by land, a second would parachute directly on Dili, and the last would seize Baucau. From there, special forces units would push inland. Victory, it was calculated, with be easy and swift. Keeping the botanical theme started with Flamboyan, Kogasgab's campaign was codenamed Seroja—Indonesian for "Lotus."

As before, Kopassandha's Group 1 was to play a pivotal role. That same month, the group had seen a change in leadership when its deputy commander, Lieutenant Colonel Soegito, was elevated to the top slot. Picking up where Samsudin had left off, he was told that he would be leading the Dili prong.

Though a tall order, Soegito was reasonably confident of success. The army headquarters promised him 500 para-commandos for the assignment: 265 would come from his own Group 1 (including a small headquarters staff), and the remainder from Group 2. These would be divided into two light detachments, each with two companies. The contingent from Group 1, termed Combat Detachment 1, was under the command of Major Atang Sutrisna; those from Group 2, dubbed Combat Detachment 2, under Major Muhidin. Both detachments, under Soegito's overall command, were codenamed Nanggala 5.

For the next two months, Soegito fine-tuned the assault plan for his portion of Seroja. Carrying through the concept conjured by Samsudin, he had elements of Combat Detachment 1 conduct parachute jumps and beach maneuvers along the Java coast.

At that point, Soegito's careful planning hit difficulties. Due to urgent Kogasgab requirements for Phase Two, all of Combat Detachment 2 was stripped from Nanggala 5 and rushed to Motaain. Two of his staff officers also left for the Timor front. Having suddenly lost half of his promised task force, Soegito was desperate for replacements. Spying the 401 Airborne Battalion ready and available at Semarang, he took the initiative to begin coordinating with the battalion staff.

A month later, army politics intervened. This was because the 401 Airborne Battalion was something of a bastard child in the Indonesian order-of-battle: having done the PKI's bidding during October 1965 while under the designation of 454 Airborne Battalion, it had been forced to change numbers and purge its leadership cadre. Though not disbanded, the battalion had never fully outlived the memories of 1965 and was the only parachute battalion not formally accepted into one of the two Kostrad airborne brigades.[8]

Rather than giving the 401 Airborne Battalion a central role in capturing Dili, headquarters had other ideas. On 17 November, Soegito was informed that the 401 Airborne Battalion was no longer available. Instead, his remaining 263 para-commandos of Nanggala 5 would be joined by the 501 Airborne Battalion from Kostrad's 18 Airborne Brigade. (Prior to 1973, the 501 Airborne Battalion was known as the 530 Airborne Battalion, the same unit that parachuted into Merauke with Benny Moerdani in 1962. Its redesignation came about during the army's restructuring campaign to smaller battalions.)

Soegito did not take the news well. He had originally been promised an all-Kopassandha task force, and now he was handed a mixed allotment that included troops not under his control. The 501 Airborne Battalion, after all, did not answer to him, but rather to a brigade commander that outranked him by a grade. This left the combined group without an overall leader. Moreover, the two halves did not have time to exercise together.

There was little opportunity to lament the imperfect marriage. On 28 November, Fretilin made its unilateral declaration of independence. Though Suharto had been delaying approval for Seroja since August, procrastination was no longer an option.[9]

Before the invasion of Timor could proceed, there was one last diplomatic hurdle to consider: U.S. President Gerald Ford planned a state visit to Jakarta on 6 December. Suharto and Ford had briefly met five months earlier near Washington, during which time Ford had been in a gloomy daze following the recent fall of Indochina to communist forces. Determined to be more upbeat this time around, Ford saw the December meeting as a way of bolstering regional confidence after the Vietnam War. The Indonesian government, the U.S. Embassy predicted, was not likely to spoil the mood by authorizing dramatic overt intervention in Timor before Ford arrived.

The embassy was correct—but only just. " I liked reading about MacArthur," said Colonel Dading, "and I remembered Pearl Harbor was on Sunday morning, December 7, when most people were at church." Using the exact same reasoning, he suggested that D-Day for Seroja should be early on Sunday, 7 December, when most of the heavily Catholic Timorese population would theoretically be attending religious services.[10]

During the intervening week before that date, the Indonesian army was a hive of activity. Recognizing that they had insufficient planes, the assaults on Dili and Baucau—originally intended for the same day—were now to be conducted in turn. As a first phase, Soegito's para-commandos, along with the 501 Airborne Battalion, would conduct a pre-dawn jump into Dili. For good measure, the 502 Airborne Battalion, also from the 18 Airborne Brigade, would jump near the town in a subsequent wave later that morning, while the marines would make a simultaneous amphibious landing.

In preparation for this, Combat Detachment 1 was briefed on the latest intelligence at Cijantung. "Sun Tzu said to know thy enemy, the terrain, and the climate," said Captain Soembodo, the Batu Jajar operations assistant now serving on Suweno's Kogasgab staff. "We did not know enough about any of these."[11]

Case in point was information fed to Kopassandha about the Komoro River. Flowing into the sea just west of Dili, the Komoro, briefing officers at Cijantung reported, was at flood stage and brimming with crocodiles. Lacking a proper bridge, the river would be all but impossible to ford given the alleged presence of these man-eating reptiles.[12]

The Kopassandha audience was also soft-sold on the resistance they would likely face. "They told us that the Timorese would see the parachute canopies and clap, and we would have a victory parade the next day," recalled Lieutenant

Luhut Pandjaitan, a company commander in Group 1. "But we had gotten word of the fighting along the border and realized it was not going to be a piece of cake."[13]

At 0800 hours on 6 December, Presidents Ford and Suharto met at the state palace. Waiting in an outer hall were General Benny Moerdani and Brent Scowcroft from the U.S. National Security Council. By then, the U.S. government had sufficient communications intercepts and other sources of intelligence to know the invasion of Timor was days, if not hours, away. Not mincing words, Scowcroft turned to Benny. "Will you be using U.S. weapons?"

Until that point, Kogasgab had been sticking with non-U.S. armaments. But with plausible deniability set to fall by the wayside with Seroja, many U.S. items—from M-16 assault rifles to landing craft—were factored into the campaign plan. "Our military is built largely around U.S. systems," Benny answered truthfully. "We have no choice."[14]

A little over one hour later, Ford and Secretary of State Henry Kissinger emerged from their tryst with Suharto. The Indonesian leader had obliquely referred to dramatic impending action in Timor, eliciting no protest from his U.S. guests. As he prepared to leave the palace, Kissinger turned to Benny. "How long do you think this little game you are playing will take?"

"A few weeks," the Indonesian general confidently responded.

Plans called for the U.S. delegation to head for the airport, with Air Force One lifting its wheels for Tokyo at 1130 hours. "Do not start," implored Kissinger, "until we have left Indonesian airspace."

Benny promised as much, then left in a rush for Kupang.[15]

Over the previous two days, Lieutenant Colonel Soegito had barely slept. On the afternoon of 4 December, he had departed to Kupang with his operations assistant, Major Theo Syafei. Huddling with the Kogasgab staff, at that late hour they were debating dropzones for the capture of Dili. It was proving an exercise in frustration. Dropzones east of the town were quickly ruled out because of the rugged high ground in between, ruining the element of surprise while they hiked to their target. Similarly, the new airstrip being constructed east of the Komoro River was deemed too far; besides, Indonesian intelligence painted the Komoro as full of crocodiles, so crossing it would be prohibitive for the lightly-equipped special forces.

Looking at closer alternatives, they next considered the town's current airfield just seven blocks due west of the Governor's mansion. This, too, was soon discounted because it was exposed to gunfire from the hills south of town.

Finally, General Suweno's deputy intelligence assistant, an artillery officer, posed the most brazen alternative of all: why not jump inside the town itself? At the very least, it would enable them to keep the element of surprise.

Not hearing any better options, those at the table concurred.

Unable to get a spare plane seat back to Jakarta, Soegito and Syafei spent a sleepless night in Kupang. Finally getting to Cijantung on the evening of 5 December, Soegito addressed Combat Detachment 1 on their impending operation. The detachment was a composite formation drawn from across Group 1; under Major Atang Sutrisna were a pair of companies led by Lieutenants Luhut Pandjaitan and Atang Sanjaya. Forbidden from telling their wives or families, both companies sorted out their weapons and parachutes late into the night.

On 6 December at 1300 hours, Soegito piled the para-commandos aboard C-130 transports and headed for Madiun, East Java. There they were to confer with the 501 Airborne Battalion to iron out details about the Dili jump. What ensued, however, was mass confusion. "There was no senior officer in charge," recalled Soegito. "The air force people held the same rank as me and did not want to take orders, and there was no clear chain of command with Kostrad."[16]

Though none recognized it at the time, the scene was a near-exact repetition of what had transpired at Madiun thirteen years earlier. At that time, Benny and his DPC had arrived to coordinate their impending jump with a company from the 530 Airborne Battalion. Fast forward to 1975, special forces were arriving for an eleventh-hour coordination session prior to a combat jump with the 501 Airborne Battalion, which was the same battalion under a new number. On both occasions, confusion reigned.

After several fruitless hours, a loose action plan was agreed upon. Four C-130 would be used for Kopassandha, while another five would carry the Kostrad battalion. In a key maneuver, the Kostrad paratroopers would theoretically shift to blocking positions in the hills south of town to prevent Fretilin from escaping inland.

The two Kopassandha companies, Soegito decided, would be divided into three teams of two platoons apiece. This would allow them to tackle three targets in the shortest possible time. One team, under Major Atang Sutrisna, would seize the Governor's mansion. The second, under Lieutenant Atang Sanjaya, would capture the docks along the beach. The last, led by Lieutenant Luhut, was to move to the town's airfield; as new information suggested that heavy mortars were present near the runway; it was deemed vital that these weapons be neutralized in the opening minutes.[17]

Because Kopassandha had more precise targets than Kostrad, they would jump in the first four aircraft. In a further call that all but guaranteed more confusion, it was decided that the three Kopassandha teams would be equally divided among these four planes. Mixed in this manner, the planes would dump their parachutists over the center of Dili, then let the para-commandos sort themselves out once they got on the ground. This allocation, it was felt, would ensure that at least part of each team would reach Dili even if some of the planes were forced to abort.[18]

Translating these plane assignments into reality proved impossible. With the aircraft parked all over the airbase, the last vestiges of order quickly disappeared as the men of Nanggala 5 tried to work out their placements as night fell over Madiun. Lacking proper sleep and not having eaten for a day, Soegito's men watched all this with frayed patience. Not until shortly after midnight on Sunday, 7 December, did they take to the air for the four hour and twenty minute journey to Timor.

Although Seroja hinged on the element of surprise, Nanggala 5 no longer held this advantage. Intercepting Fretilin radio transmissions, U.S. intelligence on 6 December determined that Fretilin was fully expecting the strike on Dili. They had already built up defenses near the capital, read one CIA report, and had moved large amounts of supplies to the interior in order to wage a protracted guerrilla war.[19]

The Indonesians hardly helped their own case. At 0130 hours on 7 December, a marine reconnaissance team landed by rubber boat along the beach just west of Dili. They were there to place markers along the shore for an amphibious assault at daybreak. Before they could depart, however, Fretilin at 0300 hours suddenly cut all lights in the town. Surmising that the Timorese correctly guessed the impending attack, the Indonesian armada loitering just over the horizon requested permission to begin shelling Dili. Thirty minutes later, after receiving approval from Suweno, naval guns began unleashing salvos toward the coast.[20]

In the air while this was transpiring, the nine C-130 transports had flown east in radio silence. They formed three triangle formations, each successive triangle flying fifteen meters higher to prevent collisions with parachutists in lead aircraft. Banking clockwise, they intended to approach Dili from over the hills to its east and make a westward run down the center of town. They would then proceed to Kupang and pick up further Kostrad paratroopers for a second sortie. Four minutes from target, rear doors opened. As the aircraft closed to within 91 meters of each other, they lowered flaps by fifty percent.[21]

At 0530 local time, para-commandos streamed from the first Hercules. After more than four exhausting hours, the men were relieved to exit into the slipstream. As the sun was only beginning to creep over the horizon, and Fretilin was enforcing a power blackout, they descended toward a town bathed in total darkness.

Seconds later, Kopassandha troops began to pour from the wingmen in the first triangle formation. After orienting themselves under olive drab canopies, the commandos scanned the approaching townscape. Though no sounds were audible apart from the drone of aircraft engines overhead, small flashes of muzzle fire began to sparkle from below. Fretilin was starting to react.

In the lead aircraft, the formation commander had finished dropping his load when the first round impacted. Smashing a window in the cockpit, shards of glass sprayed across the crew. A volley of bullets riddled his left wingman, killing an air force loadmaster inside the cabin. Immediately afterward, the airwaves were filled with frantic reports of Fretilin groundfire impacting on the planes in front. Taking evasive maneuvers, pilots in the second and third diamond formations instinctively edged toward sea; unaware they were heading away from land, jumpmasters continued to direct the parachutists out the door.

In the middle of the armada, Hercules T-1312 was particularly hard hit. As gauges flashed across his instrument panel, the pilot banked sharply toward water. Standing near the door, Lieutenant Luhut was about to exit when the jumpmaster threw an arm across his path. With its full complement of seventy-two commandos still aboard, they headed for Kupang.

At Atabae, the Indonesian forces that powered their way into that town had known for almost a week that something big was afoot. On 2 December, they had received orders to move west to the coast, then five kilometers north to the seaside village of Tailaco. Marine tanks and armored personnel carriers led the way in slow, deliberate fashion, seizing the target forty-eight hours later against no resistance.

Dading's two remaining Flamboyan teams—the third, Susi, had already returned to Cijantung on 9 November—also got word to head for Tailaco. Heeding the call, Tarub's Tuti, which had earlier exhausted itself in a vain attempt to capture Bobonaro and for the previous week had been resting at Balibo, shifted up the coast.

Sofian's Umi, however, needed to stay until replaced at Atabae by an infantry battalion from Central Java. Impatient to reach the beach, one of Umi's para-commando platoons was dispatched ahead to Tailaco; the remainder, along with their partisans, awaited the tardy infantrymen.

Not until the afternoon of 6 December did the *Teluk Bone*, an ex-U.S. landing craft, approach the Tailaco coast. As the Central Java battalion ferried to shore and made their way inland, the marines directed their amphibious vehicles into the *Teluk Bone*'s belly. Joining them was Tuti, the platoon from Umi, and twenty partisans. By dusk, all were steaming east along the coast toward Dili.[22]

The rest of Umi, with almost six hundred partisans in tow, rushed to Tailaco at nightfall. Having missed the *Teluk Bone* by a couple of hours, they stretched out on the sand and fell asleep under the stars. Their reprieve ended at daybreak, when they were jarred awake by the sound of nine Hercules aircraft passing directly overhead after the Dili drop. Surmising what had just taken place, Sutiyoso felt cheated: "I was sad to miss out."[23]

What Sutiyoso was missing was bloody mayhem. Blanketed across an unfamiliar town, the para-commandos stripped off their parachute harnesses in the darkness, then donned red berets and yellow scarves to help with identification in the urban fight to come.

Some never got that opportunity. Three commandos landed in the water and drowned. Dozens more were wounded in the opening seconds. Among them, Lieutenant Atang Sanjaya was shot as his feet touched ground a block south of the Governor's mansion. As a bullet punched through the soft leather helmet he wore for the jump, it grazed his scalp which started bleeding profusely. Moments later, a grenade exploded a few feet away, peppering both arms and legs with shrapnel. Struggling to strip off his chute with two wounded hands, he crawled for cover.

Nearby, Lieutenant Colonel Soegito landed hard next to the Governor's mansion and twisted his foot. With literally hundreds of rifles firing around the town, he tried to get a status report from his men. The news was horrifying: nearly eighty Kopassandha members were unaccounted for and feared dead. Though seventy-two of that number had actually safely diverted to Kupang, Soegito's long-distance Racal transceiver had been on the aborted drop. As a result, he was unable to communicate with the Kogasgab staff and learn of their fate.

The bad news kept coming. Rallying members of his team, Major Atang Sutrisna had maneuvered to the front of the Governor's mansion and replaced the Fretilin flag with one from Indonesia. But as he patrolled around the side of the building, a sniper from its upper floor fired off a single round. The bullet hit him high in the left temple, punching a large jagged hole out the right side of his neck. The major was dead instantly.

By the time he received word of Atang's demise, Soegito had limped north to the docks. En route, he had thrown a pair of grenades made by Indonesia's Pindad weapons factory; both were duds. Exhausted, he reached to get a drink from his canteen—only to find a bullet hole had drained it. He promptly reached down and exchanged it for a canteen from a dead soldier.[24]

Gradually, the firing began to wane. Reviewing his men, Soegito found four propped against the side of a building with bullet injuries to their arms and legs. Casualties had far outstripped what little medical equipment had been brought by Nanggala 5, and none was forthcoming given their lack of radio communications with Kogasgab. Though all four could theoretically have been saved, Soegito was forced to watch them seep blood. "We're getting sleepy, sir," they told their group commander. "Get some sleep," the lieutenant colonel replied in his most comforting voice. The four never woke.[25]

Predictably, the lack of coordination between the Kostrad and Kopassandha members proved a critical flaw. The commanding officer of the 501 Airborne Battalion could not be located in the key hour after the jump, and his deputy battalion commander had suffered serious burns. Without its own leadership and not responding to Soegito, the Kostrad paratroopers, who were supposed to move into the hills south of Dili and establish blocking positions, went nowhere. Fretilin, as a result, enjoyed a ready avenue of escape.

Sixty minutes after the parachute jump, the *Teluk Bone* approached the beach directly north of Dili's runway. As planned, amphibious vehicles, marines, Flamboyan special forces, and partisans spilled onto the sand. In a welcome contrast to the Kopassandha and Kostrad members battling inside the town, they encountered no resistance.

Meantime, the nine Hercules transports made the forty-eight-minute hop from Dili and landed at Kupang's airbase. Reviewing battle damage to the airframes, the air force determined that just five of the transports were available for continued use. Initial plans had called for the second sortie to drop the 502 Airborne Battalion, the 18 Airborne Brigade headquarters staff, and supplies. But now short four planes, half of the 502 Airborne Battalion was told to wait for a third sortie later in the day. The seventy-two Kopassandha members who aborted their jump, too, were bumped to the third sortie.

At 0745 hours, the five transports were approaching Dili for the second time. Dropping them near the east bank of the Komoro in order to avoid gunfire over town, the Kostrad paratroopers rained downward. But in yet a further example of bad coordination, the descending soldiers saw the amphibious task force that was coincidentally regrouping near the Komoro. Edgy after hearing the reports of heavy Fretilin resistance that morning, the Kostrad members began firing and tossing grenades from the sky.

Running from the friendly onslaught, some of the marines unfurled Indonesian flags. Others unslung their rifles and began shooting back. Eventually, the firefight was brought to a halt after radio messages were relayed through the Kogasgab staff. No casualties were sustained from the mistaken exchange.

Once again, the C-130 transports returned to Kupang. There they onloaded the rest of the 502 Airborne Battalion and the Kopassandha commandos. While the aircraft were taxiing along the tarmac, however, the tower called them back to the hanger. The Kogasgab staff, hearing of the gun battle between the marines and Kostrad, had placed a halt on further drops in order to avoid further friendly fire incidents.

Back in Dili, the Indonesian troops spent the rest of the afternoon consolidating their grip over the town. The Komoro River, they noted with displeasure, was barely a trickle and there was no sign of crocodiles. From Nanggala 5, fourteen were killed by Fretilin gunfire, three more were presumed drowned, and two others were missing.[26] Among Kostrad participants, thirty-six died.

The Timorese had it far worse. Official Indonesian statistics put the number of Fretilin killed at 122 and more than 365 taken prisoner. Timorese sources, probably with considerable hyperbole, placed the number of dead at 2,000.[27]

By nightfall, Soegito and his men reflected over the bloodiest single day of fighting in the history of the Indonesian special forces. Many had risen to the occasion; a few had broken down and hidden themselves inside houses. "The experience lets you see a person's true soul," said Captain Nurdin Jusuf, the assistant operations officer. "You could see who is loyal, who is brave."[28]

At Tailaco, Major Sofian's Umi had received indirect word of the pitched battle in Dili and was itching to participate. There were no ships to transport them, but they had managed to round up a few dozen Timorese ponies abandoned near Atabae. Determined to make their way by foot and equestrian mount, they pushed north toward the Ribeira Loes.

They did not get far. Unlike the Komoro, which was almost dry, the Loes was swollen at flood stage. As the first wave of commandos steered their animals into the water, the ponies struggled in the swift brown current before turning back. "The horses will drown," Major Yusman radioed to Kogasgab.

Stymied, Umi returned to Tailaco for a day. Not until the afternoon of 8 December did the *Teluk Bone* materialize off the coast. Boarding rubber boats, the special forces team, along with 479 Apodeti and UDT partisans, piled into the landing ship and headed to Dili. But rather than disembarking at the capital, they were kept at sea for a day as three similar vessels maneuvered alongside;

all four then took on two companies of marines, five PT-76 tanks, and nine BTR-50 armored personnel carriers. The next morning, said the Kogasgab staff, they would be conducting an amphibious assault to seize Timor's second largest town, Baucau. Learning from their mistake in Dili, Colonel Dading was assigned as the senior officer in charge of the entire combined force.

Under cover of darkness, the armada steamed east for two hours. At 0330 hours, 10 December, they arrived at a point 20 kilometers north of Baucau. Remaining at this safe distance in the event Fretilin had assembled artillery along the beach, the bow doors to the landing craft opened. This was the cue for amphibious vehicles and rubber boats to begin spilling into the brine for the two-hour journey to shore.

For the members of Umi and their partisans, such an amphibious assault was something novel. Many were squeezed tight into the claustrophobic interiors of the BTR-50 personnel carriers. As each of the Soviet-made vehicles exited the landing ships, it briefly plunged under the surface before the propellers activated and pushed it back above the waves. One of the nine personnel carriers, however, had a faulty propulsion unit—hitting the sea, it continued all the way to the bottom; its entire complement of marines perished.

Just as dawn was breaking, the amphibious force reached the beach. The distant approach, they discovered, was unwarranted: Fretilin forces were nowhere to be seen. Their actual landing was near the shoreside village of Laga, which was still a day's march to the east of Baucau. With Umi and the partisans patrolling ahead of the marine armor, they immediately set out for their target. The entire route was quiet, with one exception. "There was a lone Fretilin fighter with his arm snapped and brain blown across the roadside," recalls Umi's assigned doctor, Tommy Martomo. "He had tried to use a Mauser against a panser."[29]

Shortly before dusk, the column reached the edge of Baucau. With thoughts of Dili on their mind, Umi leapfrogged into town with their guns at the ready. They quickly discovered that Baucau consisted of little more than a single dirt road with a handful of colonial buildings on either side. The largest structure—Hotel Baucau—looked relatively menacing. Thinking it might be a Fretilin command post, the special forces approached its entrance with Pindad grenades. Lobbing one into the lobby, they scrambled for cover.

Seconds later, the fuse ignited in a dull pop—but the main explosive failed to detonate. "We were fortunate the grenade was a dud," said Umi's Johannes

Bambang. "When we looked back inside, we found platters of food intact."[30]

Baucau held further surprises. No sooner had Umi begin to help itself to the hotel cuisine, dozens—then hundreds—of civilians began to materialize on the main street. In stark contrast to the rude welcome offered by Fretilin in Dili, the residents of Baucau seemed genuinely pleased to see the Indonesians.

Given the benign crowd and exhausted from the long hike into town, Umi and the marines had one thing on their minds. Hotel Baucau—which, with just four rooms, could hardly qualify as a hotel—was soon claimed by Major Sofian, Captain Sutiyoso, and the two ranking partisan leaders. Colonel Dading moved into a spacious abandoned house next to the local church. The rest of the commandos, partisans, and marines spread out among the remaining dwellings. Their sleep that night was arguably the best in months.

Shortly after Dading's task force had made its beach assault at Laga, an armada of C-130 transports approached the north coast of Timor off Baucau. Aboard were 65 of the Kopassandha commandos that had been holed up at Kupang since missing the Dili jump. They were joined by 158 members from the air force's Kopasgat; their mission was to return the massive Baucau runway—the largest in the territory, and capable of accepting wide-body jets—to operational status.

After dropping a pair of mannequins strapped to parachutes—to both test wind direction and troll for Fretilin groundfire—the first wave of troops descended toward a dropzone five kilometers west of the airstrip. Regrouping on the ground with few complications, they gave the signal for the transports to return to Kupang for a second load.

By the time the planes were again nearing the coast, trouble was in store. Scheduled to make the drop was the 328 Airborne Battalion, part of Kostrad's 17 Airborne Brigade. In an inauspicious start, the jumpmasters opened the rear doors when they were nearly over the beach; mistaking this for the signal to jump, an overzealous Kostrad platoon leader launched himself over the water and drowned.

The ground proved just as hazardous. As the paratroopers exited the aircraft over the dropzone, a twenty-knot wind had picked up. Pulled across a field of sharp boulders camouflaged by tall grass, an entire company was injured.

Later that morning, the transports did a third sortie. Aboard was the headquarters staff of the 17 Airborne Brigade, as well as the 401 Airborne Battalion. The same battalion that had been yanked from Soegito's plan for Dili, it had been reinstated for the Baucau phase.[31] Again the weather was bad, and again they sustained heavy casualties from wind and rocks.

By noon, the airborne task force had covered the distance to the runway without encountering resistance. Licking their wounds, the paratroopers deemed it too late in the day to move another six kilometers east for a link-up at Baucau. That did not come until 1100 hours, 11 December, when Colonel Soegiarto, the 17 Airborne Brigade commander, arrived at the town limits. With marines and Umi commandos lined up on both sides of the main street as an honor guard, Dading gave his fellow colonel an emotional hug. Compared to the fiasco at Dili, their combined arms maneuver against Baucau had been a relative model of success.

1   Interview with Richard Sweezy, 19 September 2001.

2   Interview with Joe Garner, 23 May 2000.

3   Bambang Soembodo interview.

4   Widjojo Soejono interview; Benny Moerdani interview.

5   Benny Moerdani interview.

6   Samsudin interview.

7   Ibid.

8   In December 1974, the 401 Airborne Battalion was temporarily attached to the 18 Airborne Brigade as its third organic parachute battalion. This arrangement was only on paper: the 401 Airborne Battalion never actually operated alongside the rest of the brigade. *Tiga Puluh Tahun Bhakti Divisi Infanteri 2/Kostrad* (Malang: Tim Penyusun Sejarah Divif 2/Kostrad, 1991), p. 43.

9   On 29 November, a day after Fretilin's declaration, the Indonesian Foreign Ministry arranged for four Timorese parties to issue a joint statement declaring Timor part of Indonesia. Besides Apodeti and UDT, the two others were minor parties—Kota, which supported a traditional monarchy, and Trabalista, which purported to represent workers—that together counted but a handful of adherents.

10   Dading Kalbuadi interview.

11 Soembodo interview.

12 The crocodile briefing is widely recalled within Kopassandha. Interview with Abadi, 19 June 1999; interview with Nurdin Jusuf, 7 December 1999; Soembodo interview.

13 Interview with Luhut Pandjaitan, 30 May 1996.

14 Benny Moerdani interview.

15 Ibid.

16 Interview with Soegito, 23 August 1999.

17 Atang Sutrisna's team was dubbed Team A, Atang Sanjaya had Team B, and Luhut had Team C. Luhut Pandjaitan interview; Atang Sanjaya interview.

18 Soegito interview.

19 See December 6 entry in *The National Times* (June 6-12 1982), p. 33.

20 Of the six-man marine reconnaissance team, four attempted to swim back to the fleet and two elected to remain concealed on the beach. Of the four that took to the water, two managed to reach Alor Island, 40 kilometers away, after floating in the current for three days. Two others went missing and were presumed drowned. Hendro Subroto, *Eyewitness*, p. 148.

21 Hendro Subroto, "Drop Zone Dili," *Air Forces Monthly* (January 1999), p. 41.

22 Tarub interview.

23 Sutiyoso interview.

24 Soegito interview.

25 Ibid.

26 Within a year, bodies of both missing Kopassandha members were located.

27 Hendro Subroto, "Drop Zone Dili," p. 42; Matthew Jardine, *East Timor: Genocide in Paradise* (Tuscon, Arizona: Odonian Press, 1995), p. 34.

28 Nurdin Yusuf interview.

29 Tommy Martomo interview.

30 Johannes Bambang interview.

31 Still not formally assigned to one of Kostrad's airborne brigades, the 401 Airborne Battalion was temporarily augmenting the 17 Airborne Brigade while the latter's third organic battalion—the 305 Airborne Battalion—was in the Middle East on United Nations peacekeeping duties.

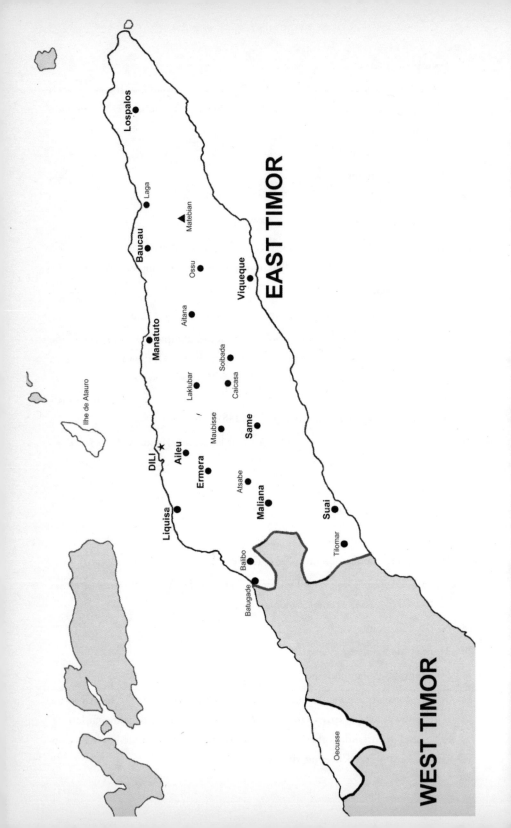

CHAPTER EIGHTEEN

NANGGALA

During the final two weeks of 1975, the Seroja campaign entered high gear along multiple fronts. From Baucau, task forces headed in two directions: one west toward Manatuto, a key town midway to Dili, the second south toward the district capital of Viqueque.

For the Manatuto prong, the bulk of the troops were from Kostrad's 328 Airborne Battalion. For added firepower, the marines lent a pair of platoons, two tanks, and another two armored personnel carriers. Kopassandha's contribution was minimal: just a platoon of partisans accompanied by two Umi non-commissioned officers. Departing the tranquil environs of the Baucau airport on 22 December, the combined task force members could have been forgiven for predicting few complications during the 45-kilometer trek ahead. The seizure of Baucau, after all, had barely rated as a combat action.

This time it would be different. After just a day on the road, the first Fretilin rounds rang out from the scrub. By the time they were halfway to their target, the sniper fire was constant and deadly. Not until nine days later, in the final hours of the last day of the year, did they push their way into the non-descript collection of houses that constituted Manatuto.

A similar story was being encountered by the prong heading south. Spearheaded by a squad of marine reconnaissance troops and a platoon from Umi, they were to blaze a path for the 401 Airborne Battalion. Their route of advance was along the main colonial road—in reality little more than a muddy cart path—that meandered in a series of tight curves up and over the central highlands.

Just ten kilometers out, the hills grew more pronounced. The surrounding limestone walls were riddled with caves; thirty years earlier, the Imperial Japanese detachment occupying Timor had widened those caves into a major logistical complex with doors affixed to seven connected entrances.

Pressing upward, they reached the halfway point near the village of Ossu. Representing the watershed between Baucau and Viqueque, both the north and south coasts could be seen from the tops of neighboring hills. But far from being able to appreciate the view, the column was by then enduring daily sniper attacks. Surprisingly, the Umi pathfinders—who had procured yellow scarves from a tailor in Baucau and were now calling themselves the Tiger Platoon— were spared the bulk of Fretilin's attention. "Fretilin was using what they called 'Mother and Son' tactics," said Umi Lieutenant Johannes Bambang. "They did not hit us in front, but struck at the main body of paratroopers that followed."[1]

As casualties mounted near year's end, the 401 Airborne Battalion was pulled back to lick its wounds. Their place was taken by the 330 Airborne Battalion, the first battalion airlanded at Baucau after its runway was restored to operational status. But with the new unit hit even harder than its predecessor, the column showed no signs of progress as 1975 gave way to 1976.

Apart from Umi, the remaining Kopassandha commandos in Timor had converged on the capital of Dili. This included all of Combat Detachment 1 (including its members repatriated from the Baucau front) and Combat Detachment 2 (which had been shipped from the western border). Giving them further critical mass was the arrival on 21 December of Nanggala 6, comprised of yet another company of para-commandos from Group 2. Paired with Major Tarub's Tuti, Nanggala 6 was assigned with rooting out what little Fretilin resistance remained around the Dili environs.

Now belatedly able to take command of both Combat Detachments 1 and 2 (which, according to original plans, together constituted Nanggala 5), Lieutenant Colonel Soegito readied them for a push south into the territory's interior. Unfortunately for him, the months of earlier combat had taken a toll on morale in Combat Detachment 2. When he instructed its Company B to begin marching over the hill immediately south of Dili, they refused to budge.

On account of their blatant insubordination, the company was bundled back to Magelang for disciplinary action.

On 24 December, the remainder finally began advancing along two lines. Their immediate target was the small town of Aileu, once host to the colony's military training center. Teamed up with a newly-arrived infantry brigade, the para-commandos of Nanggala 5, like their compatriots working their way south from Baucau, encountered stiff Fretilin resistance. Used for frontal assaults, they maintained a pace of four kilometers per day. Reaching their target by 29 December, the weary commandos were subsequently pulled back to Dili for the relatively easier duty of sector defense.

While having taken most of the northern coast of Timor, by early January 1976 a sense of malaise had set in among the Kogasgab elements. No move had yet been made against the easternmost corner of the territory, notably the town of Lospalos; the same held true for the towns along the southern coast. All of these, including several with airfields, remained in Fretilin hands.

Not until 18 January did Jakarta re-energize Seroja. The reason: a United Nations special representative had arrived in Dili; coming from New York with a mandate to speak with all parties involved, he declared his intention to visit Fretilin-controlled areas. This incensed the Indonesians, who did all in their power to frustrate his travels outside of Dili. Irritated by the stonewalling, the official departed for Australia; from there, he brainstormed ways of bypassing the Indonesians and meeting directly with Fretilin leaders in their southern strongholds.

Determined to prevent this from happening, Jakarta moved quickly to sweep into most of Timor's remaining towns and all its airfields. The first results of this boosted effort came on 24 January, when the 330 Airborne Battalion, led by Umi's Tiger Platoon, finally punched its way into Viqueque. Five days later, after an early failure by Tuti and more than a month of heavy fighting by three infantry battalions, the Indonesians evicted Fretilin's stubborn holdouts from the western town of Bobonaro. And on 4 February, the 502 Airborne Battalion—which had been involved in the friendly fire incident while jumping near Dili—made its second combat drop to seize the town of Lospalos.

One other target was handled exclusively by Kopassandha. On 31 January, Yogie Memet—who had received his brigadier's star the previous October—got orders to prepare a task force for the capture of Suai. Fashioning the largest Nanggala to date, he chose a para-commando company from Group 2 and two *karsa yudha* from Group 4. The entire 250-man contingent, dubbed Nanggala 8, was placed under the command of Major Soekiman.

Pressed for time, the members of Nanggala 8 boarded a variety of commercial airlines and military transports and rushed to Kupang's airport. Massing there by the afternoon of 1 February, they waited while some of their officers made a heliborne reconnaissance of Suai. Circling the target, the chopper encountered no groundfire; to be safe, however, they selected a dropzone 3 kilometers away near the town's coastal runway.[2]

During the pre-dawn hours of 2 February, Nanggala 8 was divided among four C-130 aircraft. Heading out to sea, the pilots looked to be over the Suai airstrip just as the sun was breaking the horizon. Though good in theory, all did not go according to plan. In a repeat of Dili, Fretilin anticipated the jump and was lying in wait with a wide range of rifles and machineguns. "We could see the muzzle flashes as soon as we exited the planes," recalls Sergeant Ramedi.[3]

With bullets pinged the bellies of their slow-moving transports, the jumpmasters rushed troops through the rear doors. Straining to see the shoreline in the dim light, several drifted short of the runway. "I landed up to my knees in water," said Ramedi, "and my parachute was pulling me away from the beach."[4] Stripping away his harness, he made it onto the sand. Two other members were not as lucky: drifting over deeper water, their heavy equipment pulled them to watery graves.

Still others had the opposite problem. Drifting inland toward the far side of the runway, one para-commando got snared in a tree; Fretilin combatants instantly materialized from the bush and swarmed around the dangling soldier, cutting him from his harness and dragging him off.

After an hour, most of Nanggala 8 had managed to converge around the airfield. From there they moved toward the town proper, only to come under heavy fire and fall backward at noon. Trading bullets for the rest of the day, the task force dug in near Suai's main church as darkness fell. In an effective bit of psychological warfare, Fretilin tortured their captive para-commando through the night, his haunting screams drifting across the Kopassandha lines.

The following morning, Nanggala 8 geared up for a renewed push into Suai. Fretilin, they found, had already melted into the bush in good order. In a macabre departing shot, they had left the mutilated body of their Kopassandha captive near the town center.

Timor was not Kopassandha's only commitment. Concurrently, three other parts of the archipelago warranted limited deployments of Indonesia's special forces. After a two year hiatus, sixteen *sandhi yudha* operatives under Nanggala 7 were dispatched to West Kalimantan in early 1976 to root out a rebel pocket detected along the border. Finding few dissidents, the action barely rated as a footnote.

In Irian Jaya—the new name given to West Irian in 1973—equally small *sandhi yudha* contingents began rotating through the province starting in August 1975. Coming after a five year interlude, the special forces presence there was deemed necessary after a noticeable resurgence in OPM paramilitary activity. This was especially true along the eastern border, across which the Australian-administered side of the island had been granted self-government in 1973; two years later, in September 1975, Papua New Guinea reached full independence.

The first Kopassandha contingent to Irian Jaya, Nanggala 1, consisted of an entire *karsa yudha* operating from Jayapura (the post-1962 name for Hollandia). Their mandate was more carrot than stick: visiting remote villages, they tried to establish indirect contact with guerrilla leaders to lure them into the government fold. Though not fully successful, they made enough headway to warrant a replacement *karsa yudha*—Nanggala 9—during 1976.

One year on, Nanggala 9 again fell short of reining in top OPM leaders from the bush. But once again, the government thought they merited replacement by a fresh *karsa yudha*. Arriving in February 1977, Nanggala 14 was led by Major Ella Bajuri, a tall, immaculately dressed officer who had earlier served as the adjutant to Ali Murtopo. One of his team members, E. Sunarya, had been to Irian Jaya twice before: in 1962 with Benny's DPC, and in 1969 with Feisal Tanjung's pre-referendum deployment. "There were more OPM this time around," he observed, "and they were also better equipped with Carl Gustav submachine guns and Garand rifles."[5]

While better equipped, the OPM soon hit hard times. Across the border, their ethnic brethren in Papua New Guinea, fearing cross-border incursions by the Indonesians, had moved to eliminate OPM sanctuaries. At the same time, Jakarta was preparing for national elections in mid-1977. To wipe out OPM bands in the runup to the polls, Indonesia had poured in troops for a major province-wide sweep. Compounding matters, Marthin Tabu, the shifty son of a former sub-district chief, rallied with a party of OPM followers at the start of the year.

The combined effect from all this was a broken resistance organization. In late 1977, Nanggala 20 arrived as Kopassandha's latest *sandhi yudha* contribution. Appealing to what they saw as the three basic human drives— mind, heart, and sex—this time they were able to entice several key secessionist leaders from the jungle to open a dialogue.[6]

But before much progress could be made, the government suffered a serious setback. On 18 May 1978, Marthin Tabu lured in a group of regional military officers—including the district commander—on the pretext of turning over further ralliers. As their chopper landed at a remote village south of Jayapura, they were surrounded by OPM guerrillas armed with arrows, knives, and rifles. Both helicopter crewmembers were killed; the passengers were taken hostage.

As word of the kidnapping reached Cijantung, Brigadier General Yogie readied emergency reinforcements. By coincidence, Major Ella Bajuri, who had led the nanggala to Irian Jaya the previous year, was preparing to leave with his *karsa yudha* for their next assignment in Timor. Plotting a new course, on 25 May Yogie accompanied Ella's contingent to Jayapura.

Their intervention proved unnecessary. No sooner had they arrived, the hostages were released after being ransomed for a shipment of antiquated rifles (which regional military officers later claimed, unconvincingly, were altered to jam after firing a few rounds). Six days after landing at Jayapura, Major Ella and his men got back on a Hercules and left for Dili. One year later, Marthin Tabu rallied for a second time; not willing to suffer an encore sting, the Indonesian authorities kept him confined to gilded quarters in Jayapura.

More serious than West Kalimantan or Irian Jaya was the stirring of resistance in Aceh. For decades under the Dutch, the Acehnese had fought a bloody, and unsuccessful, war to shake off foreign rule. Although they later battled alongside other Indonesian revolutionaries during the independence struggle, almost immediately afterward they had soured toward the republican government.

The reason for this was largely personal. Daud Beureueh, Aceh's aged religious patriarch, had declared himself military governor for Aceh during the revolution. After independence, however, Jakarta determined that Aceh would be run as a district within the larger province of North Sumatra. Because this meant he would lose his self-appointed governor's title, an irate Daud encouraged his fellow Acehnese to revolt.

In 1953, their struggle grew more serious when Daud declared common cause with the Darul Islam movement plaguing West Java. Declaring Aceh part of the Islamic state championed by the Javanese extremists, Daud and his guerrillas maintained hit-and-run attacks against government troops through the end of the year. But before Jakarta could properly address the Aceh uprising, the subsequent PRRI revolt in Sumatra and Sulawesi—which Daud and the other chapters of Darul Islam indirectly supported—consumed the attention of the central government through almost the end of the decade.

Not until 1959, with the PRRI largely spent, did the government seek to tackle Daud and his militants. Rather than a wholly military approach, however, Jakarta offered concessions. Aceh was offered "special area" status— a face-saving way of administering it as a province in all but name. Three years later, the Acehnese were allowed to implement Islamic law.

Together, these moves appeased most Acehnese. Apart from the distant gripes from a handful of diehard extremists who fled into exile, Aceh was quiet for more than a decade.

By 1976, however, the situation started to deteriorate once more. This time the reason was grounded in economics. Along with several other resource-rich provinces, Aceh felt it was being stripped of its natural wealth without proper compensation from the central authorities. "Jakarta is full of bridges with no rivers," went a common saying, "while Aceh is full of rivers with no bridges."

Anger over the disparity became more pronounced when oil companies discovered major pockets of natural gas in the district of North Aceh near the town of Lhokseumawe. With construction of pipelines taking place in 1976, local dissent saw a commensurate rise.

Fanning the flames from afar was Hasan Tiro, Aceh's self-appointed ambassador to the U.S. A charismatic orator, Hasan was prone to hyperbole. Over the previous three years, he had at various times promised likeminded kin back in Aceh that he was arranging covert American military aid deliveries via chopper or submarine. Though his promises were baseless, he was able to cultivate a receptive audience half a world away.

Perhaps believing some of his own rhetoric, Hasan infiltrated back to Aceh by the opening of 1977 to jumpstart an armed resistance.[7] Like Daud, he hailed from the northern district of Pidie. Returning there on 20 May, he presided over a clandestine meeting in which the participants put their names to a statement declaring themselves "free of the foreign regime in Jakarta." To realize this, they chose Hasan as chairman of the National Liberation Front of Aceh, soon called the Free Aceh Movement (*Gerakan Aceh Merdeka*, or GAM). Four days later, the same group selected a cabinet. In addition to being head of liberation forces, Hasan was named head of state and head of foreign affairs. Daud was chosen as Mufti Empat, the seniormost religious leader in the region.[8]

It did not take long for Jakarta to get wind of the Pidie tryst. But as the size of the threat was small—Jakarta estimated that GAM numbered no more than 125 members around Pidie and possessed about a dozen firearms in total—the military offered a muted response. That changed in early October, however, when Hasan directed a band of GAM guerrillas to attack a group of pipeline personnel in North Aceh. When an American superintendent attempted to call for help over the radio, they shot him dead. Sprinting from the scene, a second American was shot and wounded. A third expatriate, a South Korean foreman, hid in the bush for a good part of a week before being rescued.[9]

Reacting swiftly, word was passed to Cijantung to prepare a *sandhi yudha* detachment codenamed Nanggala 16. So as not to be seen as a provocation, the commandos would infiltrate without making reference to their Kopassandha affiliation; instead they would be disguised as advisors for Civil Defense auxiliaries (*Pertahanan Sipil*, or Hansip), a rudimentary home guard administered by the Department of Home Affairs across Indonesia.

Selected as head of Nanggala 16 was Major Sofian Effendi, the same officer who led the Umi team in Timor. Sofian was selected on account of his background: an ethnic Acehnese, he was fluent in their dialect and customs. He was allowed to bring along a *prayudha* and a five-man command detachment—eighteen men total—from Group 4. Several members were given extra training in religious affairs, considered important given the pious reputation of the Acehnese.

On 25 October, Nanggala 16 flew to Banda Aceh for a six-month tour. Once on the ground, they shifted east to the town of Sigli in Pidie district. There, amid sprawling prawn farms, they found Daud living openly in a villa; playing both sides, the seventy-eight year-old cleric had secretly backed the GAM proclamation but was also showing a conciliatory face toward Jakarta. Though the Indonesian government knew of his duplicity, for the time being they let him live in peace.

Rather, Nanggala 16 focused its attention on the elusive Hasan Tiro. With only eighteen members, the *sandhi yudha* team could not effectively sweep the district by conventional patrolling. For greater impact, they instead waged a psychological campaign via rumor and innuendo. Hasan, ran one bit of propaganda released by the Kopassandha team, had embezzled money solicited from the Acehnese during the revolution.[10] In another stab, they darkly hinted that Hasan was actually an ethnic Chinese—a powerful slap meant to undercut his religious and social credentials among Acehnese xenophobes.[11]

By year's end, Kopassandha dispatched a second team—Nanggala 21— consisting of a para-commando company from Group 1. While this group focused raids across the northern part of the province, Sofian's Nanggala 16 shifted its energies to raising a Hansip company. Given that figures like Daud and Hasan were seen by many locals as champions of Acehnese rights, training locals as militiamen was a delicate balancing act. Observed one Kopassandha sergeant:

> The Timorese were outstanding as partisans because they were loyal and brave. The Irianese were good as guides—limited in ability but usually not treacherous. But the Acehnese could not really be used as partisans because they were not trustworthy. They would shoot you in the back. We were leery of imparting too many skills for fear they would join GAM. We ended up mostly giving indoctrination, not paramilitary training.[12]

In late April 1978, Nanggala 16 was preparing to leave after completing its promised six-month deployment. Before departing, however, there was one last order of business. Though paying lip service to Jakarta, Daud was still giving moral support to Hasan's GAM. During the early morning hours of

1 May, five Kopassandha members and one doctor ventured to his Sigli villa after morning prayers. Injecting him with a syringe of morphine, then inserting a wooden depressor between his teeth so he would not accidentally bite his tongue, they hustled the Acehnese leader out to a waiting jeep and rushed him to a chopper. After a refueling stop at Lhokseumawe, he was bundled to a jet at Medan, then flown to the Indonesian capital. Once there, he was confronted over his support for the GAM proclamation. Away from his home crowd, Daud prudently condemned the armed secessionist movement and was resettled under watchful eyes in a government house in Jakarta.

With Daud removed from the equation, Hasan saw that his guerrilla days were numbered. Escaping on a boat to Malaysia, he resurfaced in Sweden to continue his struggle from exile. Left behind was a ragtag group of militants poorly armed with a handful of Lee Enfield rifles and apparently without any external sources of material support. Though not posing a major security threat, Jakarta was eager to erase this vestigial affront to its sovereignty. To do this, they prepared a follow-on *sandhi yudha* team to replace Nanggala 16; another para-commando company was not deemed necessary.

Over the previous year, Kopassandha had undergone considerable consolidation. Part of this was due to manpower shortfalls. Though set at two para-commando groups and two *sandhi yudha* groups, General Yogie was perpetually running below authorized strength. At the same time, several of his groups were living in borrowed quarters: Group 2 in Magelang had taken over the barracks of a regional training regiment, and Group 3's elements in Semarang had expanded into housing originally allocated to an anti-aircraft unit. In both cases, the rightful owners wanted their turf back.

Addressing both issues at once, Kopassandha in August 1977 decided to dissolve the understrength Group 3. Its men were then merged into Group 2, which then assumed a *sandhi yudha* role and relocated to Solo. Both Magelang and Semarang complexes were subsequently vacated by the special forces and returned to their original occupants.

In the second quarter of 1978, it was Group 2 that was ordered to prepare a *prayudha* for Aceh duties. Codenamed Nanggala 27, command of this went to Umi veteran Captain Sutiyoso. "It was to be my most interesting assignment in the military," Sutiyoso would later reflect. "By the time we finished, all remaining rebel leaders had run to Malaysia."[13]

Just to make sure, Major Sofian returned to Aceh for an encore engagement in June 1979 as head of Nanggala 35. Maintaining an exhausting pace, his men worked their way across Aceh's northern and eastern edges in search of GAM remnants. Six months on, they found few. Said Sofian: "We left an Aceh that was more or less pacified."[14]

By a wide margin, Kopassandha's biggest commitment remained Timor. In April 1976, the remainder of the first round of deployments—Tarub's Tuti, Sofian's Umi, Soegito's Nanggala 5, and the reserve Nanggala 6—were packing to return to Java. This left behind only Nanggala 8, the airborne task force that had seized Suai.

To that time, Kopassandha's Timor contributions had varied in terms of composition. Some were mixed units, like Tuti and Umi, which blended *sandhi yudha* and para-commando elements under a single commander. Others drew from only one half of Kopassandha, like the para-commando detachments of Soegito's Nanggala 5. In terms of size, they ranged from Susi's 72-man *karsa yudha* to the 500-man Nanggala 5. Regardless of size or composition, in all too many of the cases Kopassandha's special qualifications had been ignored in favor of using the teams as light infantry for frontal assaults and other conventional maneuvers. This was noted, and unappreciated, by several of the Kopassandha officers in the field. "There was no finesse," said one captain from Nanggala 8. "We just pushed forward with brute force."[15]

Given Kogasgab's pressing need for more troops in the field, there was little time to analyze Kopassandha operations and make adjustments. Between May and July, three more nanggala teams were readied for a second wave into the Seroja theater. Two of them, Nanggala 10 and 12, each consisted of a para-commando company; the last, Nanggala 11, was a *karsa yudha*. Very quickly, all three found themselves pooled in a string of mountaintop camps along Timor's western sector. From there, they began patrols into the valley paths running between government-held Suai and Bobonaro. These patrols soon gave way to more ambitious frontal assaults that bore little resemblance to special operations.

The most ambitious of these assaults took place in September, when all three nanggala were massed for a pincer against Lebos. The same village that had beaten back the company of Indonesian infantrymen the previous October, Lebos was now thought to be defended by as many as two companies of Fretilin regulars. With Nanggala 10 pushing from the south and Nanggalas 11 and 12 bearing down from the north, they worked their way into their target by month's end.

Predictably, the use of Kopassandha in this conventional manner came at high cost. By year's end, ten of Nanggala 12's 103 members had been killed— the highest percentage of fatalities in any nanggala to that date.

Faced with these losses, the misappropriation of Kopassandha provoked a belated reexamination of its contribution to the Timor theater. Taking the unlikely lead in this process was Hendropriyono, an opinionated special forces captain who had most recently seen action as a *karsa yudha* commander within Nanggala 8. Unimpressed with Kopassandha's role early in that deployment, he developed even bigger concerns while patrolling the Dili environs in mid-1976. Making a point of mingling with locals, he happened upon one Timorese family with siblings that had joined four different political parties. "This was not just a civil war, but an intra-family war," he concluded. "How could we understand these nuances? Only the Timorese could."[16]

Not willing to sit on his observations, Hendropriyono took them to Dading Kalbuadi. By that time, Dading had gotten his first star and was promoted to overall Timor commander. Speaking in frank terms, Hendropriyono told the general he wanted to take leave of Nanggala 8 and return with just a 13-man *prayudha* of his own choosing. He also had unconventional ideas on how to deploy them. "You are a brigadier," he told Dading. "But the Portuguese usually ruled this colony with only a major. Do you know why?"

Hendropriyono did not wait for an answer. "They kept all of the local chieftains in place," he explained. "Just like the Dutch did with the sultans in Solo and Yogyakarta." If this principle was applied to Timor, he was confident the Fretilin rebellion would peter out in no more than two years.

Dading was somewhat humored by the over-confidence of his junior. But at the same time, he did not want to dampen the captain's enthusiasm— especially one lobbying for a consecutive tour. Penning a letter of support, he sent Hendropriyono back to Cijantung to seek permission from General Yogie.

Yogie, it turned out, was not the only one that needed convincing. As word of the captain's critique made the rounds of army headquarters, he was ushered to the office of Major General Benny Moerdani. With his nerves on edge, Hendropriyono recounted his opinions to the military's intelligence chief.

Staring back with penetrating eyes, Benny's face was absolutely inscrutable. Perhaps remembering his own unconventional scheming as a young RPKAD captain, Benny made it a point of listening to any and all proposals. Finally belying a hint of interest, he gave his blessing to Hendropriyono's experimentation with a *prayudha*.

Racing back to Cijantung, the captain put word through Group 4 that he was looking for *sandhi yudha* personnel with a different state of mind. "I did not want men that would kill, but ones that would convince the Timorese not to kill," he said. "Above all, I needed men that would treat the Timorese with dignity."

After selecting a dozen, Hendropriyono alone departed in late August 1976 to make preparations inside Timor. Once in Dili, he identified two promising locals. The first, Fransisco Osorio Soares, was the younger brother of the Apodeti secretary general and a former sergeant in the colonial army. He had been in Dili when UDT had its coup; later imprisoned by Fretilin and marched into the countryside, he had made his escape just two months earlier. The second, Vidal Sarmento, was also a member of Apodeti and former colonial sergeant; he had escaped from Fretilin captivity only one month earlier.

With both of these men by his side, Hendropriyono on 1 September ventured to Laklubar. Centered along the spine of mountains that run the length of Timor, this town was surrounded by some of the most contested real estate in the territory. Just a dozen kilometers away was the village of Soibada, where Fretilin's central committee had felt sufficiently secure in May to hold a leadership conference.

At the time, an infantry battalion from North Sumatra was garrisoned inside Laklubar. With these troops patrolling the perimeter, Hendropriyono, Fransisco, and Vidal trolled for recruits. Within a day, they had forty candidates— including several Fretilin ralliers. As virtually all had either fought in the colonial army or rebel forces, or both, they were given just two days of pro forma training before officially being designated as *Ton Sus*—the Special Platoon.

In a sense, Hendropriyono was reinventing the wheel. After all, this was not the first time that Kopassandha had worked with armed Timorese: Susi, Tuti, and Umi had all fought alongside partisans. This time, however, there were differences. For one thing, they were given relatively good weapons. The mainstay of the Special Platoon was the Portuguese G-3 assault rifle, a vast improvement over the mix of antiquated arms allocated to the Flamboyan partisans.[17]

There was also the issue of giving the Timorese their dignity. In a move full of symbolism, Fransisco Osorio Soares was named *commandante* of the Special Platoon; Hendropriyono was his deputy. And dramatically demonstrating his trust in his fellow platoon members, the Kopassandha captain slept alongside the Timorese in the same quarters.

By the third week of September, word of the unique platoon had spread among the local community. Another forty volunteers soon presented themselves at their camp, though Hendropriyono had sufficient weapons for only the original forty-two. Unwilling to turn them away, he prepared the entire contingent for combat action at the nearby village of Funar.

It was to prove a defining moment for the platoon. During recent months, Fretilin had been using a so-called "Bow and Arrow" maneuver, translated as "Ramahana" in their native Tetum. This involved small rebel patrols employed as bait to lure large Indonesian contingents into valley ambushes. Catching on to the ruse, Hendropriyono coached the Special Platoon in a counter-tactic. "We had hauled a 12.7 machinegun and a mortar onto a hilltop to trick the Fretilin mother unit into thinking we were a much larger attacking force," he said. "At the same time, other parts of the platoon would infiltrate behind them on the high points."

On 23 September, the partisans moved against the Ramahana ambush. Rushing across Fretilin hill positions from the back, they managed to kill a rebel leader named Leonardo da Costa Alves Rangel. The Fretilin sector commander, Leonardo had assumed a near legendary reputation as the local version of Che Guevara. Convicted of murder by the Portuguese (allegedly for killing his male lover), Leonardo had gained his release from prison at the end of the colonial rule and soon proved his mettle on battlefields across the front; his death was hailed by Jakarta as a major victory against the insurgents.

Not until 20 October did Hendropriyono's *prayudha* arrive at Laklubar for a six-month tour. Now going by the name Nanggala 13, they fused with the existing Special Platoon. By that time, platoon was a misnomer: new recruits had expanded the unit into a full company of three platoons. Several of the new arrivals were turned prisoners or fresh Fretilin ralliers. Ever mindful of the need to empower his Timorese, Hendropriyono paid extra attention to those coming from the rebel ranks. "The first thing I did with an ex-Fretilin guerrilla was to take away his rifle," he said, "and then upgrade it to a better weapon."

At company strength, Nanggala 13's partisans scored a major victory in early November. Their target was Soibada, the heavily contested village that had hosted the Fretilin leadership conference in May. It had changed hands several times in the interim, almost always at a high cost of life. This time, Hendropriyono sent ahead just four partisan scouts; though not armed with rifles, they had grenades hidden in their pockets for emergency contingencies. Entering the village, they asked for volunteers to rally.

Soibada's collective reaction was telling. The vast majority of the population left behind their weapons and cleared out. Remaining behind were less than a dozen hardcore Fretilin, who promptly ran when the remainder of the partisans and Nanggala 13 entered from the bush. "We retook the village without firing a shot," marveled the *prayudha* deputy commander, Lieutenant Gatot Purwanto.

Remaining in the Soibada vicinity, Hendropriyono next tried his hand at psychological warfare. On 2 December, his nanggala began a black letter campaign. One of the correspondences was addressed to prominent Fretilin leader Nicolao Lobato; written from a notional government source, the letter implored Lobato to be vigilant against attacks to his position from inside and out. The implication: that the Fretilin leader was secretly conspiring with Jakarta. Two other letters were written to Guido Soares, the Fretilin deputy commander, and Jose da Silva, the Fretilin chief of staff; both consisted of nothing more than random number codes meant to sow suspicion among the rebel ranks.

On 12 December, Hendropriyono composed a fourth letter. This came after a recent firefight in which his partisans had killed Jose Berlelas, the Fretilin zone commander. Based on prisoner interrogations, they knew that the rebels intended to attack Soibada on the following day. They also knew that a local Fretilin *commandante* named Matheus, who was to participate in the Soibada attack, was refusing to let some of his men rally. Blending all of these aspects into a single letter, the captain wrote:

Matheus,
Thank you for the information. Give the body of Jose Berlelas to those that are planning to hit Soibada. Run back to us before this secret gets out.
Your brother,
Lion

The implication, once again, was that Matheus was secretly conspiring with the government. All four of the letters were given to released prisoners, with the assumption that the correspondences would be intercepted en route to their Fretilin targets.

The assumption proved correct. Thinking Matheus was an informant, he was executed by his fellow rebels. The Soibada attack, planned for the following day, never materialized. And for a period afterward, a paranoid Fretilin leadership dictated that all couriers had to pass letters through the central committee for vetting.

Later that same week, Nanggala 13 received unexpected reinforcements in the form of two dozen para-commandos. They were led by Corporal Tukiman, one of the non-commissioned officers who was part of the disgraced Company B that refused to fight near Dili the previous December. Though severely sanctioned for insubordination, Tukiman was now being offered a chance at redemption.

By the time these para-commandos arrived, other nanggalas were looking to harness Timorese manpower. Nanggala 12, which had earlier sustained heavy losses, began training three cycles of local Hansip militia in January 1977. Their instruction, however, differed in several key respects from Nanggala 13's efforts. Rather than merging directly with well-armed partisans and remaining with them for months on end, Nanggala 12 spent just one week per locale before moving to the next Hansip militia camp. Moreover, rather than offering a serious combat curriculum, they spent the largest amount of time (seven hours) practicing marching and parade drill. And once finished, the militia were turned over to the military theater command rather than retained by Kopassandha. Predictably, the results from these Timorese militia did not approach that of the Special Platoon.

In February 1977, Kopassandha got ready for yet another major rotation to Timor. Coming home were Nanggalas 10, 11, 12, and 13. Taking their place was the newly constituted Nanggala 15, a large team that included both a para-commando company and a *karsa yudha*. The turnover was not without problems. With little overlap, Captain Hendropriyono briefly introduced *Commandte* Fransisco to the Nanggala 15 commander with the intention that this new Kopassandha contingent would continue, if not build upon, the partisan concept. But more concerned with training Hansip militia, Nanggala 15 came to wield the partisans more like porters than equals. Deprived of critical dignity, Fransisco's men quickly lost interest in the war and the gains made by Nanggala 13 soon wafted away.[18]

By the close of 1977, Nanggala 15 finished its tour and another rotation was set to take place. With the Timor conflict now ending its second full year and with no end in sight, the Kopassandha headquarters had decided to standardize its deployments. From that point forward, each nanggala would stay in Timor for just a six-month tour; previously, some had remained in the territory for up to ten months. Also from that point forward, the nanggalas would either consist of a single para-commando company or a single *karsa yudha*—never the two mixed as a single entity. Lastly, Cijantung was committed to deploy three nanggala to Timor at any one time: two of these would be *karsa yudha*, and the last would be a para-commando company.

For the late 1977 rotation, Nanggalas 17, 18, and 19 answered the call. They came just as the government was instituting a military campaign of unparalleled intensity. Pouring in troops and employing OV-10 tactical strike aircraft for the first time, they focused on depriving Fretilin of food and keeping the guerrillas on the run.[19] They were greatly assisted by a critical miscalculation of Fretilin, which had resisted waging a purely guerrilla campaign and instead tried to best the Indonesians in conventional engagements. The results were horrific losses for Timorese civilians in general and Fretilin combatants in particular. So great were their losses, in fact, that the Fretilin president confided in his central committee that he desired a negotiated settlement; enraged, other party stalwarts placed him in detention and elevated Nicolao Lobato to the top slot.

With the war shaping into a conventional slugfest, Kopassandha spent most of its time on the sidelines training Hansip. This was still the case in May 1978 when the latest special forces rotation brought in Nanggalas 22, 23, and 24. Significantly, this came one month after the promotion of Mohammad Jusuf as both armed forces commander and defense minister. A native of South Sulawesi, Jusuf had been in the very first combat intelligence class in 1950, and was later one of the first army students to get airborne training.

Inheriting the festering Timor problem, Jusuf looked to make an early mark. Two infantry battalions of Timorese recruits had recently been formed, and Kopassandha had been patiently expanding the Hansip militia network over the previous year. Looking to build on this as a territorial approach to pacification (long applied in other areas of Indonesia), Jusuf seemed to be opening the door to a greater role for unconventional forces.

Presented with this opportunity, Kopassandha's response was not markedly different from what it had been already doing for a year. Dividing its *prayudha* among various militia camps, Nanggala 22's initial plan was to have each *prayudha* instruct a local militia company. But rather than maximize this multiplier effect, this nanggala once again tended to demote the Timorese as less than trusted equals. For example, when all four *prayudha* massed for a June assault against a mountain near Laklubar, the numbers were a mismatch: against fifty-five special forces members taking part, there were just thirty Hansip militiamen and another thirty Timorese relegated to carrying supplies.[20]

While Kopassandha struggled with such a half-hearted embrace of unconventional solutions, the rest of the army seemed to be getting marked results from more conventional approaches. By mid-year, Indonesian infantrymen managed to capture Fretilin's jungle radio station, along with the rebel information minister and its deposed president (who had earlier been placed in detention by hardliners). And with the Fretilin ranks sustaining unprecedented casualties around their stronghold near Mount Matebian, the endgame for East Timor—the territory's name after July 1978, reflecting its official integration as an Indonesian province—seemed in sight.

High on the government's wanted list was Nicolao Lobato, the thirty-two-year-old Fretilin president. Information from the field indicated that Lobato was roaming the hills outside Caicasa, a village near Soibada. In response, Nanggalas 22, 23, and 24 on 2 October maneuvered for a pincer against this locale. But before they were able to sweep the surrounding jungle, all three rotated back to Java and were replaced in November by the latest Kopassandha trio, Nanggalas 28, 29, and 30.

This time, there was an additional Kopassandha presence in the battlefield. Looking to inflict a deathblow against Fretilin, the armed forces headquarters authorized the creation of a special composite battalion that brought together one company each of Kopassandha para-commandos, marines, and air force's Kopasgat special forces. Known as Parikesit—the name of a noble king from the Javanese shadow puppet cosmology—this task force converged at Batu Jajar on 20 November for a week of integrated training. By 1 December, they were in Dili; ten days after that, they were being lifted by chopper to Soibada and Laklubar.

While these elite companies gave chase, Nanggala 28 was directed back to Caicasa, the same village targeted earlier in October. Consisting of a para-commando company, Nanggala 28 was led by Lieutenant Prabowo Subianto. Born with a silver spoon in his mouth, Prabowo was the son of ambitious economist Sumitro Djojohadikusumo, once the heir apparent to the Indonesian Socialist Party. When he lost out in a bitter party power struggle in the mid-fifties, Sumitro ultimately fled the capital and opportunistically backed the PRRI/Permesta rebels then combating the central government. Fleeing again into European exile when the rebel movement collapsed, Sumitro brought along his children and reared them in English, French, and German-speaking environments.

Ten years later, Sumitro, the consummate politician, lobbied from afar to offer his economic expertise to newly elevated President Suharto. Whitewashing his rebel links, Sumitro returned from exile and was named to a five-year stint as trade minister. In 1973, he served another five years as State Minister for Research and Technology. During this time, his newfound support for free market reforms was widely credited with helping reverse Indonesia's moribund economy.

Though the son of a powerful minister, Prabowo had serious difficulty when he entered the military academy's Class of 1974. Though perhaps the most widely read cadet in its history, his command of written Indonesian was marginal at best. Still, he impressed the academy's staff by his command of military science. "I was lecturing about Liddell Hart's writings on indirect attack and asked for comment," said General Himawan Sutanto. "Prabowo was the only one in class that could recite the theory."[21]

Now on his second combat tour in East Timor (he had earlier served in Nanggala 10), Prabowo, then just 26, was the youngest nanggala commander to date. Nervous from the responsibility, he maneuvered his company into Caicasa on the morning of 17 December. Guiding them, ironically, was Antonio Lobato—Nicolao's younger brother. Finding nothing over the next four days, they then received word that Nicolao had passed through a neighboring village. Rushing to this second locale, they found the information was again outdated: Nicolao had left forty-eight hours earlier.

Always one step behind, new intelligence on 23 December placed the Fretilin president near Maubisse—a mountainous redoubt fifty kilometers south of Dili. In a massive dragnet combining Nanggala 28, Parikesit, and several infantry battalions, the Indonesians immediately closed on this high ground from all directions.

After several days of uneventful patrolling, the men of Nanggala 28 woke early on the morning of 28 December expecting more of the same. When a detail of commandos ventured to a stream to fetch water, however, they ran headlong into a band of guerrillas on the opposite bank. The rebels instantly vanished, but they left behind a bag containing ammunition and two letters to top Fretilin cadre.

Upon receiving this report, Prabowo suspected ranking Fretilin leaders were in the vicinity. In the immediate area, too, was Major Yunus Yosfiah, the Kopassandha veteran and former Susi commander. Yunus was now head of the 744 Infantry Battalion, the first battalion comprised of Timorese recruits. Radioing the rebel sighting to Yunus, the major ordered Prabowo's Nanggala 28 to coordinate with his battalion for the kill.

Maneuvering as instructed, two para-commando platoons caught up with a 30-man rebel band at 0700 hours. A firefight ensured, with Timorese from the 744 Infantry Battalion engaging the Fretilin guerrillas from the opposite side. Thirty minutes later, the commandos rushed forward and snatched a prisoner. From him, they confirmed that Nicolao was among the cornered rebels; they also learned that the Fretilin president was armed with a captured M-16 assault rifle.

With the Timorese infantry advancing from the east and south, the two platoons of Nanggala 28 bore down from the north. Trading periodic rifle fire through 1100 hours, the commander of 2 Platoon approached close enough to see a pinned group of twenty surviving rebels. Among them, Nicolao was clearly visible with a seven-man escort; the unique report of his M-16 also set him apart.

As this information was relayed among the government forces, a withering amount of fire was directed in the direction of the Fretilin chief. Hit in the stomach, Nicolao attempted to cross a stream; too weak to do so, he collapsed near a tree. As Kopassandha commandos and Timorese infantrymen converged on the site, they found the rebel chief had already bled to death.

A week later, Guido Soares, the rebel deputy commander, was shot dead by Nanggala 28. With just three original members of the central committee at large, the top echelon of the East Timor resistance was all but annihilated. Fretilin looked to be in its final hours.

1   Johannese Bambang interview.

2   Dolfi Rondonuwu interview.

3   Ramedi interview.

4   Ibid.

5   Sunarya interview. The OPM insurgents were able to gain the limelight briefly during 1977 when they cut a copper slurry pipeline from the Ertsberg mine site owned by U.S. Company Freeport McMoRan.

6   Samsudin interview.

7   Hasan entered Indonesia on 13 September 1976, but soon departed for Bangkok in an unsuccessful attempt to procure arms. *Sejarah TNI*, Jilid IV (Jakarta: Pusat Sejarah dan Tradisi TNI, 2000), p. 134.

8   Although GAM was actually founded in May 1977, Hasan backdated the proclamation to 4 December 1976 because it was the anniversary of the death of his grandfather. Al Chaidar, *Gerakan Aceh Merdeka* (Jakarta: Madani Press, 1999), p. 143.

9   Reference to Hasan ordering the attack is found in Chadier, *Gerakan Aceh Merdeka*, p. 152.

10   The Acehnese were proud of the fact they had donated enough gold during the revolution to purchase a Dakota transport used to smuggle supplies through Dutch lines; this plane later became the first aircraft used by Garuda Airlines.

11   Kusnadi interview.

12   Kusnadi interview.

13   Sutiyoso interview.

14   Sofian Effendi interview.

15   Interview with Hendropriyono, 1 May 2000.

16   Ibid.

17   The Indonesians referred to the G-3 by the nickname "Getme." This nickname came from the mistaken Indonesian belief that the Portuguese-made G-3 was the same as the license-built G-36 assault rifle made by Spain's *Centro de Estudios Tecnicos de Materiales Especiales* ("Cetme").

18   Nanggala 15 divided its four *prayudha* among four sites spanning the entire territory; each *prayudha* provided instruction to a Hansip militia company.

19   The OV-10 strike aircraft were equipped with miniguns, rockets, and "Opalm," a Soviet-made copy of napalm that had been procured by the Indonesians during the 1962 West Irian campaign.

20   The commander of Nanggala 22, Major Ella Bajuri, was shot by a Fretilin sniper on the morning of 17 July while walking between two outposts. Aside from Major Atang Sutrisna, who died in the December 1975 seizure of Dili, Ella was the highest ranking Kopassandha officer to die in Timor.

21   Interview with Himawan Sutanto, 25 February 1999.

CHAPTER NINETEEN

WOYLA

On Saturday, 28 March 1981, virtually every general in the Indonesian military was gathered on the island of Ambon for a key leadership session. Chaired by General Andi Mohammad Jusuf—who held the posts of both armed forces commander and defense minister—the meeting coincided with a major training exercise spanning from East Timor to North Maluku. As part of this, the bulk of Kopassandha had ventured to Ambon to give a flashy maritime exhibition on the use of limpet mines.

Shortly after making a rousing opening speech about the need for national self-reliance, Jusuf received an emergency call from Jakarta.[1] Though details were sketchy, a Garuda DC-9 had apparently been hijacked. Christened the Woyla, the plane had left Jakarta's Kemayoran domestic airport at 0800 hours that morning bound for Medan via the South Sumatran city of Palembang. Eighteen minutes out of Palembang, air traffic controllers heard distress calls from the pilot. There had been thirty-four passengers on the flight out of Jakarta, plus another fourteen boarding at Palembang. Among them were three American executives, a Japanese engineer, a Dutchman, and a British national. The number and nationalities of those seizing the plane was as yet unknown.

By the time Jusuf got the call, the Woyla had been diverted to Penang, Malaysia. Upon landing, the Malaysian authorities conceded in providing an international route map and food. After the release of a single elderly woman—who indicated there were about six hijackers, all Indonesians—the plane again took to the air and headed for Bangkok's Don Muang International Airport.

There it came to a halt in Bay A, a largely unused section of the airfield within the precincts of the adjacent Royal Thai Air Force base. Just 150 meters away, large crowds began to gawk from the shoulder of a nearby highway.

Up until that time, Indonesia had little experience with airline hijackings. In April 1972, a passenger—depressed because he could not join the marines— had smuggled two grenades aboard on a domestic flight from Surabaya to Jakarta. And in September 1977, another passenger attempted to gain control over a Garuda DC-9 headed for Surabaya.[2]

Though both of these cases had been resolved with little fanfare—the first hijacker was quickly shot dead on the ground, the second was arrested— the Indonesian government had noted the spate of worldwide hijackings during the seventies and had started exploring countermeasures. The first to take concrete steps was the police Mobile Brigade, which in 1974 created a fledgling counter-terrorist squad. Known as Gegana—derived from the Sanskrit word *gegono*, meaning "sky"—the small team was mandated with handling explosives used by airplane hijackers rather than actually raiding planes.[3]

Three years later, an event in Somalia again prompted the Indonesians to examine counter-terrorist options. That October, a team of West German commandos stormed a hijacked Lufthansa 737 that had been diverted to the Somali capital of Mogadishu; all of the hostages were released unharmed. Elite units around the world took note of this rescue, and Kopassandha was no exception. In the February 1978 issue of its internal magazine, *Baret Merah*, an article and accompanying diagram detailed the Mogadishu raid.[4]

It was not until early 1980 that Kopassandha looked to actually raise its own counter-terrorist unit. This was prompted by two key events. During the previous November, armed extremists in the newly-founded Islamic Republic of Iran had stormed the U.S. Embassy in Teheran and taken the diplomatic staff hostage. When a rescue by a U.S. commando unit was attempted in April 1980, it ended in an embarrassing—and deadly—failure at a launchsite in the Iranian desert.

Just one month later in May 1980, commandos from the British Special Air Service raided the Iranian embassy in London. On that occasion, they succeeded in killing the armed terrorists that had seized the embassy and in freeing all the hostages.

These incidents were not lost on General Benny Moerdani, Indonesia's top military intelligence officer. Looking to preen a similar ability in his army,

Moerdani beckoned Lieutenant Colonel Sintong Pandjaitan, the same Kopassandha officer who had distinguished himself during actions around Jakarta in October 1965 and during the *karsa yudha* deployment to West Irian in 1969. Remaining within Group 4 for the next decade, it had ironically been during a training session at Cijantung that Sintong had his closest brush with death.

This had occurred while preparing for an exhibition in 1974 for the army chief of staff. Showcasing Kopassandha's novel use of mortars as a direct-fire weapon (an application that dated back to Colonel Mung's trip to North Vietnam in 1964), members of Group 4 had placed a mortar horizontally on a bed of rocks. Gathered with a crowd of commandos watching a trial run, Sintong had his eyes fixed on a target two hundred meters away.

Then disaster struck. As a sergeant pushed a round backward toward the firing pin, the recoil jarred the tube from its horizontal alignment. When the round impacted just five meters away, the concussion from the blast ripped through the crowd and severely injured a dozen people. Sintong was among them, a piece of shrapnel slicing through his web belt and into his abdomen. His driver was not as fortunate, becoming one of two fatalities from the mishap. Kopassandha subsequently shelved this technique.[5]

By the time Moerdani contacted him in 1980, Sintong had been promoted to Kopassandha operations assistant. The general told Sintong he wanted a preliminary survey of counter-terrorist training available overseas. The instruction came with two simple provisos. "He said not to go to the United States because the Americans were too technology-intensive and not appropriate for Indonesia," recalls Sintong. Rather, Moerdani was partial toward England because he felt they focused on human resources. Said Sintong, "As proof, he remarked that the British still used the old Sterling."[6]

Taking this advice to heart, Sintong gathered what little counter-terrorism material was available. While this form of training was still in its relative infancy, he managed to get some information on units in England, France, and the Netherlands. He also approached South Korea to enquire about its efforts to date.

While Sintong was looking at the issue from a theoretical point of view, Group 4 took more practical steps. On an ad hoc basis, a twenty-man team within the group began experimenting with methods of confronting aircraft hijackers. Part of this involved modifying bullets with reduced gunpowder charges, then firing them into pieces of metal to approximate aircraft skin. This was done to calculate a charge that would give a bullet enough velocity to stop a hijacker but not travel through his body and open a hole in the side of the plane; if this were to occur in flight, the rapid depressurization would rip open the aircraft.

Although this informal team had more counter-terrorist practice than any of its peers in the Indonesian military, all of its members were in Ambon when Woyla was hijacked. Apart from a few dozen commandos, in fact, the bulk of Cijantung's residents were either on combat operations or taking part in the training session alongside Jusuf's leadership meeting.

By coincidence, Lieutenant Colonel Sintong was not among them. This was because of a second close call during a training incident at Cijantung. The previous July, a U.S. Army Special Forces team had arrived at the Kopassandha headquarters to provide advanced freefall training. Although he was already freefall qualified, Sintong had elected to join the students for the first jump. Landing hard, he snapped his left ankle. The fracture was taking a long time to properly heal, leaving the lieutenant colonel still on crutches and left behind while most of his peers ventured to Ambon.

As the highest ranking officer remaining at headquarters, it was Sintong that answered the duty phone at 1245 hours on 28 March. On Jusuf's orders, he was told to assemble a full *karsa yudha* of seventy-two men for a possible hostage rescue operation. As there was no full *karsa yudha* present at the time, he relayed word to the Group 4 headquarters staff to cobble together volunteers from among those available in Jakarta.

Within an hour, Sintong was standing before twenty-nine officers and other ranks. Apart from two snipers seconded from Group 1, the remainder were from Group 4. Among the officers were Major Sunarto (the former deputy commander of Susi), Major Iznoor (formerly a non-commissioned officer who had been on the 1965 Ben Hur mission near Kuching, now a *karsa yudha* commander), Major Subagyo (Group 4's operations assistant), and Captain Untung Suroso (a Susi veteran and former member of Nanggala 13).

Heading to Kemayoran, the team looked to practice on a spare DC-9 provided by Garuda. They had few precedents to consider. To that date, commandos from other nations had attempted only two aircraft hijack rescues. One had been the successful West German operation in Somalia. The other had been a disastrous 1977 raid by Egyptian troops in Cyprus; failing to properly coordinate with the local authorities, they had gotten into a firefight with Cypriot troops that took the lives of fifteen Egyptian commandos.[7]

Looking more closely at the West German example, there were a few lessons to be learned. Though not all details had yet been released about the Mogadishu operation, it was known that the commandos had simultaneously entered through the front, rear, and four over-wing emergency doors. Speed and synchronized movements had been the key to success.

The 737 tackled by the West German rescuers was not greatly different from the DC-9. Both planes had a single aisle down the center of the plane, two toilets in the rear, and a thin partition between the front entrance and the cabin. Slightly smaller of the two, the DC-9 featured a main passenger entrance in the front, a rear ventral stairway under the tail, and four over-wing emergency doors. The front entrance was normally opened from the interior, but had an exterior control station that could be reached from the ground; the front entrance also featured a stairway and telescoping handrails that pulled out from the cabin floor.

In the rear of the plane, the DC-9's ventral stairway was hydraulically operated. Used primarily for servicing the cabin, this stairway had an exterior control station easily reached from the ground. Over each wing, the two emergency exists could be removed by a handle from the outside.

With their actions dictated by the design of the plane, the commandos began assigning duties in the Kemayoran hanger. One squad focused on the front door, a second on the rear stairway, and a third on the over-wing doors on the left side. The commandos had taken along M-16 assault rifles, which had become standard Kopassandha issue in 1978. Finding them unwieldy in the cloistered confines of the aircraft cabin, most switched to pistols by the time they called a halt at nightfall.

The next day, 29 March, the commandos were back at Kemayoran for the morning and afternoon. Further selection had narrowed down twelve members for Team A, the actual assault unit. Among the twelve, two would go in through the front door, two up the rear stairway, and two from over the wings. The remaining six Team A commandos would help open doors and provide reinforcement, while at thirteen member, Captain Untung Suroso, would provide on-site coordination from under the plane's belly. Behind them, Team B would constitute an outer ring of reinforcements; this team included the two snipers, who were to shoot the tires of the aircraft if it attempted to move on the tarmac.

Late that afternoon, Team A was called to General Moerdani's office in the Jakarta district of Tebet. Having rushed back from Ambon the previous day, Moerdani gathered the team around his desk and unveiled specialized equipment he had been stockpiling for special contingencies. This included silenced Israeli-made Uzi submachine guns, Beretta .22 caliber pistols, night vision goggles, and half a dozen white commercial bulletproof vests. Draping one of the vests on his chair, he fired a magazine into it at close range. Demonstrating the bullets did not penetrate to the upholstery, he turned the lot over to the team.

As the sun set, the rescuers ventured to Halim airbase with their new gear. Firing the Uzis into an embankment for thirty minutes, they liked its compact size and rate of fire. As only five were available, two were allocated for the squad going in the front door, one for the rear squad, and two for the commandos that would enter the over-wing doors.[8]

Receiving less generous reviews were the night vision goggles. First generation devices, they gave the user severely restricted tunnel vision. When the team used them in a synchronized rehearsal, most complained that little was discernable in the dimmed aircraft cabin.

Changing into civilian clothes at 2100 hours, Sintong ushered the task force aboard a Garuda DC-10. Along with Moerdani and three additional Kopassandha officers assigned as staff, they departed for Bangkok and were in the Thai capital shortly after midnight, 30 March.

As soon as they landed, General Yoga Sugomo, the head of Indonesia's civilian intelligence agency, was on hand for an update. Having rushed to Thailand on the same day the Woyla was seized, Yoga had been patiently negotiating with the hijackers. Much had happened during the interim, he said. While the hijackers were gathered in the cockpit on the morning of 29 March, the sole British hostage had managed a daring escape from a wing emergency exit. From him, Yoga learned that there were just five hijackers armed with a pistol, one grenade, and a stick of dynamite. Though not heavily armed, they had shown a propensity for violence. When a second hostage (an American national) attempted to escape late on 29 March, he had fallen to the tarmac with a serious bullet wound to the chest.

More details had emerged about the hijackers when they began issuing a string of demands. Initially they insisted on the withdrawal of Israeli military units from Indonesia, condemnation of Indonesian Vice President Adam Malik for allegedly taking kickbacks from a U.S. aircraft manufacturer, and the release of twenty (soon increased to thirty-four) political prisoners.

Hearing this, Yoga had been confused. For one thing, there had never been any Israeli military advisors in Indonesia.[9] For another thing, there had never been any corruption charges leveled against Adam Malik.

The last demand, however, shed much light on the identity of the hijackers. Most of the 34 political prisoners in question belonged to a shadowy Islamic extremist group called Komando Jihad ("Holy War Command"). Answering to a radical thirty-one-year-old Indonesian cleric named Imran bin Zein, the group was thought to number about a hundred members with cells in Jakarta and Bandung. They had been behind some minor disturbances during 1977-78, but had grown significantly more active after gaining inspiration from the 1979 Islamic revolution in Iran. Like the Iranians, they aimed to convert Indonesia into an Islamic state. To achieve this, they had stolen several weapons on 11 March 1981 during a deadly raid against a police post outside Bandung.

Following the Bandung attack, the government had arrested two dozen suspects. Others had escaped the dragnet, however, including two of the five hijackers. This included their leader, the Palembang-born and Saudi-educated Maharizal, and Zulfikar, a twenty-eight-year-old Medan native and karate student who had been a security guard at the Jakarta Hilton.[10] Of the remaining three hijackers, Abu Sofian and Wendy Effendy came from Medan; the last, Abdullah Mulyono, hailed from Yogyakarta.[11]

The hijackers' demands quickly became a moving target. No sooner had they demanded the release of thirty-four prisoners, they upped the number to eighty detainees. This included several persons arrested after an August 1980 attack near Bandung by a different Muslim fundamentalist group led by several aging members from Darul Islam. The hijackers were insisting that all of the prisoners be flown to Bangkok, and from there be allowed to transit through Sri Lanka for an undisclosed location (there was speculation their final destination was Libya). On top of this, they belatedly asked for US$1.5 million in cash. If all their demands were not met by 1300 hours, 30 March, they promised to blow up the plane.

From the start, the Indonesian government had no intention of meeting any of these demands. Moerdani, in fact, had received President Suharto's quick approval to stage a military operation. But playing for time, General Yoga had hinted to the hijackers that some of the demands might be negotiable. Extracting a sign of good faith, he was able to extend the deadline to 2100 hours, 30 March.

That was the situation Moerdani found upon arrival in Bangkok. Waiting until 0600 hours, 30 March, he and Yoga were ushered in front of the Thai prime minister. They were eager to receive Bangkok's approval to stage a raid, but the Thais were reluctant. They recalled a 1972 incident in which Arab terrorists had seized the Israeli Embassy in Bangkok; that event had been resolved without loss of life after meeting some of the terrorist demands and allowing them safe passage from the kingdom. When Moerdani refused to allow any room for negotiation, the prime minister promised to give an answer within five hours.

Meantime, Sintong's team had spent the morning of 30 March holed up inside the cabin of the Garuda DC-10. Though they had taken pains to keep their presence a secret, Thai newsmen had found out and filed press stories that a contingent of Indonesian commandos had arrived shortly after midnight.[12]

As promised, the Thai prime minister gave an answer to Moerdani. The Thai government, he said, would consent to an Indonesian military operation on its soil. In return, the Thai government insisted on the right to deliver any press release after the raid. And in something of a face-saving gesture, a Royal Thai Air Force counter-terrorist team was deployed to bolster security along the perimeter of the airbase.[13]

After getting this approval, Moerdani was approached by the CIA's Chief of Station from the U.S. Embassy in Bangkok. As there were still two American citizens among the hostages, Washington had a vested interest in a successful rescue. To assist, the CIA chief lent an extra bulletproof vest to the general. Also given was a piece of special audio gear that enabled conversations inside the aircraft to be remotely monitored.[14]

By late afternoon, 30 March, Moerdani quietly passed word to Sintong to prepare for action that night. A Garuda DC-9 had been flown to Bangkok for additional dress rehearsals. While they went through a final dry run, Yoga passed word to the hijackers that Jakarta had relented and the eighty prisoners would be delivered the following day. Hearing this, the hijackers—their speech slurred from lack of sleep—agreed to again extend the deadline and pledged that all hostages, except the crew, would be released once the freed prisoners arrived in Thailand. As a further sign of good faith, they allowed food to be delivered to their captives for the first time since landing in Bangkok.

As the sun set, discussions among the Indonesian military men turned toward the exact timing of the raid. Though plans initially called for the operation to be launched at 0430 hours, 31 March, Moerdani had second thoughts. With the CIA's audio device in place, he listened as the hijackers congratulated themselves over their apparent victory, ate, and then grew silent. Guessing that they were drifting off to sleep after two tense days, he wanted to hit them well before they had a chance to complete their rest. The mission, he now ruled, should be launched no later than 0300 hours.

With the timetable moved forward, Sintong's task force got their own brief rest and were awake by 0200 hours. In a last minute display of unit pride, they all donned their red berets and distinctive vertical stripe camouflage. Thirty minutes later, Team B quietly deployed in a loose ring around the plane. The two snipers were positioned to the front of the DC-9, their rifles trained on its forward wheel.

Team A, meanwhile, assembled far to the rear of the aircraft. Walking from behind at a deceptively measured pace—one journalist eyewitness described them as seemingly "strolling on a Sunday picnic"—Captain Suroso marched his men to the belly of the plane.[15]

From there, they divided into their three assigned sub-teams. Senior Cadet Ahmad Kirang, armed with a Beretta, was to be first up the rear stairway. Behind him, P.L. Tobing would be carrying an Uzi. A third commando would work quickly to activate the stairway's hydraulic release mechanism.

At the front door, another pair of commandos—Senior Cadet Slamet Riyanto with a Beretta, Sergeant Teguh with an Uzi—would be tasked with clearing the area immediately behind the cockpit. Another pair of commandos—one perched atop an aluminum stepladder they had brought for the purpose—would help yank open the door and provide cover.

Over the left wing, two commandos—Sergeants Hidayat and Suwarno, both with Uzis—led a second pair of sergeants up a ladder and onto its leading edge. Behind them, Lieutenant Rusman coordinated their efforts as they snaked along the fuselage so as not to be visible from inside the darkened cabin. Both Hidayat and Suwarno had been issued night vision goggles, but both elected to let them dangle from their necks because of their restricted range of vision.

Remaining under the belly, Captain Untung, M-16 in hand, checked the positioning of the three sub-teams. At 0245 hours, fifteen minutes ahead of schedule, he informed Sintong that they were ready. Receiving clearance to proceed, he keyed the pad on his walkie-talkie. "*Masuk! Masuk!*"—Enter! Enter!

Over the previous three days, the commandos had worked hard to synchronize their moves. This had proven difficult, especially as the various doors opened with different degrees of difficulty. The two commandos over the wing had it easiest. Pulling external releases and giving a strong shove from their shoulders, both doors immediately fell inward into the cabin.

Hidayat and Suwarno knew what to do next. During their rehearsals, Sintong had given them some simple advice. Because the British hostage had earlier escaped from the emergency exit, it was a good bet that the hijackers had moved hostages away from the nearby seats to prevent another dash to freedom. He further reasoned that at least one hijacker was guarding those exits. If there was anybody sitting near the emergency doors, they were to be shot without hesitation.[16]

Sintong's reasoning was flawless. As the two commandos peered inside, hijacker Wendy Effendy stared back. When the latter attempted to raise his pistol, he was immediately drilled with an Uzi. Vaulting in over his body, the first two commandos stepped into the aisle. With their backs together, they trained their submachine guns down both lengths of the cabin. "*Tiarap!*" they screamed. Get down!

As their eyes adjusted to the dim interior, the commandos strained to make out targets. Only seconds had transpired, and the hostages were too shocked to start screaming; most were ducking low behind their seats over fear of being hit by crossfire.

To the rear of the plane, Sergeant Cakra had worked feverishly to turn the handle that lowered the ventral stairway. Even before the stairs were fully lowered, Kirang and Tobing lifted themselves through the opening and bounded up into the cabin. Materializing at the rear of the aisle, Kirang swung his Beretta forward; cutting behind the right row of seats, Tobing leveled his Uzi. They were immediately met by a fusillade of bullets from the center of the cabin—almost certainly friendly fire from another Uzi. One round sliced through the fingers of Tobing's left hand and buried into the vest protecting his stomach. Collapsing backward, he would emerge with nothing worse than a large red welt on his lower abdomen.

Kirang was not so fortunate. The vests provided by Moerdani were commercial models, and they rode high on the hips. When a bullet impacted just above his crotch, there was no protection as the round sliced through his intestines. Bleeding profusely, he collapsed in the aisle.

At the front of the aircraft, the sub-team tackling the main passenger door required careful coordination. This entrance came with an integral staircase, as well as an inflatable evacuation slide. But because the staircase would take precious seconds to deploy, they had instead brought an extra stepladder. And because the inflatable slide would complicate their entry, one of the commandos intended to keep its cover hatch depressed so as not to cause an automatic deployment.

When Captain Untung gave word over the radio, Sergeant Mahmud, standing precariously atop one of the ladders, cracked the handle and pulled the door just enough to peek inside. From the ground, Senior Cadet Slamet Riyanto stole a glance through his night vision goggles but saw nothing but dark shades of green.

Only after hearing shots ring out further down the aircraft did Mahmud heave the door wide open. Extending his arm inside, Slamet emptied his entire pistol magazine into the dark interior as he scrambled to mount the second ladder. Behind him, Sergeant Teguh added a muffled burst from his Uzi. Reaching the partition separating the main cabin, they heard a scream: "*Ke depan*!" To the front!

A split second later, hijacker Abdullah Mulyono bounded into view and collided with Slamet. Reaching for Slamet's pistol, the two wrestled over the empty weapon. Before Teguh could get a clear shot with his Uzi, the hijacker broke free and vaulted through the open door and onto the tarmac. Getting to his feet, he sprinted past the front of the plane.

Under the aircraft, Captain Untung heard the commotion. Peering through his night vision goggles, he raised his M-16 and fired a volley at the fleeing Mulyono. Seeing the hijacker fall, he fired off another volley to ensure he would not get up.

At mid-cabin, four commandos had pushed their way inside from the emergency doors and were screening passengers when Mulyono had jumped from his seat, tossed a grenade, and sprinted toward the front. Anticipating a blast, the commandos ducked for cover. After a few seconds passed with no concussion, they realized that the Pindad factories had produced yet another dud. Locating it on the floor, the faulty grenade was gingerly handed through the wing to Lieutenant Rusman.

The commandos quickly returned to the task of identifying hijackers. This had been unwittingly made easier by the hijackers themselves. Due to the intense heat inside the cabin, most of the male hostages had stripped down to their waist. A lone Indonesian male sitting near the middle of the plane, however, was still wearing a shirt. As one of the commandos approached the passenger in question, a female hostage leveled a guilty finger in his direction. The hijacker, Maharizal, was immediately directed through the emergency door at gunpoint and onto the wing to the waiting Rusman. Struggling as he exited the plane, he was rewarded with a bullet to the head.

A fourth hijacker was soon subdued near the rear of the cabin. The last, Abu Sofian, managed to blend among the hostages as they filed out the front of the DC-9. Once on the tarmac, three of the freed passengers frantically began pointing at their former captor. Mindful of the trouble Maharizal had given on the wing, Captain Untung stepped forward and placed two rounds into Sofian's thighs to prevent him from fleeing.

Back in the plane, the commandos made a tragic discovery. Slumped in his pilot's seat, Captain Herman Rante was unconscious and bleeding from a head wound. It was never determined who fired the fatal shot—a ballistics test was not performed on the bullet—though members of Team A later speculated it came from friendly fire. Rante succumbed to his wounds nine days later.

At 0500 hours, Sintong led the victorious task force into the Garuda DC-10. Also aboard the DC-10 were five coffins; three contained hijackers killed during the rescue. Mysteriously, the remaining pair of hijackers—who were very much alive when they departed Bangkok—filled the remaining two boxes by the time they landed in Jakarta.

Left behind in Bangkok was the seriously wounded Achmad Kirang. One day later, he died in a Bangkok hospital.

In hindsight, the Woyla rescue had been every bit as spectacular as the West German operation in Somalia. Sintong's task force deserved added platitudes because they had trained for just three days prior to the raid and barely had time to familiarize themselves with their new equipment. That none of the passengers had been killed was a minor miracle; Benny Moerdani had conservatively estimated there would be forty percent casualties.

Despite their success, Kopassandha was robbed of international accolades by an accident of history. At the same time Team A was storming the Woyla, U.S. President Ronald Reagan was nearly killed by an assassin in Washington, D.C. Headlines were subsequently dominated by stories about Reagan's condition, relegating Woyla to the back pages.

Within Kopassandha, Woyla was a defining moment. Each member of the task force received an extraordinary promotion in rank. Sintong Pandjaitan, besides getting a boost to colonel, received the *Bintang Sakti*. He also received instructions from General Moerdani to formally create a counter-terrorist unit within Kopassandha rather than the previous ad hoc arrangement under Group 4.

Moerdani's order carried particular urgency due to cross-service rivalries. This came primarily from General Awaloedin Djamin, the Indonesian national police chief who had been ambassador to West Germany five years earlier. While serving as ambassador, he had capitalized on his law enforcement background and forged ties with Germany's Federal Border Police. Germany's border police, in turn, held control over GSG-9, the counter-terrorist unit that had performed the Somali aircraft rescue.

With counter-terrorism suddenly a hot topic after the Woyla operation, General Djamin had looked to have the police grab some of the limelight by boosting the abilities of the Gegana bomb squad within the Mobile Brigade. To do this, he reestablished his contacts with the German Federal Border Police and received permission to send two Indonesian police candidates for eleven months of GSG-9 training.[17]

Hearing this, Moerdani was not amused by Djamin's maneuvering. Using his considerable clout, Moerdani informed the police chief that counter-terrorism was a military function. He then notified Sintong that the two GSG-9 slots would instead be going to a pair of Kopassandha candidates; it was Sintong's job to choose the right pair.

Sintong did not have to look far. Within Kopassandha, two young officers had consistently ranked high in both mental and physical aptitude. The first was Major Luhut Pandjaitan. A Batak Christian from North Sumatra like Sintong, Luhut was a long-time member of Group 1 who had served two combat tours in East Timor (including the parachute jump at Baucau). He also showed a flair for military science, and had regularly penned articles for Kopassandha's *Baret Merah* magazine.[18]

The second was Captain Prabowo Subianto, the same Group 1 company commander who had successfully led Nanggala 28 in the hunt for Fretilin President Nicolao Lobato. Prabowo had already impressed his superiors with his grasp of military literature and was one of the few lieutenants to contribute to *Baret Merah*. Moreover, he was fluent in German—important given that the GSG-9 coursework would be in that language.

Both Luhut and Prabowo had been sent overseas together once before. In early 1980, they had been selected to attend a four-month U.S. Army's special forces course at Fort Bragg. While there, they had befriended Lieutenant Paul Arn, the senior instructor at Bragg's military freefall course.

When both returned to Indonesia, Prabowo requested Arn by name to lead a freefall training team to Cijantung. This raised some eyebrows, both because of Arn's relatively junior rank, and because foreign airborne instructors should theoretically have gone to Batu Jajar rather than Cijantung. Still, Prabowo carried a fair bit of weight because of his father's ministerial career and the request was favorably processed. In mid-July 1980, Lieutenant Arn and six other U.S. Army Special Forces freefallers arrived in Indonesia. Their mandate was to train over 250 members of Group 1 in freefall accuracy, with their graduation jump to take place in front of President Suharto during the 5 October armed forces day celebrations. Luhut and Prabowo were to act as liaison officers.[19]

Arn had his work cut out for him. On their introduction jump in front of the Kopassandha headquarters for the opening ceremony, the U.S. instructors all landed on target. The Indonesians, however, were all over the map. In addition, Sintong snapped his ankle (which had still not fully healed by the time of the Woyla operation) and Prabowo broke his tailbone. "By the time we are finished," Arn vowed, "all of the Kopassandha trainees will land like us."

In front of President Suharto, they did. After thirty-seven practice jumps during a period of two months, over one hundred students exited C-130 transports over the highway being constructed from Jakarta to Bogor. Without complications, they descended in front of reviewing stands containing the country's top leaders and dozens of foreign military attachés.

In April 1981, Luhut and Prabowo packed for the GSG-9 course. Along with five Turks, they were the first foreigners allowed to partake in German counter-terrorist instruction. It was to be a trying experience, with Prabowo missing several weeks after he fell from an obstacle course and broke his leg.[20] But eleven months later, both emerged with GSG-9 qualification wings on their chest. Luhut had also managed to make a brief side trip to Hereford, England, where he was shown the training facilities that the British Special Air Service used to hone its hostage rescue skills.

Arriving back in Indonesia in March 1982, Luhut and Prabowo were formally notified they would be the core of Kopassandha's counter-terrorist unit. The two intended to sort through volunteers from across all the groups. There was a problem, however. Although Kopassandha had eliminated one group back in 1977 because of manpower shortages, there were bureaucratic pressures to rebuild to its previous authorized strength. There was also a hint of nepotism, with General Jusuf indicating it would be nice to station a Kopassandha group in his home province of South Sulawesi.

Taking Jusuf's suggestion to heart, Kopassandha prepared plans in March 1980 to resurrect Group 3 in the South Sulawesi capital of Ujung Pandang (the new name given to Makassar in 1972). Unlike the previous Group 3—a *sandhi yudha* formation—this new Group 3 would be a para-commando unit. Finding sufficient recruits promised to be a major challenge. As a core, one combat detachment was removed from Group 1 and shifted to Sulawesi in October 1980. A scattering of additional personnel came from Group 2, Group 4, and the Kopassandha headquarters. Still chronically undermanned, the Ujung Pandang-based 700 Raider Battalion—which had been formed in the fifties when Jusuf was the South Sulawesi military region commander—offered a large number of volunteers.

On 15 March 1981, after a year of preparation, the new Group 3 was officially commissioned. Colonel Sintong, fresh off the Woyla success, was named group commander. His deputy was Lieutenant Colonel Yunus Yosfiah, who was returning to the special forces fold after heading the Timorese infantry battalion during the hunt for Nicolao Lobato.

Back up to four combat groups, Kopassandha again began to feel the pressure of manpower shortages. With all four group commanders defending their respective turf, it was a sure bet that none wanted to part with their best members for a new counter-terrorist unit. Still, with visible support from

General Moerdani, Luhut and Prabowo held enough sway to look over six hundred prospects from Cijantung, Solo, and Ujung Pandang. After a three-step process, which included a psychiatric battery and physical tests, they narrowed this field down to eighty suitable volunteers.[21]

Other important issues needed to be addressed at this early stage. From a generous initial budget approved by Moerdani, they purchased some of the best counter-terrorist gear in the world. Assault rifles were the highly regarded Heckler and Koch MP5K from West Germany. For assault suits and leather assault harnesses, they contacted Ibcol UK Limited, a subsidiary of West Germany's Ibcol GmbH; this gear was based on designs already manufactured for the British Special Air Service. A Sky Genie abseiling device was obtained from the Arkansas-based Descent Control, Inc. And recalling the fatal shortcoming of the bulletproof vest used by Achmad Kirang, they procured Bristol Armor Type 4 vests, which had ballistic protection extending down to the crotch.[22]

Luhut and Prabowo also needed to sort out how their counter-terrorist unit would be organized. In GSG-9, the basic formation was a five-man team consisting of a master sergeant and four subordinates. This arrangement was found to offer sufficient command and control, while at the same time keeping the team small enough to maneuver inside confined quarters like an aircraft cabin. Six of these five-man teams comprised a GSG-9 unit.

Keeping this same formula, the Indonesians simply reversed the nomenclature. The basic building block in the Kopassandha counter-terrorist force would be a five-man unit. "Moerdani wanted us to focus on airplane rescues," said one early member, "so the five-man unit was ideal because it allowed for two to use the ladder and crack the door, two to enter, and one to control."[23] Six of these units, plus a six-man command section, would comprise a 36-man team headed by a captain.

On 30 June 1982, the first two teams were declared mission-ready. With Luhut as commander and Prabowo as his deputy, the entire force was named Detachment 81 ("81" signified 1981, the year of the Woyla rescue). In line with their special status, the detachment had a residential block near the Kopassandha headquarters fenced off as their new secure compound; entry to outsiders was limited to Moerdani, the Kopassandha commanding general, and just a handful of other senior officers.

No sooner had Detachment 81 entered the order-of-battle, Moerdani began to expand its mandate. In particular, he was concerned about terrorist threats against coastal and offshore installations, especially the scores of oil rigs scattered across the Indonesian archipelago. Other militaries were taking proactive measures in this regard, and word had gotten to him that a special U.S. Navy SEAL team—SEAL Team Six—had been activated in October 1980 to handle such contingencies.

Upon hearing Moerdani's maritime concerns, two units quickly took shape. One of these was under the Indonesian navy, with the naval chief of operations on 4 November authorizing the formation of an ad hoc seaborne counter-terrorist formation that answered directly to him. Drawing several dozen candidates from the marine reconnaissance battalion, and a handful from the navy's Kopaska combat swimmers, the new unit was dubbed Task Force Jala Mangkara in honor of a mythical guardian of the sea.[24]

The other maritime counter-terrorist unit took shape within Detachment 81. Besides the two existing teams, Luhut immediately raised an additional three dozen men and dispatched them to Surabaya for Kopaska combat swimmer training. He could do so knowing that Kopaska and Kopassandha had long historical links, with the former having been originally formed as a sub-set of the RPKAD during the 1962 West Irian campaign. Kopaska remained a small cadre at Batu Jajar through 1967, after which the navy withdrew its personnel to Surabaya and kept a swimmer capability firmly under its thumb. Re-establishing these ties, the Detachment 81 personnel received intensive tutoring in scuba techniques and underwater demolitions through September.[25]

Now three teams strong, Detachment 81 suddenly encountered a dilemma faced by many counter-terrorist groups. In cases like GSG-9, the unit exclusively remained on standby for terrorist emergencies. By contrast, the British Special Air Service had all its squadrons rotate between refresher training, counter-terrorist alert status, and unconventional warfare stints. Although Luhut favored the GSG-9 example—that is, being reserved exclusively for counter-terrorism—this meant the detachment might go for extended periods without being used for its intended purpose. Not only would Luhut not be able to rate their performance under fire, but the stress of being on perpetual alert would probably adversely effect morale.

Before he had a chance to address the situation, Luhut in October took temporary leave of Cijantung to attend a command and staff course. Filling in his stead, Captain Prabowo took the reigns of the detachment. Almost as soon as he did so, the captain proposed a challenging first assignment—and one that was outside the borders of Indonesia.

By all accounts, 1981 had been a year of setbacks for the OPM secessionist movement in Irian Jaya. Wracked by internal feuding, short of weapons, and hounded by Indonesian military patrols, the guerrillas could offer only the slightest challenge to government rule. On the rare occasions when they tried, they were quickly beaten back to the jungle.

Desperate, the OPM tried a new tack. That October, an OPM band led by A.B. "Donald" Derey—a former subordinate of Marthin Tabu who, like Tabu, had reneged on an earlier surrender and reverted to his guerrilla habits— seized 58 hostages at a logging camp south of Jayapura. Recalling the precedent set during the 1977 kidnapping by his erstwhile mentor, Derey demanded US\$2 million in ransom and one hundred machine guns for their release. Complicating matters, one of the hostages was a Malaysian national, and Kuala Lumpur was pressuring Jakarta to rescue their citizen.

Exercising a swift military response, Indonesian infantrymen swept through the vicinity. Though they managed to hit a rebel camp and release thirty-six of the hostages, including the Malaysian national, the remaining captives were marched deeper into the jungle toward the Papua New Guinea border.

For the next seven months, the OPM kidnappers eluded government patrols. Many in Jakarta suspected they had actually crossed the border, prompting a shallow Indonesian military foray in May 1982. Though the incursion turned up little, the remaining hostages (minus five who died in captivity) were released a month later inside Papua New Guinea territory with a Papuan foreign ministry officer acting as intermediary.

All of this left a bad taste in Indonesia's mouth. Though the Papuan government denied its territory was being used as a sanctuary for anti-Indonesia rebels, Jakarta was growing suspicious about links between Port Moresby and the OPM. This was compounded by barbs thrown at Indonesia during a recent human rights "tribunal" held at the University of Papua New Guinea campus, as well as the sharp anti-Indonesia rhetoric favored by Papuan Deputy Prime Minster Iambakey Okuk.

Some suspected Papua New Guinea's links to OPM went beyond words. Confirmed in this belief was General M.I. Soetaryo, Benny Moerdani's intelligence deputy. Soetaryo and Moerdani went back a long way. Both had entered the RPKAD from the same group of student-soldiers, and Soetaryo had later served as Moerdani's deputy when the latter commanded the RPKAD's Battalion 1. In 1965, the two parted company for a time: Moerdani to head for Bangkok as an intelligence operative, Soetaryo to enter the politically-charged Tjakrabirawa Regiment. When Sukarno was deposed and Tjakrabirawa was unceremoniously disbanded, Soetaryo's star was somewhat tainted. But once Moerdani came back strong within military intelligence, he elevated Soetaryo as his key assistant.

From information gleaned by his intelligence network, Soetaryo had evidence that a jungle helipad had recently been cleared just inside Papua New Guinea's northern border with Irian Jaya. This helipad, he believed, was being used to land weapons destined for the OPM. Soetaryo wanted eyewitness confirmation of this landing zone; moreover, if a chopper was found to be using the site for arms-smuggling, the aircraft was to be ambushed.

This was the challenge posted to Captain Prabowo in early November 1982. Relishing the opportunity to field-test Detachment 81 and its equipment under combat conditions, he selected 33 members from among the three teams. Each was given sterile green civilian clothes with no manufacturer's labels, an MP5K submachine gun, and a set of night-vision goggles. They also carried one Armbrust, a 67mm one-shot, disposable shoulder-fired recoilless gun made in West Germany.

During the second week of November, Prabowo led the composite team to the Irian Jaya capital of Jayapura. After being briefed by General Soetaryo, they divided in two. One unit of thirteen men would remain in Jayapura with the Armbrust; with a chopper at their disposal, they would be on standby as a heliborne reaction force.

The remaining twenty commandos would divide in three—dubbed Bravo 1, 2, and 3—and take a trio of motorized fishing schooners east along the coast. Landing inside Papua New Guinea, they would then infiltrate inland for two days until arriving at the location of the suspected helipad from behind. They carried enough rations—including high-protein mountaineering food imported from Norway—to last for two weeks of surveillance.

From the start, the mission was plagued by Murphy's Law. Departing Jayapura at 2200 hours for a three-hour journey, the captain of the lead boat— a civilian from South Sulawesi—was reticent when they approached the shore in high swells. Showing his temper, Prabowo browbeat the captain into attempting a landing—only to have the vessel holed on the rocks. As its passengers spilled onto the beach, the boat sank under the waves. The two other boats diverted further up the coast and disgorged their passengers without incident.

Regrouping for their trek inland, the team was immediately beset by further problems. High among them was their temperamental night vision goggles, which were plagued by the searing humidity. This was compounded by the thick jungle canopy, which left little starlight for amplification. Reduced to a blind crawl, what was supposed to take two days lasted almost five.

Finally arriving at the site of the alleged helipad, they were rewarded for their perseverance. A large clearing had been cut out of the jungle just inside the Papua New Guinea border, almost certainly for use as a landing zone. To provide surveillance coverage, they divided into six observation posts, plus two roving patrols.

On their second day lying in wait, their vigil grew more interesting. Captain John Ramses, walking point on one of the patrols, spotted two Caucasian males making their way through the jungle. Both were dressed in civilian gear with yellow backpacks, and both appeared to be young and fit. Waiting until they had nearly tripped over him, the captain broke from the bush with his MP5K at the ready.

Visibly petrified, the two foreigners surrendered without resistance. Though they claimed to be Australian civilians on a trek, Ramses was suspicious. A communications officer, he noted both carried radio gear that appeared to be military issue. They also had detailed maps of the border. Rushing to the scene, Prabowo was also incredulous about their tale. "They had plausible deniability," he later surmised.

Reporting their find to Soetaryo, the general instructed Prabowo to take the pair to the helipad for exfiltration to Indonesia. Subsequently shuttled to Jayapura for an interrogation, both were later repatriated.

Back at the helipad, meanwhile, the men of Detachment 81 turned restless after nine days on the ground. Having exhausted their rations, Prabowo received orders to exfiltrate his men back north to the coast for a resupply.

Arriving there on 3 December, they saw a schooner bobbing a hundred meters offshore with fresh food. Unfortunately for them, a treacherous rocky cliff and violent breakers stood in between.

Overtaken by hunger, Sergeant Max Rohrong—a member of the detachment's scuba-trained team—volunteered to brave the swells to bring a line out to the boat. But as soon as he hit the water, the first wave flung him back on the rocks with a fierce impact. Bleeding and unconscious, the sergeant was in need of immediate helicopter evacuation. Realizing this would expose their presence to the Papuan authorities, the captain called in three helicopters to lift out the entire contingent and bring the operation to a close. Government officials in Port Moresby, aware of the aircraft incursion but unwise to the commando mission, later offered a weak diplomatic protest.

Eight months later and with no counter-terrorist assignments in sight, the decision was made to again send Detachment 81 into an operational zone. This time, they would face East Timor's Fretilin. With Major Luhut still at the command and staff course, Captain Prabowo would once again be at the helm.

Much had happened in East Timor since Prabowo had last been there with Nanggala 28. Having come close to breaking Fretilin's back after the elimination of several top leaders, the Indonesians had been frustrated by a former Jesuit seminarian and colonial civil servant named Jose Alejandro "Xanana" Gusmao. The second of nine children, Xanana had joined Fretilin at its inception and had fled Dili a week before Indonesian troops arrived in December 1975. Going on to hold a number of senior positions in the eastern part of the territory—deputy of the Viqueque zone, then head of the Lospalos sector—he took the reigns of the rebel organization after Lobato's death.

Xanana assumed command at the worst possible moment. By the time he called for a major Fretilin gathering near Viqueque in March 1981, he estimated they had lost eighty percent of their guerrilla strength and ninety percent of their weapons. Worse, Jakarta that same month was gearing up for a renewed campaign of massive proportions. Codenamed Operation Saber Kikis Baratayudha (named after a mythical war in the world of Javanese shadow puppets), it employed a technique first used during the Darul Islam insurgency in the fifties. Like beaters on an Indian tiger hunt—but multiplied hundreds of times in size—this involved 33,000 Timorese civilians backed by twelve battalions. With the civilians in front, they would be divided into two extended lines—one marching west from the beach at Laga, the second going east from Dili—with a killing zone near Aitana, a mountain thirty-five kilometers southwest of Baucau. The epitome of conventional strategy, the operation did not involve Kopassandha.[26]

For the next twelve months, the two extended lines crept across the Timorese countryside. Believing that only small pockets of rebels had managed to evade the dragnet and escape to Matebian, the same mountain redoubt where they suffered heavy casualties in mid-1978, the government saw Fretilin once more on the ropes. Declaring East Timor all but pacified, just two infantry battalions and three Kopassandha contingents—Nanggala 51, 52, and 53— were retained in the province to pursue the last holdouts.

Very quickly, it became apparent that Fretilin's epitaph was a bit premature. "The enemy had simply dispersed," said the Nanggala 52 commander, Major Gatot Purwanto. "We soon started having contact around Lospalos."[27]

For Gatot, this was his third Timor tour after serving in Susi and Nanggala 13. Having transferred to the reconstituted Group 3 in Ujung Pandang, his latest nanggala consisted of a para-commando company. This he wielded in more of a *sandhi yudha* role, using them to visit villages and put out the word that he wanted to establish contact with the Fretilin sector commander.

The offer eventually bore fruit. After three months of patient cultivation—including goodwill deliveries of food and medicine—Gatot received word that the local Fretilin chief had agreed to meet. Along with three of his men, the major marched twenty kilometers south of Lospalos near a village called Misi (so named because it had once hosted a missionary school). Waiting in the dark, they sensed movement in the forest alongside the road. Their shirts were open to show they had no hidden weapons.

After several tense moments, the Fretilin sector commander emerged from the bush. The meeting went well, as did two others that followed. As both sides grew more comfortable, more bold confidence building measures followed. At the opening of 1983, Gatot flew with the chieftain to Dili, then took a Garuda flight to Jakarta for a five-day sightseeing trip.

While a good start, Gatot had already relayed word that his real aim was a meeting with Xanana himself. This took a full three months of negotiations, during which time Nanggala 52 concluded its tour and returned to South Sulawesi. On account of his rapport with the rebels, Gatot and five of his men were retained to act as intermediaries.

The first contact with Fretilin's top commander was surprisingly easy. Given the coordinates of a desolate location near the mountain town of Ossu, Gatot and his five men departed at first light and reached their rendezvous point by noon. There they were met by a Fretilin honor guard dressed in tattered clothes but outfitted with pristine weapons. After exchanging greetings in Tetum, the Indonesians were asked to turn over their magazines but allowed to retain their assault rifles.

In an adjacent clearing, Xanana was waiting. Despite the brutal punishment his rebel movement had taken over the previous few years, Fretilin's leader was brimming with confidence. "He claimed that oil prices were down," recalls Gatot, "and Indonesia could not afford to keep troops in Timor."[28]

Three more meetings with Xanana followed in quick succession. During the last of these, on 21 March 1983, the Indonesian delegation was allowed to fly directly to the clearing in a chopper. Two days later, the governor of East Timor met with Xanana at the same locale and arrived at a verbal agreement for a ceasefire.

For the next four months, the truce held. Kopassandha maintained its normal rotation of three nanggalas, but these were singularly uneventful deployments. "We were able to visit the Fretilin base at Same," said one member of Nanggala 55. "We even took photos with the rebel pastor in that town."[29]

Despite such progress, the ceasefire was irrevocably shattered on 8 August. That night, Hansip militiamen—elements of the same formation that Kopassandha had been preening over the previous seven years—attacked a platoon of army engineers sleeping in the village of Kraras in Viqueque district. The entire platoon of seventeen soldiers—save for the chaplain—was massacred and their bodies mutilated.[30] By morning, the Hansip members had fled to waiting Fretilin guerrillas with the engineers' weapons.[31]

Accusations and counter-accusations flew in the wake of the killings. One of the more plausible was that Xanana had soured to the ceasefire because he was denied permission to meet a delegation of Australian parliamentarians.

Whatever the reason, General Moerdani—who had risen to the highest post in the military after succeeding Jusuf in late March as armed forces commander—was not in a forgiving mood. As a matter of urgency, he placed the army back on the offensive. Deadly military reprisals were staged around Kraras; Fretilin answered with attacks across the province. The war had returned with a vengeance.

This was the situation faced by Captain Prabowo when he readied 120 men—nearly all of Detachment 81—for its initial outing to East Timor. They would be going there under the codename *chandraca*, a mythical Hindu weapon of unfailing accuracy, which had replaced the earlier *nanggala* callsign. The reason for the name change: on 22 March, just a week before Moerdani took over as military commander, it was announced that Major General Yogie would pass the Kopassandha torch to Colonel Wismoyo.

This succession had been long overdue. For eight years—the longest of any commander to date—Yogie had led the special forces. It was widely known that his longevity at the post was largely due to the fact he was a favorite of General Jusuf. Yogie was such a favorite, in fact, that he earned his second star (becoming the first major general in Kopassandha) and got concurrent assignments as head of the Siliwangi military command for West Java and chief of the even larger military region covering all of Java and Madura. Wearing three hats, it came as little surprise that he often left Kopassandha leadership in the hands of deputies.

As the new Kopassandha boss, forty-three-year-old Colonel Wismoyo brought along several strengths. Unlike Yogie, he had spent his entire military career in the special forces, most recently as the Group 1 commander. And while prone to endlessly reciting canned motivational speeches before his men, he was known to have the favor of the president—in no small part because he had married the sister of First Lady Tien Suharto.

Looking to make an early mark, Wismoyo took the symbolic step of changing codenames. Out was the use of nanggala; under his watch, all Kopassandha deployments were sequentially numbered with a *chandraca* prefix. In Prabowo's case, he and his Detachment 81 contingent destined for East Timor would be Chandraca 8.

On 28 August, Chandraca 8 landed in East Timor and quickly shifted to Viqueque. To maximize coverage, they divided into four teams—named Bravo 1 through 4—and choppered into the central highlands. Armed with AK-47 assault rifles (even though Kopassandha had standardized to the M-16 in 1978, the AK-47 was still the normal weapon issued for East Timor assignments), each team took on ten armed partisans to act as guides.

Their initial movements were not without problems. Told to seize a hill near Laklubar by night, scouts for one of the Detachment 81 teams got spooked after seeing campfires in the dark and began a disorganized retreat. After a redressing by Prabowo, he led them over the hill the next day and captured several unarmed Timorese leading a line of ponies.

Eager to use his men in more challenging ways than the standard fare of night patrols and raids done by the earlier nanggala, Prabowo focused on honing ambush techniques. In this, they did well. At the cost of three Detachment 81 members killed in action, they went on to inflict far heavier losses on Fretilin patrols.[32]

Six months later, Detachment 81 returned to Cijantung to find another expansion in its mandate. At Moerdani's urging, the unit took on specialized aspects of very important person (VIP) protection. This was not exactly a new assignment for Kopassandha: ever since 1977, a limited number of special forces members had been incorporated into President Suharto's bodyguard detail.[33] In answer to Moerdani's directive, a fourth technical team was established during 1984, with an initial cadre of its members was sent to West Germany to train in VIP driving techniques.[34]

Over the span of three years, the detachment had made considerable progress. Though untested against terrorists, its members had conducted two combat assignments with better than average results. On a less positive note, however, the unit's commander and deputy commander were locked in a simmering feud. In a sense, this was because Luhut—who had since been promoted to lieutenant colonel—and Prabowo were very much alike. Both were extremely capable and ambitious. Both, too, had mentors in high places. In the case of Luhut, he had grown extremely close to Moerdani. In the case of Prabowo, he not only had the backing of his father, but in May 1983 had married the daughter of President Suharto.

By early 1985, the infighting was about to come to a head. Appealing to Moerdani, Luhut maneuvered to have Prabowo sent to Fort Benning for an advanced infantry course. When the latter left for what he thought was a temporary absence, Luhut lobbied to have his deputy's slot filled. With bad blood all around, Prabowo would instead find a new home with Kostrad.

1   FBIS, Asia Pacific edition, 31 March 1981, p. N2.

2   B. Wiwoho, *Operasi Woyla* (Jakarta: PT Meara Gading Nusantara, 1981), p. 30.

3   *Jakarta Post*, 9 February 1999, p. 3.

4   *Baret Merah*, February 1978, issue #17.

5   The other fatality was Lieutenant Mansur, a *prayudha* commander who was among the best Mandarin linguists in Group 4.

6   Sintong Pandjaitan interview.

7   The British Special Air Service had also been mobilized in January 1975 after an Iranian passenger with a pistol hijacked a plane to Essex; he was quickly arrested on the ground before a raid was required.

8   There have been assertions that Moerdani issued "special" ammunition during the Halim rehearsal; these bullets supposedly surpassed a six-month expiration date and proved to be duds (See *Benny Moerdani*, p. 358; Sintong Pandjaitan interview). In fact, no such special ammunition with a six-month shelf life exists. Moreover, Team A members recall no problems with bullet misfires during the Halim rehearsal session.

9   Six years earlier, Moerdani had given some consideration to sending two members of Kopassandha's Group 4 to Israel for commando training. This had been cancelled at the last minute, allegedly because Israel was not comfortable imparting specialized military skills to a heavily Muslim nation like Indonesia.

10   Zulfikar was later tied to a mysterious December 1980 arson attempt at the Hilton; he later went missing from his Hilton job one day before the Bandung attack.

11   FBIS, Asia Pacific edition, 1 April 1981, p. N2.

12   FBIS, Asia Pacific edition, 30 March 1981, p. J1.

13   Thailand's security forces did not exactly distinguish themselves during the Woyla raid. "Their air force counter-terrorist unit was pathetic," said George McQuillen, a U.S. Army military attaché who attended coordination sessions during the hijacking. "Their commanding general provided constant excuses why they should not get involved, such as language difficulties." Interview with George McQuillen, 22 January 1997.

14 Details of the special audio gear, which could have applications during future hijackings, will not be revealed in this book. Press accounts later claimed that the U.S. Army's counter-terrorist unit, known as Delta Force, provided assistance during the Woyla raid. This is false: the only U.S. assistance came from the CIA, not Delta Force.

15 FBIS, Asia Pacific edition, 31 March 1981, p. J1.

16 Sintong Pandjaitan interview.

17 GSG-9 operatives can spend up to three years getting fully trained.

18 Luhut's article in the February 1978 edition of *Baret Merah*, for example, concerned freefall operations, while his article in the May 1978 edition was about the structure of the U.S. Army Special Forces.

19 Interview with Paul Arn, 18 May 2000; interview with John Trantanella, 12 August 2001.

20 Interview with Prabowo Subianto, 26 July 2001.

21 Only one Woyla veteran was among the eighty. The exclusion of Woyla veterans was perhaps because many were older members of Group 4, whereas Luhut and Prabowo favored younger recruits. Others have noted, however, that Luhut and Prabowo hailed from Group 1, and both had bristled toward the elitism displayed by Group 4; in a conscious rebuff, they prejudiced their selection against members of the latter group.

22 Correspondence with Peter Harclerode, 18 June 1999.

23 Interview with John Ramses, 29 January 2002.

24 In 1975, marine reconnaissance personnel, formerly known as "Kipam" (*Kesatuan Intai Para Amfibi*, or Amphibious Airborne Reconnaissance Unit), were given the slightly less wordy acronym "Taifib" (*Intai Amfibi*, or Amphibious Reconnaissance). Although the airborne designation was taken from their title, all Taifib members remained airborne-qualified.

25 The scuba-qualified third team was called Team Paska, for *Pasukan Katak* ("Frog force"). The first Team Paska commander was Captain Tono Suratman.

26 *Baret Jingga* (Jakarta: PT Gramedia Pustaka Utama, 1999), p. 325.

27 Gatot Purwanto interview.

28 Ibid.

29 E. Sunarya interview.

30   *Gatra*, 10 October 1998, p. 30.

31   The Indonesian government initially tried to conceal the Hansip defection by claiming they had been captured by Fretilin. *Asia Watch*, Vol. 5, No. 8 (April 1993), p. 6.

32   Media accounts have falsely claimed that Prabowo went missing in the bush for several days during this deployment. Prabowo did go missing for a short period— but to quietly attend an overseas meeting with the Australian Special Air Service Regiment.

33   After the disbandment of the Tjakrabirawa Regiment in 1966, a paratrooper section within the army's military police took over security for Indonesia's top dignitaries. This remained exclusively the domain of the military police paratroopers until 1977, when the first Kopassandha members were incorporated into the bodyguard detail.

34   In practice, Detachment 81 was rarely used in the VIP escort role. One exception took place in 1995, when four members of the detachment went with President Suharto's entourage during a one-day visit to Bosnia.

CHAPTER TWENTY
KOPASSUS

W hen Benny Moerdani took over as armed forces commander in March 1983, he came to office with a vision of the future. Disturbed by what he saw as an emphasis on quantity over quality, and pomp over substance, he was determined to forge his military into something more lean, effective, efficient, and professional.

An early result of this policy was seen during the Armed Forces Day parade of 5 October 1983. Far from the garish productions of earlier years—including the mass parachute drop conducted by Kopassandha in 1980—the 1983 show was a modest, restrained event held in the parking lot of the Senayan sports stadium. Noteworthy, too, were the combat utilities worn by the troops: in order to reduce costs and sharpen discipline, Moerdani had banned the ten different camouflage patterns worn by various units and instead insisted that the entire military standardize to British disruptive pattern material (DPM) camouflage.[1]

Over the next two years, Moerdani moved beyond the superficial and began exacting tough reforms. Perhaps no unit would come to be more effected by this policy than Kopassandha. Singling out the special forces for a major overhaul, he first looked to install his own man at the helm. On 20 May 1985, Brigadier General Wismoyo—the president's brother-in-law—concluded his two-year tour and was promoted to head Kostrad. In his place came Colonel Sintong Pandjaitan, the respected Woyla veteran who most recently had been commander at Batu Jajar.

Almost as soon as he took control at Cijantung, Sintong gathered his group commanders and discussed the impending reorganization in general terms. To flesh out the idea, Colonel Yusman Yutam, the head of Group 1, was placed in charge of penning a transition scheme. It was to prove a major challenge. Instructions from Moerdani merely called for Kopassandha to pare its authorized ceiling of 6,600 men down to just 2,500 operatives. But apart from numbers, there were no clear orders on what the smaller unit would look like and what missions it was to perform. Said Yusman: "Did Benny want a return to the para-commandos of the RPKAD? Did he want something like the U.S. Army Special Forces? The British Special Air Service?"[2]

In subtle ways, Moerdani let his preference be known. First was the 1983 transition to British camouflage for the entire Indonesian military. Two years later, he went out of his way to scuttle ties with America's special forces. Said Moerdani:

I asked the U.S., 'What will you teach us? You failed raiding the island off Cambodia [during the 1975 Mayaguez incident]. You failed in rescuing the hostages in Iran and at the Son Tay prison in Vietnam. Will you teach us about that?' The U.S. government got mad, so there was no more U.S. Army Special Forces training during my time.[3]

Reading into these moves a bias toward the British model, Yusman looked closely at the Special Air Service. In terms of organization, the SAS regiment was broken into four squadrons, each consisting of 72 men and 6 officers. Each squadron had a staff and four troops, with each troop consisting of one officer and fifteen men. Troops, in turn, were broken into four patrols of 4 men apiece.

The key to the SAS's success, Yusman found, was the versatility of its members. Each trooper was cross-trained in two or more specialist skills. This allowed all of its squadrons to be equally adept at conducting missions like conducting raids, pathfinding, and counter-terrorism. In the ultimate display of quality over quantity, England retained less than six hundred members in the entire regiment, including administrative staff and support units.

Extrapolating from the SAS example, Yusman proposed a new table of organization for Kopassandha. The basic building block would be a ten-man unit capable of being broken into two five-man patrols. Each unit would be led by a lieutenant, and all its members would be cross-trained in more than one specialization. Three units would comprise a team (roughly analogous to an SAS troop) led by a captain, and three teams would comprise a detachment (akin to an SAS squadron). Taking this one step further, three detachments would be grouped into one battalion. This new structure would apply to all elements except Detachment 81, which from its inception was organized roughly similar to the SAS.

Like the British model, Yusman's proposal to have each Kopassandha member cross-trained in more than one specialization would make for a marked increase in versatility. Once this was done, no longer would there be a need to differentiate between *sandhi yudha* or para-commando groups. In addition, the *prayudha* and *karsa yudha* nomenclature—which had always confused the army's more conventional officers—would be rendered obsolete.

Presented with the plan, Sintong liked what he heard. Winning quick approval from Moerdani, the restructured Kopassandha would from that point forward be known as the Special Forces Command (*Komando Pasukan Khusus*, or Kopassus). To meet Moerdani's lower personnel ceiling, Kopassus would include no more than two combat groups, plus Detachment 81. In addition, the Batu Jajar school, which had been administratively under the army's Training and Education Command during the Kopassandha period, would be placed directly back under the Kopassus commander.

While ratified on paper, the plan to rebuild Kopassus promised to be a long, challenging campaign. Beginning in August 1985, all personnel from Groups 1, 2, 3, and 4—everybody from lieutenant colonel down to private—were rotated through a battery of individual and unit tests. This was done to determine which members had sufficient aptitude to receive multiple specialist qualifications. The hundreds that came up short were then directed to Group 3 in Ujung Pandang. This process was completed in April 1986, at which point Group 3 was officially removed from the Kopassus order-of-battle and transferred to Kostrad as the newly-established 3 Airborne Brigade. Named as the brigade's first commander was Colonel Tarub, the Tuti commander in Timor, who symbolically exchanged his red Kopassus beret for Kostrad green.

Having stripped away Group 3, Kopassus was left with a lean and able core. More cuts were necessary, however. In May 1986, all remaining members were rotated through jungle warfare and counter-guerrilla training. In addition, they began receiving specialization instruction in such topics as intelligence, mountain climbing, demolitions, sharpshooting, communications, medicine, freefalling, combat swimming, computers, and English.

By the end of this process, attrition had taken a heavy toll. With Groups 1, 2, and 4 all far below authorized strength, it now became easy to consolidate their remaining personnel into just two groups of two battalions apiece. Group 1, consisting of Battalions 11 and 12, would be posted to new barracks at Serang in West Java. Group 2, comprised of Battalions 21 and 22, would remain in Solo. The Batu Jajar school, now directly under the Kopassus chief, would be renamed Group 3. Detachment 81 would stay unchanged at its secure compound in Cijantung.

On 27 December 1986, the restructuring process was complete. Officially retiring the Kopassandha banner, a new Kopassus standard was unfurled in its place. Meeting the 2,500-man limit placed by Moerdani, Groups 1 and 2 were in theory—now equally adept at performing a full range of unconventional missions.[4]

As an addendum to Moerdani's push for quality over quantity, the general took great pains to root out overlapping mandates within his military. This was readily apparent in the area of elite units, where several of the services had maintained similar formations that competed for limited budgetary resources. Determined to stamp this out, Moerdani forced two early changes. In the police Mobile Brigade, he dictated that its airborne ranger regiment (*Resimen Pelopor*) be disbanded. And in the air force, he insisted that the Kopasgat special forces— which had once rivaled the RPKAD during the Sukarno era—be strictly limited to the missions of forward air controlling, airbase defense, and combat search and rescue.[5]

An exception to this rule were the maritime counter-terrorist commandos of Jala Mangkara. Since its formation in 1982, Jala Mangkara had remained an ad hoc unit that specialized in counter-terrorism in name only. On 13 October 1984, Moerdani looked to change this by cutting orders to convert it into a permanent force with a rigorous selection and training process. This was codified on 16 April 1985, when Task Force Jala Mangkara was upgraded to Detachment Jala Mangkara with an authorized strength of seventy members.

As before, the bulk of Detachment Jala Mangkara would be drawn from the marine reconnaissance battalion. The remainder would come from the navy's Kopaska. Though limited in size—they expanded in 1985 to a single squadron in Surabaya, plus a smaller detachment in Jakarta—Kopaska had spent recent years making notable gains in expanding its capabilities. In 1983, for example, they started practicing covert exits from submarine torpedo tubes (they packed up to three swimmers per tube). And in 1985, they played host to a U.S. Navy SEAL training team.[6]

Unlike the previous task force arrangement, Detachment Jala Mangkara adopted a new set of selection principles that bordered on the impossible. This became apparent from the opening psychological evaluation: just seven marines and two navy frogmen passed. Taking aboard six others that came close, the detachment had its first fifteen members. They were housed in a small, segregated barracks within the marine brigade compound in South Jakarta.[7]

With this thin roster, the ranking officers within Jala Mangkara looked to map out a course of training. In this, the U.S. Embassy provided some notes on the organization of its own maritime counter-terrorist formation, SEAL Team Six. Like Team Six, Jala Mangkara adopted a flexible organization of assault teams numbering between four and six operatives.

Jala Mangkara also came up with some innovative training techniques. To practice parachuting onto the deck of a moving ship—a tactic that was reportedly being considered when SEAL Team Six was mobilized to raid the hijacked Achille Lauro cruiseliner in 1985—the detachment fixed a wooden platform atop a Land Rover. With the vehicle at first remaining stationary, the commandos practiced landing on its roof. After perfecting this, they did so while it was on the move. By the end of 1986, they graduated to jumps onto oil rigs and moving ships at sea. Showing a hint of mission-overlap, they also practiced aircraft assaults.

Smitten with the unit, Moerdani provided it with a generous budget to buy specialized gear. Once more showing his partiality toward England, he sent them there in 1987 to purchase a pair of Sea Riders and a trio of Sub Skimmers. The former was a rigid inflatable boat with a pair of outboards that could reach speeds of forty knots and carry ten passengers. The latter was an unusual hybrid of surface vessel and sub: an inflatable boat with a waterproof outboard that could submerge by deflating some tubes and carry four men underwater at three knots.[8]

After patiently preening subsequent groups of volunteers, Jala Mangkara reached its authorized seventy-man ceiling after five years. But as with many dedicated counter-terrorist forces, it had yet to face a terrorist situation and had not been used in combat. Recognizing the mental exhaustion this would exact, members were allowed a maximum of six years with the unit before being returned to Kopaska or the marine reconnaissance battalion.

Just like Jala Mangkara, Detachment 81 had yet to be used for its intended role. But on two occasions under Captain Prabowo's watch, they had sought out other opportunities to be tested in combat. In mid-1986, Lieutenant Colonel Luhut made preparations for their third combat outing. Once again, it would be in East Timor. Going by the codename Task Force 86 (and given the second Tetum codename of *Railakan*, meaning "Water and Fire"), he would be given joint control over three teams from his own Detachment 81 and a company from Group 1. Their deployment was scheduled for a full year.

From the start, Luhut looked to use Task Force 86 as a testbed for new tactics. One of his innovations was tracking by long-range reconnaissance patrols. Sleeping by day and moving only by night, five-man units from Detachment 81 were deployed for five-week intervals far from other friendly units. To take on the guerrillas, Luhut insisted that they become guerrillas. "There was no shaving, no brushing teeth, no combing hair," said Luhut. "They smelled like animals."[9]

Much of their time was spent staking out water holes. In the dry season, the number of water sources in the hills was limited. "Fretilin might not come to a certain pond next week," continued Luhut, "but they're certain to come to the next, or the next."

A smaller number of Detachment 81 operatives were used to revisit the partisan concept, but with a twist. During previous attempts to arm Timorese— such as with Susi, Tuti, Umi, and Nanggala 13—the partisans were mainly Apodeti or UDT supporters; only a few were former Fretilin. Under Task Force 86, the numbers were reversed: nearly all of the Timorese it employed were former Fretilin guerrillas. They were also afforded the best equipment to date; most of their partisans carried either M-16 or AK-47 assault rifles. And much like the U.S. Army Special Forces fighting alongside Montagnards in the highlands of Vietnam, just a handful of Kopassus members were assigned to far larger Timorese formations.

To fill its partisan ranks, Detachment 81 recruited heavily from among fresh Fretilin prisoners. Luhut, known for his direct and persuasive personality, was especially adept at changing attitudes. "Within three hours," said one task force officer, "he could take a prisoner and convince him to lead a singleton raid against Fretilin." Once having drawn blood during such a raid, the ex-detainee was unlikely to return to the rebel fold.

For most of the recruits, Detachment 81 then prepared a short training primer to shore up lagging skill sets. "They were good at fighting but could not read a map," said Hotma Marbun, a captain in the detachment. "They only knew how to march along established trails between two points."[10]

With the training class concluded within a month, the task force unveiled its first two partisan formations. Team Alfa—named after its Timorese commander, Alfonso—took shape in Lospalos. Team Sera—named after its young leader, Sera Malik—was raised in Baucau. In both cases, a fluctuating core of no more than nine Detachment 81 operatives stood alongside twenty-one former Fretilin guerrillas. And in most cases, they acted as pseudo gangs by dressing and acting like Fretilin.[11]

The combined effect of the long-range patrolling and ex-Fretilin teams was potent. During the first three quarters of 1987, Team Sera was credited with more Fretilin kills (6) and more prisoners captured (22) than any other element within Task Force 86. Having proven the concept, a third partisan team—Saka—was raised in the central highlands near Ossu.[12] Even more telling, the Kopassus headquarters elected to maintain Task Force 86 for a second straight year (rotating in new special forces contingents) with Luhut at the helm.

The task force had not been without its moments of frustration. One of Luhut's obsessions was tracking down Xanana Gusmao. Xanana had been particularly active over the previous year, heading an effort to widen Fretilin's appeal by papering over its leftist image and forging a new resistance council that welcomed former members of UDT. Xanana was elected president of this council in March 1986; he also remained in command of Fretilin's guerrilla forces.[13]

On three separate occasions, Task Force 86 came close to intercepting Xanana in the bush. Each time, the former seminarian had slipped away just prior to the arrival of the Indonesian commandos.

The fourth time, Luhut looked to be lucky. Among the Sera partisans was a fifteen-year-old guerrilla nicknamed Junior. Never seen without his

AK-47 and a Fretilin-style headband, Junior was leading a patrol when they happened upon a large rebel band. Firing off a volley from his Soviet-made assault rifle, he hit Xanana's adjutant—an older guerrilla named Ernesto—in the buttocks.

When Detachment 81 evacuated the wounded guerrilla to a field hospital for treatment, Ernesto revealed his role under questioning. Surmising that the Fretilin chief was still in the vicinity, Luhut pressed him for details of Xanana's local base camp. Reluctantly, Ernesto gave coordinates atop a neighboring mountain.

With this information, several units from Detachment 81 were whisked to the slopes of the mountain to raid the outpost. But as the commandos approached the summit after an exhausting climb, they came across just two fresh sets of footprints. This was not welcome news: the Indonesians knew Xanana almost never traveled in groups of less than nine persons, including several minders that tended to him during bouts of rheumatism.

By that time, Ernesto had been shuttled in a chopper back to Luhut's forward camp at the base of the mountain. Wearing a catheter and unable to sit upright from his wound, the guerrilla was being afforded good care from Detachment 81's medical staff. Perhaps feeling indebted for the attention, he quietly called over the doctors and made a confession. Xanana's camp, he admitted, was on a different mountaintop.

Hearing of the ruse, Luhut was furious. Though artillery and OV-10 strikes were quickly vectored against the new target, it was too late. For the fourth time, Xanana had escaped the noose.

As the first rotation from Task Force 86 returned from East Timor in the third quarter of 1987, new training opportunities were in store. In yet another example of Moerdani's preference for things British, he had arranged for Detachment 81 to host an SAS squadron during the first joint unconventional warfare training exercise on Indonesian soil.

The exercise was coached in secrecy. The British commandos landed at Halim airbase and, in a first for foreigners, were whisked directly inside Detachment 81's secure compound at Cijantung. There they offered some briefings on shooting techniques and the latest in satellite communication gear.

After that, commandos from both sides departed for Sukabumi, the district south of Jakarta near the Indian Ocean. In the event of any injuries among the British, two rooms in Jakarta's Pertamina Hospital had been reserved for employees of a "foreign oil company."

Once at Sukabumi, the Kopassus troops were in their element. Dividing into mixed teams, they offered the SAS pointers on jungle warfare and jungle survival. After two weeks, the British commandos packed up and returned to England. Rated a major success, two British contingents came over the next two years to conduct further joint training exercises with Indonesia's counter-terrorists.[14]

The SAS were not the only foreign advisors with Kopassus. In 1988—at the same time Benny Moerdani finished his tour as armed forces commander and was named defense minister—he passed orders for Detachment 81 to upgrade its technical team to include an intelligence-gathering capability. To accomplish this, detachment members penned plans for a 34-man contingent to be preened over the next five years. In a highly sensitive move, the primary instructor was a rotund advisor from Mossad, Israel's foreign intelligence organization.

By all accounts, the Mossad instruction was thorough. Unlike other Indonesian intelligence bodies—which normally afforded their members a few months of abbreviated instruction, if at all—the Detachment 81 students were given an intensive foundation on the theory behind intelligence collection and analysis.

At the same time the Mossad advisor—who went by the nickname "Arizona"—taught theory, a second foreign advisor arrived in 1991 to coach in the use of hardware. Hailing from MI-6, Britain's foreign intelligence agency, he offered the men from Detachment 81 tips on audio and video surveillance. "He showed us how to place a microphone in a clove cigarette," recalled one participant. This same British officer then sold the unit a range of surveillance gear.[15]

Although Detachment 81's intelligence training was originally scheduled to last through 1995, politics intervened. Two years short of that date, Moerdani, who was widely viewed as the second most powerful man in Indonesia, fell from grace with President Suharto (allegedly because he counseled against the mushrooming business excesses of the First Family). With surprising speed, he was axed from the cabinet.

Within Kopassus, repercussions from the removal of Moerdani were immediately felt. The Mossad connection was quickly severed. Far more significant, Lieutenant Colonel Prabowo Subianto made a strong return to the special forces. Having been unceremoniously drummed out in 1985, he had spent the intervening years with Kostrad. Four of them had been as commander of the 328 Airborne Battalion, where he had gotten high marks for improving morale and sharpening discipline within the unruly battalion. Now back in the Kopassus fold, he was named commander of Group 3 in Batu Jajar.

For the next five years, Prabowo would leave an indelible imprint on the corps. Named the Kopassus deputy commander in 1995, and the commander a year after that, he became the first special forces chief to wear major general's stars since Yogie Memet. Under his tenure, he hosted a record number of foreign training teams (primarily from the U.S.), and also trained a record amount of foreign students at Batu Jajar. He also oversaw a string of notable Kopassus successes (the 1996 hostage rescue in Irian Jaya, for example, when Detachment 81 was finally used in its intended role), and saw the size of Kopassus expand well beyond the pre-1985 cuts.

Recounting the history of Kopassus during this more recent period, however, becomes exceedingly difficult. Coming during the waning years of his father-in-law's regime, Prabowo and his Kopassus became lightning rods for charges of human rights abuses both real and alleged. Lines were often blurred, with Kopassus operatives being seconded for intelligence operations for which they were not trained or intended. Especially after 1997, it often became impossible to say what was a bona fide operation sanctioned by the army chain of command, and which were missions with Kopassus personnel moonlighting on behalf of political interests. For much of the latter, written orders were never issued.[16]

Not surprisingly, then, documentation of this recent period is a problem. So while there is considerable speculation about the Kopassus role in pivotal events like the 1998 riots in Jakarta, the 1999 upheaval in East Timor, and excesses in Aceh and Irian Jaya (now Papua), hard facts are elusive because many officers are still active, trials are pending, and there is only limited political will to seek closure. For all these reasons, a second volume addressing the post-1993 history of Kopassus must necessarily await the passage of time to allow for better historical perspective.

1   As of October 1983, different camouflage patterns were being used by Kostrad, the marines, the police Ranger Regiment, Kopasgat, the Jakarta military region, the West Kalimantan military region, the Irian Jaya military region, the cavalry, military police paratroopers, and Kopassandha.

2   Yusman Yutam interview.

3   Benny Moerdani interview. In fact, there were three U.S. Army Special Forces training teams during the first two years of Moerdani's term as armed forces commander. During August-September 1984, a U.S. team taught High Altitude High Opening (HAHO) and High Altitude Low Opening (HALO) techniques at Batu Jajar. In June 1985, a second U.S. team coached Kopassandha in the use of scuba gear. And in September 1985, a U.S. pathfinder team was dispatched to Batu Jajar. After this third team, no further U.S. Army Special Forces teams were allowed into Indonesia for the remainder of Moerdani's tenure as armed forces commander and later defense minister.

4   Perhaps hedging its bets, the Kopassus headquarters elected to keep a residual *sandi yudha* capability intact by pooling the best members from the disbanded Group 4 within Group 2's Battalion 22.

5   To symbolize the new, reduced mandate of Kopasgat, it was renamed the Air Force Special Forces (*Pasukan Khas Angkatan Udara*, or Paskhas AU) on 11 December 1984.

6   In 1976, the first U.S. Navy SEAL training team had come to Surabaya to teach jungle warfare and scuba tactics to a mixed group from the marine reconnaissance battalion and Kopaska. The next team did not come until 1985. Interview with Hasan Hariadinata, 13 January 2000.

7   Although Jala Mangkara is a joint unit under the navy headquarters, the influence of the marines is overwhelming. Not only is it housed in a marine compound— and is therefore reliant on the marines for administrative support—but the majority of its members are always marines, its commander is always a marine officer, and all members (even those from Kopaska) are required to wear purple marine berets.

8   The Sub Skimmers proved to be a poor choice. Coming with an expensive price tag—"one was equal to six Mercedes," said a member of the purchasing team— they were plagued by maintenance difficulties. Even the British gave it poor reviews. "It tried to be a boat and a sub," said one senior British officer from the

Special Boat Service, "but was not very good at either." Hariadinata interview; interview with Michael Hitchcock, 4 October 2001.

9   Luhut Pandjaitan interview.

10 Interview with Hotma Marbun, 5 April 2001.

11 For administrative purposes, the partisans in Alfa and Sera were interchangeably classified as Ratih (*Rakyat Terlatih*, or Trained Population) or Wanra (*Perlawanan Rakyat*, or People's Resistance). Both are generic terms for militia. This set them apart from Hansip, the other militia formation that administratively answered to the provincial authorities.

12 The three partisan teams raised by Task Force 86 proved enduring, and played prominent roles during the final chaotic months of Indonesian rule in East Timor. Ten members of Team Alfa were later charged with 13 counts of murder, assault, kidnapping, torture, and persecution of Timorese independence activists between April and September 1999.

13 Jakarta had tried hard to draw attention to Fretilin's leftist leanings, and had started to regularly refer to the rebels by the abbreviation MLF—for Marxist Leninist Fretilin. (See *Jakarta Post*, 23 February 1984).

14 In 1988, the British contingent, which included both SAS and Special Boat Service commandos, offered counter-terrorism instruction at Cijantung to a mixed class of Detachment 81 and Jala Mangkara. The last SAS contingent went to Kalimantan to practice riverine operations in a mangrove swamp.

15 During this same period, Detachment 81's technical team added several members who were demolition specialists.

16 In an interview with the author in August 1997, Prabowo stated, "Indonesia is the best country for conducting covert operations because there are no written orders."

GLOSSARY

Apodeti A Portuguese abbreviation for the Timorese Popular Democratic Association.

Bakin Indonesian for *Badan Koordinasi Intelijen Negara*, the State Intelligence Coordination Agency.

DI Darul Islam, the militant Islamic movement that fought for a non-secular Indonesian state.

DPC Indonesian for *Detasemen Pasukan Chusus*, or Special Forces Detachment.

Fretilin A Portuguese abbreviation for the Revolutionary Front for an Independent East Timor.

GAM Indonesian for *Gerakan Aceh Merdeka*, or Free Aceh Movement.

Hansip Indonesian for *Pertahanan Sipil*, or Civil Defense auxiliaries.

KAMI Indonesian for *Kesatuan Aksi Mahasiswa Indonesia*, or Indonesian Student Action Group.

karsa yudha A term for 72-man units within the RPKAD/Kopassandha special warfare groups. Comprised of six prayudha, the karsa yudha is roughly analogous to a U.S. Army Special Forces B-Team.

Kesko Indonesian for *Kesatuan Commando*, or Commando Unit. Formed in April 1952 under the West Java military region, it was later expanded into the KKAD.

Kipam Indonesian for *Kesatuan Intai Para Amfibi*, or Amphibious Airborne Recon Unit, the elite marine formation created in 1961.

KKAD Indonesian for *Korps Komando Angkatan Darat*, or Army Commando Corps. Prior to January 1953, known as Kesko.

KNIL Dutch for *Koninklijk Nederland-Indisch Leger*, the Dutch East Indies Army. Founded in 1830, it consisted of Indonesian recruits led by European officers. KNIL units served only in the Indonesian archipelago and were distinct from the Royal Dutch Army.

Kogasgab Indonesian for *Komando Tugas Gabungan*, or Combined Task Force Command.

Kopasgat	Indonesian for *Komando Pasukat Gerak Tjepat*, or Quick Reaction Force Command. Prior to 1966, known as PGT. In 1984, Kopasgat was renamed Paskhas AU (*Pasukan Khusus Angkatan Udara*, or Air Force Special Forces).
Kopaska	Indonesian for *Komando Pasukan Katak*, or Frog Force Command, the elite combat swimmer unit created with RPKAD assistance in 1962.
Kopassandha	Indonesian for *Komando Pasukan Sandi Yudha*, or Special Warfare Force Command. Prior to 1971, known as the RPKAD. During the Kopassandha period, the school at Batu Jajar was known as *Pusat Sandi Yudha dan Lintas Udara*, or Special Warfare and Airborne Training Center.
Kopassus	Indonesian for *Komando Pasukan Khusus*, or Special Forces Command. Prior to 1985, known as Kopassandha.
Kostrad	Indonesian for *Komando Cadangan Strategis Angkatan Darat*, or Army Strategic Reserve Command.
KY	An abbreviation for *karsa yudha*.
Menparkoad	Indonesian for *Resimen Para Komando Angkatan Darat*, or Army Para-Commando Regiment. This abbreviation officially replaced "RPKAD" between 1962 and 1966. Unofficially, "RPKAD" remained in favored usage throughout this period.
MSSR	Malaysian Special Service Regiment.
NCO	Non-Commissioned Officer.
OPM	Indonesian for *Organisasi Papua Merdeka*, or Free Papua Organization.
Opsus	Indonesian for *Operasi Khusus*, or Special Operations, the name for the office headed by General Ali Moertopo that specialized in managing covert operations.
Paraku	Indonesian for *Pasukan Rakyat Kalimantan Utara*, or North Kalimantan People's Force.
Permesta	Indonesian for *Piagam Perjuangan Semesta*, or Charter of Inclusive Struggle, the name of the movement centered in North Sulawesi that fought a campaign to secede from the republic.
PGRS	Indonesian for *Pasukan Gerilya Rakyat Sarawak*, or Sarawak People's Guerrilla Force.

PGT	Indonesian for *Pasukan Gerak Tjepat*, or Quick Reaction Force, the name for the air force's elite troops prior to 1966.
PKI	Indonesian for *Partai Komunis Indonesia*, or Indonesian Communist Party.
Prayudha	A term for 13-man units within the RPKAD/Kopassandha's special warfare groups; roughly analogous to a U.S. Army Special Forces A-Team.
PRRI	Indonesian for *Pemerintah Revolusioner Republic Indonesia*, or the Revolutionary Government of the Republic of Indonesia.
PY	An abbreviation for *prayudha*.
RMS	Indonesian for *Republik Maluku Selatan*, the South Moluccan Republic, an armed secessionist movement in the Malukus that was active during the early fifties.
RPKAD	Indonesian for *Resimen Pasukan Komando Angkatan Darat*, or Army Commando Force Regiment. Prior to July 1955, known as the KKAD. While keeping the same initials, in 1959 it was renamed the *Resimen Para Komando Angkatan Darat*, or Army Para-Commando Regiment.
RRI	Indonesian for *Radio Republik Indonesia*, or Radio of the Republic of Indonesia.
RTP	Indonesian for *Resimen Team Pertempuran*, or Regimental Combat Team.
Sandi Yudha	An Indonesian military term that literally means Secret Warfare, but is analogous to the U.S. Army Special Forces concept of Special Warfare.
SAS	Special Air Service
SPKAD	Indonesian for *Sekolah Pasukan Komando Angkatan Darat*, or Army Commando Force School. While maintaining the same initials, in 1959 the school was renamed *the Sekolah Para Komando Angkatan Darat*, or Army Para-Commando School.
Ton Sus	Indonesian for *Pleton Khusus*, or Special Platoon.
TNKU	Indonesian for *Tentara Nasional Kalimantan Utara*, or North Kalimantan National Army.
Tropas	A Portuguese term for its colonial troops.
UDT	A Portuguese abbreviation for the Timorese Democratic Union.

INDEX

Aceh 25, 41, 51, 57, 59, 111-112, 217, 260-265, 275
Agum Gumelar 221
Aircraft types:
  AC-47 224, 231, 233, 235
  An-12 120, 149
  B-25 45
  B-26 48, 123, 224, 231, 233
  Bell-206 (Jet Ranger) 220
  C-47 (Dakota) 30, 40, 43, 45, 47, 74, 84, 97, 224, 233
  C-54 43
  C-130 (Hercules) 64, 66, 76-77, 79, 80, 83, 94, 96, 98, 101, 116, 120, 122, 151, 161, 165, 175-176, 184, 243, 245-246, 248, 251, 258, 260, 290
  DC-3 185-186
  DC-9 277, 278, 280-281, 284-285, 288
  DC-10 282, 284
  DHC-4 (Caribou) 116-117
  Il-28 82
  Mi-6 117
  OV-10 271, 276, 312
  P-2 (Neptune) 66, 72, 86-87
  P-51 (Mustang) 45, 48
  Tu-16 82
Ali Murtopo see Murtopo, Ali
Atang Sutrisna 239, 243-244, 247, 253, 276
Atmodarminto, Wiyogo 29, 56
Bambang, Johannes 219-220, 250-251, 256
Bambang Soembodo see Soembodo, Bambang
Banteng Raiders 46, 51, 68, 103
Barlian 39, 40
Battalion:
  1 (RPKAD) 92, 98, 103, 111, 113-115, 118, 128, 132-133, 137, 147-148, 154, 158, 169, 178, 296
  2 (RPKAD) 57-58, 69, 79, 83, 85, 91-92, 94, 96-98, 103-104, 118, 147, 154, 158, 163, 166, 169, 177
  2C (RPKAD) 158
  3 (RPKAD) 103, 113, 129, 133, 137, 146, 147, 154, 155, 163, 167, 169, 171, 177, 182
  305 Airborne 253
  328 Airborne 251, 255, 314
  328 Raider 78, 80, 83, 85, 96-97, 107, 130, 137-138
  330 Raider 68, 83, 85, 123
  330 Airborne 112-113, 123, 216, 256-257
  401 Airborne 144, 240, 252, 253, 255-256
  436 Airborne 83, 85, 103
  441 "Banteng Raider III" 103
  454 Airborne 75, 83, 85, 106, 130-131, 133-137, 140, 144, 146, 240
  454 "Banteng Raider II" 68
  501 Airborne 240-241, 243, 248
  502 Airborne 241, 248, 257
  530 Airborne 76-77, 83, 130, 133-138, 240, 243
  530 Raider 68
  700 Raider 291
  744 Infantry 274
  Special Warfare 162, 165, 166, 169
Brigade:
  1 Infantry 134-135, 138
  2 Infantry 226-227, 231
  3 Parachute 68, 75-76, 82-83, 85, 114, 130, 137, 167
  3 Airborne 307
  4 Infantry 146, 148
  5 Infantry 168
  17 Airborne 238, 251-253
  18 Airborne 240-241, 248, 252
Central Intelligence Agency 41-43, 47-49, 51, 64, 79, 139, 244, 284-285, 303
Cham (Cambodian Muslims) 154, 190-191, 200
CIA see Central Intelligence Agency

Company (RPKAD):
   A   22, 26, 31, 33-35, 40, 43, 45-48, 55,
    57, 59, 69-70, 98-101, 107, 118-119, 163
   B ("Ben Hur")   29, 34, 45, 48, 55, 57,
    69-70, 98, 101, 104-105, 128, 137-138,
    141, 147, 149, 151-152, 154, 155, 163
   C ("Cobra")   98, 101-103, 115-116,
    128, 138, 163
   D ("Dracula")   128, 137, 154, 163
   E   128, 138, 147, 149, 163
   I   129, 133, 137-139, 141, 146, 147

Dani, Omar   109, 134, 136-137, 139-140,
   143, 153-154, 177
Dading Kalbuadi   *see* Kalbuadi, Dading
Darul Islam   13-15, 20-21, 25, 51, 55, 57-
   58, 83, 107, 111-113, 261, 283, 297
Daud Beureueh   261-264
Detachment 81   292-297, 300-301, 304,
   307-308, 310-314
Detasemen Pasukan Chusus   71-78, 86-87,
   89, 91-92, 157, 162, 170, 180, 181, 183,
   243, 259
DI   *see* Darul Islam
Djaelani, R.E.   24, 28, 32-35, 39
Djajadiningrat, H.   45-46, 51, 56, 123
Djanbi, Mochamad Idjon   16-24, 26, 28-
   29, 35
Djasmin   149
Djohor, Junus   32
DPC   *see Detasemen Pasukan Chusus*

Ella Bajuri   259, 260, 276

Fadillah, R.A.   26, 46

Garuda Airlines   40, 45, 277-278
Gatot Purwanto   269, 298
Group (RPKAD/Kopassandha):
   1   169, 188, 190, 217, 238-239, 242, 263,
    280, 290, 291, 300, 303, 306, 307
   2   169, 172, 173, 188, 193, 199, 206,
    211, 224, 239, 258, 264, 291, 307
   3   169, 175, 178, 188, 217, 264, 291,
    298, 307

   4, 169-172, 175, 179-181, 182, 188, 192,
    193, 206, 217, 258, 262, 267, 279-280,
    289, 291, 302, 303, 307, 315
Guerrilla Force:
   PG 100, 63-64
   PG 200, 65
   PG 300, 66, 72
   PG 400, 75
   PG 500, 78, 80
   PG 600, 85, 88
Gunawan Wibisono   *see* Wibisono,
   Gunawan
Gusmao, Jose Alejandro "Xanana"   297,
   299, 311-312

Handjono, Soerjo   120
Harseno, Kentot   95, 115-117, 119, 123,
   128, 151-153, 175-176
Hartono, Seno   57-58, 69, 83, 85, 96, 190,
   193-194
Hasan Tiro   262-263, 275
Hatta, Mohamad   28, 37, 41
Hendropriyono   193, 266-270
Hernoto, Agus   73-74, 114
Husein, Achmad   38, 39, 40

Jala Mangkara (Detachment)   293, 308-
   310, 315
Johannes Bambang   *see* Bambang,
   Johannes
Jusuf, Andi Mohammad   271, 277, 280,
   291, 300

Kalbuadi, Dading   43-44, 198-199, 205,
   211, 217-218, 223-228, 230-231, 241,
   250-252, 266
Kartosuwiryo, Sekarmaji Marijan   14
Kawilarang, Alex   8-10, 13, 15-16, 19-22,
   25, 33, 37, 41, 50-51
Kentot Harseno   *see* Harseno, Kentot
Kesko   20-21
Kipam   82, 88, 303
Ki-Pas-Ko   15-16
Kissinger, Henry   242
KKAD   *see Korps Komando Angkatan Darat*

KNIL *see Koninklijk Nederlands-Indisch Leger*
Kodim, Achmad 51, 56, 69, 96, 222
Kogasgab 223-226, 232-233, 234, 239-242, 247, 248-250, 257, 265
Koninklijk Nederlands-Indisch Leger 4-8, 20, 21
Kopasgat 173-174, 251, 272, 308, 315
Kopaska 82, 84-85, 88, 141, 144, 293, 308-310, 315
Korps Komando Angkatan Darat 22-26, 28
Kostrad 114, 129-133, 135-137, 140, 199, 237-238, 243, 245, 248-249, 251, 255, 305, 307, 314
Kuntara 182-183

Lubis, Zulkifli 32, 34, 37, 39, 46
Luhut Pandjaitan *see* Pandjaitan, Luhut

Magenda 62, 64-67, 72, 75
Malaysian Special Service Regiment (MSSR) 191-192
Martomo, Tommy 230, 232, 250
Meadows, Richard 236-237
Moerdani, Leonardus Benjamin "Benny" 23-24, 28, 48-49, 128, 153, 160, 201, 223, 295, 301, 305, 315
    and counter-terrorist units 278-279, 292, 293
    and DPC 69-71, 73, 76-78, 80, 86, 170, 240, 243, 259
    and East Timor 194-195, 198-199, 207, 225, 238, 242, 267, 300
    and Kopassus 306, 308, 312-313
    and Woyla rescue 282-285, 289, 302
    as Battalion 1 commander 92, 98, 113-115, 124
    as Company A commander 33, 40, 43-45, 51, 55, 59
MSSR *see* Malaysian Special Service Regiment
Mulyono Soerjowardojo 95, 106, 146, 148
Mung Parhadimuljo *see* Parhadimuljo, Mung
Murtopo, Ali 196-199, 201, 202, 205-206, 208, 259

Nanggala:
    1 216, 259
    2 216
    3 216, 218
    4 216, 218
    5 239-240, 244, 247, 249, 256-257, 265
    6 256, 265
    7 259
    8 258-259, 265-266
    9 259
    10 265, 270, 273
    11 265-266, 270
    12 265-266, 270
    13 268-271, 298
    14 259
    15 270-271, 275
    16 262-264
    17 271
    18 271
    19 271
    20 260
    21 263
    22 271-272, 276
    23 271-272
    24 271-272
    27 264
    28 272-274, 290, 297
    29 272
    30 272
    35 265
    51 298
    52 298, 299
    53 298
    55 299
Narto Coolie *see* Sunarto
Nasution, Abdul 31-35, 37, 44-45, 46, 64, 67-68, 72-73, 93-94, 103, 132, 136, 142, 143
Nasution, Kaharudin 39, 42, 48, 54, 163

Operation:
    Flamboyan 199, 205, 211, 217-218, 220-225, 227, 232, 235, 239, 248
    Gawaru 193
    Komodo 197-199, 202, 205-209, 217, 221

Linud X 175
Mangkok Merah 174
Merapi 148
Merdeka 53
Saber Kikis Baratayudha 297
Sadar 118-119, 170, 181-182
Sapu Bersih 173
Sapu Bersih II 173
Seroja 239-241, 244, 255, 257, 265
17 Agustus 47
Tegas 42-43, 47
Tertib 173
Trisula 172, 189
Ubaya 122
Wibawa 182, 185, 187
OPM see Organisasi Papua Merdeka
Organisasi Papua Merdeka 118-119, 170, 181-184, 186, 187, 259-160, 275, 294-294

Pandjaitan, Luhut 242, 243-245, 290-293, 297, 301-302, 303, 310-312
Pandjaitan, Sintong 138-139, 141, 182, 185-186, 193, 279-280, 282, 284-286, 288-291, 305, 307
Paraku 172-174, 192-193
Parhadimuljo, Mung 54-55, 57, 68-69, 82, 83, 88, 91, 97-98, 110-111, 113-114, 116, 119, 120, 123, 124, 175, 279
Parikesit (composite battalion) 272-273
Partai Komunis Indonesia 41, 109-110, 127, 130-131, 133-136, 145-149, 154, 156, 158-159, 162, 163, 166, 168, 170-173, 181, 193, 197, 224
Pasukan Gerak Tjepat 30-31, 39, 40, 42-43, 45, 47, 48, 56, 72, 73, 75, 80, 83, 85, 106, 110, 118, 121, 139-140, 143, 161, 173-174, 177
Pasukan Gerilya Rakyat Sarawak 155-157, 160, 172-175, 192-193
PGRS see Pasukan Gerilya Rakyat Sarawak
PGT see Pasukan Gerak Tjepat
PKI see Partai Komunis Indonesia
Prabowo Subianto 273-274, 290-297, 300-302, 303, 304, 310, 314, 316

Pranoto, Prijo 59, 115, 150, 168
Prawira, Alex 24
Prijo Pranoto see Pranoto, Prijo

Rangers, Indonesian Police 59, 72, 75, 79, 85, 97, 184, 187, 308, 315
Regiment Speciale Troepen 5, 20
Republik Maluku Selatan 7-10, 13, 15, 40
Riyadi, Slamet 9-10, 16, 18
RMS see Republik Maluku Selatan
Royal Dutch Army 4-5, 17, 26

Said 215-216
Samsudin 173, 239
Santosa, Chalimi Imam 128-129, 132-133, 141-142, 147, 169, 178, 202
Sarwo Edhie Wibowo see Wibowo, Sarwo Edhie
Seno Hartono see Hartono, Seno
Setiabudi, Alex 101-102, 115, 175-176
Sigarlaki 49-50
Simbolon, Maludin 37-39, 45
Sisnodo, Heru 73-75, 86, 154, 158, 163, 181
Soebandrio 93-94, 150-153, 155-156, 178
Soedarto 80
Soediro, Herman 129, 131-132
Soegito 239-244, 247-249, 252, 256, 265
Soejono, Widjojo 55-57, 68, 75, 82-83, 110, 122, 167-168, 170, 180, 188-189, 238
Soelaiman, Marzoeki 24, 32-35
Soembodo, Bambang 192, 237, 241
Soetaryo, M.I. 152, 295, 296
Sofian Effendi 217, 246, 249, 251, 262, 265
Special Air Service (SAS) 107, 108, 124, 164, 278, 293, 302, 304, 306, 312, 316
Special Forces (U.S. Army) 59, 69-70, 72, 79, 158, 169-170, 179-180, 187, 206, 236-237, 280, 290, 303, 306, 310, 315
Special Troop Regiment see Regiment Speciale Troepen
Sudrajat, Edy 118, 123
Sugiyanto, Aloysius 18, 33-35, 196-197, 202, 208-209, 217

Suharto 153, 160, 167-168, 171, 181, 194, 196, 200, 290, 301, 304, 313-314
  and East Timor 198, 210-211, 223, 239-242
  and Mandala Command 71, 77, 106, 114
  and Woyla rescue 283
  as Kostrad commander 129-133, 137-138, 141-142, 146-147, 150
Sukarno 6, 31-32, 37, 41, 55, 57, 59, 62-65, 71, 73, 79, 81, 92, 105, 109-110, 120-121, 127, 130-131, 134, 136-137, 140, 143, 145, 149-150, 152-157, 160, 167, 171-172, 201
Sumardji 111, 158, 162
Sumual, Herman "Ventje" 41, 49
Sunarto 212-214, 280
Supardjo 132-136
Supomo 22, 24, 25, 35, 163
Suroso, Untung 95, 212-213, 215, 227, 280, 281, 285-288
Sutiyoso 218-220, 246, 251, 264
Sutopo, Bambang 87
Suweno 223-224, 226, 236, 241, 243, 245
Syafei, Theo 242-243

Tahril 50
Tanjung, Feisal 123, 171-172, 182, 184-186, 259
Tarub 217, 218, 221, 246, 256, 265, 307
Tentara Nasional Kalimantan Utara 93-103, 107, 137, 155, 174-175, 207
Tjakrabirawa Regiment 110, 123, 131, 134-135, 142, 143, 150-152, 171, 296, 304
TNKU see Tentara Nasional Kalimantan Utara

Umar Wirahadikusumah see Wirahadikusumah, Umar
Untung Syamsuri 85-86, 130-134
Untung Suroso see Suroso, Untung
Urip Sucipto 154

Visser, Rokus Bernardus see Djanbi, Mochamad Idjon

Westerling, Raymond "Turk" 5-6, 11, 15
Wibisono, Gunawan 56, 73, 84
Wibowo, Sarwo Edhie 103, 181, 184-186
  as RPKAD commander 114-115, 124, 127-129, 131-133, 137-141, 147-153, 155-158, 161, 163, 167-168, 177
  as SPKAD commander 56, 64
Widjojo, Soejono see Soejono, Widjojo
Wirahadikusumah, Umar 127, 129, 131, 133
Wiriadinata, A. 30, 42
Wismoyo Arisunandar 182-183, 300, 305
Witarmin 189, 216
Wiyogo Atmodarminto see Atmodarminto, Wiyogo

Yani, Ahmad 46-47, 56, 68, 71, 76, 103, 110, 113-115, 121-122, 127, 129, 131, 156-158, 164
Yoga Sugomo 194, 201, 282-284
Yogie Soewardi Memet 216, 222, 258, 260, 264, 266, 300, 314
Yunus Yosfiah 192, 206-207, 211-216, 227, 230, 234, 274, 291
Yusman Yutam 58, 211, 218, 220, 227, 232-233, 249, 306-307